TOLSTOY'S FALSE DISCIPLE

Pegasus Books LLC
80 Broad Street, 5th Floor
New York, NY 10004

Copyright © 2014 by Alexandra Popoff

First Pegasus Books cloth edition November 2014

Interior design by Maria Fernandez

Library of Congress Cataloging-in-Publication Data is available.

ISBN: 978-1-60598-640-1

10 9 8 7 6 5 4 3 2 1

Printed in the United States of America
Distributed by W. W. Norton & Company

TOLSTOY'S FALSE DISCIPLE

THE UNTOLD STORY OF
LEO TOLSTOY AND VLADIMIR CHERTKOV

ALEXANDRA POPOFF

PEGASUS BOOKS
NEW YORK LONDON

TOLSTOY'S
FALSE
DISCIPLE

To the Memory of My Father

To the Memory of My Father

ACKNOWLEDGMENTS

F or a biographer, uncovering archival material, which you are the first to read, is exciting. Research is where the story begins. Later, one needs to put all the pieces of information together and bring them to life.

Many people helped me during the five years of research and writing of this biography. My thanks go to the trustees and curators of the L.N. Tolstoy State Museum in Moscow, who gave me exclusive access to the full collection of Vladimir Chertkov's letters to Tolstoy. I am particularly grateful to the museum director, Natalia Kalinina, for facilitating my research over the years and for permission to publish the photographs in the book. I relied on the expertise of the museum curators Marina Loginova, Tatyana Nikiforova, Svetlana Novikova, and Yuliya Yadovker. The veteran librarian, Valentina Bastrykina, made valuable suggestions to further my reading. Olga Golinenko, one of the oldest museum employees, told me of her encounters with Vladimir Chertkov's son and of working under Tolstoy's former secretary and follower, Nikolai Gusev. Through her stories about Gusev, who spoke of Tolstoy's wife, Sophia, with animosity, I could feel Chertkov's strong influence over the followers, which extended into the 1950s.

The Manuscript Department at the Russian State Library holds 250 boxes of Chertkov's papers. Because the catalog is said to be incomplete, researchers are denied access. Permission to read this catalog and request documents was given to me exclusively. I am indebted to Victor Molchanov for permission to access Chertkov's extensive archive and to Irina Pyattoeva, who helped facilitate my research. I also want to thank the curators of sculptor Anna Golubkina's Museum in Moscow, which preserves the atmosphere of her working studio intact. This is where Chertkov would arrive in his old age to pose for a bust. My research would be incomplete without materials obtained at the Russian State Archive for Literature in Moscow (RGALI) and from my local University of Saskatchewan Library.

My special thanks go to my husband, Wilfred, who has edited all of my books and whose suggestions were vital, as ever. This book employs a story about his people, the Russian Doukhobors, whose migration to Canada Tolstoy had sponsored.

I will always remember discussing this book in Moscow with my father, writer Grigory Baklanov. Every evening, as I would return from the archives, he would listen to my stories about Chertkov—first in disbelief and later with fascination and amusement. In the end, he told me, "I want this book written." This was five years ago, and his phrase kept me going when my father was no more.

I want to thank my editor at Pegasus Books, Jessica Case, and my agent, Don Fehr for their unfailing support. I am grateful to Pastor James Dimitroff, whom I consulted about religious references, and to Professor Lisa Vargo, who has been a great stimulus from the very beginning. She had suggested the literary parallel with Dr. Johnson and Mr. Savage, which I use in the book's opening.

Finally, this book would have been impossible without the grants from the Canada Council for the Arts and the Saskatchewan Arts Board, and I am thankful to them for supporting my project.

A NOTE ON RUSSIAN NAMES

I n the Russian language, a formal address requires the use of both a first name and patronymic (derived from the father's first name). In the text I use mostly first names as this is more familiar to the Western reader.

Women's names have feminine endings in the Russian language: Anna Karenina, Elizaveta Chertkova, Alexandra Tolstaya, Sophia Motovilova, Tatyana Sukhotina, etc. Sophia Tolstoy's name in Russian is Sophia Andreevna Tolstaya.

Among family and friends, a diminutive of the first name is commonly used; for example, Tanya for Tatyana, Masha for Maria, Sasha for Alexandra, Dima for Dmitry or Vladimir (as with Vladimir Chertkov, who called himself Dima). Sophia called Tolstoy by his diminutive Lyovochka. He called her Sonya. In the footnotes and in the index their first names appear in full.

In this book Lev is used interchangeably with Leo, since there is no consistency in sources.

"There are false heroes—and false devotees . . .
What! Will you find no difference between
Hypocrisy and genuine devoutness?"

—Molière, *Tartuffe*

PROLOGUE

T here are two sides to every attachment: one loves, the other allows himself to be loved; one kisses, the other gives his cheek to be kissed . . . And in our friendship it was I who kissed and Dmitry who presented his cheek; but he too was ready to kiss me." These lines from Tolstoy's early novel, *Boyhood*, may help fathom the strangest relationship of his late life, his admiration for a man to whom he became bound by love and their joint pursuit of religious ideals. Like the hero of his novel, Tolstoy subordinated himself to the influence of his single-minded friend, who was incomparably inferior to him intellectually and morally.

Tolstoy was fifty-five when he met Vladimir Chertkov, a handsome ex-officer of the Guards, a generation his junior. Their first encounter in 1883 sparked an intimate friendship; as contemporary biographer Aylmer Maude writes, "An attachment immediately sprang up between the two men, which lasted all Tolstoy's life . . ."[1] A man of forceful personality, Chertkov appealed to Tolstoy and won his trust, becoming the writer's closest companion and confidante for three decades.

It was a paradoxical union between the ingenious writer and a dogmatic man, who was a foe to creativity, but nevertheless attracted and fascinated

Tolstoy. Contemporaries, who met both, regarded their closeness as nothing short of mysterious. Tolstoy alone refused to recognize the obvious gap between them, repeatedly describing Chertkov as his best friend and alter-ego.

Chertkov was dominant in Tolstoy's life during the writer's religious phase. Following publication of *Anna Karenina*, Tolstoy experienced a profound spiritual crisis, rejecting his literary achievement, and former life as a family man and landowner as sinful and futile. He sought a deeper meaning of life in strong faith, but existing religions did not satisfy him. After years of toiling to retranslate the Gospels, Tolstoy formulated his own, practical religion, devoid of mystery. It was based on the ethical principles, which Tolstoy believed Christ had taught, but Christians failed to practice. The most vital among them was the precept of not resisting an evil doer by force. It inspired Tolstoy's doctrine of non-violence, which in turn led him to renounce all existing social institutions as coercive.

At the time he met Chertkov, Tolstoy felt isolated in his intellectual milieu where his new religious writings failed to make an impact. Unlike those in Tolstoy's circle, Chertkov grew up among Russia's first evangelicals and expressed keen interest in his philosophy. Their first meeting lasted into the night: the writer read him chapters of his recently completed work, *What I Believe*. Chertkov concurred with Tolstoy in all questions that mattered to the writer and immediately struck him as a like-minded man. Regardless of what happened later, he would never revise this impression. Tolstoy yearned for a strong follower to keep him steady on his chosen path, and found such an adherent in Chertkov.

Their relationship was enmeshed in faith, but extended beyond Christian brotherly love. During the first year, Chertkov became Tolstoy's confidante to whom the writer even told his marital troubles. Tolstoy kept no secrets from Chertkov, allowing him to read his diary, a privilege given in the past only to his wife, Sophia. His exchange with Chertkov was intense and intimate, and the two men had each other's permission to destroy the occasional letter. Tolstoy assured Chertkov that their relationship was "beyond trust."[2] Later, he would have other followers and befriended some of them, but only with Chertkov did he form an exclusive and non-transparent union.

Despite his insignificance, Chertkov claimed a prominent role in Tolstoy's life. Tolstoy wrote him over 930 letters, more than to any other person, including Sophia. However, many things in Tolstoy's letters are just implied and the story of the relationship emerges only from the disciple's letters, of which over one thousand survive. But Chertkov's part of the exchange has been long inaccessible. The disciple had made a special arrangement with Tolstoy asking him to return his letters immediately upon reading; later they were suppressed by the Russian archives.

During the atheistic Soviet era Tolstoy's religious writings could not be promoted, and this period of his life and his relationships with his followers remain the least known. This particularly concerns his association with Chertkov. Even today, the materials that could shed light on the character of Tolstoy's friend are guarded, almost like a state secret. More than a century later, Moscow's archives are still denying access to Chertkov's papers, even to his letters to Tolstoy—and when the Russian archives are hiding information, there is something the public is not supposed to know.

In Russia, there is a tradition of portraying its national writers as flawless. Chertkov's love-friendship correspondence with Tolstoy, some of which was destroyed at the writer's insistence, suggests their relationship was homoerotic. This is, of course, a sensitive subject in Russia. But it alone does not explain why Chertkov's papers were suppressed.

From his letters to Tolstoy, which I had been able to access exclusively when researching Sophia's biography, Chertkov emerges as a manipulative and unscrupulous man. But how could Tolstoy maintain a close and lasting friendship with his moral opposite? This question is impossible to answer without knowing the whole story.

Chertkov had exacerbated Tolstoy's marital discord. He was at the center of events that generated lasting controversy—Tolstoy's signing of a secret will, his flight from home at eighty-two, and his pathetic death at Astapovo. The secret will was drafted by Chertkov himself and signed in dubious circumstances at his insistence. "Why write about Chertkov?" asked a librarian at the L.N. Tolstoy State Museum. "He was a shady character." This observation, or at least the second part of it, was on the mark. It exposes the need for the cover-up. Without access to full information

Chertkov can be presented as a suitable companion to Tolstoy, who inexplicably described him as the man he "most needed" and "the person closest" to him. Although Tolstoy had emphasized Chertkov's dedication to his teaching and causes, the disciple's devotion was wishful thinking on the writer's part.

In fact, the relationship was complex and troubled. While Chertkov indeed spent decades publishing Tolstoy's works and propagating his teaching, he hindered rather than helped him. His involvement in the writer's public affairs was a source of annoyance and grief. Chertkov demanded privileges and promotions from Tolstoy, which he received because the writer could never refuse him. Faced with this relentless pressure, Tolstoy turned over all his public affairs to his disciple, also appointing him to be his sole representative abroad. As such, Chertkov devoted his time to intrigue and acquiring personal influence. He attained the exclusive right to publish the writer's most profitable first editions—despite Tolstoy's renunciation of copyright, which enabled all publishers to produce his works on equal terms. Chertkov argued that his publishing enterprise employed Tolstoy's moral principles, making it superior to the rest. This helped him to establish a monopoly on publishing Tolstoy's latest writings. One of his major quarrels in the publishing world occurred during Tolstoy's work on *Resurrection* and jeopardized it. There were also Chertkov's disagreements with other disciples and even the writer's daughters. Although Tolstoy was frustrated by the strife, he took Chertkov's side in all disputes and in his conflict with Sophia, who was the disciple's main rival.

A despotic man, Chertkov was a poor choice to promote Tolstoy's message of universal love and unity. But he ironically used the non-resistance teaching to influence the writer himself. Over the years, he insisted on maintaining his exclusive and extraordinary privileges to copy Tolstoy's diary and his entire correspondence. His ingenious argument was that he needed these letters and entries for the compendium of the writer's thoughts he was compiling. In fact, he used them as mind control. When Tolstoy would express some thoughts that disagreed with his own doctrine, he would immediately receive a stern letter from Chertkov. As Tolstoy practiced submission, Chertkov gained power over him. He surrounded Tolstoy with secretaries whose job it was to send him a copy of everything the writer produced. These people, to whom Chertkov paid salaries, were also spying on the writer. Chertkov's obsessive desire to know even Tolstoy's intimate thoughts had a detrimental effect on his creativity. Chertkov meddled in his work, told him what to write, and often nipped Tolstoy's ideas in the bud. He carried on with his activity despite Tolstoy's objections that this perennial reading over his shoulder "stifled and paralyzed" him.

Some of Tolstoy's most important decisions, which were also the ones the writer would come to regret, were made under his disciple's pressure. Among them were Tolstoy's public renunciation of copyright, which only fueled competition between publishers and in the end did not benefit readers. The secret testament, in which he appointed Chertkov sole executor of his literary estate, generated conflict with Tolstoy's family.

During Tolstoy's final years Chertkov emerged as being in complete control of the elderly writer. Dushan Makovitsky, Tolstoy's personal doctor, describes this influence as "tremendous and despotic." The disciple took away Tolstoy's manuscripts and he alone decided who should publish and translate his works. Having witnessed this state of affairs, Mikhail Sukhotin, the writer's son-in-law, later explained to Tolstoy's last secretary, Valentin Bulgakov, that Tolstoy "loved Chertkov with exceptional tenderness, partially and blindly; this love drove L.N. [Tolstoy] to become completely subordinated to Chertkov's will."[3] The fact that Tolstoy loved Chertkov can be sensed from his many letters including the one he had written in 1910, shortly before leaving Yasnaya forever: "Today, for the first time I felt with a special clarity—and sadness—how much I miss you . . . There is a whole sphere of thoughts, feelings, which I cannot share with anyone as naturally as with you, knowing that I'm completely understood."[4] If Chertkov loved Tolstoy in return, his love was selfish and pathological: it inspired his vain desire to possess and control the writer's spiritual legacy, which belonged to all.

As Maude remarks, Chertkov pushed Tolstoy to his extremes. And so it was with Tolstoy's flight from his ancestral estate, which Chertkov had long anticipated and urged him to make. Tolstoy's fanatical followers yearned for a lasting legend of their own, expecting him to go out into the world to preach, like Christ and Buddha. By abandoning his home and the so-called "conditions of luxury," Tolstoy would validate his extreme material renunciation. Chertkov also had a personal agenda in his long struggle with Sophia, attempting to prove that he was closest to Tolstoy. Without his intrusion and scheming the ailing writer would have not left home.

Chertkov brought many inexplicable things into Tolstoy's life. The daughters, with whom he was closest among the children, were unable or unwilling to disclose all they knew. The eldest, Tanya, had admitted that she was being bound by her "promise of silence."[5] Tolstoy remained exceptionally protective of Chertkov to his last days. In a farewell letter to his eldest children, written in Astapovo, he reminded them that Chertkov occupied "a special position in relation to me."[6]

A man of striking personality, Chertkov commanded attention. His photographs with Tolstoy show him towering over the writer. Tolstoy, a little old man, labors at his desk. Chertkov, sitting behind him to record his pronouncements, is a powerful and impressive figure. These photographs are evocative of the relationship where Chertkov was dominant.

His story is intriguing. Although a close friend of Tolstoy, he was also close to the tsars and was even believed to be an illegitimate son of Alexander II. Chertkov's ancestors were influential courtiers and his father was a general in the Tsar's suite. His uncle, Peter Shuvalov, was an adviser to the same Tsar and an all-powerful chief of the secret police. Unlike his claim, Chertkov never severed his ties with the establishment. He was a lifelong friend of Dmitry Trepov, a chief of the gendarmes and an assistant minister of the interior, who was effective at eliminating political dissent.

New evidence suggests that Chertkov, whose loyalty Tolstoy never doubted, had ties to the tsarist secret police. This book will tell the little-known story of police surveillance over Tolstoy, whose works against the Orthodox Church and the authoritarian state made him into Russia's most prominent dissident. One year before meeting Chertkov, Tolstoy was placed under permanent secret surveillance. Chertkov's arrangement to keep a copy of everything Tolstoy wrote, including his correspondence and diaries, should be seen in this context. Tolstoy was not entirely blind to Chertkov's dark side. One day, he discovered that the disciple was deceiving him: he was not the only one reading his diaries. On another occasion, he learned that Chertkov had deposited his papers at the private residence of the chief of the gendarmes, Trepov. But even such painful discoveries would not disillusion Tolstoy, who wanted to believe that the man he loved and who shared his faith, was devoted to him.

Despite his proximity to the tsars, Chertkov did not emigrate after the 1917 Bolshevik Revolution. Instead, he made another swift rise, acquiring new patrons in dictators Lenin and Stalin, with whom he met and corresponded. He also describes his meeting with the head of the Bolshevik secret police, Felix Dzerzhinsky, in a short reverential memoir. Close to the tsars, to Tolstoy, and to the Soviet government, Chertkov had reinvented himself many times. Whether as a Tolstoyan or a near-Communist, he was seen as fighting for the good cause. All the while, he was a man of dark passions, consumed with ambition and greed, and living a double life.

Drawing from new evidence, this biography will re-examine different aspects of Tolstoy's paradoxical alliance with Chertkov and reveal the strange magnetism it held for the writer. Among the enigmatic relationships in literary history, from Dr. Johnson's with Mr. Savage to Somerset Maugham's liaisons with his secretary friends, Tolstoy's strange and enduring affair with his moral antipode stands out as the most surprising.

CHAPTER ONE

BORN TO PRIVILEGE

"We who are the descendants of oppressors and tyrants . . ."
—Tolstoy, in a letter
to Sergei L. Tolstoy[1]

"If Chertkov did not become what he became, he would
have been a governor general and would hang people."
—Tolstoy, in a conversation
with Valentin Bulgakov[2]

Vladimir Chertkov's aristocratic family was close to court for generations and linked to the ruling dynasty with many visible and invisible ties. A few distant members of his family were related to the Romanovs—and what is more, Chertkov was believed to be an illegitimate offspring of Alexander II. The Tsar had many fleeting affairs and fathered at least seven children out of wedlock. Chertkov met him as a child, at his parents' home, and later, as a young man, craved the Tsar's personal attention.

After centuries of absolute monarchy, Russian aristocracy depended on the Tsar's favor, which placed an indelible mark on the Machiavellian characters of courtiers. This was Chertkov's milieu as he was growing up. At the remark of Russia's first Prime Minister, Sergei Witte, "military types" at court advanced in rank by looking after the royal kitchens, "horses, dogs, and the like."[3] Since the sixteenth century, the Chertkovs produced a succession of military generals and high-ranked administrators, whose influence and wealth was obtained through such court service. Both of Chertkov's grandfathers were generals who held court titles as equerries; managing the royal stables was an influential position, providing direct access to the Tsar. (One equerry in Russia's history, Boris Godunov, even rose to the throne.)

In the eighteenth century, when the aristocracy's wealth and status were measured by their number of male serfs, favorites of Elizabeth I, Catherine II, and Paul I received princely handouts. They were granted millions of rubles, vast estates, and thousands of serfs. Some of Chertkov's ancestors belonged to this privileged group of courtiers. Before the emancipation of 1861, his paternal grandfather, Count Ivan Dmitrievich Chertkov, was among the top sixty-three serf owners in Russia, owning 6,838.[4]

Chertkov's father, Grigory Ivanovich, inherited twenty estates, the largest of which were in the vast Voronezh province in Russia's south. Among the hundreds of serfs who worked for the family was Egor Mikhailovich Chekhov, the writer's grandfather. Egor raised Count Chertkov's cattle and drove them to market. As a clever salesman he was allowed to share the profits. However, it took him thirty years to save enough money to buy freedom for himself, his wife, and three sons. The daughter's freedom was added as a bonus, out of Count Chertkov's generosity.[5]

Born in 1828, the same year as Tolstoy, Grigory Chertkov studied at the elite Imperial Page Corps, which produced future generals, statesmen, and court officials. Upon graduating he chose aristocracy's oldest and most respectable profession, war. Grigory Chertkov served under three reigns, beginning as an aide-de-camp in the suite of Nicholas I. His career was launched under Alexander II who led a military campaign against Poland from 1863–1864. Despite his moderate attitude towards minorities, the

Tsar suppressed the Polish uprising for independence. The campaign launched many careers including that of Grigory Chertkov, who was promoted to major-general and remained in the suite of Alexander II.

The name "Chertkov" first appeared in Tolstoy's letters in the early 1860s, during his work on *War and Peace*, when he conducted research in the newly opened public libraries. Emancipation of the serfs in 1861 and other great reforms of Alexander II inspired a surge in public activity. This is when the first libraries—the Rumyantsev Museum and the Chertkov Library—were opened in Moscow for public use. Count Nikolai Petrovich Rumyantsev spent two million rubles[6] to renovate his palace, the Pashkov House, damaged during Napoleon's invasion. After the renovations it was home to the biggest library and archive. The splendid neoclassical palace of white stone topped the hill opposite the Kremlin and from its windows one could see the churches' cupolas on Cathedral Square. Tolstoy spent many hours in this building reading Masonic manuscripts and other documents. In 1865, he also read historical materials in the Chertkov Library. The library's owner, Alexander Dmitrievich Chertkov, was a distinguished historian and archeologist, who belonged to the Moscow branch of Vladimir Chertkov's family. His library had a special collection of manuscripts and books on the war with Napoleon and portraits of military generals, which Tolstoy came to research for his novel. Alexander Chertkov donated his precious library to the city as a way to give back some of his wealth, generated by serfs. (He owned 13,888 male serfs before the emancipation. Female serfs were not counted.) Alexander II's reforms preceded Lincoln's Emancipation Proclamation by two years. In Russia, the reforms stirred public consciousness and inspired the notion of "noblesse oblige." In 1856, with the Tsar's emancipation still at the discussion phase, Tolstoy began to free serfs at his estate, Yasnaya Polyana.

During his research Tolstoy came across Chertkov's maternal ancestors as well. Chertkov's mother, née Countess Elizaveta Chernysheva-Kruglikova, was related to several Decembrists. Tolstoy read their history for his planned novel *The Decembrists*, which he drafted before *War and Peace*. In December 1825, a group of young aristocratic officers, heroes of the war with Napoleon, had attempted to overthrow the absolute monarchy and establish a constitutional regime. After suppression of the Decembrist

Uprising, five of its leaders were hanged, and scores of others sent to Siberia. Tolstoy interviewed them when, after decades of exile, the Decembrists were allowed to return to European Russia. Although he never completed this earlier novel, the altruism of the rebel aristocrats would inspire him for decades.

The story of the Decembrist Zakhar Chernyshev, closely related to Chertkov's mother, made it into Tolstoy's notebooks. The Chernyshev clan, which rose to prominence in the eighteenth century, owed their wealth to Peter I's favorite batman, Grigory. During subsequent reigns the former valet was promoted to major-general, received valuable estates and the title of Count. His son, Ivan Grigorievich Chernyshev, was a favorite of Peter III, who granted him two state-owned copper smelting factories in the Urals. Peasants assigned to work at these factories, which produced artillery, were mercilessly exploited: the Urals were an epicenter of peasant rebellions.

Ivan Chernyshev's influence increased under Catherine II, who appointed him as ambassador to London, senator, and Field Marshal. Chernyshev's fashionable wife, née Anna Islenyeva, wore jewels worth £40,000.[7] Court aristocrats led opulent lifestyles: the Chernyshevs owned Mariinsky Palace in Petersburg worth 3 million rubles and a palace outside the capital, known as Chernysheva dacha.

The ill-fated 1825 uprising changed the family's luck. The sole heir to an immense fortune, Zakhar Chernyshev was sentenced to hard labor in Eastern Siberia. For a year, he worked in the silver mines wearing shackles, in conditions far worse than those of the serfs at his grandfather's smelting factories. Zakhar was the uncle of Chertkov's mother, Elizaveta; her aunt, Alexandra Grigorievna Muravyova (née Chernysheva), the wife of a prominent Decembrist, had voluntarily followed him to Siberia.

Elizaveta's connection to the exiles did not affect her standing at court: many aristocrats had family members involved in the revolt. A beauty, she was introduced to Nicholas I at her coming out ball. The Tsar, who had deported her uncle and other relatives to Siberia, chatted with her graciously. In 1851, Elizaveta married the fabulously rich Grigory Chertkov, who became an aide-de-camp to the same Tsar.

Prince Alexander Ivanovich Chernyshev, also her relative, was Nicholas I's Minister of War and Field Marshal. His story is fascinating. A reactionary, he helped suppress the Decembrist Uprising and insisted on harsh penalties for the leaders. Alexander Chernyshev is depicted in *War and Peace* as an aide-de-camp to Alexander I, when during an early stage of the Napoleonic wars he is stationed in a fortified camp in Drissa on the River Dvina.

Alexander Chernyshev's career was launched at fifteen: he was introduced to Alexander I during a coronation ball in 1801. The boy impressed the Tsar with his intelligence and was chosen as an imperial page. At twenty-two, as an aide-de-camp in the Tsar's suite, Chernyshev was trusted to deliver Alexander I's personal messages to Napoleon. Later, he co-managed an espionage operation in Paris. Before Napoleon's invasion in Russia, he procured secret military reports about the redeployment of the French army eastwards. He obtained this information through his paid agents, officials employed in Napoleon's government and military administration. An adventurer, Chernyshev even infiltrated Napoleon's family. While in Paris, he became a lover of Pauline Borghese Bonaparte, Napoleon's younger sister. In 1812–1813, during the final stage of Napoleon's invasion in Russia, Chernyshev commanded several Cossack regiments, known as "flying detachments," which operated behind enemy lines and made deadly raids on the Grande Armée.[8] Alexander Chernyshev's story was undoubtedly known and told in the family when Chertkov was growing up, although this alone cannot explain his opportunism later on and his knack for conspiracy.

Chertkov's parents had a close relationship with Alexander II even before he became Tsar. In 1852, as heir to the throne, Alexander Nikolaevich baptized the couple's eldest son, Grigory. Having the Tsar as godfather brought certain privileges, such as a grant for the boy's education; on attaining his majority the young man could claim a post in the Ministry of Court.[9]

Alexander II visited the Chertkovs' home unaccompanied, arriving in a one-horse sleigh. His intimacy with the family fueled the gossip that he had sired the couple's second son, Vladimir. Born on October 22, 1854, Vladimir, or Dima, as they called him at home, was alone among a family of three brothers to survive adolescence. The others both died of consumption: Grigory at 17 and Mikhail, the youngest, at 10; the family witnessed his death in the south of France.

Tolstoy also lost two of his brothers to the same disease, which was rampant then. In 1860, Tolstoy was traveling with his eldest and beloved brother, Nikolai, when he too died in the South of France, at Hyères. As Tolstoy wrote a friend, "Nothing in life had made such an impression on me."[10] His brother's death inspired Tolstoy's thoughts about the need for religion, devoid of a metaphysical side. At his brother's funeral he got an idea to write "a materialist Gospel," a life of Christ without miracles.[11]

As a child, Dima Chertkov had practically no exposure to ordinary people, growing up among the children of Russia's ruling elite. The future Alexander III was among his playmates, as he would like to mention later on. Such an upbringing left him with a peculiar picture of the world and a strong sense of his own exclusiveness. He would become forever drawn to those in positions of the highest authority.

In contrast, Tolstoy did not meet a single government official until in his late teens. His father, Nikolai Ilyich, a participant in the war with Napoleon, had no ambition to pursue a military career in court, remarking he would not become a court equerry. As a liberal, he despised government service and, upon marriage, settled at his wife's country estate Yasnaya Polyana where Tolstoy would spend most of his life. The estate belonged to Tolstoy's maternal grandfather, Nikolai Volkonsky, vividly portrayed in *War and Peace*. Promoted to full general under Catherine the Great, Volkonsky later fell in disfavor. According to a family legend, this happened after he refused Catherine II's request to marry her lady-in-waiting, Varvara Engelgardt. This young woman was the mistress of Catherine's favorite, Grigory Potemkin, and by marrying her, Volkonsky would do him a favor, which would be undoubtedly returned with interest. When Varvara Engelgardt married Prince Sergei Golitsyn (related to the Chernyshev clan), the latter was promoted to General of the Infantry. In 1903, Tolstoy related this incident in his memoir with obvious pride that his grandfather did not seek advantages at court.[12]

Tolstoy was orphaned early and did not remember his mother. In childhood, he prayed to his mother's soul: his need for her love became inseparable from his faith in God. Later he would say that love was the essence of the human soul and that the ultimate goal of humankind was to become united in love.[13] Among Tolstoy's earliest influences was his peasant nanny and Yasnaya's housekeeper, Praskovia Isaevna: he describes her selfless love in his first novel, *Childhood*. His German tutor, who handled his early education, was unsophisticated but truthful and kind, qualities Tolstoy would come to value most.

Chertkov's nannies and governors came from England; he was educated at home by tutors he shared with the royal family. Among his tutors was Charles Heath, who taught at the Imperial Alexander Lyceum, the school for future diplomats and high officials. Heath would also educate Russia's last Tsar: in 1894, on a visit to Britain, Nicholas II introduced him to Queen Victoria.[14]

In 1884, remembering his lessons with Heath, Chertkov told Tolstoy: "He was an expert of English literature, a fan of Shakespeare, and also a talented water-color painter. He was noble, straightforward, and remarkably passionate . . . I remember, during his lessons we would forget all about spelling, and become carried away by heated discussions of various subjects, which lasted several hours."[15] Heath introduced Chertkov to painting, which would become his lifelong hobby.

Chertkov's family would spend much of their European vacation in England. When recalling "the comfortable and isolated little world" of his childhood, Chertkov would write how "after a tiresome journey by rail, our whole family settled in for lodging for the night at one of the best hotels of the foreign city."[16] Later in life, he would stay in Angleterre when abroad and when in Moscow—at the fashionable hotel, Slavyansky Bazar.

In 1864, when Dima was ten, Count Peter Shuvalov married his father's sister, Elena Ivanovna. Influential in the interior ministry, Uncle Shuvalov soon rose to become the closest adviser to Alexander II. In 1866, after the first assassination attempt on the Tsar, when a strong man was needed to fight revolutionary terrorists, Shuvalov was swiftly appointed the chief of gendarmes and head of the secret police (or the Third Section of His Imperial Majesty's Own Chancellery). But Shuvalov's repressive policies failed to discourage revolutionaries who made persistent attempts on the Tsar's life, until succeeding in 1881.

The all-powerful chief of the gendarmerie, Shuvalov never failed to remind the Tsar he was responsible for his safety and that of the empire. Alexander II trusted him completely: Shuvalov's influence was such that he even selected government ministers (notably from among his family and friends, e.g., Count Vladimir Bobrinsky and Count Konstantin Palen).

The Tsar endorsed all his appointments even though Shuvalov, a conservative, opposed the abolition of serfdom. Shuvalov was the real power behind the throne, which is why he was dubbed "Peter IV," after an epigram by a poet Fyodor Tyutchev. At the height of his influence Shuvalov established surveillance over government ministers and the Tsar himself. This action also became responsible for his fall from grace. Like other courtiers, Shuvalov disapproved of Alexander II's morganatic union with Catherine Dolgorukaya.[17] He spied on the couple during their European travel and, overstepping his authority, destroyed the negatives of the Tsar's portrait with his secret wife. In 1874, Shuvalov received a prominent but distant post as ambassador to Britain.

Uncle Shuvalov's influence over the Tsar impacted Chertkov's imagination. When he became Tolstoy's close friend and publisher, he resorted to similar tactics, reminding the writer about his own role promoting his religious creed. Chertkov repeated this so many times and so persuasively that eventually Tolstoy felt indebted to him. During Shuvalov's ambassadorship, Chertkov visited him in London, and later benefitted from his uncle's connections abroad. Upon Shuvalov's retirement in 1879, Chertkov would join him on hunting expeditions.

In his teens, Dima Chertkov hunted on the prairies that stretched around his parent's Voronezh estates. Lizinovka's estate manager, Vladimir Shramm, advised his young master, in Petersburg, about the availability of foxes and rabbits and new arrivals in their kennel where he cross-bred English hounds with the borzoi.[18] One summer, while riding on the hot prairie, Dima suffered sunstroke. Doctors forbade him strenuous mental activity and later blamed his violent mood swings and temper tantrums on this hunting incident. In a letter to Chertkov, Tolstoy eloquently describes his mental imbalance: ". . . Your mood is changeable—sometimes you are feverishly active, other times apathetic."[19]

At nineteen, Chertkov was enlisted as an officer in the Horse Guards. Handsome, taller than average—of guardsman's height—he was nicknamed *le beau Dima*. Because the Guards' barracks were in Petersburg, his manservant regularly delivered him clean linen, supper, and wine.

Chertkov's friend in the Guards, Dmitry Trepov, would remain his lifelong companion and best government contact. A son of Petersburg's governor general, Fyodor Trepov, he would surpass his father's career success and enjoy great favor in the court of the last Tsar.

Like other gilded youth of Petersburg, Chertkov took part in carousals with the gypsies, activity also favored by the sons of Alexander II, the Grand Dukes Alexei and Vladimir. (The Grand Dukes' behavior is known to have scandalized public opinion.[20]) Describing his pastime as an officer, Chertkov would write, "All three classical vices—wine, cards, and women—I gave myself without a restraint, living in a daze, with rare interludes of staidness."[21] Rich and with big connections, which made them feel impervious, the Guards had unlimited opportunities for amusement as well as vice.

They did daily drills to prepare for parades, frequented the officers' club, and attended balls in the capital. Although officers were expected to attend balls, they rarely received a personal invitation. The regiment was informed how many Guards would attend and the officer in command named those who would take on the duty. The senior colonel would instruct them before a ball: "You must not think about having a good time . . . You have got to dance with the ladies and do your best to keep them amused . . ."[22] But for a willful man like Chertkov, there was pleasure in defying these rules.

Unlike most other Guards, *le beau Dima* received a personal invitation to the Anichkov Palace where the Grand Duchess Maria Fyodorovna held small, select dances for three hundred guests. (The annual balls at the Winter Palace would host two to three thousand.[23]) Those who attended were royalty and the cream of aristocracy; officers were invited only when extra dancing partners were needed. It was under such circumstances that Dima Chertkov attended; but when the hostess herself invited him to a waltz, he abruptly refused. The ballroom went silent, but Maria Fyodorovna, a close friend of Chertkov's mother, forgave the prank. She smiled and fastened a rose to *le beau Dima*'s chest.

Such behavior would have been unthinkable for Chertkov's father: a dutiful servant of the royal family, he would remember a single rebuke for years. At a ball given by German ambassador Prince Reuss, General Chertkov danced with Maria Fyodorovna and sat beside her, on her orders, failing to observe that Alexander II had entered the ballroom with the German emperor. The Tsar publicly reprimanded Chertkov for his oversight. Years later, under the new Emperor, the incident was still remembered at court. By then, General Chertkov's legs were amputated due to gangrene, but he attended balls in a wheelchair. He sat surrounded by the ladies of the imperial family when Alexander III entered the ballroom. The courtiers whispered that now Chertkov could not be reprimanded for remaining seated.[24]

Dima Chertkov rebelled against his father's influence. A military administrator, General Chertkov attained top awards, to which his rank entitled him, including the Order of Alexander Nevsky with diamonds. But he was only a general-adjutant in the large imperial suite, which swelled under Alexander II to an unprecedented 385 people.[25]

The Guards would meet the Tsar and his suite during the Sunday review of their regiments, which took place at the Mikhailov Manège. It was anticipated by all the officers, who were vying for the Tsar's personal attention. The guards would be lined up, waiting for the moment when the gates opened and Alexander II would appear, leading his gray horse Ovid. The Guards immediately hushed. "The command, 'Be on guard!' resounded through the enormous hall . . ." The officers presented their reports, while the rest anticipated the show of horsemanship to follow. Officers from different regiments—the Cavalier Guards, the Horse Guards, and the Don Cossacks of the Guard—galloped in three straight lines, never losing their distance, then all at once came to a halt before the Tsar. The Cossack riders performed acrobatic stunts and the Tsar, delighted, shouted, "Thank you! Good fellows!"[26] After the review Alexander II chatted with the Guards, whom he knew by name, and praised their performance. On one occasion, Chertkov tells, he outcompeted the other officers with his show and the Tsar, impressed, rode up to him, an act that was "unprecedented in the history of the Guards' Sunday ceremonial reviews."

> Stopping directly opposite me, he [Alexander II] looked at me with sympathy, nodded, and made a throaty sound of approval. Then, looking around, he asked, "Where is Grigory Ivanovich?" This was my father. All at once, members of his

entourage began to summon Grigory Ivanovich. In a while, my father, who did not like to sit in the front row, arrived. The Tsar told him, "But he is more handsome than you were." "I do not contend, your Imperial Highness!" "You do not contend! You do not contend!" the Tsar replied.[27]

Having recorded this story in 1932, as an old man, Chertkov still relished the Tsar's special attention. In fact, Alexander II had casual relationships with his adjutants-general and baptized their children, which is why the Guards called him their "leader-father."[28] But Chertkov apparently believed that the Tsar was his actual father, which may explain his grandiose sense of self-worth, that would later enable him to treat Tolstoy as his equal. As Chertkov wrote in another memoir, "Alexander II was well-disposed to me . . . and I was looking forward to a new meeting with him, face to face."[29]

Chertkov would tell of how he and his parents were invited to the Livadia Palace in the Crimea where the royal family spent their holidays.[30] An invitation to Livadia was considered a sign of imperial grace. However, Chertkov later altered his diaries and such accounts cannot be verified. Uncle Shuvalov indeed visited Livadia: in the 1860s, at the height of his influence, he was seen accompanying Alexander II's young sons, Sergei Alexandrovich and Paul Alexandrovich, to the Crimea. Witte, then the head of the Odessa railroad, was surprised that the powerful chief of the gendarmerie was looking after the Grand Dukes as their tutor.[31]

Tolstoy had encouraged Chertkov to write his recollections, and in 1909 he produced a short memoir about his time in the Guards. At eighty-one, Tolstoy read it with tears of joy.[32] It was a story Chertkov had partly told during their first meeting, when he spoke of experiencing a religious awakening while still in the army. He had begun to proselytize in the military hospitals where junior officers were assigned inspection duties. This is also where Chertkov for the first time encountered simple folk: he read the Gospels to the sick and dying soldiers.

Chertkov remembers himself at twenty-two, on duty at the enormous Nikolaevsky Military Hospital, which accommodated over a thousand patients. Although it was patronized by the Tsar, corruption was rampant.

Junior officers, who knew nothing of accounting, were entrusted with checking the books. Administration routinely confiscated money from soldiers, and because they were afraid to complain, such violations usually went unreported. Chertkov launched his own investigation, finding that the cash ended up in the desk drawer of the hospital treasurer. When he challenged the official, the latter produced the requested sum with indifference.

Soon he learned that there were political inmates among the patients. They were kept separately, in sweat-boxes, and routinely tortured by exposure to extreme cold and heat. Contact with politicals was forbidden, and the fact of their existence in the hospital was a secret, but this only fueled Chertkov's curiosity. He prevailed on a guard to open one of the boxes. Upon finding a consumptive prisoner in an overheated cell, Chertkov demanded his transfer. The terrified guard fled, obviously to report the case, of which Chertkov was aware. Meanwhile, he entered the cell, took out the Gospels, which he kept in his pocket, and began reading to the inmate, who turned out to be a revolutionary radical of some prominence. Later, realizing that he exceeded his authority, Chertkov admitted that he simply "forgot" that he had officers above him. In fact, he was accustomed to being in command. When called before the general in charge, Chertkov was amused: "I perfectly realized that nobody would punish me because of my parents' high position in society . . ." Upon learning his name, the head of the hospital, who was a classmate of Chertkov's father at the Page Corps, dropped the case. It was Chertkov who complained about the inadequacy of the hospital administration. He took the case to his regimental commander, Baron Vladimir Freedericksz, who would become minister of the imperial court. Proving his noble intentions and impressing Freedericksz seemed the main point of his visit. "As we parted, we both felt that we belong to the same exclusive circle of 'decent people,' for whom acting like the hospital administration was just as unthinkable as bad table manners . . ." As for the political inmates, their fate was not assuaged: they were placed under tighter security.

Chertkov preached the Gospel in military hospitals at the time of a religious revival in Petersburg. His circle of upper aristocracy had recently undergone spiritual conversion and begun to engage in charitable activities.

Chertkov's mother opened sewing shops, shelters, tea rooms, and visited women's prisons and hospitals where she also proselytized to the terminally ill.

Two years earlier, in 1874, an English evangelical preacher, Lord Radstock,[33] made his first, phenomenally successful visit to Petersburg. Like many in his milieu, Chertkov was influenced by Radstock's message of personal salvation through independent Bible study. His mother had heard Radstock in Europe, shortly after the death of her youngest son, and found solace in his sermons. Upon becoming Radstock's follower, Elizaveta invited him to Russia. In Petersburg, she introduced him to family and friends, becoming responsible for his instant success.

An English aristocrat and Oxford graduate, Radstock had worked among the poor in London's East End and conducted missionary activities in India. Arriving in Petersburg in spring of 1874, during Holy Week, Radstock turned fashionable salons into prayer homes. Each day he would speak to two or three gatherings and would have individual appointments in between. This unremarkable red-haired man with blue eyes and childish laughter was casually dressed and spoke without eloquence, in faulty French. But his simple message, that salvation was open to all who desired it, was eagerly received. Meetings were held in some forty mansions and palaces. Radstock would begin with a silent prayer for divine guidance, then read and discuss passages in the Gospels, never preparing his comments. At the end of each gathering, he knelt in front of his audience to an improvised prayer, uttering it with deep conviction; he concluded with a hymn. He led people to Christ, rather than to the Church. His sermons were accessible, unlike services by the Orthodox clergy, still held in Church Slavonic, which was incomprehensible even to men with university education. Radstock's audiences would exclaim, "How simple! How clear!" His role was compared to that of a nanny.

Front pages of Petersburg newspapers began to praise Radstock as well as attack him, all of which boosted his fame. Because his success created tensions with the Orthodox Church, his adherents were cautious about revealing their names. Among them were many prominent aristocrats: Countess Elena Shuvalova (née Chertkova), statesman Baron Modest Korf, Count Aleksei Bobrinsky (minister of ways and communications), Princess

Vera Lieven and her sister, Princess Natalia Gagarina. Alexander II and his personal physician were said to have been among Radstock's friends. According to a senior Orthodox priest, "Not to be a Radstockist meant to lower oneself in the eyes of society and risk the danger of becoming labeled a backward person."[34]

Novelist Ivan Turgenev wrote that despite official harassment, Lord Radstock was winning hearts with his "awkward and ineloquent sermons."[35] Writer Nikolai Leskov remarked that Radstock "indeed must have true faith; how different from our clergy who function like civil-service men."[36] In March 1876, during his work on *Anna Karenina*, Tolstoy met Count Bobrinsky, who was his neighbor in the Tula province. As Tolstoy wrote to Alexandra Tolstaya, his relative and lady-in-waiting at the Petersburg court, Bobrinsky "struck me very much by the sincerity and ardor of his faith."[37] Tolstoy asked Alexandrine, as he called her, to describe her impressions of meeting Radstock. Alexandrine spoke of him as "a dear and kind sectarian. . . . According to his system, every human being can divest himself in no time of all his passion and evil inclinations provided he has the desire to follow his Savior. . . . He often talks of such cases . . . in which the conversion took place in about an hour's time. This is his weak point. But then, what devotion to Christ, what warmth, what immeasurable sincerity! His message resounded here like a bell, and he awakened many who before never thought of Christ and their salvation."[38] Tolstoy, who also believed that "sudden conversions rarely or never happen,"[39] used her account for an ironic depiction of the missionary Sir John and his circle of devotees in the novel: "It was a circle of elderly, unattractive, virtuous and pious women and of intelligent, educated and ambitious men. One of the intelligent men who belonged to this circle called it 'the conscience of Petersburg society.'"[40] Tolstoy mocked Radstock's converts because they maintained privileged lifestyles.

Radstock's missionary activities came at a time when the Orthodox Church's influence was declining. Whereas Western church-state separation had begun in the early sixteenth century with Martin Luther's two kingdoms doctrine and Henry VIII's break with Rome, the Russian Orthodox Church remained closely allied with the government. If anything, church-state relations in Russia were going in the opposite direction of those in Europe. The Church had lost its independence back in 1721 when Peter I replaced the Moscow Patriarchate with the government appointed Holy Synod. The Synod was directed by the Chief Procurator, the lay head of the Orthodox Church and a member of the Tsar's cabinet. In 1880, the reactionary Konstantin Pobedonostsev was appointed to this post, which he would occupy for twenty-five years. It was also in the early 1880s that Tolstoy began to challenge the Church's authority, complaining of its continued alliance with the state. During Pobedonostsev's time in office the Orthodox Church was subservient to the autocracy and did not make any independent decisions. Everything, from repair of church buildings to selecting priests and disbursing Church funds, was decided by lay officials. Priests were expected to assist the police, reporting anything suspicious or disloyal learned during confession. Moreover, the Church joined the state in the persecution of sectarians and other minorities. The largest group of religious dissenters, the Old Believers, had caused a schism in the Church in the 1660s, after they refused to accept Patriarch Nikon's reforms to rituals. Some sectarian groups, such as the Doukhobors, or "spirit wrestlers" (they would become one of Tolstoy's causes) were continually harassed and displaced by the government. Although by some estimates sectarians comprised a quarter of the empire's population, they all experienced discrimination.[41] The abusive policies of the state and the Church led to general disillusionment with official religion. Beginning in the 1860s, Russia saw the spread of nihilism among young radicals: they preached materialism and atheism. Most intellectuals would leave the Church by the early twentieth century.

While educated society was becoming more secular, Tolstoy believed in the importance of religion; however, he also stopped attending church. In 1859, at age thirty, he wrote Alexandrine that he read the Gospels and prayed in his own room, "but to go to church, to stand there and listen to unintelligible and incomprehensible prayers . . . that I *absolutely cannot* do."[42]

In fact, the Orthodox Church had suppressed the spread of the New Testament: it only became widely accessible in Russia in 1876, when it was distributed by Radstock and other missionaries. Although the New Testament had been translated into modern Russian back in 1823, it was available marginally. The first complete Bible was not published until 1882.[43]

The Church was alarmed with Radstock's popularity: in 1878, he was banned from Russia. After his expulsion, Chertkov's uncle, Colonel Vasily Pashkov, took over his missionary activities, becoming the leader of his own movement.

Immensely rich, Pashkov owned factories and vast estates around Novgorod, Moscow, Tambov, and Orenburg. In addition, his wife (Elizaveta Chertkova's eldest sister, Alexandra) had inherited most of the immense Chernyshev fortune. In 1909, Tolstoy would visit Kryokshino, their lavish estate near Moscow: it was where Chertkov would have him sign the first redaction of his secret testament.

While in the past, the Pashkovs' Petersburg palace had accommodated balls for two thousand with Alexander II attending, in the 1870s, it drew aristocrats and peasants alike, for regular prayer meetings. Unlike Radstock, Pashkov preached to all classes indiscriminately. In the words of a contemporary, the motley crowd in his residence resembled "Noah's gatherings of pairs from every kind of living creatures."[44] After the sermons, Pashkov gave elaborate meals and distributed cash to anyone who asked. The authorities viewed Pashkov as a safer alternative to the spread of populist and socialist ideas. The governor of Petersburg, General Fyodor Trepov, even provided police protection during Pashkov's prayer gatherings. Trepov indefatigably fought the revolutionary movement and in 1878, was sentenced to death by a group of radicals. A revolutionary named Vera Zasulich shot and wounded him to avenge the flogging of a political prisoner.

Pashkov and his followers, among whom Chertkov's mother was most active, formed "The Society for the Encouragement of Spiritual and Ethical Reading." Their religious propaganda became unprecedented in the empire: the society produced millions of pamphlets and other spiritual literature, selling it for less than a kopeck, and distributed the Bible. Chertkov would adopt many of his uncle's practices when launching Intermediary, his publishing enterprise with Tolstoy.

In 1879, Chertkov took a sabbatical to engage in Christian study in England. As a personal favor to General Chertkov, Baron Freedericksz permitted an extended leave of eleven months without quitting the regiment. Chertkov settled outside London, in a house of a rural minister, but did not shut himself from society. He frequented London's Piccadilly

Club where he could meet members of the English diplomatic service and the Foreign Office. At the residence of Uncle Shuvalov, in his last year as ambassador, Chertkov even met European royalty. Later, he told Tolstoy an anecdote from his time in London: he was invited to a supper at the Russian embassy for the Prince of Wales, the future Edward VII. The supper was served on small separate tables. The tables were swiftly removed before the dance, revealing that the Prince of Wales and a lady beside him sat with their legs joined. Tolstoy, eighty-two, was laughing heartily and asked Chertkov to repeat the story to his eldest daughter, Tanya.[45]

Upon returning to Petersburg, Chertkov joined a Christian study group, one of many that sprang up in the capital. Among its members were talented young aristocrats, such as Prince Boris Golitsyn, a physicist and future academician; Paul Biryukov, a naval officer and Tolstoy's future biographer, and Count Alexander Geiden, another naval officer, who would become Admiral of the Fleet. Chertkov's close friend in the Guards, Dmitry Trepov, was the group's leader. Much like his father, Trepov Jr. would brutally suppress student demonstrations in his capacity as the governor general of Petersburg. The Gospel's message was apparently lost on him, but Chertkov would always insist that Trepov was a decent man.

Later, Chertkov would tell that he left the army because of his pacifist beliefs. While this may be true, his deep disdain for discipline and authority made him unsuitable for a military career. In 1880, Chertkov submitted his resignation and left for Lizinovka, his family's estate. As Tolstoy suggests in *Resurrection*, using Chertkov's background for Dmitry Nekhlyudov, there was also his dream of becoming an artist. Tolstoy's hero resigns from the army, believing "he had a talent for art." Nekhlyudov's well-appointed studio, in which Chertkov's is recognizable, was "a large, lofty room fitted up with a view to comfort, convenience, and elegant appearance." Like Nekhlyudov, who was aware of his "inability to advance in art,"[46] Chertkov lacked the talent and perseverance to become a portraitist.

In 1881, two major events rocked Petersburg: Fyodor Dostoevsky's death and the Tsar's assassination. After publication of his final novel, *The Brothers Karamazov*, Dostoevsky was treated as a prophet: tens of thousands came for his funeral. Tolstoy had mixed feelings about his great literary rival whom he had never met. Days after Dostoevsky's death on February 9, Tolstoy wrote he was "the very closest . . . and most necessary man for me."[47] But two years later, he told critic Nikolai Strakhov, that Dostoevsky's "elevation into a prophet and saint" was "false and erroneous."[48]

To Chertkov, who was fascinated with Dostoevsky as a Christian writer, his fame illustrated phenomenal spiritual power. He wanted to see Dostoevsky and even made arrangements for the meeting. As Chertkov later told Tolstoy, Dostoevsky's death came "as a great personal privation to me—I was about to meet him. I think I've never heard of a better and loftier interpretation of Christ's teaching in terms of its practical application as in *The Idiot* and, mainly, in Alexei Karamazov."[49]

The following month, Alexander II was assassinated by members of the revolutionary organization the People's Will. Chertkov's reaction to this event is veiled in mystery: years later, he made the strange and impersonal remark that the Tsar's murder reawakened his monarchist sentiments.[50] On March 1, the Tsar attended the regular Sunday parade of the Guards' regiments. As he was driving back along the Catherine Canal towards the Winter Palace a terrorist bomb was thrown, injuring his Cossack convoy. The Tsar was unharmed in his bomb-proof carriage, a present from Napoleon III of France. But when he left the carriage to look at the injured, a second explosion fatally wounded him.

Following the assassination the aristocracy vowed to defend the monarchy. Three million rubles were raised to fund a conspiratorial monarchist society, the Holy Brotherhood, formed to hunt down revolutionaries at home and abroad. Chertkov's other uncle, Paul Shuvalov, was a co-founder of Holy Brotherhood, which recruited members from among the government ministers and the military. But membership was kept secret even from the police. The Guards were likely to join this short-lived organization: it was their duty to defend the monarchy. Around this time, Chertkov briefly returned to his regiment.

Uncle Peter Shuvalov was assigned to inform the European courts about Alexander III's ascension to the throne; Chertkov was included in his delegation. But in the end, he did not go, dashing his family's hope for his military career. Chertkov's parents were particularly close to Alexander III, a nationalist Tsar, who pursued repressive policies.

In March, Tolstoy wrote to the new Tsar asking him not to execute his father's assassins, but to forgive them in the name of Christian law. "One cannot fight them by killing or destroying them. It is not their number which is important but their ideas . . . There is only one ideal which can be opposed to them . . . the ideal of love, forgiveness and the returning of good for evil."[51] However, Alexander III began his reign with executions, much like his grandfather Nicholas I, who had executed the Decembrist leaders. The terrorists, including one woman, Sofia Perovskaya, a general's daughter, were hanged on April 3, 1881. Revolutionaries retaliated by plotting to assassinate Alexander III on the sixth anniversary of his father's death.

Later that year, Chertkov's resignation from the army became official and he returned to Lizinovka, at once plunging into activity as a landowner and a preacher. A vast estate, Lizinovka was surrounded by villages with a total population of 5,000, but the inhabitants had no access to education or medical care. Chertkov's mother had opened an ambulatory and a village school at the estate. Chertkov made further improvements, opening village stores, reading rooms, and the community savings bank. He also transformed the village school into a trade school for sixty boys, hired teachers, and himself gave religious instruction. When Chertkov moved from the mansion into the student dormitory, his mother wrote that he was confusing Christianity with democracy.[52]

Simultaneously, Chertkov became involved with *zemstvo*, the local government, established during the liberal reforms of Alexander II to build roads, promote public education, and provide medical service. The judicial reform created Justice of the Peace courts to try lesser cases, and jury trials—for more important offenses. Shortly after the Emancipation, Tolstoy served as the Arbiter of the Peace, resolving arguments between the gentry and peasants. Tolstoy settled land disputes in peasants' favor, which earned him the gentry's wrath. Chertkov wanted to serve as an Honorary Justice of the Peace, an unpaid position to which local landlords were entitled. Justices were confirmed in the Senate, so Chertkov wrote to both his father and Uncle Shuvalov, urging them to speed up his nomination.[53] This was unnecessary, but Chertkov wanted influential people to become involved, even if his family belonged to the opposite political camp from his present milieu.

Chertkov's new associates were liberal landowners; one was his Petersburg friend Rafail Pisarev, who was also working for the local government. Pisarev had assisted Tolstoy with educational projects, opening and inspecting schools in the Tula district. The two were so close that Tolstoy mentioned him affectionately in his diary. It was through Pisarev that Chertkov soon entered Tolstoy's intimate circle of friends.

When in 1883, Chertkov's mother asked him to consider civil service, he refused: a formal career was against his beliefs. Besides, by joining a government service he would only lose money. In fact, his allowance of ten thousand rubles exceeded a salary of a high government official. (The director of the Department of Railroad Affairs then received an annual salary of 8,000 rubles.[54]) Chertkov preferred to be his own master, writing his mother that he would achieve greater influence if the initiative and the course remained in his hands.[55]

Having made costly improvements in Lizinovka, Chertkov was heavily in debt. His mother complained about the bills, which he expected his family to pay. Chertkov was unsuccessfully trying to raise money by selling his hunting rifles and Persian carpets from the Lizinovka manor. (His intended buyer was Aunt Shuvalova.) Afraid that he would squander the family's fortune, General Chertkov amended his will, leaving the capital to his wife. Chertkov would continue to receive an allowance, which his mother doubled.

Earlier that year, describing a glamorous reception with the Tsar at their Petersburg apartment, Elizaveta listed their guests. The Chertkovs entertained Alexander III and Empress Maria Fyodorovna; Grand Duke Mikhail Nikolaievich[56] and Grand Duchess Olga Fyodorovna[57]; General Pyotr Cherevin (friend of Alexander III and chief of palace security), General Adjutant Nikolai Levashov (former Governor General of Petersburg); Count Illarion Vorontsov-Dashkov (Alexander III's friend, then minister of the imperial court), his wife Countess Alexandra Vorontsova, and Countess Elizaveta (Betsy) Shuvalova (née Baryatinskaya). Countess Betsy Shuvalova, who could trace her ancestry further than the Romanovs, lived in the eighteenth century palace on Fontanka 21, where she hosted some of the most splendid balls in the capital. The previous owner of the Fontanka palace, Maria Naryshkina, was a mistress of Alexander I.

Dinner was served in the red living room, where Elizaveta Chertkova sat between the Tsar and Countess Vorontsova. "After the tea, everyone went into Papa's study and walked around the room for a long time . . . and finally sat down to play cards. The Tsar with his party sat at your round antique table of Louis XV, which was dragged from your room and which everyone admired."[58] The Empress played cards at a separate table with the ladies. Elizaveta and Aunt Sophie Chertkova, who did not take part in the game, were watching and admiring "the grand spectacle" from their "ordinary armchairs."

Chertkov was twenty-nine when he received this letter. That fall, he met Tolstoy, finding a new patron and a proxy father in the writer whose fame made him an equal of the Tsar.

CHAPTER TWO

UNLIKELY FRIENDS

"I have a weak character and submit easily to the influence of people I love."

> —Tolstoy, in a letter to Alexandrine
> (Alexandra Tolstaya), 1863

"I love him and I believe in him."

> —Tolstoy, *Diaries*, 1884

"Little did he [Maugham] know that he was about to enter the longest, most miserable, and most miserably destructive relationship in his life."

> —Selina Hastings,
> *The Secret Lives of Somerset Maugham*

Chertkov's first meeting with Tolstoy, in late October 1883, was opportune: the writer felt increasingly isolated in his intellectual milieu where his religious works failed to make an impact. Chertkov, keenly interested in his teaching, struck Tolstoy as a man "of one mind" with him. Their immeasurable differences—in intellect, character, and age—only strengthened mutual attraction: Chertkov soon became his confidante.

When, after the universal success of *Anna Karenina*, Tolstoy turned to religious writing, his friends and family were disappointed. His new dogmatic style was a far cry from his artistic works, and his preoccupation with the Gospels, an attempt to prove that the official Church teachings were incompatible with Christian ideals, was of interest to few. In mid-life, Tolstoy had experienced a profound spiritual crisis, which affected his views, character, work, and lifestyle, compelling him to reject his literary achievement and former life as a family man and landowner. In 1880, he refused to participate in the Pushkin festival in Moscow with the unveiling of the poet's monument. The event drew rapturous crowds: Dostoevsky and Turgenev were among the speakers. Tolstoy dismissed the event's importance, which generated a rumor in the writers' milieu that he no longer wrote fiction and that he had gone mad.

In *A Confession*, which he wrote at the time, he describes his struggle with suicidal thoughts and his search for a deeper meaning of existence, a truly spiritual life that alone could escape destruction by death. Religion promised salvation from doubts in a simple truth: we do not live for ourselves. Tolstoy did not believe in sudden conversions, and existing world religions did not satisfy him. True faith could be found "through work and suffering," he wrote Alexandrine. "You say you don't know what I believe in. Strange and terrible to say: not in anything that religion teaches us; but at the same time I not only hate and despise unbelief, but I can see no possibility of living, and still less of dying, without faith."[1] Tolstoy did not accept the Christian doctrines of redemption and resurrection. He sought a religion that could withstand his rational scrutiny. The idea of creating a practical religion, which would guide his conscience, had first occurred to him at twenty-seven. When formulating it in his diary, he wrote that he could devote his life to implementing this dream:

> This idea is the foundation of a new religion corresponding to the development of mankind—the religion of Christ, but purged of dogma and mystery, a practical religion, not promising future

bliss but providing bliss on earth . . . Working consciously to
unite people with religion is the foundation of the idea which
I hope will occupy me.[2]

Tolstoy had never labored with such intensity as in his fifties. Immersed in
translating the four Gospels (from the Greek), he worked to recapture Jesus'
messages in their purest and earliest form, before they were corrupted by
the Church's interpretation. He said he was conducting "an investigation
of the teachings of Christ" based "on what has come down to us" from
Jesus.[3] Eventually, he focused his attention on the moral imperatives in the
Sermon on the Mount, which he viewed as the blueprint for building the
Kingdom of God on earth. In St. Matthew's Gospel Jesus tells that the
old law of "an eye for an eye, and a tooth for a tooth" should be replaced
by a non-violent response: "But I say unto you, That ye resist not evil . . ."
Tolstoy thought this message was key to understanding Christianity. He
argued that no physical force can be used to compel another human being, a
belief that enabled him to renounce not only violence and war, but all social
institutions as coercive. When he met Chertkov, Tolstoy was completing
his book *What I Believe* in which he formulated his non-resistance doctrine.

In summer 1883, at the wedding of his friend Pisarev, whose estate
was near Yasnaya Polyana, Chertkov met an old friend of Tolstoy, Nikolai
Davydov. As prosecutor and president of the Tula circuit court, Davydov
handled Tolstoy's petitions on behalf of the peasants and was a source for
his fiction. During a long nocturnal conversation Chertkov told the judge
of his belief that Christ's teaching was incompatible with military service.
Davydov was struck that on other issues that mattered to Tolstoy, such
as his attitude to the Orthodox Church, Chertkov also sounded precisely
like the writer. He was even more fascinated when Chertkov told him
he had never read Tolstoy's works, but arrived at the same conclusions
independently.

Davydov at once wrote Tolstoy that he should meet the young like-
minded aristocrat. By then, Chertkov's name was familiar to Tolstoy:
Gavriil Rusanov, another acquaintance and member of Tula's district court,
had also spoken favorably about him. Chertkov had befriended people close
to Tolstoy, thus setting himself above the writer's many visitors and acolytes.

Davydov also helped with the arrangements: at Chertkov's request, he sent a telegram informing him when Tolstoy was in Moscow. Chertkov was already there, staying at the fashionable Slavyanski Bazar Hotel not far from the Kremlin. The hotel and its restaurant were favored by wealthy landlords, Petersburg ministers, and owners of Siberian gold mines.

Tolstoy's Moscow residence was in Khamovniki, a working class neighborhood on the outskirts of the city. The century-old, two-story wooden house was surrounded by a large garden and shady park. Tolstoy's upstairs study was at the back of the house, isolated from noise, its windows facing the garden. A heavy desk of dark mahogany with a wood railing dominated the small study, and two black leather armchairs stood beside it.

Chertkov was neither an intellectual, nor, as he claims, had he read Tolstoy's works before they met. But he knew enough about the writer to impress him, and began with a confession. He told about his dissolute life as an officer in the Guards, his interest in the Gospels, which had produced his spiritual transformation; all of this had a perfect pitch for the writer. When Chertkov mentioned he quit the military upon becoming a pacifist, Tolstoy picked up the manuscript of *What I Believe* and began reading. During the last week of October, Chertkov returned to Tolstoy's house several times. They discussed the Gospels and Tolstoy's teaching; Chertkov asked detailed questions and recorded the answers in his notebook. Chertkov belonged to circles close to court and Tolstoy was glad that his ideas were making an impact on the very rich.

Tolstoy believed that the teaching of the Orthodox Church was in conflict with Christianity. For example, the Gospel says, "do not kill," "do not be angry," while the Church sanctions the army and therefore murder. Christ's moral imperatives were unifying, whereas the official Church had caused divisions and persecuted dissenters throughout its history. To show that Jesus' moral imperatives in the Sermon on the Mount were meant to unite, rather than divide people, Tolstoy reduced them to the five he thought most inclusive: do not be angry, do not lust, do not swear oaths (according to Tolstoy, Christ had rejected courts and the judiciary), do not resist evil by force, and love all people alike. Tolstoy's non-fiction, which was critical of the government and the Church, could not be published in Russia. People who read the underground copies were mainly revolutionaries, who, though sympathetic with his anti-establishment message, rejected Tolstoy's belief in non-violence. He had recently met a serious follower in the prominent painter, Nikolai Gay, with whom he struck up an instant and close friendship. Tolstoy experienced moments of "indescribable joy" when his correspondents or visitors expressed ideas similar to his own. He understood this as a sign that he had uncovered an essential truth, which would have universal appeal: "These thoughts are not mine, this is God's truth, and it's in your heart, and in mine and in the hearts of all people."[4] With Gay, a talented artist, who would paint him in his Moscow study at work on *What I Believe*, Tolstoy exchanged ideas on religion and art. With Chertkov, who was to become his most important follower, such intellectual exchange was impossible. If Tolstoy did have something in common with Chertkov, it was his dogmatic streak and a tendency toward moralizing. But mainly, he was drawn to the younger man, who was keen to absorb his ideas.

On October 31, returning from Tolstoy in the early hours of the morning, Chertkov sat down to reply to his mother's letter in which she warned him against promoting Tolstoy's alien doctrine. So he reassured her that he was having a good time with Tolstoy, but they had "significant differences" in their perception of God. They agreed mainly on the practical application of Christ's teaching, on how Christians should live.[5]

Back in Lizinovka Chertkov collected his books on theology, which he had studied in London, and sent them to Tolstoy. This only produced a cooling off in the relationship. Skimming through the voluminous *Life and Words of Christ* by John Geikie, Tolstoy was bored, describing it as "a tedious compilation." The anonymous *Ecce Homo*, which surveyed the works of Christ, was more promising, he told Chertkov. While the books did not interest him, Tolstoy read Chertkov's penciled notes in the margin, trying to understand the man. "Dear and kind, and nearest to me, Vladimir Grigorievich, I received your books, and I thank you for them," Tolstoy began his first letter to Chertkov. He sensed Chertkov's attempt to explain religion to him, but nothing could repel Tolstoy more than such attempts. As he had written earlier, "The more they explained [religion], the more obscure it became to me."[6]

Tolstoy told Chertkov about his relationship with God through a parable of a master and a laborer. A good laborer, eager to do the work, wants to grasp his master's instructions. A lazy one will stick around the kitchen asking questions about his master's life and in the end will confuse it all and will accomplish nothing. It's important to recognize Jesus as your master and understand what he wants from you. As for Jesus' life, "I'll never know it, he is not my equal: I'm a laborer, not a master."[7] Referring to Chertkov's books about resurrection, Tolstoy asked, "Are you really interested in this?" He rejected the metaphysical side of the Gospels, thinking it only distracted attention from Jesus' message and from the changes one had to make in one's own life.

Chertkov believed in the teachings of resurrection and redemption, but was quick to reassure Tolstoy: "I agree with you almost on every point, and recognize you as the expounder of my best aspirations."[8] But two weeks earlier, he told his mother a different story: "Your remark . . . that you were happy to know I didn't agree with Tolstoy on everything surprised me and made me smile. Do you really think, Mama, that my convictions . . . are so unsound that I will embrace the views of a chance acquaintance?"[9] Chertkova's evangelical circle believed Tolstoy's interpretation of the Gospels to be harmful and she kept advising her son not to spread his views, for "one would answer to God for this."[10] Chertkov responded evasively that actually nobody knew he kept Tolstoy's "articles."

In November 1883, Chertkov and his mother were reading *War and Peace*, published a decade and a half earlier. Tolstoy's satire on high society and his conception of history, which allotted a prominent role to the people, not their leaders, had discouraged them from reading it earlier. Chertkov wrote his mother that, historical views aside, the novel contained "wonderful artistic passages" and revealed the author's long-standing interest in religion.[11]

Coming to Moscow before Christmas, Chertkov visited Tolstoy informally as a friend, arriving at his house direct from the station. He charmed the entire family. Sophia's first impression of the man, who later would become her rival, was favorable: she describes him as handsome, manly, and "a true aristocrat." In her memoir she remarks that Chertkov was steeped in Tolstoy's new writings. Tolstoy was fond of him and "loved him to the end, and highly valued him for his sincere and keen admiration of everything Lev Nikolaevich wrote and thought."[12]

In winter 1884, Chertkov was reading *What I Believe* and instructing his peasant students in Lizinovka to accept Tolstoy's interpretation of the Sermon on the Mount as the only correct one. "I have a strong need to commune with you," he told Tolstoy, inviting him to Lizinovka. "You are very busy, you have your own family and work, and I cannot count on your visit here." Chertkov needed Tolstoy's counsel to guide his students: "What will become of them if I lead them on a wrong path?.. No, Lev Nikolaevich, come, cheer up, help. You are needed here."[13]

Tolstoy thought Chertkov was trying to abnegate his own duties and to engage him in proselytizing. There was only one teacher—Christ, he replied. And besides, one should be doing God's work without expecting praise. "I love you very much, and your life is important to me, as part of mine, but I unlikely will visit you this winter."[14] Chertkov accepted Tolstoy's criticism humbly and admitted his selfishness. He also admired Tolstoy's plan to mass-produce edifying books for the people.[15] Tolstoy was assuaged: "What a splendid cheerful letter you wrote recently—and a kind one."[16]

As part of his effort to promote public education, Tolstoy had decided to produce books that could be accessible even to semi-literate peasants. He had discussed the idea with Pisarev, whom he trusted, having written in his diary: "Pisarev is close . . ."[17] But Pisarev was procrastinating, while Chertkov had energy and initiative.

Chertkov was keen to assist Tolstoy in his projects, writing him in February: "I constantly want to know where you are and what you do."[18] That month, Tolstoy's treatise *What I Believe* was banned by government censors. The head of the Moscow Civil Censorship Committee, Evgeny Feoktistov, wrote that the treatise "undermines the foundations of social and governmental institutions and wholly destroys the teachings of the Church."[19] The police seized most of the copies from the printers, but unlike other banned literature, *What I Believe* was not burned. Instead, it was distributed among the top government officials. Learning about this, Tolstoy was pleased that his message reached the government. The book also began to circulate illegally: in fact, it proved impossible to ban Tolstoy's works; someone would always smuggle a copy from a printing shop. There was also growing interest abroad: in 1885, *What I Believe* came out in German and French translations. Chertkov became useful to Tolstoy by orchestrating an English translation. A team of translators he employed included the Petersburg University professor Charles Turner and his former tutor, Charles Heath.

Chertkov also advised Tolstoy to produce a popular summary of the Sermon on the Mount. Written in simple language, it would explain the "correct" meaning of Christ's five commandments and warn against "false interpretations."[20] He referred to the moral imperatives, which Tolstoy thought were at the heart of Christ's moral law. Chertkov imagined that the compilation should only take "a few hours." Tolstoy briefly considered writing such a summary, but he was not up to it.

Their relationship was beginning to occupy Tolstoy: that spring, he frequently mentioned Chertkov in his diary, with growing affection: "A fine letter from Chertkov . . ."[21] "I love him and I believe in him."[22] "A letter from Chertkov—splendid . . ."[23] On March 9, Tolstoy wrote him the first in a series of spontaneous and intimate letters, asking to destroy it upon reading. Chertkov obeyed, but recorded Tolstoy's instruction and preserved the part where the writer discussed his teaching.

Only months into their relationship, Chertkov confessed his sexual fantasies to Tolstoy. His letter, of which only one line survives, is quoted in Tolstoy's reply. "I got drunk and I had depraved thoughts,"[24] Chertkov told him. "Any letter of yours disturbs me," Tolstoy replied. He thought, however, that Chertkov deliberately exaggerated "what is shameful, and in this respect I always make you an example for myself; but this is frightening."

Their exchange was consistent with the intimate friendship Tolstoy describes in his early autobiographical novel, *Boyhood*. The narrator, Nikolenka, in whom Tolstoy depicts himself, promises to confess even his most shameful thoughts to his close friend, Dmitry Nekhlyudov, deciding to be completely open with him. "'But you see, our most important and interesting thoughts are just those that nothing would induce us to tell to one another.'"[25] Carried away by their revelations, the two boys "make quite shameless confessions" and later are afraid to part, bound to each other by their "moral secrets."[26]

Despite the tremendous gap between them, Tolstoy told Chertkov many things he did not confide to anyone else. But he was always interested in young men's sexuality. Son Ilya remembers that when he was in his teens, his father asked whether he was still a virgin and wept upon learning that he was. During his final year, Tolstoy would ask young men coming to him for advice, about their sexual lives. "He would usually ask this intimate and delicate question at the end of their discussion," remembers his last secretary Valentin Bulgakov.[27] In 1910, in a letter to a female correspondent, Tolstoy spoke of his sensuality as his greatest vice, which made him feel most guilty and repulsive to himself.[28] There was a gulf in his mind between spiritual and sensual love: Tolstoy considered the sexual act to be sinful and debasing.

Returning to *Boyhood* and "the rule of frankness," which Nikolenka and Nekhlyudov established: they shared an ideal of moral perfection and a belief that the purpose of human life is continual self-improvement. "At that time it seemed very possible . . . to destroy all the vices and miseries of mankind, and it seemed very easy to improve oneself, to assimilate all the virtues, and to be happy . . ."[29] Tolstoy had written this thirty years before he met Chertkov, with whom he would pursue the same ideal. In Nekhlyudov, Tolstoy depicts the type of idealist which always appealed to him. As he tells in his next novel, *Youth*, Nekhlyudov was "cold, severe with himself and with others, proud, fanatically religious and pedantically moral."[30] When developing this character, Tolstoy wrote in his notebook that Nekhlyudov was also stubborn and "artistically obtuse."[31] (This also perfectly described Chertkov, who was a pedant and viewed literature only as a tool to propagate religious ideas.) Tolstoy who perceived himself as inconsistent and full of doubts, was attracted to his opposite, a domineering and single-minded type. In *Boyhood*, Nikolenka willingly submits to the influence of his cruel and "adored friend," Nekhlyudov:

> Karr[32] has said that there are two sides to every attachment: one loves, the other allows himself to be loved: one kisses, the other gives his cheek to be kissed. That is perfectly true; and in our friendship it was I who kissed, and Dmitry who presented his cheek; but he too was ready to kiss me. We cared for one another equally . . . but that did not prevent his exerting an influence on me and my submitting to him.[33]

Chertkov shared many of Nekhlyudov's traits including his cold-heartedness, and it was not coincidental that Tolstoy would call him Dmitry, or Dima. In 1884, Chertkov repeatedly confessed that he could not love people, no matter how hard he tried.[34] "I cannot feel empathy towards another person, as a brother, a neighbor . . . Christ and his teaching are only a theory to me, and I'm beginning to think that one can study Christ's teaching, but remain spiritually further away from Christ than many simple souls . . . Christ is love. But I can't love, therefore I'm not a Christian."[35] Tolstoy refused to believe this, since in his view, every person possessed a "free, creative, divine power" of love.[36] This especially concerned the pupils of Christ, who chose to live unselfishly for others.

Tolstoy would soon learn that Chertkov possessed a full array of human weaknesses—vanity, greed, vindictiveness—but none of these faults would deter him. As Tolstoy once wrote, "the goodness of a dove is not a virtue."[37] Apparently, it made more sense for him to set out on a road to self-improvement with a man who also struggled to suppress his lust and conquer his vices, rather than with a virtuous one, who had no passions to overcome. Mutual confessions strengthened the bond between the two men; Chertkov wrote:

> Ah, Lev Nikolaevich, I should not be discussing lofty . . . sub-jects. I'm so low, so vile, so repulsive to myself . . . In reality my inner life is base and dirty. My imagination is filled with beastly and impure thoughts. At night . . . I live in the imagi-nary world of most disgusting and unnatural depravity . . . There are two men in me; one is so sordid and depraved that he would make the most dissolute man ashamed of his company; the other soars high above . . . I'm possessed by the devil.[38]

This verbal self-flagellation, repenting sins, appealed to Tolstoy, who wrote: "I value your truthfulness and I'm learning from you. I behave worse and don't talk about it. . . . I love you very much."[39] In turn, Tolstoy told Chertkov about his struggle with sensuality, beginning his letter with the words: "I am weak, I am evil, I have a vice . . . a terrible vice which I am struggling against." He told of how he made an assignation with a young woman, employed as a cook at Yasnaya, but as he walked out of the house, son Ilya called him from the window to remind him they had a lesson that day. "I came to my senses and didn't keep the appointment. Clearly it can be said that God saved me."[40] This letter was preserved, while others had to be destroyed. Chertkov wrote that it was painful for him to tear up Tolstoy's letters.[41] Tolstoy replied he had to think about himself.

In spring 1884, Chertkov traveled to see his family in Petersburg and visited Tolstoy en route. In April, they spent two days together and met Tolstoy's acquaintance Alexander Prugavin, an expert on Russia's sectarian movement. The topic keenly interested Chertkov, who spent his youth among Radstock and Pashkov followers. Uncle Pashkov was now facing expulsion from Russia: the Church objected to his broadening religious propaganda. The tyranny of the official Church was one of the topics Tolstoy discussed with Chertkov, writing in his diary, "Chertkov is remarkably in coincidence with me."[42] Following this meeting in Moscow, Tolstoy sent another intimate letter, asking Chertkov to destroy it.

As Maude would say, Chertkov resembled Tolstoy with his intolerance of the things he disliked.[43] From Petersburg, Chertkov wrote disapprovingly of the aristocracy lavishly celebrating Easter: "Here, in the memory of Christ, everyone is clad in silks and ribbons, they send expensive flowers and gifts to each other . . ."[44] Chertkov said that the sums they spent on bouquets could sustain a poor family for a year. This followed Tolstoy's train of thought: he often spoke of money in terms of what it could buy for a peasant family, so he rated Chertkov's letter in his diary as "splendid."[45]

On April 23, Chertkov's father died of a stroke at fifty-six. Chertkov again set out for Petersburg. Tolstoy met him at the station in Moscow as he changed trains. "Chertkov is firm and calm, just the same. He said he was little upset."[46]

There was a private ceremony in the Chertkovs' Petersburg apartment on Sergievskaya Street. Alexander III and the Empress, accompanied by the palace commandant, Vorontsov-Dashkov, came to pay their respects. State Secretary Alexander Polovtsev wrote in his diary that Elizaveta Chertkova, who objected to the Orthodox rituals, decorated the apartment with posters addressed to the ghost, such as, "Don't be afraid, it's me."[47] Still, a Church funeral was unavoidable. (Five years later, when Peter Shuvalov died, his widow, also an evangelical, refused to attend the Church ceremony.) Describing his father's funeral, Chertkov wrote Tolstoy: "Requiems, gold, ribbons, the deacon's recitations, hordes of people, the Grand Dukes, my father's body in his coffin is decomposing . . ." He complained of having to buy a top hat for 15 rubles, an unnecessary expense. A peasant lad would have to work all summer to make this amount.[48] (This also reflected Tolstoy's own pronouncement: that year, he gloomily complained in his diary that daughter Tanya's ball gown cost 250 rubles and that peasants could buy twenty-five horses with the amount.)

Tolstoy responded he was struck with the death of Chertkov's father— "with its significance for you. I cannot explain how and why, but I feel that it was needed for your sake."[49] Perhaps, this was necessary for Chertkov's liberation from his former life. He had acquired a spiritual father in Tolstoy.

Around this time, Chertkov became attracted to his peasant student Pyotr Apurin, a clever boy of nineteen, who was a son of the village drunkard. Chertkov was keeping Tolstoy informed about his relationship with the boy, who slept in his bedroom and accompanied him on all trips. Apurin was Chertkov's convert and best pupil, having grasped the five moral imperatives Tolstoy had formulated in *What I Believe*. When Chertkov shared the joy of his student's progress, Tolstoy responded that he was getting carried away with his proselytizing.[50] "You should get married," Tolstoy also advised.[51] However, there were no women in Chertkov's life: "I know your remedy, but cannot accept it. There are many reasons why I cannot marry."[52] His fear of marriage was apparent from the lengthy and evasive explanations that followed. Chertkov imagined that marriage involved finding a like-minded woman, who would also share in his work. (This reflected Tolstoy's view of marriage.) But a helpmate was unlikely to be found among the aristocracy, the milieu where Chertkov's mother wanted him to seek a wife. This was a good excuse, but Chertkov was not telling the whole story. He had intimate relationships with young men and, before visiting his mother, would ask her permission to let his friend sleep in his bedroom. Tolstoy did not leave it there: in the years to come, he would continue to insist on Chertkov's marrying. He then believed that a man was only safe from sin on a narrow path—marriage and hard physical work—and prescribed these remedies to Chertkov to curb his desires.

Tolstoy preached renunciation of ambition, simple toil, and self-suffi-ciency, and his ideas were beginning to make an impact. In spring 1884, he learned that Nikolai Gay Jr., the artist's son, had decided to abandon his degree in criminal law at Kiev University along with a potential career, and was learning a trade to support himself through physical labor. Tolstoy wrote Chertkov that the young man was entirely of "the same faith as us." He also sent a passionate letter to Gay Sr., the artist, explaining how his son's decision affected him: "It's not that I agree with his every word, sen-timent, and thought. These words, sentiments, and thoughts are like my own . . . As long as I live I'll never stop watching him with special feelings of a throbbing heart and love . . ."[53]

But Tolstoy's ideas of building paradise on earth were untested by reality. Many of his young followers, who were determined to live a morally good life on Tolstoyan lines, would form agricultural colonies. These were short-lived. The young city intellectuals knew little about agricultural labor and, in addition, would find themselves helpless in practical situations. When faced with land disputes, Tolstoyans could not resolve them because of their rejection of the judiciary. Since they also rejected bureaucracy, police, and the use of force, they could not protect their communal property from pillage. They were following the premise: "Give to him that asketh thee!" Naturally, peasants would take advantage of such an outlook. Gay Jr., who was then an ardent follower of Tolstoy, did not join an agricultural commune. Having settled on his father's estate, he married a peasant woman and worked the land. But a decade later, entirely disillusioned with Tolstoyism, he abandoned this primitive way of life and emigrated to Switzerland.[54]

At first, Chertkov also wanted to engage in farm work. He persuaded his mother to give him 270 acres of land and 2,000 rubles to buy cattle and inventory, but never tilled the land himself; instead, he hired laborers. He was only an ignorant observer on his farmstead, he wrote Tolstoy. Far more interested in Tolstoy's publishing affairs, Chertkov kept reminding him about the idea of mass-producing moralizing literature. It would be better "if you'd write stories for the people and let me handle the editorial and the publishing side."[55]

In May, learning that Chertkov had decided to accompany his mother to England, Tolstoy asked whether they could see each other before his departure. He wrote something for Chertkov's eyes alone, instructing him: "Tear up this letter."[56] Chertkov copied it out without intimate passages and then destroyed the original. The relationship was growing more secretive. In his diary, Tolstoy continually praised Chertkov and made disparaging remarks about his wife and children. He referred to Sophia as his cross to bear and described the atmosphere in his family as depressing and deadly. Later that year, in a show of trust, Tolstoy gave this diary to Chertkov, along with permission to delete unwanted information. Chertkov had precipitated the move by sending pages from his private journal to Tolstoy.

That summer, Tolstoy complained about his loneliness in a family where no one shared his beliefs. He told Chertkov that at night he was praying to God to touch his wife's heart "and suddenly it occurred to me: I suffer because my wife does not share my convictions."[57] The relationship with his wife was far more complex than he was prepared to admit; he was creating a simplified narrative for Chertkov in an apparent attempt to win his sympathy and approval.

Tolstoy was doing an injustice to Sophia, who had helped him attain celebrity. Having married him at eighteen, she assisted Tolstoy in all his projects—from literature and teaching peasant children to farm work. His novels, for which he was famed, were written during the first two decades of marriage and drew closely from family life. Sophia was his model, copyist, and first editor and, in addition, Tolstoy used her articulate letters and entries to depict his heroines' motherhood in both novels. In *Anna Karenina*, he employed her experiences when creating Dolly, Kitty, and Anna. Sophia's heart-rending letters and entries after the deaths of their baby sons, Petya and Nikolenka, went into *Anna Karenina* almost unchanged to depict Dolly's grief at the loss of her child. Anna Karenina's near escape from death, when she contracts puerperal fever after the birth of her daughter, recounted Sophia's experiences after Masha's birth. The infection was then fatal in ninety-nine cases out of a hundred, as Tolstoy tells in the novel, but Sophia's health pulled her through, and so it was with his heroine. Sophia was artistically gifted, and Tolstoy relied on her intuition when reading his chapters to her. But it was her emotional support and her love that mattered most. Later, when acknowledging her impact on his art, he would remark: "You gave me and the world what you were able to give; you gave much maternal love and self-sacrifice, and it's impossible not to appreciate you for it . . ."[58] But when Tolstoy had dismissed his art, he also rejected their past and her contribution to him. Conflict arose when Sophia refused to abide by his new Christian principles, regarding them as unfeasible for the family. In his turn, Tolstoy continually criticized her for holding onto property, even though he himself was living on their estate. There was some duplicity in this attitude. Tolstoy would never reproach Chertkov for maintaining his privileged lifestyle. Chertkov became his main ally: he was helping Tolstoy to promote his faith and to wage the struggle with his wife. The two men would eventually frame Sophia as the enemy of their movement.

Though Chertkov was now traveling abroad, he was spiritually present in the Tolstoy family drama. Tolstoy complained to him of disagreements with Sophia, whom he now viewed only as an obstacle to implementing his new beliefs. His intimacy with Chertkov exacerbated the conflict. On June 18, Tolstoy stormed out of the house after a petty argument with Sophia over some property, which he no longer wanted. She was pregnant with their twelfth child and was soon to give birth. But as Tolstoy walked away, she caught up with him in the alley to ask where he was going. He replied that he was leaving forever. However, he returned the same night when Sophia bore daughter Sasha.

A month later, on July 14, Tolstoy again attempted to leave Yasnaya. He was in a despondent mood and was treating Sophia contemptuously. Waking her in the middle of the night, he poured out accusations "that she had ceased to be a wife" and no longer was even his helpmate. Although Tolstoy stayed at home, he vowed in his diary that he eventually would realize his intention to flee. Chertkov was in England and the two men carried on their intimate exchange. On June 6, Tolstoy wrote him with emotion, "I repeat to you what I've written and told you before—I need your letters, they make me very happy." On July 12, days before his outburst with Sophia, Tolstoy received two letters from Chertkov, and wrote in his diary: "I had a dream about Chertkov: he suddenly started dancing the cancan."[59]

Tolstoy's social and religious writings did not interest Sophia as much as his literature had in the past, and she no longer assisted him. Chertkov replaced her as Tolstoy's dedicated copyist and audience. In spring, Tolstoy told him a story he would later use in his treatise, *What Then Must We Do?* This work employed Tolstoy's impressions from participating in the Moscow census and witnessing abject poverty. In a letter to Chertkov, Tolstoy related his encounter with a drunk teenaged prostitute, led away by the police. The girl was about the same age as Tolstoy's daughter Masha, and, in contrast with his family's privilege, the sight inspired his remorse: "They took her away, and I didn't take her home, didn't give her a meal, didn't do anything at all for her . . . I'm ashamed to write this, ashamed to live. At home a dish of sturgeon, the fifth course . . ."[60] *What Then Must We Do?* where he included this episode became his most passionate work against social injustice, its title inspired by the lines of the Gospel from Luke: "And the people asked him, saying, What shall we do then? He answereth and saith unto them, He that hath two coats, let him impart to him that hath none . . ."[61]

As Tolstoy's publisher, Chertkov received special privileges no one else would have before or after. In 1884, he told Tolstoy of his intention to produce *What I Believe* with his own excisions. At first, Tolstoy was taken aback: the unabridged version was about to appear in French. "The readers will be unhappy," he told Chertkov. But with a change of heart, Tolstoy gave him carte blanche to make the revisions. Moreover, Tolstoy wrote that he was prepared to endorse Chertkov's changes even before seeing them.[62] Chertkov's like-mindedness explains Tolstoy's blind trust: his disciple and friend could do no wrong.

Tolstoy was zealously wrestling with his pride. He explained to Chertkov that his first impulse was to see his entire text produced. But he rejected this temptation as vanity. He was no longer a writer, but a laborer for God. "Even now I'm afraid I'm guided with vanity, so it's better that you do not discuss [the changes] with me; just do as you wish." He also encouraged Chertkov to criticize him: "I have a strange feeling towards you: your disagreement does not upset me at all . . . it only interests me. This must be because I love you truly . . ."[63]

Allowed all this freedom, Chertkov removed the vital parts of *What I Believe*, which concerned Tolstoy's rejection of the metaphysical side of the Gospels and the resurrection—ideas that were important to the writer.[64] When in September 1884, Tolstoy received a revised copy of his book, he claimed that he did not experience an unpleasant feeling; "on the contrary, I felt only great love—and curiosity towards you."[65] Chertkov explained that he distributed a limited edition of *What I Believe* among his friends and family. They believed in the resurrection, redemption, and the afterlife, so there was no need to undermine their faith.[66] People can practice the five commandments and still believe in resurrection, Chertkov wrote persuasively. Tolstoy soon repeated the idea in a letter to Sophia, telling her that he revised a chapter about the redemption and divinity of Christ in his previous work, *A Critique of Dogmatic Theology*. He now realized that this question was still important to millions of people.[67] In 1885, Chertkov produced English translations of *What I Believe*, *A Confession*, and *The Gospel in Brief* under the general title *Christ's Christianity*.[68]

Tolstoy had not allowed abridging of his text in the past. In 1878, when the *Russian Herald* was publishing *Anna Karenina*, the magazine editor, Mikhail Katkov, asked Tolstoy to eliminate his attacks on the Russo-Turkish war. Tolstoy refused to publish the epilogue with such excisions, so the editor had to print a notice to the readers that the final chapters would not appear in the magazine. Katkov was Tolstoy's and Dostoevsky's editor of many years, whereas Chertkov had no publishing or editing experience at all. Now that Tolstoy's literature became subservient to his causes, Chertkov had permission to make any changes he liked.

While Tolstoy believed that Chertkov fully accepted his non-resistance doctrine, this was only wishful thinking: in reality there was little concurrence between them. Tolstoy preached extreme material renunciation and called property an "anti-Christian invention," since it had to be protected by force.[69] Chertkov replied evasively: "It seems we have a lot in common in our understanding of property . . . But I'm not sure I entirely understand your view. I think that for a Christian, property does *not* exist and cannot exist. Everything belongs to one master—god." [Sic.][70] Property is slavery, thundered Tolstoy. Property is an illusion, a matter of perception, responded Chertkov in his melodious voice. Tolstoy proclaimed that money was sinful, responsible for inequality and suffering. Chertkov insisted that money should not be destroyed: "I receive 20,000 rubles [£ 2,000] annually from my mother. Receiving it does not involve any coercion on my part. My mother gives it to me, and how she obtains the money, is not my business . . . For me, there's a tremendous convenience in this . . . Money simply makes its way into my pocket without an effort on my part and as long as nobody takes it away from me I don't have to resist . . ."[71] Tolstoy commented gloomily in his diary that Chertkov is simply afraid to renounce his property. "He doesn't know where his 20,000 comes from . . . I know—it comes from oppression and from people tired out with work."[72] He intended to tell this to Chertkov, but never did. At the time, Chertkov was staying at uncle Pashkov's villa near London and, naturally, could not think of renouncing property. Pashkov and a few prominent members of his sect had already been exiled from Russia; Chertkov and his mother briefly joined them in England, out of solidarity.

Chertkov likely sensed that Tolstoy's views were too extreme to attract a popular following. Although he did not say this directly, he sent Tolstoy a few pages from his diary where he recorded a conversation with his relative, an evangelical and a follower of Pashkov. Having read *What I Believe*, she agreed with Tolstoy's formulation of Christ's moral principles, but thought one needed Tolstoy's resolve to practice them.[73] For Tolstoy, compromising his ideal was unthinkable: "It was terribly unpleasant—painful for me to learn that you disagree with the demands of Christ's moral law, with his 5 commandments, that you find it possible to circumvent, to soften any of them . . . This [disagreement] would be painful for me because I'd feel that we were not one."[74] Such was Tolstoy's desire for concurrence that he was asking Chertkov to agree with him. It was just as Tolstoy had written earlier to his friend and editor Nikolai Strakhov, with whom he discussed his definition of moral truth: "I would very much like you to agree with me."[75]

Chertkov was steering their conversation from property to intellectual property, writing Tolstoy that it was important not to consider one's intellect or talent to be one's personal possession.[76] He referred to publishing Tolstoy's popular fiction, which the writer would naturally now submit for free. Chertkov was now trying to persuade Tolstoy to write stories and parables to illustrate his interpretation of the Gospels. Tolstoy had written a moralizing story, *What People Live By*, for a children's magazine: it told about an angel who was sent to earth by God. Hugely successful, the story was read even by semi-literate peasants. If Tolstoy would give him another such story, Chertkov would launch their publishing venture. He promised to look after the organizational and financial side: "As long as my mother is alive, I'll have financial means at my disposal."[77] Tolstoy did not reply, which only inspired Chertkov to develop a more detailed plan that included publishing a popular periodical; he also began to assemble a publishing team.

Tolstoy considered all practical affairs unimportant, which he told Chertkov: "Naturally, I'm glad to support a good cause when I have a chance, but this is your undertaking, not mine. I have my own—and in my work, I know that nobody can help me."[78] Tolstoy was working on a new treatise, *What Then Must We Do?* and was afraid to make another commitment. However, as he had intimated to Chertkov, he could never demand doing things his own way: "I could never insist, not only on actions, but even on words."[79] But it was the opposite with Chertkov, who was unyielding even on small matters. Tolstoy, who valued their close relationship, would have to learn to do things Chertkov's way.

On August 28, his birthday, he wrote Chertkov, who had returned from England, "I want to know all about you. I often think of you, as people think of those who are dear."[80] Chertkov had been sending pages from his diary, but there was almost nothing personal in his notes, and his letters lacked warmth: "One more thing—your letters have little genuine love for me, a man who loves you."[81] Chertkov responded that he loved individuals little, "with the exception of children, particularly boys, whom I love very much."[82] He corrected himself in another letter: "I definitely love you, although I'm a bit afraid of you."[83] His genuine feeling for Tolstoy was tainted with a vain satisfaction that he had a great man for a friend; it was just "what I felt when the Tsar or some Grand Duke gave me special attention . . ."[84]

In October, when Tolstoy's family left for Moscow, he invited Chertkov to visit Yasnaya. But Chertkov was silent, perhaps, punishing Tolstoy for his failure to commit himself to the publishing project. "I haven't written to you because I expected you here any day," Tolstoy said. "How's your project? Now it seems more attractive to me than before. I'm so used to you and so value your company, and I miss your letters very much."[85] From Moscow, Tolstoy sent Chertkov a telegram, "I want to see you very much."[86]

Also in October, Tolstoy spent a week with Gay Jr. on his farm in Ukraine. Cherkov was unpleasantly surprised when, arriving to Moscow, he found Tolstoy in the company of this young man. Immersed in discussion about Gay's farming, the two paid little attention to Chertkov. To make things worse, Gay started taunting him about his privileged lifestyle. Actually, Chertkov had his own agenda: he wanted Tolstoy to travel with him to Lizinovka to meet his mother who agreed to sponsor the publishing project. Tolstoy bluntly refused to go. Chertkov spent the night in Tolstoy's study and left early, without saying goodbye. Tolstoy wanted to mend frictions and even apologized for sleeping in. "Your practical affairs are unimportant," he preached in a letter to Chertkov. ". . . You are so restless, my dear friend . . . I'd wish you more calmness and idleness, good-natured, kind, and a forgiving attitude to people; calmness and idleness. I'd love to live with you and, if we are still alive, I shall live with you. Never cease to love me, as I love you."[87] But having written this, he began to think that he had sent an insensitive letter. During a sleepless night, Tolstoy wrote again:

> . . . I'm in torment that I hadn't seen you before your departure, that I hadn't traveled along with you and that I'd written you a bad and cold letter. Please don't be cross with me. You are terribly dear and close to me. I feel this now and suffer because I think that I gave you pain . . . I will dispatch this letter in the morning and will also send you a telegram to find out whether you have forgiven me.[88]

Chertkov responded with a telegram and two letters, which were destroyed. Tolstoy's letter that followed reveals Chertkov was jealous of Gay.

In December, putting aside his treatise, Tolstoy spent a day working for Chertkov. He agreed to support the publishing project and was writing some text to accompany a reproduction of *The Flagellation of Christ* by the French artist William-Adolphe Bouguereau. Chertkov wanted to produce a series of popular picture booklets and had sent this illustration. Tolstoy's first instance of writing on assignment was unsuccessful and, after a day's toil, he conceded defeat. But he promised Chertkov to keep trying.[89] Beginning to refer to the publishing venture as "our undertaking," Tolstoy saw its benefits: it was important "for the cause and for you."[90] Indeed, their joint undertaking, Intermediary, would establish Chertkov as Tolstoy's editor and close associate. For Tolstoy, these years were marked with hard work and further withdrawal from creativity.

That same month, in a letter to Chertkov, Tolstoy elucidated on the distinction between love, a boundless feeling that knew no rules, and rational Christian love. In love one is vulnerable, unlike in Christian saintly life and love: "I cannot write all that I think and feel about you . . . Perhaps, you think I love you less than I really do."[91] Chertkov had outlined a Christian relationship that established a stronger bond than within one's family: "Everything must be communal . . . no secrets or secret thoughts. To speak one's mind directly . . . to break all barriers . . ."[92]

CHAPTER THREE

A LABORER FOR GOD

"I've just understood that my life is not mine, that I was sent into the world to do God's work."
—Tolstoy, *And the Light Shineth in Darkness*[1]

"The only true, everlasting and supreme happiness comes from three things: work, self-denial, and love!"
—Tolstoy, in a letter to Valeria Arsenieva, 1856

One fine day in November 1884, a young aristocrat in an elegant fur coat entered a bookstore in Moscow's downtown. The store owner was Ivan Sytin, a publisher of peasant descent who mass-produced cheap calendars and chapbooks that sold at the city market for a kopeck. The visitor was Vladimir Chertkov. He made an attractive offer: "Do you want to publish serious literature for common people?" The publisher would receive Tolstoy's short fiction for free, which would compensate him for occasional royalties to other authors. Illustrations would come from prominent painters, such as Ilya Repin. Chertkov would deliver this material to the publisher, but there were two conditions: brochures could not be copyrighted and had to sell at the same price as Sytin's chapbooks. "I heard this offer with great interest," remembers Sytin who began his career as a shop boy at thirteen and opened his first bookstore at twenty-five.[2] The contract with Chertkov would turn his enterprise into the largest publishing house in pre-revolutionary Russia. Launching the venture were Tolstoy's "What People Live By," "God Sees the Truth But Waits," and a folk story by the talented writer Nikolai Leskov.

While Chertkov was the mastermind, the man who managed Intermediary during its first, most successful years, was Paul Biryukov. A graduate of the Page Corps and Petersburg's Naval Academy, Biryukov had sailed around the world and briefly worked as a physicist in Petersburg's main observatory. He had met Chertkov through their Gospel readings in the Society for Christian Help, presided over by Dmitry Trepov. One of the meetings was at the Chertkovs' family apartment in the large mansion on Sergievskaya Street. Biryukov would later describe Chertkov's comfortable and spacious study appointed with Persian carpets, a fireplace, and several leather armchairs. Everything in the study was tailored for "convenient reading." The most memorable were a pair of electric lamps with lampshades (in Petersburg electricity was introduced in 1879) that stood beside each chair. Invited to stay after the meeting, Biryukov sat down with his host by the fire. Charming in his velvet jacket, Chertkov, sipping sherry and smoking, asked meticulous questions: "Would you tell me your opinion on military service—is it against Christ's teaching or not?" Upon learning that Biryukov was of the same mind, Chertkov, as always in such cases, took his notebook and wrote down his full name and address. "I have a friend, who also thinks so, his name is Lev Nikolaevich Tolstoy. Do you know him?" Biryukov had read *Anna Karenina* and *A Confession*, neither of which impressed him. (Biryukov remembers that the manuscript of *A Confession* was brought to one of the Christian Help gatherings. This is significant because Chertkov most definitely read this work before meeting Tolstoy, which would explain why he had impressed the writer with his like-mindedness. *A Confession* was a story of Tolstoy's spiritual transformation, providing insights into his mind and soul.)

Chertkov had a gift for hiring selfless and hardworking people. On November 21, he took Biryukov to Tolstoy's Moscow residence and the three discussed launching Intermediary. Biryukov soon left his naval career and began to work under Chertkov's supervision without pay. Chertkov had a commanding personality and like many others, Biryukov fell under his influence.[3]

Intermediary would become Tolstoy's and Chertkov's most successful undertaking together. Within the first four years, it issued twelve million booklets, boosting public education in a predominantly peasant and illiterate country. Tolstoy's idea was to make quality reading widely accessible. They would produce two lines of books: literature by Russian and Western authors in adaptations and Christian literature. According to Maude, Intermediary's literary production inspired the inexpensive World's Classics series in England.

For Tolstoy, this enterprise was an extension of his ongoing public education campaign. Some of the best writers and artists soon recognized it as a worthy cause and lent their support. Among them was the celebrated portraitist Ivan Kramskoy whom Chertkov first approached on Tolstoy's behalf. Kramskoy was a spiritual leader of a new democratic movement in art and a founder of the Wanderers, a group of painters who, for the first time in Russia's history, took their exhibitions across the country to bring art to the people. One of Kramskoy's most famous paintings was *Christ in the Desert*, showing Jesus in deep contemplation. In 1873, the year it received wide acclaim, Kramskoy was commissioned by the Tretyakov Gallery to paint prominent Russians and made a portrait of Tolstoy at work on *Anna Karenina*. Now, Kramskoy inspired Repin and other artists to illustrate Intermediary's editions. The Wanderers made the enterprise instantly popular and helped take Tolstoy's campaign to the national level.

Tolstoy would write some twenty stories for Intermediary with characters and situations drawn from peasant life. His publishing program was broad: their literature should not be against Christian teaching.[4] As he explained to the renowned playwright Alexander Ostrovsky, "Our aim is to publish what is accessible, comprehensible and necessary to all, and not to a small circle of people, and has a moral content in accord with the spirit of Christ's teaching."[5]

Chertkov, however, had a much narrower agenda, viewing Intermediary as a platform to promote the Gospel and Tolstoy's doctrine.[6] At Maude's remark, Chertkov "did not care for works which lacked a religious tendency. In authorship he demanded religious sermonizing . . ."[7] The writer who suffered most from this approach was Tolstoy himself.

At Intermediary, Chertkov emerged as Tolstoy's zealous editor—the one who watched that his message remained consistent with his doctrine. Tolstoy extended carte blanche to Chertkov, despite his editorial inexperience and poor Russian. (Chertkov spoke with a foreign accent, the result of his aristocratic upbringing, and misinterpreted the meaning of some words.) It was a strange collaboration between the writer of genius and his religious censor, who was a foe to artistic complexity.

In January 1885, Chertkov persuaded Tolstoy to change the ending of his story "God Sees the Truth." Tolstoy had written it a decade earlier when he composed his *ABCs* and the *Russian Readers*. It was a story about a village merchant, Aksyonov, who is accused of a murder he never committed and is sentenced to hard labor in Siberia. After three decades there, Aksyonov meets the actual murderer, who arrives at the same barrack. A moral quandary opens for Aksyonov when this man is planning to escape and his tunnel is discovered by prison authorities. An investigation begins and, after a struggle in his heart, Aksyonov decides not to betray his foe to the camp authorities. When asked who dug the hole under the barrack, he replies, "I don't know, I haven't seen it." Chertkov was troubled that the hero of the tale, a religious man, tells a lie, so he persuaded Tolstoy to change the ending.[8] Tolstoy agreed, and the story appeared in the version Chertkov approved: Aksyonov says that God doesn't allow him to reply.[9] The difference was significant: Tolstoy focused on the struggle in the man's heart, while in Chertkov's version there was no room for doubt: it was replaced with a sanction from God.

Tolstoy's story "Prisoner of the Caucasus" also came out with Chertkov's redaction. An amusing episode where Zhilin, the hero of the tale, treats a sick man with a mixture of sand and water, and his patient recovers, was cut. In a long and tedious letter to Tolstoy, Chertkov explained the negative impact his message might have "on the impressionable reader." Typically, Chertkov had misinterpreted the story, thinking it justified using any means to attain one's goal. But even so, Tolstoy agreed to make the excisions. He wrote to Chertkov that he "happily agreed" with his suggestions and was grateful to him.[10] During the years of their collaboration the moralist in Tolstoy would prevail over the artist, and the popular stories he wrote for Intermediary were tendentious and weak. Chertkov held the typical view of censors that literature was one thing and life—another. In life, he would have no moral scruples when it came to getting what he wanted. But as Tolstoy's editor he demanded political correctness.

Tolstoy's stories for Intermediary were meant to illustrate his five commandments, which were laid out in *What I Believe*, among other works. "The Candle" demonstrated the principle of non-resistance to an evil doer. It was Tolstoy's major belief that evil can be extinguished by good. Despite these ideological constraints, his peasant characters were convincing. Strakhov, who had edited *Anna Karenina*, liked "The Candle" and its denouement where the bailiff's death is depicted in graphic detail. Chertkov, who did not care for artistry, prevailed on Tolstoy to rewrite the ending. "The Candle" was based on a factual incident, which took place during serfdom. The bailiff, a former serf, who has risen to power from slavery, abuses peasants under his authority. He administers beatings for any minor offense and some die after sadistic floggings. Eventually, the peasants decide to kill him and contemplate his gruesome violent death. But one man, Mikheich, opposes the murder. When the bailiff learns that the peasants are plotting against him, he forces them to work during a holiday. Mikheich alone takes this punishment meekly: he sings his psalms as he ploughs the field, and a wax candle stuck onto his wooden plough does not go out in the wind. (Here Tolstoy creates a new peasant saint.) When faced with meekness, not hatred, the bailiff for the first time experiences remorse. But that same day, he dies in a violent accident when a horse throws him against a wooden fence and he punctures his belly on a stake.

Chertkov argued that once the bailiff is reformed, there is no reason for him to die: it's important to show the triumph of good over evil. On November 8, Chertkov sent Tolstoy two versions of the new ending—one he himself wrote and another composed by a junior editor. Tolstoy was annoyed and replied frankly that their versions sounded false. He wrote another ending for Intermediary, but in later editions restored his original.[11]

It did not take long for the Russian censors to discover that Intermediary was Tolstoy's undertaking. In 1885, when Tolstoy's latest work *What Then Must We Do?*, was banned, Chertkov wrote that in the Petersburg Censorship Committee they feared Tolstoy "like fire."[12] Once censors in Petersburg and in Moscow became alert, authorization for publishing Intermediary brochures could be obtained only in the provinces. Chertkov worked out a whole strategy and used his family connections at the Ministry of Internal Affairs to approach chief censors in Warsaw (then a part of the Russian Empire), Odessa, and Kiev, in turn. His uncle, Mikhail Chertkov, was a governor general in Kiev.

All censors scrutinized Intermediary booklets for subversive messages, finding such subversion even in the Gospel itself. Maude tells that when Intermediary published the Sermon on the Mount as a reading lesson, the booklet was refused a license until the injunction to "take no thought for the morrow" had been removed.[13] Chertkov instructed Tolstoy not to send anything to censors on his own: "Leave censorship to me."[14]

A project to which Chertkov gave much attention was the Lives of the Saints series. There was a popular demand for such literature and Sytin published it willingly. Under Chertkov's supervision a team of Intermediary employees stripped the Orthodox Saints of their miracles and created peasant-like saints of the Tolstoyan faith. Chertkov's future wife, Anna Dieterichs, was also on this team, churning out several booklets a day. So as not to attract the censors' attention, the Tolstoyan version of Lives of the Saints appeared under the same blue and pink covers as the Orthodox saints. Because Chertkov's strategy was to replace the "harmful" Church brochures with his own, his employees produced a steady stream of hagiographies.[15]

The enterprise was growing. Chertkov opened an Intermediary warehouse and a shop in Petersburg adjacent to his editorial office. He was also opening a shop and an editorial office in Moscow where he came once a month to meet Tolstoy on business. Attempting to cut their expenses, Chertkov and his mother moved to a less lavish Petersburg apartment, although situated on Millionnaya, or Millionaire's Street. Tolstoy's letters now mostly concerned publishing matters, which he discussed with Chertkov in a telegraphic style. Only occasionally, did he include a personal line: "I kiss you, dear friend. May God give you the same peace and happiness, which I'm enjoying more and more, regardless of all external circumstances and even regardless of health."[16]

A flood of manuscripts and editorial assignments left little time for Tolstoy's own writing. Chertkov's staff had no literary experience, and Tolstoy had to be consulted on every matter. He read submissions to decide what should be published, edited peasant writers' manuscripts, and read and revised the "badly written" Lives of the Saints: "All lives of saints, once they are translated into plain language, strike one at once by their artificiality. They can only be read in Slavonic or in an ancient language. And hence they can deceive."[17] When a freelancer compiled a biography of Socrates, Tolstoy not only revised it but also anonymously contributed a chapter, after thoroughly researching the subject. The work took him a few months, and the Intermediary staff complained about the delay. There were other assignments, which Chertkov sent, with the insistence that Tolstoy alone could handle them. For example, he wanted Tolstoy to supply ideas and themes for illustrators. Chertkov instructed him to submit not fewer than ten ideas simultaneously, so that illustrators could choose. "Can't you really jot down a few ideas for illustrations during your breaks from writing?"[18] (Tolstoy was absorbed with a new novella, *The Death of Ivan Ilyich*.)

Reading adaptations of his work by Intermediary employees was undoubtedly disagreeable for Tolstoy, even if he did not say so. Nikolai Ozmidov, a former agronomist and shopkeeper, was adapting his *Sevastopol Sketches* for a popular edition. Chertkov praised his adaptation, writing Tolstoy that although Ozmidov did not have a grasp of style, he definitely strengthened the antimilitary message by cutting "everything unimportant."[19] Tolstoy did not change a word in Ozmidov's version, since Chertkov wanted him to approve it as fast as possible. "I think you shouldn't make many revisions there," Chertkov proposed. "It would be better if you'd use your time to write another story in a military setting."[20] He now casually advised Tolstoy on what to write, although sometimes felt the incongruity of his position: "I'm amused, it looks as if I'm teaching you . . ."[21]

After the ban of *What Then Must We Do?* Chertkov suggested that Tolstoy stop writing "long articles" and instead produce more stories and parables for Intermediary, which they badly needed.[22] Millions of people will read these popular stories, as for pamphlets and articles, workers and peasants did not need them. "Write short—text for illustrations, for the booklets . . ." Alluding to Tolstoy's boot making, Chertkov wrote that people needed his stories, like boots, "and we are asking you to produce them because you alone can stitch them. They're more important than boots—they're bread, daily bread."[23] Tolstoy never questioned Chertkov's desire to speak on behalf of the people. This likely happened because Chertkov repeated some of Tolstoy's own thoughts back to him. While in the past, Tolstoy wrote for an educated minority, he now believed he should produce literature for the masses, compensating them for their hard work. "What indeed do I want?" he wrote in *What Then Must We Do?* "I want to do good, to arrange that people should not be cold or hungry, but should live in a way fit for human beings. I want this, and I see that by violence, extortion, and various devices in which I participate, the workers' bare necessaries are taken from them, while the non-workers (of whom I am one) consume . . . the fruits of the labor of those who toil."[24] Strange as it may seem, Tolstoy looked down on intellectual work, believing it was a privilege of the upper classes. He felt bad that he was not giving enough of what the people needed, and Chertkov learned to exploit his sense of guilt.

Simultaneously, Chertkov pressed Tolstoy to release his early literary works to the public domain. But this would inevitably produce conflict with Sophia, to whom Tolstoy had given power of attorney to publish his writings up to 1881, the year of his conversion. Sophia began to bring out Tolstoy's collected works in 1885, when he and Chertkov launched Intermediary. So far, Chertkov had persuaded Tolstoy to let Intermediary have his stories from the *Russian Readers*, which Sophia was also publishing. "This will not hurt the Countess financially," Chertkov assured, although realizing this would not be the case. By mentioning Sophia's publishing profit, he cleverly juxtaposed her operation with Intermediary, which ran entirely on Tolstoy's moral principles. He had succeeded in making Tolstoy feel guilty.

In summer 1885, the two discussed whether Tolstoy should publicly renounce the copyright on his latest works, written after his spiritual transformation. Bizarrely, the conversation took place in a bathhouse. As apparent from Chertkov's letter of July 7, Tolstoy mentioned his desire to relinquish his copyright, but changed his mind soon after. Chertkov would not leave it there, insisting that Tolstoy explain "why one evening (in a bath-house) you acknowledged the need of placing your works into the public domain but the day after, you completely abandoned the idea?"[25] He sent another letter, which Tolstoy rated as "bad" and which was destroyed. As Maude would remark, Chertkov pushed Tolstoy to extremes.

Chertkov may have been acting in the interests of their cause, but his ability to create trouble for Tolstoy was unmatched. In May 1885, before the bathhouse discussion, Chertkov learned that Tolstoy had authorized his wife to publish his collected works; he demanded clarification. Tolstoy said that, four years earlier, he gave Sophia power of attorney to manage all his business affairs. Actually, he did this in 1883, only two years prior to their conversation. Apparently, Tolstoy wanted to avoid further questions and to appear less inconsistent in his disciple's eyes, so he moved the matter further into the past.

Although Tolstoy had written against money and property, he continued to eat, travel, and accommodate scores of visitors and guests. With nine children in the family (three others died in early childhood), their needs were growing, while their income had shrunk. Tolstoy's recent non-fiction was not published in Russia, he no longer wrote novels, and Yasnaya produced negligible revenue. The family had to live and pay the bills, and, when presented with such facts of life, Tolstoy allowed Sophia to issue his works. She alone supported their large family with her publishing proceeds.

Tolstoy's permission to Intermediary to produce stories from the *Russian Readers* generated conflict with Sophia's editions. Since Intermediary's prices were unbeatable, Sophia ended up with most of her copies unsold. Her losses amounted to one thousand rubles, a significant sum for their family. To resolve this, Tolstoy asked Sytin, the publisher, to buy her editions. Sytin agreed, although he ended up paying about half of the agreed sum. Tolstoy did not care about his family's losses, only worrying about Sytin's; he assured Chertkov, "I will not let Sytin suffer a loss."[26] (But Tolstoy's concern over Sytin's business was unjustified. One year after launching Intermediary, Sytin bought a new printing shop and was producing 50,000 copies of prints and brochures daily. Three years later, he opened a book shop in Petersburg and later branches in other cities. In 1899, he bought the Moscow newspaper, *Russian Word*.)

After the issue with Sytin was resolved, Chertkov continued to discuss it and tactlessly offered to send some money for Tolstoy's wife. Any mention of his family's finances was unpleasant to Tolstoy, who had wished they had given up their money and property altogether. Chertkov was exploiting his disagreements with Sophia and adding fuel to the fire. All this came in the middle of Tolstoy's revision of the novella *The Death of Ivan Ilyich*.

Artistic work provided respite from other projects, Tolstoy remarked. Although absorbed with the novella, he now considered his literature a mere diversion. It was the opposite with Sophia, to whom he read chapters from *The Death of Ivan Ilyich*. She continued to regard his art as his most important vocation, and was happy he had returned to literature, which had united them in the past. He wrote this powerful work while handling routine assignments from Intermediary. The novella depicts the agonizing loneliness of a man dying of cancer. The course of the disease, the physical signs of progressing cancer and its impact on the mind and soul are described with great power. Tolstoy was a healthy man in his fifties, but his mental suffering, alienation from a family that did not share his religious beliefs, and deep sense of gloom that winter made him feel like someone facing death.

In mid-December 1885, deeply divided in his heart, Tolstoy wrote letters to Chertkov and to Sophia. These two people mattered most to him. But while with Sophia he shared his past, which he did not want to remember, Chertkov represented his present. Therefore, his letter to Chertkov was written as one can write only to an intimate friend: "I am sorely heavy at heart, and there is nobody I wish to share this heaviness with as much as you, dear friend, because it seems to me that nobody loves the good that there is in me as much as you . . ." The good in Tolstoy, as he himself saw it, was his religion. He agonized over the conflict between his ideals and his family's practical life and, mainly, the incongruity of his own position. Sophia was about to profit from his collected works, which, given his renunciations, would make him appear hypocritical: "I would go downstairs and meet a customer who would look at me as though I were a fraud, writing against property and then, under my wife's name, squeezing as much money as possible out of people for my writings . . ." Tolstoy was also deciding whether he should remain with his family or should make "a complete break and free myself." With all this, he needed Chertkov's advice. "Why am I writing this to you? I just want to, because I know you love me, and I love you . . . If it is *absolutely clear* to you what it is better for me to do, write and tell me."[27] Tolstoy did not mail this letter, deciding to hand it over to Chertkov and have him read it in his presence. He also imagined an idyll, having Chertkov visit him in Yasnaya. But this was not to be: ". . . Despite all my love for you and the joy of seeing you—such a joy that if you came to Yasnaya, I'd be happy; but now, as I reason, I see and I know that it's more important for me to stay alone."[28] Tolstoy was going through a crisis, being torn between his ideals and his love for Chertkov on one side, and his duty towards his family, on the other.

His letter to Sophia was unyielding. In it, Tolstoy accused her of violating his principles and of deliberately opposing him: "I renounced my property, began to give what people asked of me, renounced ambition for myself and the children . . . You pulled in the reverse, in the opposite direction: sending the children to grammar schools, bringing out your daughter, making friends in society . . . it was all going on in the field of activity I regarded as evil."[29] Tolstoy discussed their disagreements at length, but he neither sent this letter to Sophia nor did he hand it over to her. Instead, he hid it, expecting it would be read in posterity.

Shortly after writing to Chertkov and to Sophia, Tolstoy burst into his wife's publishing office and, after shouting and pouring out accusations, threatened to divorce her and leave for Paris or America. For Sophia, who had been busy with Tolstoy's edition, proofreading at night, this outburst came as a bolt from the blue. Insulted, she considered leaving home. But as she tells in a letter to her sister, "the children ran in, sobbing . . . He [Tolstoy] pleaded: "Stay!" So I stayed; but he suddenly began to sob hysterically . . . imagine—Lyovochka—is all trembling and shaking of sobs. I felt a rush of pity for him; the four children, Tanya, Ilya, Lyova, and Masha, were all weeping and wailing."[30] The following day, realizing that Tolstoy was having a bout of depression, Sophia dispatched him to their friends' estate, herself staying in Moscow with the children. The estate of their friends Olsufievs was far more luxurious than Yasnaya and although this family had close ties to court, they escaped Tolstoy's criticism. Unpredictable in his attitudes, he would frequently return to this estate to work and to relax.

Sophia's publishing conflicted with Tolstoy's intention to renounce his copyright. Actually, her editions were among the most inexpensive and satisfying to the reader, and she worked to further reduce their price. At first, Tolstoy took interest in her publishing and even helped with proof-reading. In 1885, he gave Sophia his novella *The Death of Ivan Ilyich* as a present for her editions and allowed her to publish it exclusively in the collected works. But later that year, he distanced himself from her money-making operation. Chertkov demanded consistency from Tolstoy, who was becoming a spiritual leader of his own religious movement. And because Tolstoy's image was at stake, he expected his family to fully comply with his moral principles. Tolstoy had a different standard for Chertkov, whom he did not ask to renounce property and money.

At this stage in life, Tolstoy was surprisingly dogmatic: even Chertkov could not persuade him to relax some of his moral rules. When the disciple suggested revising the five commandments to include one more, *one shalt not lie*, Tolstoy was hurt. In a sarcastic letter to Chertkov, he wrote that the *five* commandments came down to us from Christ and could not be softened or revised. "You're saying, these commandments are insufficient. Then tell me which [you find] sufficient and I'll take yours." But before Chertkov invented some of his own, "as Christ's adversaries do," it was better to implement the actual rules Christ had provided. Tolstoy did not send this letter, although he showed it to Chertkov when they met. (Having replied in an impulsive and angry way, Tolstoy violated his own principles. So, he wanted to let Chertkov know that he worked to suppress his pride. Chertkov was becoming a teacher and Tolstoy—a pupil.) Instead, Tolstoy sent a meek letter to Chertkov: "I hug you and I love you. Let's try before God to seek Him, e.g., truth, and then we'll be always together."[31] Around this time, Tolstoy wrote an acquaintance who was involved with Interme-diary: "There is a man in Petersburg who is very close to me, Chertkov . . . We are completely in accord in our views and convictions."[32] Apparently, Tolstoy wanted Chertkov to become an extension of himself, his alter-ego.

Their collaboration at Intermediary revealed, however, that there was little agreement in their program and goals. Tolstoy suggested publishing a broad list of titles, practically all famous European literature and philosophy, mentioning Miguel de Cervantes' *Don Quixote*, Jonathan Swift's *Gulliver's Travels*, Friedrich Schiller's *The Robbers* as well as his beloved Voltaire, Rousseau, and Gotthold Lessing.[33] Chertkov found this list unsuitable, arguing that Intermediary should only publish literature that was spiritually close to Tolstoy's teaching. "We must raise and hold high the banner of Christ's truth, so that all who recognize this truth would see whom to join." In publishing, Chertkov continued, they should avoid "the slightest disagreement with Christian teaching."[34] Tolstoy did not reply to this. Such definition of truth was undoubtedly constraining for him, even if he admired Chertkov's pure and uncompromising attitude.

Chertkov's agenda prevented some talented writers from publishing with Intermediary. When Tolstoy asked the satirical writer Mikhail Saltykov-Shchedrin to contribute his stories, Chertkov found an excuse not to publish them. Saltykov's stories exposed corruption, and Chertkov argued the subject was unsuitable for Intermediary, since it dealt with money. "One should tell him [Saltykov] that we do not want to touch any economic or social questions," Chertkov wrote Tolstoy, "but that we want to discuss general questions of interest to humanity . . ." He did not want to publish social satire because it was unkind to particular groups; satire should expose human weaknesses and vices inherent to all.[35] Russia's government censors also did not allow social criticism.

Tolstoy wanted to publish Nikolai Leskov's "excellent" tale about friendship between a Jew and a Christian without changing a word in it.[36] Chertkov disagreed and insisted they could not publish it until Leskov excluded references to lending money and getting rich. (This would be hard to accomplish since much of the tale was about a Jewish merchant helping his Christian friend in need.) "If it's necessary to say that a Jew helped a Christian, it's enough to say it in a few words."[37] In the end, Russian censors banned a separate Intermediary edition of Leskov's stories and Tolstoy suggested publishing them in Leipzig along with other suppressed works.[38] Whether the volume came out with Chertkov's revisions or without them is not known.

A pedant in art, Chertkov expected literature to illustrate Tolstoy's non-resistance doctrine. Tolstoy's little-known, tendentious parable "Walk in the Light While There Is Light" was a result of his collaboration with Chertkov. Set in the time of early Christians, "in the days when apostles of the apostles of Christ were still living and the Christians firmly observed the law of the Teacher," the story romanticizes early Christian communes. Tolstoy made a rough draft of this parable and put it aside. Chertkov, who was always searching Tolstoy's papers for something to publish, unearthed it. He made a clean copy and returned it to Tolstoy requesting specific revisions. As was his habit, Chertkov left spaces in the manuscript where he wanted Tolstoy to insert text. Tolstoy gave it a try, but soon abandoned the parable, becoming absorbed with his new philosophical work, *On Life*. Chertkov, who still wanted the parable for Intermediary, asked Tolstoy whether he himself could complete it. So, Chertkov was soon writing pages of insertions and complaining to Tolstoy of the difficulty handling historical topics: "Looking up sources is an awful and unnecessary waste of time . . ."[39] Chertkov composed tedious dialogues between the "good Christian" and the "bad" heathen. In July 1887, Tolstoy received this version of the parable and replied, "The style is very bad, very bad." He stopped short from criticizing Chertkov for his style and only asked him to condense the insertions.[40] Chertkov struggled to shorten the dialogues. But as he explained, the heathen's arguments could not be left unanswered: each had to be countered with a detailed exposition of Christian views.[41] "The absence of what you call artistry doesn't eliminate this work's importance," Chertkov argued. While some people may find it boring, for others it would provide answers on how to live.[42] The parable was published in 1893 and, according to Maude, inspired the founding of Tolstoyan agricultural colonies.[43] Chertkov was understandably proud of his input. Tolstoy, however, later admitted to Maude that he could not bear the mention of this parable without feeling ashamed.

During the first years of Tolstoy's involvement with Intermediary, Chertkov gained substantial influence over his publishing affairs. Assured of Tolstoy's moral support, he made decisions without consulting the author. In 1886, he placed Tolstoy's stories written for Intermediary in several literary magazines, only later informing him about this. Tolstoy did not care who published his works, as long as there was no conflict for him. He asked to avoid frictions with Sophia: "I'm so glad when you are in agreement with her."[44] Because Sophia had power of attorney, Chertkov needed at least to inform her of what he was publishing. When her rights were violated she was quick to point it out. On April 17, she wrote: "Vladimir Grigorievich, I see that you are handling my husband's works as your own property, even though he always reminds you that this matter concerns me. When it came to *the people's* benefit and their reading, my sympathies were on your side . . . But now I see that you're taking it upon yourself to help the magazines, and I have no sympathy at all for this . . . Unfortunately I have to remind you that all *rights* were transferred to me . . ."[45] Chertkov was furious and forwarded her letter to Tolstoy, along with his comments. This had an immediate effect on Sophia, who wrote a conciliatory letter to Chertkov: "It's impossible for us not to be friends: we love and respect the same man who loves both of us."[46] It was now apparent that Chertkov could easily tip the delicate balance in her marriage and, as long as it was possible, she was trying to keep peace.

In summer 1886, Tolstoy injured his leg while carting hay, his wound became infected, and he narrowly escaped blood poisoning. He remained bedridden for three months, and Sophia nursed him with the help of medical celebrities she brought from Moscow. During this time Tolstoy wrote a play, *The Power of Darkness*, which Sophia was copying and admiring: "It is very good. The characters are wonderfully portrayed and the plot is full and interesting . . ."[47] A psychological drama from the peasant life, *The Power of Darkness* was based on a criminal case Tolstoy learned from his friend Davydov, the very judge who had acquainted him with Chertkov. The play describes two murders and adultery in a peasant family. A laborer, Nikita, seduces his sixteen-year-old stepdaughter and kills the baby from this union. At the stepdaughter's wedding, which is arranged to hush things up, Nikita publicly confesses his crimes. It was a strange play for Tolstoy revealing the brutality of the very people he idealized. Having written it for the Moscow Skomoroh folk theater, Tolstoy wanted to test his play on a peasant audience. He arranged a reading at Yasnaya for the local peasants, and himself participated in the reading, but his listeners failed to understand the work.

Tolstoy's family and friends attempted to get the play approved for publication, but Chertkov alone succeeded with the support of his influential family: the play was read at their homes before important officials. His mother met the Empress and arranged for a reading at court. It was held in January 1887 at the apartment of the minister of the Imperial Court, Count Vorontsov-Dashkov with Alexander III and the royal family attending. The reader, Alexander Stakhovich, was a courtier and Tolstoy's acquaintance. He had a difficult task of charming this refined audience with a play about peasant life, written in coarse language and depicting violence. Stakhovich read an adapted version and succeeded beyond expectations: Alexander III exclaimed that the play was "a marvelous work" and promised to allow Imperial Theaters to stage it.[48] Days before the reading, Chertkov received permission to publish the play at Intermediary. By March, they had launched five editions and sold 100,000 copies. (Because of the haste to produce it first, the play was not properly proofread and mistakes abounded.)

Just as the theaters began to rehearse the play, the Procurator of the Holy Synod, Konstantin Pobedonostsev, who controlled religious censorship, gave his mighty opinion to Alexander III: "I just read L. Tolstoy's new play and cannot get over the horror." In his long diatribe the procurator called the play an insult to public taste and morality. The play was impossible in its cynicism, nothing of the kind had been ever created in the world, and even Zola had not descended to the same level of crude realism as Tolstoy had. Permission to perform it would spell "the downfall" of the Russian stage. Embarrassed by the strong rebuttal, the Tsar agreed there were too many horrors in the play. Soon after, in a letter to the Minister of Interior, Alexander III called Tolstoy "a nihilist and heretic" and suggested prohibiting the sale of his play.[49] *The Power of Darkness* was banned from production and distribution. In 1888, it premiered in Paris, in the Théâtre Libre where Émile Zola watched and admired it. Within a few years, the play was staged in major European theaters. In Russia, it was produced in 1895, in Petersburg's Alexandrinsky Theater, but three years later was banned again.

The Power of Darkness became the first literary work on which Tolstoy renounced his copyright. Chertkov made it inevitable, having told publishers they could reprint his play for free, as any other work produced by Intermediary. In February 1887, he informed Tolstoy that he recently gave his consent to launch an expensive edition of the play for the benefit of the Literary Fund. ". . . I've been telling everyone who comes with similar requests that all your writings, which Intermediary has published or is publishing, cannot be copyrighted and anyone can reproduce them in whichever form . . . Unless I hear from you otherwise, I'll assume that I acted correctly."[50] In response, Tolstoy wrote a brief statement saying that he releases the play into the public domain and renounces royalties on it for himself and his heirs. He asked Chertkov to publish it. Chertkov drafted a more comprehensive statement, saying that Tolstoy's works produced by Intermediary can be reprinted without payment. Tolstoy endorsed this version and it was published on March 7 by *The Russian Gazette* and later carried by other newspapers. Chertkov needed this statement to justify his willful publishing practices.

He also persuaded Tolstoy to make a small change in the play's finale where the hero confesses his crime. In Tolstoy's version, Nikita says: "It was my *plan*, my doing." Chertkov proposed changing one word: "It was my *fault*, my doing." He proceeded to explain over several pages why this revision was necessary and why it was more in tune with the Christian message of the play. Tolstoy agreed to make the change, but only for the Intermediary's edition. "I think you are pedantic in this," he wrote, meaning Chertkov's attitude to art.[51] Chertkov replied, in a perfectly pedantic way, that he would remember Tolstoy's remark and would try to avoid pedantry in the future.[52]

The play's epigraph from the Gospel from Matthew illustrates Tolstoy's belief in biblical inerrancy and his changing attitude towards women, whom he now viewed as a source of temptation: "But I say unto you, That whosoever looketh on a woman to lust after her hath committed adultery with her already in his heart."[53] Tolstoy's attitude to women is revealed from the contrast between his play and the criminal case, which inspired it. Tolstoy took great interest in the trial and met the thirty-seven-year-old murderer, the model for his hero Nikita. Witnesses described him as a drinking and violent man, who raped his stepdaughter and continually abused her when drunk. Tolstoy employed the horrific detail of how he killed the baby in the cellar by crushing him with a board. However, in the drama he vindicated Nikita and made his female characters unattractive.

In the play, Nikita is twenty years old and manipulated by older women, his wife Anisya and his mother Matryona, who directs him to murder the baby. In contrast to the real-life rapist and murderer, Nikita is an almost sympathetic figure. An implication is made that his step-daughter is cohabiting with him willingly. Tolstoy presents the girl as sensual and crude, quite unlike her prototype. All female characters are unappealing, suggesting that a man's sinful thoughts are incited by a woman. Tolstoy would return to this theme in *The Kreutzer Sonata*, his controversial novella about sexual love.

The subject of sensuality dominated Chertkov's letters: abstinence from sex only made him more obsessive about it, and he informed Tolstoy of his sexual fantasies and masturbating. Back in 1885, outlining the moral rules for sexual relations, Tolstoy wrote Chertkov that one must not make sex an amusement but must not suppress sexual urge, either. According to Tolstoy, a man was only safe when sexual drive was controlled through marriage, physical work, and vegetarian diet.[54] This narrow path protected one from temptation and sinning. "Why don't you marry?" Tolstoy asked Chertkov in another letter. "You can't live contrary to the law of nature—God. This [would be] tempting God."[55] (Tolstoy used the word in the meaning it appears in the Gospel from Matthew, e.g., in the parable "The Tempta-tion of Jesus," when Jesus tells the devil: "Though shalt not tempt the Lord thy God."[56] Chertkov argued: "You say—tempting god. [Sic.] But do you know that's precisely what I want to do—to tempt god, my own god, my understanding of him and my interaction with him." During his struggle with lust, when he prayed for deliverance, he "felt closer to god."[57] A willful Chertkov disregarded the words of Holy Scriptures and Christ, which Tol-stoy pointed out: "You're saying: but I want to tempt God. That's not good."

Tolstoy's views on sex would continue to change, but in the meantime, he still believed that living a morally good life was impossible without mar-riage. "You'd say: and what if a man doesn't have a calling for marriage. If he doesn't have a calling, he also doesn't lust. You'd say: and what if he hates this lust and wants to overcome it? Overcoming it is only possible through one means: go and live, like a laborer, working the way he works and eating what he eats. But to live, as you live, with your mother, and to struggle with lust means tempting God."[58] In his thirties, Chertkov was still under his mother's wing. For a sensual man, who had plenty of money and did little work, it was easy to slip into dissipation.

Yielding to Tolstoy's pressure, Chertkov decided to marry. In July 1886, while vacationing in England with his mother, he wrote Tolstoy, "I am hoping to marry soon, although I don't yet know whom to."[59] Upon his return, Chertkov proposed to Anna Dieterichs, his coworker at Intermediary. (She called herself Galya.) On September 2, Chertkov wrote that he was expecting Galya's reply without trepidation: "I'm not thinking much about it." Galya's response arrived just as he was finishing his letter to Tolstoy. Galya said that she loved Chertkov, but doubted she could make a good wife because of her poor health. Having survived typhus, a serious bacterial infection, she suffered various complications, which left her disabled. (She was eventually confined to a wheelchair.) Undeterred by this admission, Chertkov forwarded Galya's letter to Tolstoy.

Tolstoy now had conflicting feelings about Chertkov marrying, being jealous and protective of him as well as fearing for the outcome of this experiment. In a letter to his follower Ozmidov, who had recently founded an agricultural colony, Tolstoy said that he thinks of Chertkov's future marriage "with love and dread."[60] Tolstoy shed some light on this comment in a letter to Gay Sr., the artist: "I have a strange feeling of dread before the most important events in life. That's how I feel about the founding of Ozmidov's colony, Chertkov's marriage, Feinerman's life, and your new project."[61] Isaak Feinerman was a young fanatical follower of Tolstoy, who gave his money and property to the poor, leaving his pregnant wife and child without means. Chertkov's loveless marriage to a like-minded Tolstoyan, was another of the writer's ideas put to test.

On October 12, Tolstoy's eldest daughter, Tanya, twenty-two, wrote in her diary that "Chertkov does not look like a bridegroom. He is to be married almost at once, but says he hardly thinks about it...I hardly know if he is more pitied or admired for his views on marriage. He has found a woman who shares his convictions and who loves him, and as he thinks he ought to have children and a wife to help him in his work, he has decided to marry her, although he is not in love. I hope it turns out well, but it seems risky."[62] Chertkov was simply implementing Tolstoy's theories. Tolstoy advised his followers to "marry without sensual love, but from the calculation . . . that your future wife will help you, and not prevent you from living a humane life."[63] A good Christian was expected to live an entirely spiritual life, unsullied by sexual passion, which is why Chertkov and Galya could be expected to become a model couple.

On October 19, they were married in a chapel of a Petersburg gymnasium. The church wedding was against Chertkov's and Galya's beliefs, but was meant to placate her traditional family. Tolstoy was soon advising the newlyweds not to become attached to each other and not to quarrel, thus cautioning them against the mistakes he had made in his marriage.[64]

Elizaveta Chertkova was pleased with her son's choice. Galya belonged to a respectable family of military generals and government officials. Her father was a graduate of the Page Corps, like Chertkov's father, and her sister, Elena, was married to Ivan Shcheglovitov, whose family was related to the Romanovs and who became a minister of justice. Possessive of her son, Chertkova was also pleased that Galya would not capture his heart.

Galya was educated at the Bestuzhev's Courses in Petersburg. This was the first Russian institution of higher education for women. Opened in 1878, the Higher Women's Courses offered instruction in philology, history, mathematics, and natural sciences; subjects were taught by the leading scholars, such as the chemist Dmitry Mendeleev, who developed the periodic classification of the elements, and physiologist Ivan Sechenov. Graduates received the right to teach at female academies and also at male educational institutions at a lower level. Nadezhda Krupskaya, Lenin's future wife, was among those who attended these courses. During this time, the artist Nikolai Yaroshenko, a member of the Wanderers, captured Galya in the painting *Kursistka* (A Girl Student). The painting, which shows her walking down the street with a book under her arm, became symbolic of a new generation of Russian women who attained higher education and careers. Yaroshenko also painted Galya as she was recovering from typhus: sitting in an armchair, propped by pillows, she is a shadow of her former self.

In her twenties, Galya sympathized with the revolutionary Populist organization Land and Freedom and was an atheist. After the assassination of Alexander II, she became disillusioned with revolutionaries. Her interest in Tolstoy's teaching of non-resistance brought her to Intermediary in 1885 and she became the only female staff member. People who knew Galya as a free-spirited woman would watch her become a submissive wife, a mere echo of Chertkov.

In September of 1886, Galya wrote a long letter to Tolstoy, whom she had met on a recent visit to Yasnaya. Asking Tolstoy to give her a "blessing" for marrying Chertkov, she wrote: "For me, my future husband is a pupil of Christ and a man of one mind with you."[65] It was a carefully crafted letter, which betrayed a cold and pedantic mind, like Chertkov's own. Galya stated her attitude to property, which "doesn't matter" to a Christian, and her rejection of Church ritual. Because Tolstoy was recovering from the injury to his leg, Galya asked to explain his attitude to death. (The question was likely suggested by Chertkov himself. Tolstoy's attitude to death was of great importance to him because of their different views on afterlife.) Galya wrote that she was struck by the idea that Tolstoy could die, like the rest of us. Chertkov's influence could be sensed in her blunt question, "What would better promote the spread of your teaching of Truth—your long life or your timeless death?" She believed that Tolstoy would transcend death, having impacted the spiritual life of the entire mankind—"I know you are immortal."[66] Tolstoy, instead of replying to Galya, for which he apologized to Chertkov, began to draft his philosophical treatise, *On Life and Death*. In November, Chertkov was reading the first chapters of it.

In this work Tolstoy discussed the meaning and purpose of life, as expressed by philosophers from antiquity to modern times. He also explored an idea whether life can escape destruction by death. The question of his own mortality always deeply concerned Tolstoy. Upon completing the treatise he concluded that death did not exist and removed the word "death" from the title. It was also in this work that he first expressed his belief in a future life. This would become Tolstoy's permanent view, a major change of attitude from his earlier work *What I Believe* where he proposed that Jesus "never asserted a personal resurrection and personal immortality beyond the grave."[67] Chertkov closely followed the progress of his book *On Life*, reminding Tolstoy to discuss his attitude to afterlife in the conclusion and even insisting that Tolstoy should explain *how* he understands a future life.[68] In one of his letters Chertkov wrote, with great confidence, that for people who live "a true" spiritual life death does not and cannot exist.[69] Including this point mattered to Chertkov as a promise (needed for himself and for the followers) of personal salvation through Tolstoy's faith.

Although Chertkov's letters were extraordinarily banal, making it difficult even to quote them at length, Tolstoy was apparently influenced with his message. As he stated in the concluding chapters of his work, by renouncing material, personal life for the benefit of others, one enters into a new relationship with the world, in which there is no death. In 1891, in a letter to Hamilton Campbell, a minister of the Free Church of Scotland, Tolstoy wrote that he had expressed his views on personal immortality in the last chapters of his book *On Life*: "I think that . . . the less we live our own personal life, the more we feel sure of immortality, and the reverse . . . immortality must coincide with complete renunciation of self."[70] Thus, Tolstoy came to believe that by dedicating one's life to attaining a higher spiritual goal, one would transcend death.

Unlike with his literature, which captured the world's complexity, in religion Tolstoy sought simple truths, which could withstand a rational analysis: "Religion is the awareness of those truths which are common and comprehensible to all people in all situations at all times, and are as indisputable as $2 \times 2 = 4$. The business of religion is to find and express these truths, and when the truth has been expressed, it inevitably changes people's lives . . . Religion is like geometry."[71] In the years to come, Chertkov would act as a schoolmaster, assigning his pupil, Tolstoy, to formulate his views in a popular and concise way. A genuine exchange of ideas between them was impossible. Chertkov was feeding on Tolstoy's ideas, collecting his utterances, to present them to others as expressions of absolute truth.

Absorbed in his work *On Life*, Tolstoy could no longer collaborate with Intermediary as before. Once he withdrew from their undertaking, the interest was also lost for Chertkov. In June 1887, he wrote Tolstoy that he wanted to leave the management of Intermediary to someone else. Tolstoy was shocked that Chertkov could abandon their venture. It was God's work, and Chertkov should continue pulling his load with love and joy until the Master himself removes the harness. Tolstoy told Chertkov a parable about the Tsar who was wondering why he wasn't successful. He asked three wise men to give him advice. The first told the Tsar that he didn't know the right time to do things; the second—that he didn't know who was the man most necessary to him; the third—that he didn't know what task was the most valuable of all. The Tsar tried to un-riddle the advice of the wise men, but nobody could help him. "And then a young girl answered the riddle for him. She said that the most important time of all is the present, because there is no other time exactly like it. And the most necessary man of all is the one you are now dealing with, because he is the only man you actually know. And the most valuable task of all is to do good to this man, because this is the only task that will certainly be of advantage to you."[72] In this letter Tolstoy actually shared one of the secrets to his own success: he always labored by focusing on the task at hand and believed his current work to be most important.

CHAPTER FOUR

HAPPY AND UNHAPPY FAMILIES

"But now he's like
A man besotted, since he's been so taken
With this Tartuffe. He calls him brother, loves him
A hundred times as much as mother, son,
Daughter, and wife. He tells him all his secrets
And lets him guide his acts, and rule his conscience."
—Molière, *Tartuffe*

"And now he has revealed the most intimate details of our
life in his diaries and letters to Chertkov and Co., and this
repulsive man draws his own conclusions . . . from these
letters and diaries, which are often written merely to please
him—and often in his tone of voice too . . ."
—*The Diaries of Sophia Tolstoy*

O n September 23, 1887, the Tolstoys marked their silver wedding
anniversary. There was a modest celebration at Yasnaya: family
and guests assembled outside at a long table. Sophia's eldest
brother, Sasha, who had been best man at their wedding, gave the couple

a silver goblet. When Dmitry Dyakov, Tolstoy's close friend from student years, proposed a toast to their happy marriage, Tolstoy retorted: "It could have been better!" Hurt by his remark, Sophia commented, years later, that these words exemplified Tolstoy's impossible demands, which despite her best efforts she could never satisfy. In fact, their family was fortunate in many ways. In that span of twenty-five years their twelve children were born and Tolstoy's celebrated novels were written.

Back in the days when Tolstoy wrote *Anna Karenina*, projecting his ideal of family happiness, he and Sophia were in agreement in all their beliefs. The book's publication made Tolstoy the most famous and wealthiest writer in the land. As he had written in *A Confession*, "Had a fairy come and offered to fulfil my desires I should not have known what to ask . . . I had a good wife who loved me and whom I loved, good children, and a large estate which without much effort on my part improved and increased." It was at this time that his religious transformation prompted him to renounce his former life as not sufficiently serious and spiritual.

Becoming more aware of social injustice, of living blissfully in the midst of poverty and oppression, Tolstoy wanted his family to show "the greatest possible renunciation of the self and one's egotistical pleasures."[1] His new demands were extraordinary: he wanted his wife and children to radically change their lives. As Sophia explained in her diary, "I am expected to renounce everything, all my property, all my beliefs, the education and wellbeing of my children—things which not only I, a fairly determined woman, but thousands of others who *believe* in these precepts, are incapable of doing."[2] Because the family did not follow him on his path, which he believed offered nothing but goodness, Tolstoy continually criticized them for their vile and privileged lifestyle. Yet, they still lived precisely as in the days when he wrote *Anna Karenina* and depicted their way of life as exemplary.

As a mother, publisher, and estate manager, Sophia handled more work and responsibility than noble women of her day. There were also her charities: she provided free medical help in their district (with skills learned from her father, a court physician) and assisted peasant women in labor. Tolstoy ignored all her independent activity, having written uncompromisingly in 1885 that there can be no agreement between them until she came to his view of life.[3] Although Sophia could not accept his sweeping renunciations, she was interested in Tolstoy's philosophy and read every work he produced.

In 1887, copying Tolstoy's treatise *On Life*, her favorite among his philosophical works, she disagreed with the idea that "one should have to renounce one's personal life in the name of universal love. I believe that there are obligations which are ordained by God, that no one has the right to deny them, and that these obligations actually promote, rather than hinder, the spiritual life."[4] In her view, raising their family was no less important than pursuing Tolstoy's ideal of universal happiness. In any case, she had lived for others: her young years were spent assisting Tolstoy in his work and bearing their children in endless succession. At forty-one, she became a publisher and handled all material responsibilities, allowing Tolstoy to live and work as he wished.

That summer, Tolstoy was preparing *On Life* for publication: Sophia included it in a separate volume of collected works, although realizing that if the treatise was prohibited she would lose her investment. To meet the printers' deadline, Tolstoy organized family and guests to copy his revisions. He divided his helpers into groups: some took his dictation in his study, while others copied in the drawing room. Alexandrine, with whom he discussed religion over the years, philosopher Nikolai Grot, and public prosecutor, Alexander Kuzminsky, married to Sophia's sister Tanya, were among his distinguished copyists. He allowed them to correct his style, but Kuzminsky argued that "simple mortals" should not revise Tolstoy's prose.[5] Professor Grot, whose expert opinion on the manuscript Tolstoy sought, having engaged him to proofread the entire work, offered his revisions cautiously and only after consulting the author.

The following year, when censors banned *On Life* and six hundred copies were confiscated, Sophia was left with the printers' bills. However, that year the book was published in New York in an English translation by Isabel Hapgood. Sophia translated *On Life* into French and in 1889 her translation appeared in Paris. Later, Chertkov was surprised when he found out that she had translated the book and even asked Tolstoy to confirm this.

Tolstoy did not send *On Life* to Intermediary and Chertkov felt excluded from the project. He reproached Tolstoy for resuming his old habit of "writing for an educated audience. If you were to write again in your old style, it would be very sad, and you'd say many unnecessary things. Everything people *need* can be expressed in a popular form."[6] Although Tolstoy had many helpers, Chertkov wanted Intermediary employees to copy his revisions: "I have many copyists here—and all these people are of the same spirit as you."[7]

Deciding to adapt *On Life* for a popular audience, Chertkov collaborated on the project with Galya. He wrote Tolstoy, "Galya is now simplifying some of your particularly complex thoughts." They condensed passages, retold chapters, and occasionally misinterpreted Tolstoy's ideas. In 1890, Chertkov sent Tolstoy the adapted version, along with his own introduction. Tolstoy tried correcting it, but gave up: "Something is wrong with the adaptation."[8] Chertkov published his adaptation of Tolstoy's book in 1916, in a journal he edited. It appeared under the title "About Lev Tolstoy's True Life."

In the fall of 1887, there was also commotion in the Chertkov household: Galya was soon to give birth. Tolstoy was consulted on whether to christen the future baby, whether Galya should breastfeed it herself, and whether she could use anesthetics during labor. Because Tolstoy sneered at doctors and medicine, Chertkov sought his opinion on the use of narcotics. Doctors in England were beginning to employ laughing gas (nitrous oxide) for pain-free childbirth. Chertkov explained that laughing gas was different from chloroform or ether and had only a passing euphoric effect on patients, who remained conscious.[9] Tolstoy's opinion was inflexible, although he only spoke for himself: "I'd be decidedly against both chloroform and laughing gas. God gives childbirth and God will give strength."[10] But in the end, he thought that protecting oneself from pain and suffering was a moral issue, which offered constant dilemmas, and believed the decision lay in each person's heart.[11] Sophia also advised against the anesthetics, but for a different reason: laughing gas was a novelty in Russia and unless administered by someone experienced could do more harm than good.

Despite Tolstoy's mistrust of medicine, he was in favor of producing popular literature on a broad range of medical subjects. Intermediary published books and brochures by experts on venereal diseases, midwifery, and child rearing. Tolstoy himself edited a brochure on infant care by the pediatrician Egor Pokrovsky.

On November 1, Galya bore a girl, of which Chertkov informed Tolstoy in a telegram. (She did not use anesthetics: Chertkov wrote that her opinion coincided with Tolstoy's.) The Tolstoys wrote to congratulate and Sophia gave her advice to the new mother. Before the girl was named, Chertkov referred to the baby as Tolstoy's granddaughter. "I kiss you and the granddaughter," Tolstoy replied.[12]

Tolstoy acquired a second family with Chertkov and treated it more considerately than his own. Three years earlier, when Sasha was born, Tolstoy complained a letter to Chertkov that Sophia hired a wet nurse. He called his wife's refusal to suckle her own child "the most inhumane, unreasonable, and unchristian act."[13] (She was launching a publishing business and could not afford sleepless nights with the baby. Tolstoy, no longer interested in his family matters, judged her severely.) Chertkov did not allow any criticism of his wife, and demanded Tolstoy's attention and sympathy to his family's needs. He routinely reported Galya's problems nursing his daughter, Olya, and Galya's lack of breast milk.

Over a few months, Tolstoy traveled twice to visit the Chertkovs, who were staying at the well-appointed Kryokshino estate near Moscow. (This was Uncle Pashkov's estate before his exile.) They moved to Kryokshino for Galya's birth, taking their large entourage—family, servants, and a wet nurse. Maria Schmidt, a former superintendent in a female gymnasium and Tolstoy's follower, was summoned from Yasnaya as a nanny for Chertkov's baby. (Tolstoy quietly objected that they should engage a peasant woman for a nanny.) A female doctor, Ekaterina Goncharova, who was qualified at the Sorbonne, was looking after Galya.

Tolstoy believed wet nurses were harmful, having first discussed this in *War and Peace*. Testing his patience, Chertkov wrote profusely about the wet nurse they hired. She was a destitute single mother, who left her baby for adoption in a Moscow orphanage. Upon finding employment with the Chertkovs, the woman wanted her baby back. Chertkov delegated the task of retrieving her baby to none other than Tolstoy, since he was in Moscow. In December, despite being unwell, Tolstoy went to the orphanage, found the child, and arranged for a female escort to deliver him to Chertkov's estate. Reporting that the baby safely arrived, Chertkov contemplated how the assignment would make Tolstoy feel. Because of their closeness,

Chertkov thought that Tolstoy was unlikely to be annoyed: "I noticed that regardless of how irritated I get, even during the worst moments, I'm *never* annoyed with myself. And so, it's *impossible* to become annoyed with someone you love as much as yourself. It turns out that I don't love anyone in the world as much as myself . . . What about you?"[14] Chertkov wanted proof of Tolstoy's unconditional love, and the writer was ready to provide it.

The Chertkovs were planning to stay in Moscow before relocating to their Voronezh estate. Although the couple had servants, Chertkov asked Tolstoy to find him an apartment. This stole Tolstoy's time (he was drafting *The Kreutzer Sonata*), but he responded that he was "very, very glad" to help.[15] Although Tolstoy did not help Sophia at home, he was running Chertkov's errands. He inspected several furnished apartments in the fashionable Arbat district inhabited by university professors. (It was where Tolstoy had dreamt to buy a house for his own family back in the days when he was writing *War and Peace*.) In January, upon arriving from Kryokshino, southwest of Moscow, where he traveled at Chertkov's insistence, Tolstoy returned to the same district to see furnished rooms in *Stolitsa*. An eighteenth-century three-story house near the Praga restaurant, it had thick soundproof walls, which is why many writers liked to stay there. Tolstoy also recommended the place for its inexpensive restaurant, but the Chertkovs ended up spending only ten days there. In February, already at his Voronezh estate, Chertkov wrote with another request.

He presented their family predicament: the baby was crying, apparently from not getting enough milk, and Galya was suffering. They suspected that the wet nurse was feeding her own child and did not give enough to *their* child. Chertkov, of course, could resolve this without troubling Tolstoy: a new wet nurse could be easily found in the villages around his vast Voronezh estates, the size of a small European country. But he simply wanted Tolstoy to be involved, if only to secure the healthiest nurse for his child. He instructed Tolstoy to meet pediatrician Pokrovsky at the Moscow children's hospital and have him find a new mother whose child recently died: there are many such destitute women in the city, he wrote selfishly. (There was something nasty about this request: the rich taking advantage of the poor, precisely what Tolstoy preached against.) Chertkov's letter arrived the day after the Tolstoys celebrated their son Ilya's wedding. Just twenty-two, Ilya was the first among their children to marry, but neither Tolstoy nor Sophia attended the church ceremony. Tolstoy, rejecting the ritual, stayed at home and Sophia, far into her difficult new pregnancy, was unwell and embarrassed about her appearance.

On March 4, after he met the doctor at the children's hospital Tolstoy informed Chertkov about developments, sending three letters on the same day. In the last one Tolstoy exploded, fully revealing his annoyance. He wrote that Chertkov and Galya relied on medicine more than on God, that if the baby cries, they should be patient, that he did not believe in hiring wet nurses, paying doctors, etc.[16] Chertkov responded in a forceful letter: "Is it fair to cruelly accuse people of godlessness only because their attitude to medicine is different from your own?..I feel sorry for you that you've written such a letter."[17] He sent a page from his diary to show how Tolstoy had hurt his and poor Galya's feelings.

Tolstoy at once admitted that he had written a bad letter; it was "very painful for me to realize that I hurt both of you . . . I hurt people I love . . . Forgive me."[18] On March 19, Tolstoy informed Chertkov in a telegram that the wet nurse was on her way to his Voronezh estate. Tolstoy paid for the woman's transportation with Sophia's money.[19] (A year later, on April 24, 1889, the Chertkovs had a son, Vladimir. Tolstoy was again forced to interrupt his work and spend a day at a children's hospital, consulting a young doctor on Chertkov's behalf about a wet nurse, something he would have not done for his own family.)

On March 31, 1888, Sophia bore their thirteenth and last child, son Vanechka. This last birth was the most difficult, as she confided with sister Tanya: "Never before did the suffering drive me so insane. Lyovochka [Tolstoy] and the nanny wept—they stayed with me the entire time . . . A quarter to nine, a boy was born. Lyovochka took him in his arms and kissed him, a miracle unseen before! He is happy it's a boy and treats him with special care and protectiveness."[20] Although the birth of his youngest son was a joy to Tolstoy, he did not inform Chertkov about it until later on, nor did he stay in Moscow to help Sophia. Some two weeks later, on April 18, Tolstoy left for Yasnaya Polyana on foot in company with his young follower and Sophia's publishing assistant, Gay, Jr. Sophia stayed in the city to look after the children and her publishing affairs: she was producing a new edition. Her letters to Tolstoy revealed her nervousness and overwork.

That summer, after a fire in the village, Tolstoy with his follower Biryukov and Nikolai Gay (the artist) decided to build a new hut for a peasant widow. Daughter Masha, eighteen, the closest to Tolstoy among the children, helped in the construction. They cut the straw, pounded the clay, sprinkled it with water, mixed them together, and tossed the mixture onto the walls with spades. It took Tolstoy and Gay some time to figure out how to build a stove, but in the end, they accomplished their task well. Tolstoy engaged a carpenter to do the less interesting work—to make the ceiling, install widows, and doors. Nearing sixty, Tolstoy spent this summer hauling water, chopping wood, and working in the field.

Chertkov, who wanted Tolstoy to keep contributing popular stories for Intermediary, reasoned that "a man of your age should not be mostly doing physical work."[21] Tolstoy usually made a break from mental activity during the summer and enjoyed working outside. "Don't reproach me," he asked Chertkov. "I am working a lot with my hands: we are now building a house of straw and clay for the victims of a fire, and on Monday, will be tilling the land and mowing."[22] Of Masha, who was assisting in all his labors, Tolstoy wrote they were inseparable.

In late November, Tolstoy resumed *The Kreutzer Sonata*, the story of "how a man killed his wife." A novella about sexual love, it was inspired by evenings of storytelling and playing Beethoven at the Tolstoys' houses in Moscow and Yasnaya Polyana. A year earlier, the actor Vasily Andreev-Burlak told Tolstoy a story of marital infidelity he had heard from a man on a train. There was also a direct musical inspiration. During a large artistic gathering at their Moscow house with the painter Repin present, the Tolstoys' eldest son, Sergei, an accomplished pianist, and a young violinist named Yuly Lyasotta played Beethoven's Violin Sonata No. 9. Tolstoy said that the music expressed every conceivable emotion and proposed that the guests collaborate, each developing the theme in their own genre. He would write a story, which Andreev-Burlak would read on stage; Repin would make a painting inspired by the leitmotif of the Kreutzer Sonata, and display it as Tolstoy's story was read. The proposal was accepted, but in the end, Tolstoy alone produced a work. His intense novella tells about human passions and the cruelest of them all, the sex urge.

Tolstoy, who had idealized family happiness in *Anna Karenina* and only recently disapproved "of a celibate life for those who are ripe for marriage,"[23] now preached that virtuous marriages did not exist. In *The Kreutzer Sonata*, he drew from his betrothal, as he had in *Anna Karenina*, but now his goal was to show the disastrous consequences of sexual love. Throughout this work he argues that physical love is an obstacle to the Christian ideal of brotherly love: ". . . The prophets have said, that all mankind should be united together in love . . . what is it that hinders the attainment of this aim? The passions hinder it . . . If the passions are destroyed, including the strongest of them—physical love—the prophesy will be fulfilled, mankind will be brought into unity . . ."[24] Having repudiated sex even in marriage, Tolstoy proclaimed complete chastity to be his new ideal.

He now viewed Sophia as a source of temptation and when he succumbed, hated her for the passion she inspired. After insisting that they should have sex, he would denounce it in his diary as sinful: "Slept badly . . . Slept sinfully . . . Slept terribly badly . . . Thought: what if there should be another child? How ashamed I should be, especially before the children. They will reckon up when it was, and will read what I'm writing."[25] Sophia felt that Tolstoy's sexual moralizing was hypocritical: "One should not be an animal, but nor should one preach virtues one doesn't have."[26] The novella remains the most extreme and unfathomable among Tolstoy's fictional works. The writer later admitted that his conclusions came as a surprise to him as well and that he even felt "horrified" at the start.[27]

Tolstoy's demand of continence even within marriage also surprised Chertkov, all the more so because he had recently married at the writer's insistence. In November 1888, just before Tolstoy resumed *The Kreutzer Sonata*, Chertkov asked him to articulate his views on marriage and sex: what he considered lustful, whether he justified sex for procreation, etc. Chertkov was defining aspects of Christian doctrine, which is why he often asked Tolstoy to clarify his views. His questions usually inspired Tolstoy's moralistic response, as happened this time. Referring to the passage in the Gospel from Matthew where Christ says there are "eunuchs for the kingdom of heaven's sake,"[28] Tolstoy wrote that both men and women should aspire to absolute chastity. This pronouncement precipitated a flood of Chertkov's questions, to which Tolstoy responded in a long letter containing his inflexible conclusions. The ideas on marriage and sex developed in this letter would travel into *The Kreutzer Sonata* almost unchanged. To Chertkov's question, whether married couples should sleep in the same bed, Tolstoy replied that, of course, they should sleep separately. It was shameful to enjoy sex; disgusting and shameful for "every man with a conscience" to have sex when his wife was pregnant or nursing. Tolstoy preached that a husband and wife should live together as brother and sister, but could have intercourse during interludes of "falling in love." He compared the sex urge with a steam engine: when pressure could not be contained, a safety valve would open. Anticipating the objection, "But then the human race would cease to exist," Tolstoy argued that because the safety valve would function there would still be children. At any rate, the annihilation of the human race was no big loss and if the two-legged animal, homo sapiens, would vanish, he would not regret its extinction more than the extinction of the Ichthyosaurus. The ideal of humanity was not fertility, but spiritual love, so people should renounce lust for the sake of this ideal.[29] Tolstoy later found similarities to his views among religious sects that practiced chastity, such as the Skoptsy (self-castrators) in Russia and the Shakers in America. Around this time, he received Dr. Alice Stockham's *Tokology: A Book for Every Woman*. An obstetrician and gynecologist, Dr. Stockham believed that women should not have continual pregnancies and that men should be able to control their sexual desire. But Tolstoy's message in *The Kreutzer Sonata* was far more radical.

In the novella, Tolstoy advances his extreme view that virginity is the only righteous condition for both sexes. In life, however, he failed to even marginally control his desire. Sophia, who was reading his novella, was aghast with his contradictions and felt, as she would mention in her memoir, that he was utterly unconcerned with her experiences. In his diary, which she also read at the time, Tolstoy only explored his own feelings and moods: ". . . Slept *badly*. It was so disgusting, I felt I'd committed a crime . . ."[30] Tolstoy invested his hero, the wife murderer Pozdnyshev, with some of his own features, such as marital jealousy, sensuality, and revulsion after the sex act.

In 1908, Tolstoy confided to his son-in-law, Mikhail Sukhotin, who was writing a biographical article about him, "You're collecting various trifles about me, and will publish them; others are even trying to write my biographies. But here's what I have to say to you: all accounts will remain inaccurate and one-sided until the biographers will explore the most vital part of my youth, which had a tremendous influence over the rest of my life; I mean my relations with women. But, of course, the most important will remain unknown to biographers and, to tell you the truth, not everything is appropriate to write about. Of course, after my marriage I did not have carnal relations with other women and did not indulge in debauchery."[31] According to this admission, something vital about his private life remained untold. This was despite documenting his exploits in his diaries and in his works, and revealing such intimate occurrences as his loss of virginity in a bordello where his brothers brought him at fourteen.

The Kreutzer Sonata produced an uproar in Russia, where it began to circulate in underground copies even before Tolstoy completed his final redaction. The novella discussed relations between the sexes with unprecedented openness and by spring 1890, entire households had read it. *The Kreutzer Sonata* sparked discussion, argument, and a flood of written response. Strakhov wrote to Tolstoy that instead of saying, "How are you?" people would ask, "Have you read *The Kreutzer Sonata*?"[32] Chekhov sent his copy of the novella to Modest Tchaikovsky, the composer's brother. Describing how the work made him feel, Chekhov wrote to a friend: "Aside from its artistic merits, which are in places stupendous, we must above all be grateful to the story for its power to excite our minds to their limits. Reading it, you can scarcely forbear to exclaim: 'That's so true!' or alternatively 'That's so stupid!' There is no doubt that it has some irritating defects."[33]

As writer Ivan Bunin recalls, the public found it unfathomable that "a man who had fathered thirteen children could rise up against conjugal love and the continuation of the human race itself. They said that *The Kreutzer Sonata* could be best explained by the fact that Tolstoy . . . 'hated his wife.'"[34] A young follower, Andrei Butkevich, told Tolstoy that some people thought he had composed "a description of a sexual maniac." Tolstoy was shocked, writing in his diary: "I'm sexually disturbed." But then he thought that at least these experiences would be useful to some people and "at least it had stirred up something that needed stirring up."[35] As Maude would point out, the novella could inspire one to think, for example, that "the world suffers from excessive lust."[36]

In 1889, Sophia herself read *The Kreutzer Sonata* to their children. She understandably disliked the work, with its description of marriage as "nothing but copulation" and Tolstoy's exploitation of their intimate experiences. Attending that reading, Tolstoy heard daughter Tanya's remark that the heroine's crime (flirting with a guest musician) was small compared to her punishment. Tanya, twenty-five and unmarried, admitted in her diary that the novella made her feel "lost, unhappy and lonely."[37]

Because contemporaries assumed that Tolstoy once again drew from his marriage, Sophia came to be seen as a victim: her acquaintances and Tolstoy's brother Sergei Nikolaevich empathized with her. Told that the Tsar, upon reading *The Kreutzer Sonata*, remarked that he was sorry for Tolstoy's poor wife, Sophia became determined to prove that she was not at all a victim. She decided to publish the novella in the collected works.[38]

Chertkov learned about the novella in spring 1889, when Tolstoy mentioned he was writing "a story about sexual love."[39] He immediately asked that Tolstoy allow Intermediary to bring out his new fiction and thus support their undertaking.[40] At first, Tolstoy agreed, but changed his mind when other publishers approached him with the same request. In the end, none of them would attain official permission to produce the novella. When in December, Tolstoy first learned that the censors would likely ban *The Kreutzer Sonata*, he confessed in his diary that he was pleased with the news.[41] He wanted to avoid arguments, jealousies, and having to benefit financially from the novella's publication if Sophia produced it in the collected works.

In February 1890, the Procurator of the Holy Synod, Pobedonostsev, gave his opinion in a letter to the Chief Administrator for Press Affairs, Feoktistov. The procurator described the novella as a "powerful" work and thought it impossible to penalize the public for reading it, but found official publication unacceptable.[42] Although the novella could not be banned for moral reasons (it called for higher morality than sanctioned by the Church), it challenged the institution of marriage.

Sophia was hoping that censors would allow producing *The Kreutzer Sonata* in her limited subscription. But in February of 1891, the volume with the novella was seized by police from the printing shop. Informed that the volume was irrevocably banned, she decided to appeal to the Tsar, who alone could permit publication. Opinion about the novella in the royal family was divided: Alexander III liked the work, while the Empress was shocked.

But before Sophia traveled to Petersburg to petition the Tsar, Tolstoy told her of his intention to give up the copyright on his latest work: "This morning I told Sonya with difficulty and trepidation that I would announce that everyone would have the right to print my writings. I saw she was distressed . . ."[43] Actually, Tolstoy's friend Strakhov first suggested that he give up royalties on this new novella and allow publishers to freely reprint it. Distancing himself from Sophia's efforts to lift the ban on the novella, Tolstoy ridiculed her in a letter to Strakhov: "Sophia Andreevna is petitioning for the publication of this volume apparently for my sake, while everything to do with its publication is merely unpleasant to me . . ." What displeased him most was that "my works are for sale."[44]

While Tolstoy expected his wife to give up her profit, other publishers in Russia and abroad were making fortunes from his writings. In January 1890, a Danish translator, Peter Gansen, told Chertkov how a charitable organization raised significant funds by producing Tolstoy's minor story "Where Love Is, God Is." Gansen allowed the charity to issue 10,000 copies of his translation of this story. It published a booklet, which was distributed free of charge. With that, the charity provided an address where the public could send donations and in the end it collected a significant sum. Chertkov was laughing when he heard the story.[45]

Sophia's audience with Alexander III took place on April 13, 1891, in Petersburg. The Tsar allowed her to produce the novella exclusively in her collected works, which she recalls with understandable pride: "I cannot help secretly exulting in my success in overcoming all the obstacles, that I managed to obtain an interview with the Tsar, and that I, a woman, have achieved something that nobody else could have done!"[46] She could not share her triumph with Tolstoy, who was indifferent to her publishing and worldly success. Chronicling the audience in her diary, she describes

Alexander III who, she apparently thought, was related to Chertkov: "The Tsar is rather shy and speaks in a pleasant melodious voice . . . He reminded me a little of Vladimir Grigorievich Chertkov, especially his voice and manner of speaking."[47]

Sophia produced 3,000 copies of *The Kreutzer Sonata* in the collection, which did not nearly satisfy the demand. In summer, she received permission to print an additional 20,000. This is when Tolstoy made a final decision about renouncing copyright on his latest works. Sophia received the text of his copyright statement, which he asked her to send to the newspapers *The Russian Gazette* and *New Times*. Tolstoy's statement that he was placing his latest works, written after 1881, in the public domain was printed on September 19. Although Sophia complied with his request, she believed it was unfair to deprive their large family of income: "I knew that rich publishers, like Sytin [Intermediary's publisher], would profit from my husband's work . . . And it seemed to me that for God, in whom I believed, it did not matter whether it was I who sold Tolstoy's works or it was Sytin and Suvorin."[48] Tolstoy came to regret his decision. Because everyone could produce his works, competition between publishers increased. Trying to be first, they issued editions and translations of poor quality. In addition, publishers would approach Tolstoy by the back door, asking to let them have the most profitable first editions. Tolstoy complained to Maude that after he renounced copyright, publishing his new works became a source of trouble and annoyance.

Upon completing the novella, which he wrote simultaneously with an article on art, and the comedy, *The Fruits of Enlightenment*, Tolstoy began to draft *Resurrection*. Chertkov did not allow him to move on, however, asking to revise the novella along the lines he suggested. He wanted Tolstoy to show the spiritual growth of his hero, the wife murderer Pozdnyshev, and his eventual transformation into "a true Christian."[49] Tolstoy wrote in his diary that "Chertkov criticizes *The Kreutzer Sonata* very justly; I wish I could follow his advice, but haven't the inclination."[50] Chertkov was also urging Tolstoy to explain his views on sex, either in the novella or in an afterword. But Tolstoy felt so strongly on the subject that he could not reason; he could only express his emotions and thoughts through art. He invested some four months writing the afterword, but upon failing to clarify his ideas, decided to abandon it: "Although I've started writing an afterword, I probably won't finish it . . . I simply can't do it," he pleaded with Chertkov.[51] His friend persisted, however, sending additional suggestions for the afterword in which he expected Tolstoy to relax his ideal of complete chastity. Chertkov gave copies of the novella to the Danish and Anglo-American translators and now felt personally responsible for the impact Tolstoy's message would make around the world. Arriving in Yasnaya in January 1890, Chertkov copied the latest draft of Tolstoy's afterword, thus urging him to complete it. He was adamant that Tolstoy write at least a paragraph to justify moral Christian marriage. This was important "for the hundreds of millions of contemporaries who did not yet rise to the level of a chaste marriage." If the afterword would appear without this paragraph, millions of people would turn away from Christ.[52] Although Tolstoy was afraid to anger Chertkov with his refusal, he replied that he could not make "rehabilitation of an honorable marriage . . . There is no such marriage."[53]

In the afterword Tolstoy expressed the same uncompromising view: "The Christian ideal is that of love of God and one's fellow man . . . whereas sexual love, marriage, is a service of self, and consequently in any case an obstacle to the service of God and man, and therefore from a Christian point of view a fall, a sin . . ."[54] He now believed that his marriage prevented him from attaining his moral ideal, having written in his diary: "I often told myself: if not for my wife and children I would have lived a saintly life . . ."[55] Tolstoy loved humanity, but viewed his own family as only an obstacle on his spiritual path.

At the same time, he was lenient with his followers who were his spiritual children. Tolstoy had infinite patience for troubled men, who flocked to him for guidance. Chertkov was a difficult man, Tolstoy would say, and it was with great patience that he endured his friend's mental imbalance. In his letters to Tolstoy, Chertkov described his extreme moods, fluctuating from euphoria to apathy, and his delusion of persecution. Once, when traveling by train, Chertkov was overcome with fear of being pursued by police spies. Ever after, when he traveled alone, his fear returned, leaving him agitated and suffering.[56] Tolstoy had a similar experience. Traveling alone after completing *Anna Karenina*, he was overcome with fear of death and madness: "I remember long ago, I boarded a train at night, a 1st class coach; it [the carriage] was empty, and I became terrified that I would go mad."[57] Tolstoy advised Chertkov "to accept your illness and weakness" as God's will.[58] Actually, he was more considerate with Chertkov than with Sophia, whose mental and physical strength began to break under the weight of her responsibilities and perennial motherhood. Sophia suffered from anxiety and neuralgia, which Tolstoy occasionally mentioned in his diary with irritation. But he dutifully read his friend's letters reporting occurences. He consoled Chertkov when his infant daughter died of dysentery in summer 1889. Later that year, when the Chertkovs wanted to stay in Tula, Tolstoy secured a doctor and a massage therapist for Galya. Chertkov seemed to be deliberately asking Tolstoy to do what he most disliked, to deal with doctors and medicine.

It was also with surprising patience that Tolstoy endured Chertkov's obsessive meddling in his work. One of Chertkov's fixations was his desire to read Tolstoy's diaries. Knowing that Chertkov was reading them changed what Tolstoy wrote there about his wife and children: he continued to disparage them for anything that contradicted his ascetic ideal. In his diaries, Tolstoy also recorded plots for future work, thoughts about God, prayer, government, sex, etc. Back in 1887, Chertkov first proposed creating a compendium of Tolstoy's thoughts. He wanted to extract the writer's pronouncements on various subjects from his drafts, letters, and diaries and vowed to dedicate himself to this task.

Tolstoy was indifferent to the idea of a compendium, but Chertkov kept bringing it up: "I believe that you should definitely record your thoughts, in the roughest form, as they occur to you, and not for polishing them later on, but for making them available to people who are following in your path and who can understand you from a hint."[59] At the start, Tolstoy was reluctant to pass on his thoughts to Chertkov, who absorbed them "so greedily." But he also thought that Chertkov's project might be useful to others. "Oh yes, about the collection. Perhaps, it will be good, but certainly not [to publish it] under my name . . ."[60] However, when in winter 1890, Chertkov's messenger arrived to fetch Tolstoy's current diary, the writer refused to submit it. A while earlier Sophia had discovered that Tolstoy shared intimate family information with Chertkov and he promised not to do this again. To appease Chertkov, Tolstoy also promised to mark passages of general interest in his diaries and have Masha copy and send him the extracts.[61]

This fell on deaf ears: in May 1890, another of Chertkov's couriers arrived, with the same instruction to fetch Tolstoy's diaries. Tolstoy could not satisfy their request, explaining to Chertkov: "I am very sorry that I cannot send you my diaries . . . Not to mention the fact that it would upset my attitude to what I write, I can't send them without causing unpleasantness to my wife or keeping secrets from her . . . I'll copy out extracts for you, as I have started doing, and send them." Because Chertkov worried that Tolstoy's letters and diaries could be destroyed by fire, the writer replied that his family was safekeeping the papers and that "nothing of God's can be destroyed."[62]

At twenty, Masha was her father's secretary and confidante. She had to copy extracts from Tolstoy's diaries for Chertkov, but felt awkward about prying into her father's intimate thoughts. When during the summer, Chertkov nagged her to keep sending the extracts from the diaries and to remind Tolstoy to mark passages to copy, Masha responded, "Actually, it's unpleasant for me to copy these extracts, I'm ashamed to intrude into his spiritual, very intimate, godly work. I'm not asking him to mark the passages . . . I think it's unpleasant for him." Chertkov would not relent, so Masha wrote him firmly: "I'm confident that he [Tolstoy] doesn't want anyone to read these diaries during his life. He even writes about this somewhere. And so let's leave it at this."[63]

Tolstoy took his daughter's side: "Masha has written you that she will no longer copy my letters and diaries. She is right, and she is doing this for my sake. Don't be angry with me, dear friend, but try to understand, it's not only difficult for me, but it paralyses my spiritual activity; knowing that everything will be copied at once and sent out paralyzes me. Don't give me different reasons, but loving me, enter my situation, which *is* love . . . And I'll be writing you more often."[64] Back in 1884, Tolstoy impulsively trusted his diaries to Chertkov, allowing him to keep them and make revisions. Now, he wanted to cancel this arrangement, which had become tedious and difficult.

Faced with determined opposition, Chertkov relaxed his control. He assured Masha that he would not insist on copying Tolstoy's diaries. But he still had one request concerning Tolstoy's correspondence. Masha should meticulously record dates and names of people to whom Tolstoy wrote. In time, when Tolstoy's followers would be collecting his every line, Masha's records would come useful.[65] In a letter to Tolstoy, Chertkov agreed to "lovingly submit." However, he still had a small request. If all of Tolstoy's correspondence and diaries cannot be copied for Chertkov, at least some less intimate letters should be copied and sent to him: "Please keep doing this . . . for the sake of my project . . . Make sure to send me your thoughts . . . for my Compendium of your thoughts."[66]

Collecting and systematizing Tolstoy's pronouncements would occupy Chertkov and his assistants for three decades. It justified Chertkov's desire to read over Tolstoy's shoulder. The narcissist in Tolstoy seemed flattered with the attention: as he mentioned to daughter Tanya, Chertkov "shows even excess of respect, collecting anything to do with him [Tolstoy], but at the same time lets nothing slip."[67] Chertkov genuinely loved collecting Tolstoy's utterings, or "recipes" for "spiritual nourishment,"[68] as he called them. But the result was disappointing. In the words of Vladimir Bonch-Bruevich (Chertkov's friend and Lenin's future secretary), the compendium was "the most boring treatise, which no one needed."[69]

Chertkov used the compendium to impose uniformity among the followers. Maude, who joined Tolstoy's following as a young man, would observe that in the Tolstoyan movement "there sprang up a form of mental coercion. When under the stress of Tolstoy's doctrine some person of tender conscience adopted for a while Tolstoy's point of view regarding sex, or property, or Government employ, it was made hard for him ever to readjust himself. As soon as he tried to do so, he was accused of 'going back on his principles . . .'" And yet these principles were nothing more than "honest and strongly felt opinions of a man of genius," views that "had temporarily hypnotized" Tolstoy.[70] As the leader of their movement Tolstoy experienced pressure to comply with his own views and was accused of backsliding when developing new ideas.

Maude tells of how Tolstoy's principles created problems for him in daily life. In 1886, Anton Rubinstein, the pianist Tolstoy knew personally and loved, gave a concert in Moscow. Although Tolstoy would have immensely enjoyed the performance, he decided not to go. Rubinstein's music was for the educated minority, which contradicted Tolstoy's new belief that art must be accessible to all. On another occasion, Tolstoy had to sacrifice his love of chess to his austere principles. In 1894, the world's chess championship took place in Moscow with Emanuel Lasker playing against Wilhelm Steinitz. Tolstoy wanted to go, but Maude, then a devout Tolstoyan, objected, saying that professional chess was competitive and involved jealousies, which was against his teaching. As a result, Tolstoy did not attend the match, which Maude remembers with shame.

In his family life, Tolstoy's ideals created a lasting conflict. Having shifted all practical affairs to Sophia, he expected her to implement his principles in daily life. This would mean, for example, that while managing their estate, she could not protect it from plunder. She was also expected to give peasants in nearby villages what they asked. As a publisher, she was under pressure to give up her profit. As a mother, she was faced with Tolstoy's disapproval for sending their children to school where they received religious instruction from a priest. Tolstoy wanted her to educate the children in accordance with his new beliefs, even though he himself withdrew from their upbringing. As he had written Sophia in 1885, "I would like to help you, but you know yourself that I can't do so . . . All those things—or at least the majority of them—which disturb you, namely; the children's schooling, their progress, money matters, book matters even—all those things seem to me unnecessary and superfluous."[71] Since Tolstoy viewed all her activity through the prism of his religious beliefs, she was criticized even for striving to support their family. In a letter to her sister, Sophia describes their family predicament: "Our entire life is in conflict with Lyovochka's convictions and to concur with them . . . in our daily life is impossible . . ."[72] Being independent-minded, Sophia could not follow Tolstoy blindly, as his disciples had attempted. She also could not accept his views out of conviction, believing them impracticable and even harmful for the family.

Chertkov, on the other hand, claimed that he and his wife adhered to Tolstoy's principles in daily life. This gave him the advantage of presenting his family as morally superior to Tolstoy's. One year into his marriage, describing Galya as his sister in spirit and collaborator, Chertkov boasted: "I don't know how to thank god [sic.] for the goodness I receive from the communion with my wife. I always remember people who are deprived of the chance to experience such spiritual communion with their wives, but who deserve this happiness more than I do."[73] Tolstoy did not dispute this point, even though Sophia's assistance to him, when he wrote novels, was incomparably more valuable.

Chertkov, who continued to live as luxuriously as before, accepted Tolstoy's teaching in word only. His wife made financial transactions on his behalf, so he could claim to live without money. His mother provided a generous allowance and although it came from their estates, which employed unpaid peasant labor, Chertkov argued he exploited no one. Tolstoy turned a blind eye to Chertkov's spending habits: his inability to carry out Christian precepts mattered less than his attempt to fulfill them, his striving towards perfection. At the same time, Tolstoy disapproved of his own family for their supposed "luxury" and "idleness." Because he used them as a negative example in his non-fiction, his readers assumed that the Tolstoys lived like aristocracy, which was not the case.

Beginning in the mid-1880s, visitors to Yasnaya, such as Maude and the American explorer and journalist George Kennan, would describe the simplicity of life there. Kennan was surprised to discover that the Yasnaya mansion was utterly unimpressive: "It would be hard to imagine a simpler, barer, less pretentious building."[74] Maude recalls "old fashioned, rather plain furniture, worn bare-board floors . . . and window-frames that needed repairing."[75] During his visits Maude was also struck with the genuine "atmosphere of love and respect that surrounded Tolstoy...People have spoken much of discord between Tolstoy and his family, but at that time I saw many more proofs of the affection and esteem in which he was held by them."[76]

In 1891–1892, after a massive crop failure in Russia, which caused severe famine, Tolstoy's family worked alongside him to provide relief. The two eldest sons, Sergei and Ilya, became involved with the local Red Cross. Son Lev organized relief in Samara, southeastern Russia. Tolstoy's eldest daughters, Tanya and Masha opened canteens and distributed aid with their father in the most afflicted areas between Tula and Ryazan. In November 1891, at the start of Tolstoy's work on the famine, Sophia wrote an appeal for donations, which was carried by newspapers across Russia and reprinted in the West. According to her estimate, in two years their family collected 200,000 rubles (some 30,000 rubles were sent directly to her). What is more, the Tolstoys and their volunteers distributed aid directly to the starving. Sophia contributed some of her publishing profit, solicited donations, and dispatched carloads of grain and vegetables to Tolstoy, their sons, and to the artist Nikolai Gay and his son who dispensed relief near Petersburg. The Tolstoys helped save many people from starvation and provided a moral example that was followed across the country.

But Tolstoy also doubted his involvement early on. In fall 1891, when a follower pointed out to him that distributing aid contradicted his idea that money was evil, he apologetically replied that he had been "dragged into this work of feeding the starving . . . My wife wrote a letter asking for donations, and without my noticing it I've become a distributor of other people's vomit . . ."[77] Yet, it was during this calamity that the principle of universal love could actually be tested and when the entire nation became united in its compassion. Sophia wrote to her sister that work on the famine was beneficial for Tolstoy, since he was surrounded by "ordinary people," not his fanatical followers.[78] While some disciples participated in the relief, Chertkov remained at his Voronezh estate, copying Tolstoy's new work, *The Kingdom of God Is Within You*. His correspondence with Tolstoy reveals that he was more concerned about abstract religious ideas than the issue that was consuming the nation—how to feed the starving.

CHAPTER FIVE

EVIL GENIUS

"Uriah Heep can worm his way into the confidence of an experienced man of affairs, gradually get the upper hand of his weaknesses, and reduce him to subservience."
— Charles Dickens, *David Copperfield*

"It is in our power to turn evil into good, but often one is not up to it."
— Tolstoy, in a letter to Aylmer Maude, 1897

O n Christmas Day 1889, Chertkov made a "huge request": Tolstoy had jotted down his ideas and plots for future works, and "one can say with full confidence that you'll never have the time to develop them into full-fledged stories. So, here is my request—that you occasionally devote two hours to relate these plots in your letters to me, recording them roughly, as if telling me a story..." These drafts were to be copied and returned to Tolstoy for one final revision, Chertkov proposed. "I assure you this will be good. At least you won't hide this tremendous capital, which you've accumulated and which people need, inside you; at least they will receive it as raw material . . ."[1] (Apparently, Chertkov perceived Tolstoy as a copper or gold mine he could exploit. And since he was asking for drafts, not finished works, he could dispose of this raw material as he wished.) He often complained that Tolstoy was taking too long to perfect his prose, contradicting his promise to give up literary ambition.

When visiting the writer, Chertkov would dig through a pile of papers on his desk, unearthing new drafts, which he would take away to copy. Once, he returned a freshly copied manuscript with some original pages missing, which the daughters detected at once, pointing this out to Chertkov. Afraid he would get annoyed, Tolstoy assured him that he did not notice the missing part.[2] Occasionally, Chertkov snatched papers without letting Tolstoy know. He was collecting Tolstoy's archive, but he also planned to publish some drafts and sought the writer's permission in such a way that it was difficult to refuse. Tolstoy would begin to search for an opening of a new work, only to discover his draft was missing. And as it happened in January 1887, he would have to write Chertkov asking whether he had the piece. Chertkov apologized: "If I inconvenienced you by taking away these manuscripts, I'm terribly sorry, and I'll never do it again."[3] He promptly sent Tolstoy copies of his unfinished short fiction, "Notes of the Madman," and the article "Nikolai Palkin," which the writer needed. The article was deplorably copied: Chertkov's scribe failed to decipher Tolstoy's scrawl and left blank spaces. "Nikolai Palkin" (Nikolai the Stick) was a story about corporal punishments in the army under Nicholas I, an account Tolstoy heard from an old soldier. It describes the time in the army when soldiers were beaten to death with rods for the slightest offense and had dubbed the Tsar, who approved of such punishments, "Nikolai the Stick." The stolen article caused trouble when Chertkov's young assistant, Mikhail Novoselov, produced copies on a hectograph and began to distribute them. Novoselov wrote Tolstoy after the fact: "I didn't ask your permission, since I've always heard that you have nothing against your works being distributed."[4] Within days of Novoselov's letter (it was likely perlustrated), the police searched his flat, confiscated copies of the article, and arrested the owner and his friends. Tolstoy petitioned for Novoselov's release and confronted the chief of the Moscow constabulary, arguing that he was the author of the article and they should arrest him. The chief supposedly replied that Tolstoy's fame was too enormous for their prisons to contain it.

In January 1890, replying to Chertkov's questions about his writing plans, Tolstoy wrote he had ideas for different works: "There's a lot that I not only want to write now, but am writing, and it's all artistic. Please don't tell anybody," he added as if confessing a sin. Struggling to suppress his artistic nature, Tolstoy went so far as to declare that art was "a soul-degrading occupation."[5]

Soon after, when Chertkov was in Yasnaya, Tolstoy wrote in his diary: "Chertkov is still close to me, even more so."[6] They went for walks, Tolstoy spoke about art and death, and Chertkov absorbed his words, like a sponge. Tolstoy enjoyed his stay, but was disturbed by "Chertkov's agitated state."[7] That winter, in a letter to his disciple Biryukov, Tolstoy wondered about Chertkov's restlessness, "What's troubling Chertkov? Why doesn't he have inner peace?" Answering his own question, Tolstoy concluded that Chertkov was honest and was earnestly struggling with his passions, wrestling his vice.[8] Chertkov got hold of this letter and responded that he indeed was struggling with his sensuality and hated his "disgusting body."

During Chertkov's stay Tolstoy promised to send an idea for a new story. In February, he was in a mood for fiction and began his letter lightheartedly: he would tell Chertkov a story he might otherwise forget. This was the plot for *Father Sergius*, a novella about the seduction of a monk. Chertkov was not the first to hear it: Tolstoy spoke about the story in his brother's family and had a good laugh over it with Masha, Sergei Nikolaevich's wife. He also visited Optina Monastery to refresh his impressions and gather material about monastic life. Chertkov received an eight-page draft of the planned novella. In it, Tolstoy for the first time employed some of Chertkov's background for his hero. Like Chertkov, Prince Kasatsky is a young and handsome aristocrat, an ex-officer of the Guards, who has been devotedly religious since his youth. He also doubts whether he is made for an army career. Kasatsky discovers that his fiancée was a concubine of an important person. (Later in the novella Tolstoy makes the young woman a lover of Tsar Nicholas I.) Kasatsky breaks the engagement and, soon after, experiencing a spiritual transformation, resigns from the army and joins a monastery where he is ordained as Father Sergius. From this moment in the story Tolstoy projects his own desire to lead an ascetic life and control his passionate nature.

After seven years as a monk, discovering that he failed to tame his pride, Father Sergius leaves the monastery to become truly humble and live as a hermit. Ironically, after decades of ascetic life, he gains greater fame, to become widely regarded as a saint. People expect him to have supernatural powers and heal the sick. So, he finds himself in a "false circle where humility turns out to be pride. . ."[9] (Tolstoy was also describing his own predicament: he had attempted to renounce ambition, but became a leader of a religious following in his name. Some disciples—and Chertkov—compared him with Christ.) Father Sergius also fails to suppress his lust and nearly yields to temptation. At Shrovetide, a merry company is riding on troikas. A beautiful and eccentric divorcee bets with her lawyer friend that she would spend a night in the monk's cell. Tolstoy ended his draft: the party continues on troikas towards the hermitage, bells tinkling.

Upon receiving the outline, Chertkov made a copy of it with extra spaces between the lines where Tolstoy should insert revisions. He sent Tolstoy this copy in summer, attaching a few blank sheets of paper for Tolstoy's convenience. (Tolstoy referred to this copy as "Chertkov's manuscript" and scribbled some revisions on it.) Chertkov expected him to complete it quickly: Tolstoy should not perfect it, like a literary work. He should record the second part of the story in rough form and send it to Chertkov. And if *Father Sergius* "would be ever published, I'd make sure it remains an artless story . . . not a polished writer's work . . ."[10] Chertkov interpreted the piece as an instructive story on how to control sensuality, an account told by a brother in faith to his less experienced brother. To urge Tolstoy to complete it along these lines, he had another follower, an Intermediary employee, send the writer a similar request.

With Chertkov's meddling, Tolstoy postponed writing *Father Sergius* and was soon absorbed with other projects. "I don't want to do it hastily," he explained. "I put it aside because it's dear to me. Struggle with lust is only an episode, or a stage here, the main struggle is with love of fame."[11] Tolstoy could not stop thinking about *Father Sergius* and his idea for this novella was growing more complex. He wrote in his diary that "the whole interest" was in the psychological stages his hero was going through—first as an aristocrat who abandoned a promising career, then as a monk, who found his superiors in the monastery too frivolous, and finally as a hermit, fanatical in his asceticism, but still unable to defeat his passions: "But the holiest man is as much of a devil as the most sinful one."[12] Over the years, Tolstoy would return to the novella sporadically. He was not letting himself write what he would enjoy and *wanted* to write, but worked on the projects he *needed* to write. So, he did not complete the novella. In 1902, Tolstoy explained to Chertkov, who kept inquiring about the draft, that he had finished the story outline and left it unpolished.[13]

There were many causes that were important to Tolstoy and articles he *needed* to write, such as an introduction to a book *On Drunkenness* by a medical doctor, Pyotr Alexeev. Tolstoy, who had given up tobacco and wine, spoke out against stimulants and narcotics. He had also given up hunting, believing that killing animals for amusement was bad sport. When in October 1890, Chertkov sent his own article about the evils of hunting, Tolstoy agreed to revise it. It took several days for him to condense Chertkov's piece, to which he also wrote a brief introduction. Chertkov was "touched to see how much labor you invested revising this article."[14] From this moment on he would ask Tolstoy to write introductions to his articles.

Tolstoy's current project, which interested him most and took three years to complete, was his tract *The Kingdom of God*. It was inspired by the works on non-violence by two American abolitionists, the social reformer William Lloyd Garrison and the pastor Adin Ballou. Tolstoy, who had formulated his non-resistance doctrine in *What I Believe*, was unaware that the Quakers had held and practiced such beliefs 200 years before him. After his book came out Tolstoy received letters and publications containing ideas similar to his own. He began *The Kingdom of God* by citing Garrison's declaration of non-resistance. Written 50 years earlier, this document rejected world governments, which waged wars, and even resistance in self-defense, and proposed treating enemies in the spirit of Christ's teaching. Garrison claimed that this was to be the path to universal peace. The starting point for Tolstoy's book was the *Catechism of Non-violence* by Ballou, to which he had begun to write an introduction; however, his ideas could not be contained in an article.

Tolstoy wrote *The Kingdom of God* during his work on the famine, witnessing mass starvation and government incapacity to handle the crisis. He argues that governments are fundamentally corrupt and rest on force: they conduct wars, maintain prisons, rob people by making them pay taxes, and pass laws for the advantage of the rich. The book denounces all forms of violence, especially state violence; it makes a powerful indictment against war, and argues that all governments are incompatible with true Christianity. Tolstoy calls on individuals to withdraw support from government institutions, which in his view are responsible for inequality and oppression. However, practical application was always the weakest aspect of Tolstoy's philosophy, and here he essentially preached Christian anarchism.

Intensely interested in this project, Chertkov became involved in it at an early stage, at once trying to influence Tolstoy to soften his criticism of government. Although Tolstoy's daughters were copying for him, Chertkov sent secretaries to fetch each chapter; these were delivered for copying to his Voronezh estate. But Chertkov did more than copy; he proposed major revisions. In the first chapter, he eliminated the paragraphs discussing government repressions against recruits who refused conscription. He also deleted a sarcastic remark about Alexander II. Chertkov cleverly argued that Tolstoy's "censorious and dry" tone was against his message of love; it would provoke angry responses from his opponents.[15] Chertkov's revisions annoyed Tolstoy; his pride was hurt. But he overcame this emotion, replacing it with feelings of goodness, gratitude, and humility. In spring 1891, Tolstoy promised Chertkov to take out "everything unkind" and provocative from his tract.[16] Chertkov wrote in response that he could not understand why his "little" remark was "a tiny bit" unpleasant to Tolstoy, but also praised him for taking it meekly.[17]

When in the fall, Tolstoy left to work on the famine with his two older daughters, they were staying near the village of Begichevka, at the estate of his friend Ivan Raevsky, which was one hundred miles southeast of Yasnaya. The Tolstoys and their volunteers were opening soup kitchens in two provinces, between Tula and Ryazan. At sixty-three, Tolstoy would travel to distant villages to assess need and inspect distribution centers. In winter, he would make the hazardous prairie journey in a cutter, with temperatures ranging from minus 20 to minus 30 degrees C. Once, returning to Begichevka at night, he was caught in a blizzard and lost his way; he was rescued by a peasant, an experience he describes in the story "The Master and Man."

Beginning in November 1891, Tolstoy produced a series of articles on the famine, urging the Russian government to act. It was from these articles that the authorities became aware of the scale of the calamity. The first article, "A Terrible Question," concerned the vital issue: was there enough bread in Russia to feed the hungry? The Minister of Internal Affairs reprimanded *The Russian Gazette* for publishing the disquieting piece. But at the same time, the government issued an order to estimate the country's wheat stocks. Tolstoy's participation in the relief also attracted world attention to the crisis. A committee for famine relief was created in the West, which asked Tolstoy to act as intermediary for distributing money and aid. Replying to a member of this committee, London publisher Fisher Unwin, Tolstoy wrote, "It is a great joy to me to see that the brotherhood of people is not an empty word, but a fact."[18] Aid began to arrive from England where the Quakers collected funds and from America where Tolstoy's translator Isabel Hapgood had launched a fundraising campaign.

Tolstoy wrote *The Kingdom of God* while torn between Moscow, Begichevka, and Yasnaya. He was making slow progress with this book, which frustrated Chertkov who impatiently anticipated new installments. Chertkov's couriers and scribes waited on Tolstoy to finish the chapters, staying at Begichevka for weeks on end. Living amid epidemics and want, Tolstoy refused to relax accusations of the government, which he held responsible for the crisis. He wrote Chertkov, who kept asking him to tone down his anti-government message, that relaxing his style would weaken the impact of the book.[19] Undaunted, Chertkov continued to provide revisions and even proposed a conclusion.

Tolstoy's final chapters were inspired by an incident he witnessed in the fall of 1892. He was traveling to Begichevka when he saw a train carrying soldiers on a punitive mission: they were sent to suppress a mutiny among the starving peasants. A local landowner, Count Vladimir Bobrinsky, asked the Tula governor to send the troops and conduct floggings of the peasants with whom he had a legal dispute over possession of a forest.[20]

The incident had shaken Tolstoy as much as the public execution by guillotine that he had watched in Paris as a young man. He was in tears when, upon returning to Begichevka, he told the story to his friend and disciple Biryukov. The punitive expedition during the famine validated Tolstoy's argument in the book. He describes the floggings in graphic detail and goes on to indict the government, which sanctioned them. Since it was not the only case, he was able to tell of similar incidents in other provinces during the famine when government troops were called in to suppress peasant uprisings. (Tolstoy's description of the floggings in the Tula province led to the governor's dismissal.) He also talks about greed: Bobrinsky, a young aristocrat with an income of around 100,000 rubles, had swindled the peasants out of the forest, which was worth only 3,000 rubles. (The Bobrinskys were among the wealthiest Russians and, like Chertkov's mother, adherents of Lord Radstock.)

In the conclusion Tolstoy expresses his long-standing belief that the well-being of the dominant classes is maintained by violence and rests on sufferings of the majority. Throughout history, those who rise to power, the most evil, violent, and corrupt, establish their authority over the meek. Chertkov objected to this paragraph and expected his scribes to report whether Tolstoy heeded his revisions. During the months when Tolstoy labored intensely on the concluding chapters, Chertkov's scribes were trying to hasten his work. One of them reported to Chertkov, after waiting for weeks, that Tolstoy was still writing with no end in sight. Tolstoy told this man he was not as concerned with finishing the book as he was with improving it.[21]

Chertkov was relentlessly demanding that Tolstoy replace criticism of the authorities with the message of love. This had some influence on Tolstoy, who wrote Chertkov that he was "weeding out" the unkind words from his conclusion. However, he believed it was impossible to absolve a system founded on violence and maintained through murder; impossible to speak about Christianity, love, and fairness, if this system had no morality.[22] Chertkov kept pressing. In a letter, which does not survive, he asked persistent questions; Tolstoy quoted some of them back: "'Am I fair in accusing the highest authorities of corruption and hypocrisy?'" Replying to this, Tolstoy wrote that he could not judge whether he was fair or not: he simply expressed what he felt on the subject.[23]

About a month later, Tolstoy received another missive from Chertkov, who was still at his Voronezh estate and who continued to interrogate him.

(Typically, this letter also does not survive.) Tolstoy replied: "To your questions, do I regard my coarse and angry disapproval of people to be good? Do I believe myself guilty before my conscience that [by making these] condemnations I deviated from the eternal truth revealed to me through Christianity? I will reply, thank God, completely sincerely and humbly, that I believe myself guilty and that it's painful to me that I've . . . deviated from the meek and loving style of Christian discourse." Tolstoy then proceeded to say what Chertkov expected to hear all along, that he felt ashamed for the angry passages in the book. "But such is my character, it springs up everywhere, I know it's bad and I wish and hope to change it."[24] With this admission in hand, Chertkov began to coerce Tolstoy to write "a little afterword," saying he regretted his "coarse and critical style." This would inspire good feelings: his readers would be moved by "a sincere admission of your mistakes."[25]

If the government could not deter Tolstoy from speaking his mind, Chertkov had this power. He reminded Tolstoy that by getting angry, irritating the authorities, he was sinning against God.[26] "Humility is a marvelous medicine for the soul," Tolstoy agreed.[27] In the end, Chertkov prevailed: Tolstoy was persuaded to think there was "lots of anger" in *The Kingdom of God* and an afterword should be written to assuage the impression. He even asked Chertkov to outline "what you think needs to be admitted as wrong."[28] The result was the following paragraph written either by Tolstoy or by Chertkov himself: "My chief mistake in this book, the mistake, which I repent before God and for which I ask people to forgive me, is the passion enabling me to depart from the very law of love, for the sake of which I've written what I've written; and my unfair and severe judging of people."[29] However, Tolstoy did not include this passage in the book and did not complete the afterword, which Chertkov pressed him to write. The passage is found today among the drafts to *The Kingdom of God*, written in Chertkov's hand, and is yet another example of his meddling in Tolstoy's work.

Years later, daughter Tanya's husband, Sukhotin, would remark that Chertkov acted as Tolstoy's personal censor. In Russia's history writers never enjoyed freedom of expression. Tolstoy's predecessor, Alexander Pushkin, was officially prohibited to publish or even publicly read his work without government approval. Everything Pushkin wrote had to be first sent to Tsar Nicholas I and the chief of his secret police for inspection. Chertkov (who may have been a grandson of Nicholas I) was proud of a similar role beside Tolstoy, remarking in 1901 to his friend Bonch-Bruevich: "I often postponed publication of his [Tolstoy's] works until we agreed on how to phrase certain passages . . . With that, I'm not trying to say, of course, that I consider myself to be a mentor or a censor of Lev Nikolaevich . . ."[30] Actually, Chertkov was the only censor whose revisions Tolstoy seriously considered. This happened because Chertkov used Tolstoy's own doctrine to persuade him. Chertkov struggled for the purity of his teaching, Tolstoy thought. Because of this belief Tolstoy was in a unique position to be influenced. Aspiring to suppress his pride and tame his passions, he even welcomed Chertkov's censure, having written him: "I'm asking you to point out my sins more often."[31]

Around this time, Chertkov asked Tolstoy to keep his letters in a separate folder, not letting anyone read them. (Ever pedantic, Chertkov actually provided a special folder where his letters and extracts from his diaries would be kept.) With hundreds of correspondents, Tolstoy made this special arrangement for Chertkov alone. Later, Chertkov also got Tolstoy to agree to have his letters returned to him. Nobody was supposed to peek into his relationship with Tolstoy or read his instructions to the man of towering authority.

Tolstoy's dedicated work on the relief made him the most influential unofficial person in Russia.[32] Witnessing the immensity of the need, he was often disappointed with what he was accomplishing, even though thousands were saved from starvation. Tolstoy and the daughters continued to visit the affected regions until the good harvest of 1893. During this time Chertkov established surveillance over Tolstoy and his family. Chertkov's scribes, who copied revisions to *The Kingdom of God*, were also spying on the writer. Once, Tolstoy misplaced some of Chertkov's articles, and was embarrassed to admit he did not know where to look for them. Shortly after, Chertkov wrote that Evgeny Popov, an Intermediary employee who also copied for Tolstoy, said that the missing papers were in the writer's desk drawer in Moscow. This reveals how well he had familiarized himself with its contents.

While Tolstoy was in Begichevka, Chertkov's messengers and scribes even read his private letters. In 1892, Mikhail Novoselov (the very man who had circulated the "Nikolai Palkin" article without the writer's permission) sent Chertkov a copy of Tolstoy's letter to Sophia. Additionally, in the manner of a police informer, Novoselov attached a detailed report, beginning with the words: "It [Tolstoy's letter] was written under the following circumstances . . ."[33]

This letter was written in winter 1892, during the scandal that broke out after Tolstoy's article "On the Famine" was banned by Russian censors. Tolstoy had asked Sophia to send the piece to Emil Dillon, a correspondent for the *Daily Telegraph* in London. "Let them publish it," he instructed Sophia, adding that the Russian newspapers would later reprint it.[34] Dillon translated and serialized it, beginning in January, in the form of Tolstoy's letters to England, entitled "Why Are the Russian Peasants Starving?" The *Moscow Gazette*, a conservative daily Russian newspaper, translated portions of Tolstoy's article back into Russian. A subversive phrase, "people will rise," which did not appear in the original, was introduced through double translation. The phrase implied revolution, and the newspaper accused Tolstoy of advocating an uprising.[35] The matter caused a government uproar. Alexander III was offended by Tolstoy's exposé and allegedly remarked that he had been betrayed to the English. There were rumors that Tolstoy would be put under house arrest in Yasnaya or exiled, either abroad or to Solovki, the notorious prison-monastery on an island in the northern White Sea. The Tsar was against exile, however, saying it would turn Tolstoy into a martyr.

During this time, many people (including those closest to him, Chertkov and Sophia) asked Tolstoy to publish a refutation and explain that he preached the opposite of revolution. Tolstoy blamed the misunderstanding on government censors, who prevented him from publishing his original article in Russia. In his letter to Sophia, which got the attention of Chertkov's scribe, Tolstoy wrote he had nothing to apologize for: the problem was created by the Russian government, which prevented him from expressing his ideas freely. "For already 12 years I write what I believe in, and what cannot appeal to either the government or the privileged classes . . ." And only "those ignorant people, of whom the most ignorant are found at court" can confuse his ideas with revolutionary propaganda.[36] Tolstoy wanted to circulate this letter, but Chertkov learned about it and did not let him. Sometime later, Tolstoy received a copy of this letter to Sophia from Chertkov, with passages underlined. The disciple, who did not even explain how he got hold of Tolstoy's letter to his wife, chastised him for his provocative style. He accused him of departing from the ideals of Christ and becoming ensnared by the devil.[37] Chertkov alone could write such insulting things, expecting Tolstoy to turn the other cheek. Tolstoy responded meekly that, upon receiving this "anxious" letter from Chertkov, he was grateful because it prevented him from yielding to temptation. It "showed your love . . . for me."[38] However, Tolstoy's admission sounded forced. In fact, he went on to say that the "help" he received from some of Chertkov's scribes felt "oppressive." He had little in common with these men, even though they called themselves his followers: "The majority of these people are alien to me . . . I love them, I value their good qualities, but I see and I know they don't love me."[39]

Around this time, Tolstoy's letter to his follower Popov was lost in the mail. Chertkov, who learned at once, used the incident to impose a system of copying everything Tolstoy wrote. He began by expressing his unhappiness that the vanished letter could contain important thoughts. "Ah, how good it would be if you allowed someone close to you to copy your letters before mailing them . . ."[40] Tolstoy ignored this request and denied there was anything important in this letter, but to no avail. Chertkov was becoming only more insistent: "Your work keeps you busy, but in the evenings . . . you occasionally write letters, and if you'd want to give me pleasure, you'd ask someone to copy your letters and send me these copies. You'd then provide one of the greatest joys accessible to me, revive our communication, and supply additional material for my Compendium of your thoughts . . ."[41] Thus, Chertkov's project was more important than Tolstoy's wishes. The compendium was an ingenious ploy that allowed Chertkov to know the writer's intimate thoughts and to influence him when he expressed them.

Despite the many miles separating them, Tolstoy constantly felt Chertkov's presence. Once, he apologized that his letter to Chertkov was brief. He wrote it at the end of the day, tired after having written six other letters.

Chertkov's heart sank when he learned "about your letters I am unfamiliar with . . . How sad that not all of them are being copied . . ."[42] Chertkov was relentlessly pursuing his goal—establishing surveillance over Tolstoy, which the writer thought was dictated by love.

If Chertkov loved Tolstoy, his love was selfish, obsessive, and pathological. It drove him to try to establish total control over Tolstoy's work and personal life. Attempting to isolate him from his beloved daughters, friends, and other disciples, Chertkov complained to Tolstoy that he surrounded himself with a narrow circle of "courtiers." His daughters and a few followers belonged to this "privileged little circle." (Of course, this was against Tolstoy's teaching of equal love to all, as Chertkov was quick to point out.) He went on to complain about all members of Tolstoy's close circle, especially daughter Masha who is "closest to you," but who was ill-disposed to Chertkov.[43] Whatever Tolstoy's daughters were saying at home about Chertkov was immediately reported. Because this was done supposedly for Tolstoy's benefit, to warn the writer about temptations, Chertkov did not conceal that his assistants and scribes who stayed with the family were spying on them.

Sophia remained Chertkov's biggest rival and he treated her with animosity, looking for every opportunity to drive a wedge between husband and wife. During Tolstoy's work on the relief Chertkov kept sending him writing assignments and his own articles, which prompted Sophia to interfere. She wrote Chertkov that Tolstoy was "*a tired and nervous old man*" and asked that Chertkov not load him with requests. Chertkov responded by upbraiding her for her ideological disagreements with Tolstoy and, after outlining their differences, said she was her husband's cross to bear. (Sophia would recognize this expression of Tolstoy's, which appeared in his diaries. The two men referred to her as Tolstoy's cross.) Sophia replied to Chertkov that only God could judge a husband and wife: "I have nothing more to tell you except to wish you more kindness and simplicity, and less meddling in other people's lives."[44] Chertkov did not spare Tolstoy this detail of his feud with Sophia. In addition to sending copies of their exchange, he was able to report Sophia's exclamation after she read his letter: she told someone in her house that her relationship with Chertkov was over.

But Chertkov would worm his way back and again enjoy Sophia's hospitality. When Tolstoy was in Moscow over Christmas, Chertkov asked his permission to stay with the family. This would make him genuinely happy, unless, of course, his presence was "repulsive" to Sophia. The house was crowded with guests, but Chertkov phrased his request in such a way that Tolstoy felt compelled to reassure him. They would find room for Chertkov, he replied, and Sophia was disposed to receive him.[45]

By then, Chertkov was on bad terms with people close to him, including writers such as Leskov, as well as the Tolstoyans. Even Chertkov's couriers and scribes, to whom he paid salaries, did not stay long with him. Popov criticized his love of power and money, and made unflattering remarks about his character.[46] Gay Jr. was upset with his hypocrisy, pointing out that Chertkov continued to live lavishly, despite the moral principles he advocated. Mutual denunciations were common with the followers, and Chertkov himself encouraged these exchanges, but rarely forgave those who disapproved of him.

Sophia, who now had a good grasp of Chertkov's cold and cunning nature, had written Tolstoy early on, "Will you continue to shut your eyes *deliberately*, as not to see anything but good in some people? That's blindness!"[47] Her attempts to open Tolstoy's eyes were futile. Tolstoy knew about Chertkov's dark side, but their relationship was unaffected by this knowledge. Two years after their first meeting, Tolstoy wrote Chertkov that he did not disapprove of him because "you are too dear to me. And this is why, perhaps, I don't see much that is bad in you."[48] A decade into the relationship, Tolstoy continued to trust and idealize him. He was lenient with all his followers, but particularly with this man, because of the special bond that united them.

Years later, defending Chertkov from other disciples who attacked his character, Tolstoy told his secretary Bulgakov: "If Chertkov did not become what he became, he would have been a governor general and would hang people."[49] True, Chertkov did not follow in the path of his extended family who became military and government officials close to court. Here Tolstoy may have influenced his choice, but he could not change Chertkov's Machiavellian character; rather he only succeeded in giving him a more benign outlet.

In fall 1893, when *The Kingdom of God* was banned in Russia, Nikolai Strakhov wrote Tolstoy that the censors considered his book to be the most harmful of all they had ever prohibited for publication.[50] By then, Tolstoy's acquaintances traveling to America and Europe had delivered his manuscript to publishers and translators.

During this time, Chertkov tried to dissuade Tolstoy from publishing this book abroad. He suggested that Tolstoy inform his translators that he had changed his mind about *The Kingdom of God* and offer them another book. What Chertkov was proposing, however, was not really Tolstoy's book, but Chertkov's compilation of Tolstoy's drafts and pronouncements on art: "Translators can be satisfied with *your* other book, on art . . . It turned out *splendidly*, and with my own introduction, explaining that it's not your work, but my compilation of your drafts etc. Nothing but good can come out of this."[51] Tolstoy did not want this compilation to be published because he felt his ideas in it were not clearly defined.

Chertkov used another argument to stop translation of *The Kingdom of God*. In a series of letters to Tolstoy he implied that his future was linked to the fate of this book. Its publication in the West would irritate the Russian government and because of Chertkov's proximity to Tolstoy, as well as his ties to court, he could face persecution. "I'd like to know when the book will be sent to France because, I imagine that a few days later they may learn about . . . it in our government circles, and . . . I'd be compelled to change my situation and activity."[52] Tolstoy dismissed his fears as completely unfounded.[53] A French edition of *The Kingdom of God* came out in December 1893 and the following year the book was published in America.

Chertkov was likely afraid of displeasure at court, of losing some valuable contacts. His mother would be also offended by a book condemning the government, and could even stop paying Chertkov his allowance. There may have been a connection between the publication of the book in France and Chertkov's resignation from Intermediary that year. He even wanted to shut down the enterprise, but Tolstoy would not allow it.[54] But from this moment on Chertkov no longer dealt with government censors, arguing that censorship was a coercive institution and he would have nothing to do with it.[55]

After resigning from Intermediary, Chertkov withdrew the capital investment of 10,000 rubles, which his mother had advanced, thus dealing a financial blow to the enterprise he had founded with Tolstoy. Apparently, Chertkov's mother did cut off his allowance, if only temporarily. That year, Chertkov attempted to support himself with editorial and translating work and wanted to reduce his expenses. He tried to negotiate a salary for himself with Biryukov, who took over his managerial duties, but his friend wrote that Intermediary could not afford this. Unless, of course, Chertkov would agree to share an honorarium with another editor who was paid 50 rubles for eight hours' work.[56] In the end, nothing came of Chertkov's idea to become a writer; nor did he cut down expenses. Instead, he purchased high-priced writing implements, ordering fountain pens from England. He gave one to Tolstoy, who used it for his letters to Chertkov, while murmuring, "See, how well your pen is writing."[57]

After three years of intense labor on *The Kingdom of God*, Tolstoy was suddenly free from his major commitment. As he wrote Chertkov, he was tempted to return to artistic work, but felt guilty about it.[58] (Around this time, he began drafting an autobiographical play, *And the Light Shineth in Darkness*, which depicts conflict in his family over his decision to give up their property. He returned to this play over the years, but left it unfinished.) Upon hearing that Tolstoy was free, Chertkov was back at his door with his compilation of pronouncements on art. Chertkov could not help pushing the project he considered to be his own. Asking Tolstoy to approve the volume for publication, he assured him there was "no need" to change anything or "add a single word to this book." Permission to publish Tolstoy's views on art would bring "a great joy to me personally . . . and help readers at home and abroad to understand this important question."[59] Chertkov was in a hurry to publish his compilation in England, so Tolstoy invested three weeks to revise it, although he knew that his raw drafts and random pronouncements were too "vague" and did not represent his actual ideas.[60] In November 1896, when the time was ripe, Tolstoy drafted his famous treatise, *What Is Art?*, taking five days to complete 80 pages. Although the bulk of it was written with surprising ease, it took him two more years to polish the book.

"If I could influence you in terms of what to write next," Chertkov proposed in his faulty Russian, "I'd strongly suggest that you dedicate a few days to the *sex question*."[61] He wanted Tolstoy to contribute an article to his collection on the evils of sex, which Intermediary was producing. These were articles to which Chertkov had written an introduction and which were assembled under the general title, "A Secret Vice: Sober Thoughts on Sexual Relations." In his ambiguous introduction Chertkov failed to explain what he meant by "secret vice." He advised young men and boys to struggle against temptation and assured them that "individuals and whole groups of people" are already working "beyond strength" to promote chastity between the sexes.[62] Tolstoy read this piece and suggested cutting its length, but he did not contribute to Chertkov's collection. (Such articles failed to promote chastity among members of the movement, which may have been Chertkov's intention. On the contrary, the Tolstoyan agricultural colonies were notorious for sex scandals. In 1891, Nikolai Karonin, a populist writer, published "The Borskaya Colony," a story about intellectuals who founded a commune with the idea of helping peasants. Published in the journal *Russian Thought*, the fact-based account told about a rape of a peasant girl, who later committed suicide.)

Chertkov wrote articles on sex, vegetarianism, and other issues that mattered to Tolstoy, supposedly to popularize his ideas. His independent projects included his magnum opus, "On Christian Thinking," later renamed "On the Rectitude of Thinking," which he worked on over the years, but left unfinished.[63]

In spring 1894, Chertkov pleaded with Tolstoy to visit him in Rzhevsk, his other estate near Voronezh. Galya was seriously ill and Chertkov was summoning close friends and family for support. The writer wanted to go: "I cannot tell, my dear friend, how much I love you and how much I'd want to be with you now." But he could not leave his son, Lev, who became severely depressed at twenty-five. Lev had undergone treatment, but lost hope of recovering and talked only of dying.[64] Nonetheless, only a few days later, Tolstoy set out for Rzhevsk with daughter Masha, leaving his son in Sophia's care.

Chertkov had likely exaggerated the danger to Galya's health. Upon arrival, Tolstoy found that too many people were fussing over her and that Chertkov's mother had also arrived. Within a week, the duration of Tolstoy's stay, Galya's condition improved. But her illness had provided an excuse for Tolstoy and Chertkov to be together. Tolstoy wrote Sophia how much he enjoyed Chertkov's company: "I'm very happy that I came . . . We are so spiritually close, we have so many common interests, so rarely see each other, and feel so good together. She [Galya] is very pitiful and sweet, spiritually strong . . . At first I felt ashamed thinking that too many of us have come all at once, but there are many cottages here . . . everyone is comfortable, and we feel even too good."[65] Masha and Tolstoy stayed in a modest cottage near the manor, in a picturesque setting. Tolstoy enjoyed his walks in a forest and near a ravine where he picked snowdrops.

Upon returning to Moscow, Tolstoy wrote Chertkov that the visit would remain among his most precious memories. And he also wrote to criticize: "Only three things are not good: 1) that you're unhappy with your lives; 2) that you, AK [Galya], are ill and 3) that you, VG [Chertkov] are restless." Chertkov spoke angrily about people and Tolstoy advised him to be more forgiving.[66]

Soon after the visit, Chertkov sent Tolstoy a writing assignment. A year earlier, Tolstoy mentioned that it was possible to express the essence of Christ's teaching in just 60 words. Chertkov was now asking him to record and send "these 60 words." Tolstoy replied in one sentence, covering what he had said before, that the essence of the teaching was in the awareness that "my life—is not mine," "my goal" is not my personal benefit, but that of other people; he believed he was sent into the world to do God's work.[67] Back in 1888, Chertkov wanted Tolstoy to write a catechism of his beliefs, explaining how to apply his principles to various situations, e.g., what people should do, what they should not do; how to choose a husband or wife, etc. "You alone can write such a statement," Chertkov assured.[68] Tolstoy replied that writing a catechism would be an act of "insane pride," which would be punished by failure.[69] Now, upon returning from Chertkov's estate he took on the project. In addition, he had to fulfill Chertkov's practical requests, which he confirmed to his demanding friend: "Two things, dacha and asparagus."[70]

Chertkov had asked Tolstoy to rent a cottage near Yasnaya: he and his family wanted to spend summer in the neighborhood. In addition, he assigned Tolstoy to send him ten pounds of asparagus, which he apparently could not acquire at his estate. Tolstoy himself bought the needed quantity from a merchant, but failed to check whether the asparagus was fresh. Chertkov at once complained that it was wilted. According to daughter Tanya, Tolstoy was upset, went back to the merchant and rebuked him for his deception. Chertkov soon received a box of top quality asparagus.[71]

In April and May, Tolstoy was looking for a suitable cottage to accommodate Chertkov and his family. He eventually found a newly built log cabin near the village of Dyomenka, three miles from Yasnaya. Tolstoy described its advantages: there was a good view to a field and a forest, a fruit orchard on the lot, and the cottage was relatively inexpensive. He drew up a floor plan to show that the family and their maid would each have a separate room, but "I'm afraid this might be small [for you]."[72] (Two decades earlier, during his work on *Anna Karenina*, Tolstoy had his family join him on the Samara prairies, where he bought a small, shabby cottage. He then wrote a similar letter to Sophia, describing advantages and disadvantages of the place and sent her a floor plan: the cottage had only two bedrooms. But the Tolstoys and their six children would spend several summers there, leading a Spartan life in the midst of the arid prairie.) Chertkov decided to buy the cottage and asked Tolstoy to build an addition. Tolstoy replied in a telegram: "The dacha is yours. Building an addition . . . Delighted."[73] In May, a tired Sophia, who was alone handling the schooling of their teenaged boys, the upbringing of the small children, and publishing new editions, arrived in Yasnaya. She was managing all these material responsibilities to let Tolstoy write in peace; upon arrival, she discovered he was running Chertkov's errands. Moreover, Tolstoy just bought a cottage for Chertkov: so much for renouncing property and money! She again wrote Chertkov, asking him not to burden Tolstoy with requests. Chertkov responded almost in a sermon, but his long sentences were hiding a sting: "So, if Lev Nikolaevich undertook various trips in connection with preparing an accommodation for us, he did this on his own initiative and undoubtedly because he found it pleasurable for himself."[74] Chertkov and Galya were looking forward to spending summer in close communion with Tolstoy, expecting to benefit from his spiritual guidance. To maximize the impact of his letter, Chertkov sent it through Tolstoy, who was expected to read it before forwarding it to his wife.

Tolstoy was annoyed with Sophia for interfering in his relations with Chertkov. His friend implied he could cancel his summer plans, if Tolstoy's wife was unhappy. Tolstoy at once wrote to reassure him: "If you'd ask me: does she want you to come? I'd say: no. But if you'd ask: do I think you should come? I'd say, yes."[75] In his diary, Tolstoy expressed frustration with "Sophia's dismal escapade over Chertkov. It's all understandable, but it was very painful; the more so because [I] . . . was glad of my restored—even newly established— good, strong, loving feeling for her. I was afraid it would be destroyed. But no, the thing blew over, and the same feeling has been restored."[76]

Meanwhile, Sophia despaired that her summer would be ruined, that Chertkov would visit daily and that he would draw a throng of followers to Yasnaya. The family called them "the dark ones." Typically, these were morose-looking bearded men, who sat around Tolstoy listening to him preach. Sophia feared they would drive out all other visitors from Yasnaya. The daughters were also unhappy that Chertkov would spend the summer in the neighborhood. As Tanya explained in her diary, Chertkov "will try to meddle in Papa's work and our way of life, and almost by force will require us to follow his advice and instructions."[77] Chertkov had recently attempted to turn Tanya against her mother. In February, he wrote Tanya suggesting that she give up her inheritance and "fine clothes." He also advised her on how to denounce her mother. First, she had to spend time with Sophia, drawing closer to her, to win her trust. When the "maximum of mutual softening" was reached, Tanya should condemn Sophia for opposing Tolstoy's doctrine. Tanya felt it was "wrong to condemn and expose one another . . ."[78] That summer, Chertkov and Galya were jointly trying to persuade her that it was wrong for Tolstoy's children to inherit property. To Tanya's question whether the Chertkovs' son, Dima, would be left with funds or without, Galya replied, "Of course, with."[79]

Back in 1892, Tolstoy had divided the estate, allocating it to family members, as people do before dying. Vanechka, the youngest, and Sophia received Yasnaya because Tolstoy would continue to live there. Masha, the most idealistic among the children, refused to accept her share. This annoyed her siblings, who attacked her for trying to appear better than the rest. (Upon marriage Masha changed her mind, requested and received her inheritance.) Tolstoy took the incident personally and complained to Chertkov about his children's greed, asking that it remain confidential. Shortly after, Chertkov chastised Tolstoy for making "a big mistake" by dividing his property among his family. He should have handed it over to the peasants, in accordance with his beliefs.[80]

In mid-May 1894, Chertkov settled in his newly-renovated cottage, at walking distance from Yasnaya, and began to meet Tolstoy almost daily. There were important developments in their movement: a peasant school-teacher, Evdokim Drozhzhin, who was arrested for refusing to enlist, had recently died in solitary confinement. He became the first martyr of the movement and Chertkov arranged for his hagiography to be written by the Tolstoyan, Evgeny Popov. In June, the police confiscated Popov's manuscript during a search; the news was carried to Yasnaya by other followers. But a copy survived, so Tolstoy wrote an introduction to this book, which was published in Berlin the following year.

In July, Chertkov contracted malaria and was too ill to walk; he would arrive in Yasnaya in a light spring-carriage. On August 9, after visiting Chertkov, Tolstoy wrote in his diary that his friend was "physically ill, but spiritually strong." In the same entry, Tolstoy reproached Sophia for her supposed lack of humility and love.[81] He wrote this on the day when Sophia traveled to Tula to find a doctor for Chertkov.

While she was still in Tula, Chertkov urgently requested that Tolstoy's latest diaries be sent to him. They were now locked up in a portfolio, an arrangement made at Chertkov's insistence. Masha was also away and she alone kept the key to the portfolio. (She was again copying her father's entries for Chertkov, a fact she had to keep secret from her mother.) In Masha's absence, Tolstoy could not access his portfolio. With Chertkov's messenger pressing him to send the diaries before Sophia returned, Tolstoy wrote Chertkov that his daughter did not explain to him how to open the portfolio, so he was sending the entire case.[82]

The story of the diaries took a dramatic turn in October when Tolstoy lived in Yasnaya with his two eldest daughters. By then, Chertkov was recuperating at his Voronezh estate, and he wrote Masha asking her to ship him a box of papers he left behind. When ill with malaria and afraid he might die, he entrusted this box to Masha for safekeeping. Before sending it back, Masha examined the contents and discovered Tolstoy's diary for 1884, copied in unknown hand. Reading it for the first time, she was appalled with Tolstoy's harsh judgment of her mother and brothers. It was the diary which Tolstoy allowed Chertkov to keep and revise. It was filled with disparaging comments about Sophia: "Tried to talk to my wife after dinner. Impossible . . . The one thorn, and a painful one . . . Lord, help me. If this is my cross, so be it; let it weigh me down and crush me." Tolstoy also did not spare his eldest son: "Seryozha is impossibly obtuse. The same castrated mind that his mother has."[83] Apparently, Tolstoy had only a vague recollection of what he had written ten years earlier. When Masha gave the notebook to Tolstoy he reread his entries with embarrassment and disbelief.

Having entrusted this intimate diary to Chertkov, Tolstoy suddenly realized that information about his family was likely circulated among his followers who could use his criticism to attack Sophia. He wrote Chertkov how the discovery affected him:

> My diary for 1884 has just come into my hands in Masha's room
> . . . Reading it aroused in me a very painful feeling of shame,
> remorse and fear for the grief which the reading of these diaries
> may cause to the people about whom such bad and cruel things
> are said in many places. It's unpleasant—more than unpleasant,
> it's painful—that these diaries have been read by people other
> than you—even by the person who copied them—painful because
> everything that was written in them was written under the impres-
> sion of the moment, and often terribly cruel and unjust, and fur-
> thermore because they speak about the sort of intimate relations
> which it was vile and odious of me to record, and still more odious
> to allow anyone except myself to read. You will surely understand
> me, and help me to destroy everything that has been copied, and
> leave the original with me... As it is, I am horrified at the thought
> of the use which enemies may make of words and expressions in
> this diary directed against people mentioned there.

But Tolstoy was also letting Chertkov know that their relationship would be unaffected by the incident: "Forgive me if you find my letter unpleasant . . . I constantly think about you and I love you." Hurt and confused, he was unable to solve a problem: what should he do with the copy of the diary Chertkov had made? Should he destroy it or should he send it to Chertkov and ask him to destroy it? This was not a small matter since it involved trust. Tolstoy kept changing his mind and in the end, chose the more complex option, deciding to send the copied diary to Chertkov and have him destroy it. Then, remembering that Chertkov still had his portfolio with a few notebooks in it, Tolstoy asked: "Please don't let anybody copy the diaries you have, but copy out thoughts of a general nature . . . How many exercise books do you have?"[84]

Chertkov replied that he was sorry and ashamed to have upset Tolstoy, but expressed his remorse in a cheerful and confident way: "I would have begged you to forgive my blunder, if I did not see it from your letter that you're not angry with me, as everyone else would have been in your place, myself included...Thank you, dear friend, that you treated me with such love and forbearance. This only amplifies my sense of guilt." He was promising to be "pedantically careful" with the diaries from now on. Perhaps, his good intentions could absolve him. Chertkov went on to explain that a year earlier, when concerned with the safety of Tolstoy's papers, he made copies of everything he had on hand. While in a hurry to deposit the duplicate of the archive (and some originals) with his "trusted friend" in Petersburg, he overlooked that Tolstoy's diary should not have been copied. But no harm was done: Chertkov's scribe was "completely loyal" to him and actually, "did not learn anything essentially new from this diary . . ." (This suggested that Tolstoy's disparaging remarks about Sophia were by then common knowledge among his followers.) Now, because of this unfortunate incident Chertkov was "tormented by fear" that Tolstoy would stop trusting him with his papers. He was still expecting Tolstoy's latest diary, which Masha has already agreed to send him, and was hoping that Tolstoy would not "hinder" this arrangement, but would remind his daughter to send the notebook. Chertkov promised to copy only the passages of a "general nature."[85] A few weeks later, Chertkov was reading and revising Tolstoy's latest diaries. He was asking the writer's permission to remove some passages and instructed him to destroy the letter where he made this request. As apparent from Tolstoy's response, these segments unfavorably described Chertkov. Tolstoy allowed their removal and agreed to destroy Chertkov's letter.[86]

But Chertkov did not return the original diary for 1884, which was harshly critical of Tolstoy's family. Tolstoy's request would have to wait, Chertkov reported matter-of-factly. The diary (or the diaries, to be precise since there were two notebooks) was still at the Petersburg residence of Chertkov's "reliable friend." There was no need to worry, since Tolstoy's papers were kept "in a special trunk" under lock and key where they were just "as safe" as in Tolstoy's own house. All bundles were marked with serial numbers and Chertkov had a list of codes to the packages. "If you want I can ask my friend to fetch and send . . . the parcel with the diaries," he casually offered. But it was more prudent to wait until he himself traveled to Petersburg and retrieved the notebooks from his friend's trunk.[87]

Chertkov's "reliable" friend was General Dmitry Trepov. In 1893, when Chertkov deposited Tolstoy's archive at Trepov's residence, Sophia was the first to find out. "I have just learned from Chertkov that most of Lev Nikolaevich's manuscripts are either with him or in St. Petersburg—with General *Trepov* of all people. Our children must be told about this at once."[88] Chertkov, of course, did not ask the writer's permission when taking his papers for safekeeping at Trepov's house, which in fact was an abominable breach of trust. General Trepov Sr. had a notorious reputation: Russians associated his name with police brutality. In the 1860s, when a strong man was needed to fight Russia's revolutionary movement, Uncle Shuvalov promoted him to head of the Petersburg Police Department. In 1877, as the Governor of Petersburg, Trepov Sr. ordered the flogging of a political prisoner who refused to greet him by removing his cap. Revolutionaries vowed revenge. The following year, Vera Zasulich shot and wounded Trepov. In a highly publicized trial Zasulich was found not guilty.

Son Dmitry Trepov, with whom Chertkov was close in the Guards and who would remain his life-long friend, was then a general in the imperial suite. His career was on the rise. Two years later, in 1896, he was promoted to head the Moscow police where he worked closely with Sergei Zubatov, a famous provocateur and director of the Special Section of the political police, Okhranka. The Trepov family was known for its close ties to the interior ministry and secret police. It was at their residence that Chertkov deposited Tolstoy's papers and intimate diaries.

When Sophia protested, Chertkov argued that Trepov's house was the safest place to hide Tolstoy's illicit papers from possible police search. Tolstoy's archive, however, was safe in his own house: in fact, Yasnaya was the safest place to keep it. (Tolstoy's manuscripts for *War and Peace* and *Anna Karenina* were by then in the Rumyantsev Museum where Sophia had deposited them in 1887.) Although Chertkov's intricate scheme cannot be fully known, he apparently cared about the safety of *his own* archive. The papers he hid at Trepov's residence, including the writer's original diaries, were *his* personal possessions, he believed, and it was only logical for him to arrange for a safe storage. As a result, Tolstoy's papers and diaries remained in the residence of the future chief of gendarmes for some two years, a bizarre occurrence, but one that demonstrates Chertkov's duplicitous role, his lack of loyalty to Tolstoy, and his continuing ties to the establishment.

In Russian, Chertkov's surname translates as "the son of the devil." Playing on the word, Sophia ascribed Tolstoy's blindness to the supernatural forces unleashed by "the devil" Chertkov: "The man I love has been taken over by evil spirits, but he does not know it."[89] A year later, in October 1895, Sophia discovered the disappearance of some of Tolstoy's diaries. He admitted he was again sending them to Chertkov. After Tolstoy's urgent request to return the diaries, Chertkov dispatched several notebooks, but not all. He now argued that Tolstoy had given him the diary for 1884 as a gift and informed the writer that he had destroyed the original notebook covering the dates from March 18 through September 25, 1884. (These entries were made during the most intense stage of their relationship, when some of their exchanged letters were also destroyed.) "I've told you this summer that I preserved only a copy. According to your wish, I am rereading it, while crossing out and cutting out the unwanted spots."[90] Given Chertkov's revelation that part of the original diary for 1884 was destroyed and that he kept revising the copy, it should not be trusted at all. It contains Tolstoy's intolerant entries about his family, of which he was later ashamed and which he did not want published. Chertkov, however, attributed "tremendous importance" precisely to these entries.

Having disclosed sensitive information to Chertkov, Tolstoy found himself at his mercy. He was now afraid to record his intimate thoughts, grumbling: "They spoiled my diary for me . . . I write with a view that the living people would read it."[91]

In the fall 1894, the discovery that Chertkov was not alone to read his private diary threw Tolstoy off balance. It was at a time when he resumed writing fiction in Yasnaya, with his two loving daughters copying for him. In September, he was drafting "The Master and Man," the story about a rich village merchant and his servant, Nikita. Lost in a snowstorm, they spend the night in the field where both are certain to freeze to death. The merchant is hoping to buy a forest for a third of its value and, afraid to miss the deal, insists on driving out in blizzard. During the ravaging snowstorm the merchant and Nikita become hopelessly lost within only a mile from a village. Now, money loses its power: both men are facing God.

When Tolstoy mentioned the story to Sophia, she sensed that "it will be *genuine*, e.g., very good. How strange are these sparks of creativity," she wrote. ". . . I cannot renounce my love of your *artistic* work, and today I clearly felt that this is because I experienced it . . . in my youth. And the daughters, in their youth, are experiencing another side of your creative work and they will love it more than all the rest."[92] Tolstoy completed the story in January 1895, but doubted if it was good. He sent it to his friend Strakhov, asking whether his ability had weakened. "I haven't written anything artistic for so long that I really don't know the result. I wrote it with great enjoyment . . . If you'll say it's not good, I won't be offended at all."[93] Strakhov replied that he could not tear himself away from the story: "It's a whole drama, most simple, clear-cut, and stunning!"[94]

Publishers were already approaching Tolstoy by the back door, and he promised exclusive publication to Lyubov Gurevich at the *Northern Herald*. (Sophia objected and the story was produced simultaneously—in the collected works, Gurevich's magazine, and Intermediary.) Chertkov put forward his request: he wanted to translate the story with the English pastor, John Kenworthy, and to publish it abroad. As usual, he requested revisions, asking Tolstoy to show, "with a few small strokes," that Nikita "is not just a kind-hearted Russian peasant," but that he bettered himself by reading the Gospels. "It looks as if I'm instructing you, especially in the artistic sphere. But of course, I didn't want to do this; I merely wanted to share my little doubt . . ."[95]

Simultaneously, Chertkov discussed a recent quarrel over a group photograph: he had persuaded Tolstoy to pose for a picture with his followers, which was against his family's wishes. Chertkov had a talent for antagonizing people, and now there was a feud between the two sides. Sophia and the daughters found it absurd that Tolstoy should be photographed with his disciples. Sophia said Chertkov was trying to institutionalize Tolstoy's following. "Group photographs are taken of schools, picnics, institutions, etc., so I suppose that means that the Tolstoyans are an 'institution'! The public would seize on it, and they'd all want to buy pictures of 'Tolstoy with his pupils' . . . "[96] The disciple prevailed and the photograph was made, but Sophia went to the studio and obtained the negative plates. Later, she tried to scratch Tolstoy out with her diamond earring but failed and then smashed the negatives. Chertkov organized an entire campaign against her, with followers coming to the door to berate her; he also wrote angry letters to Tolstoy. A month after the photograph incident, Chertkov was still brooding over it, blaming his hurt feelings on the daughters, who took their mother's side, and demanding their apology. He again chastised Tolstoy for dividing property among his heirs.[97] Tolstoy was struck with Chertkov's "poisonous lack of love."[98] But Chertkov would not be appeased, writing Tolstoy in mid-February, that the daughters should give in and make "a full admission" of their mistakes; only then would the kind feelings in his heart be restored.[99] Masha wrote him she could not find any genuine remorse in her heart and considered the matter blown out of proportion. Tanya sent a meek letter, saying she regretted offending people who might think they did not deserve to be photographed with Tolstoy.[100] Chertkov would likely have continued the feud, if not for a misfortune.

On February 23, 1895, the Tolstoys' youngest son, Vanechka, died from scarlet fever at seven. His death brought the family together and extinguished disagreements. Tolstoy wrote Alexandrine, "We have none of us felt as close to each other as we do now, and I have never felt either in Sonya or in myself such a need for love and such an aversion towards all disunity and evil."[101] He received a rare "kind, heartfelt letter" from Chertkov "and I wept, while reading it, having sensed the very thing that unites us, and all people with each other and with God."[102]

CHAPTER SIX

TOLSTOY UNDER SURVEILLANCE

"The Thought Police would get him just the same."
—George Orwell, *1984*

It's little known that Tolstoy was under police surveillance for fifty years and that he was never free from it until his last hour in 1910. In 1862, after he made generous settlements with his peasants, police conducted a two-day search of Yasnaya. Arriving in Tolstoy's absence gendarmes arrested the teachers in the peasant school he had opened there and searched his home for subversive materials. The officials sat in Tolstoy's study, reading his correspondence and diaries. They told his sister, Maria Nikolaevna, that they acted "on the highest authority."[1] Insulted, Tolstoy protested this violation of his privacy in a letter to Alexander II; he considered leaving Russia forever. The Tsar did not reply to Tolstoy, but ordered a formal investigation, which only legitimized the actions of the gendarmes.

Scrutiny was intensified in September 1882 when Tolstoy was placed under permanent surveillance. This was a consequence of his interest in sectarian religions and his own subversive writings against the Church and the state. Russia's prominent intellectuals were always watched; yet, there are more police reports on Tolstoy than on any other public figure. Three police departments—in Petersburg, Moscow, and Tula—kept constant surveillance. Today, there are 1,180 police files in the Central State Historical Archive of St. Petersburg alone.[2]

In 1918, soon after the Bolshevik Revolution, two sizable volumes of Tolstoy files were unearthed in the Petersburg Police Department. The inscription on the cover read: "To preserve in perpetuity." (A literal translation is even more ironic: "To preserve eternally.") Only few police records were then kept longer than fifteen years. According to an expert, the exceptions were made either "on the highest authority" or when the police department itself took a particular interest in a case.[3] Tolstoy was the most eminent man in the land, and the interior ministry and the police prized his records.

A contemporary memoirist tells that undercover police agents were ever-present around the Tolstoys' Moscow residence. This is confirmed by Tolstoy's acquaintance of many years, the writer and artist Dmitry Grigorovich. One day, coming to see Tolstoy at his house in Moscow, Grigorovich was struck that the writer could be seen from the outside sitting at his desk. He asked Tolstoy why he didn't draw the curtains. Tolstoy replied: "I want the police to see who is visiting me. They are watching over me, and it's awkward to peep through a hole."[4] Undercover agents penetrated the Moscow residence and Yasnaya estate, occasionally posing as Tolstoy's followers.

Sergei Zubatov, the very police provocateur and political detective, who later worked under Dmitry Trepov, visited Tolstoy in Moscow in 1887. Wearing tinted glasses, Zubatov sat in Tolstoy's study, pretending to be interested in the teaching of non-violence. This was shortly after Tolstoy's draft for the "Nikolai Palkin" article was stolen from his desk and began to be circulated in hectographed copies. Zubatov, who had obtained it from a Tolstoyan, was sent to investigate an allegation that the writer kept a clandestine printing press at home and was himself disseminating his illicit works. (Zubatov would have an extraordinary career, rising from informer to head the Moscow security bureau. At the height of his career, Zubatov was director of the Special Section of the political police, Okhranka. Like

Trepov, he was a convinced monarchist, which may explain why he was assigned to investigate the matter with Tolstoy's "Nikolai Palkin," the article that defamed three Russian emperors at once.) Zubatov, who later employed spies to infiltrate the revolutionary movement, used provocation as his main technique. Although the task of the political police was to prevent the spread of illicit literature, Zubatov also helped disseminate it so as to incriminate political opposition.[5]

In June 1896, a plainclothes gendarme, Prokopy Kirillov, penetrated Yasnaya. Posing as a nihilist, he expressed interest in Tolstoy's latest works and the writer discussed his beliefs with him. Kirillov felt so remorseful about deceiving Tolstoy that he returned the same day with a written confession, in which he admitted that he was an officer on a spy mission. Upon reading his letter Tolstoy told son Lev that he at once "felt sorry, disgusted, and pleased."[6] When the account reached Chertkov, he requested (through Intermediary employee Ivan Tregubov) that Tolstoy make a detailed record of the incident and send it to him. Kirillov, his identity exposed, was promptly fired from the corps of gendarmes.

The Petersburg Police Department diligently collected information about Tolstoy, his family, friends, and followers. By 1897, their records described Tolstoy's following as a "religious-political sect."[7] The gendarmes needed to know who visited Tolstoy and who wrote him, and collected extracts from his correspondence. Perlustration of correspondence (the practice of secretly opening private and business letters to extract information) was vital to the police state. All letters in the empire could be opened and read, save those from the Tsar and the interior minister; even correspondence by the imperial family. Letters by prominent public figures, members of political opposition, newspaper editors, and courtiers were always perlustrated. This activity was carried out in the so-called "black offices" by employees of the Special Section of the Police Department. Among these employees was Chertkov's Petersburg friend Vladimir Krivosh, an expert cryptographer fluent in 21 languages.[8] Chertkov's activity of habitually copying Tolstoy's correspondence and diaries should be seen in this context.

In 1891–1892, during Tolstoy's work on the famine, the district police was instructed to watch whether the writer was engaged in political propaganda among the peasants. The government feared mass discontent because the calamity affected 40 million people. Beginning in November 1891, when Tolstoy and his daughters arrived in Begichevka, local gendarmes began to send regular reports about their activity. This information traveled from the provincial police department to the headquarters in Petersburg. In December 1891, the gendarmes reported that Tolstoy and his family had opened bakeries and canteens feeding 400 people. Tolstoy's daughters also provided medical help during epidemics. Their activity contained "nothing illegal," the gendarmes wrote. The scale of the relief was growing by day, and so did the police surveillance. Tolstoy distributed donations, clothing, and books (Intermediary editions with his stories). The alerted gendarmes followed Tolstoy, confiscating the booklets. In January 1892, the Petersburg Police Department issued a secret order to increase surveillance over Tolstoy's relief operation and provided additional funds.

During his last decades Tolstoy lived under double surveillance: in addition to the police scrutiny his disciple Chertkov maintained a close watch. In 1894, the disciple supplied a press to daughter Masha, especially to make copies of all Tolstoy's correspondence for Chertkov. A Compendium of Tolstoy's Thoughts, which justified this need, was a clever ruse. Chertkov never relaxed his control. Later, he employed secretaries, who aside from helping Tolstoy, copied for Chertkov. His method of collecting intelligence strangely resembled that of the secret police. Actually, his traits as a schemer, his love of secrecy, and lack of moral qualms made him ideally suited for such clandestine activity.

By 1886, Tolstoy's illicit pamphlets and articles circulated widely and were found during searches of the homes of his followers, revolutionaries, and students. While the authorities did not touch Tolstoy because of his fame, his followers were arrested. Tolstoy was distressed when learning about people who were persecuted for reading his works and sharing his views. He would attempt to become actively involved in every case, trying to lessen the punishments. Chertkov did not share his sense of guilt: he welcomed martyrs into the movement.

In the fall 1895, Chertkov told Tolstoy of his decision to relocate with his family to England. Chertkov was planning to resume his publishing activity and propagate Tolstoy's illicit works. Upon learning this, Tolstoy wrote emphatically that he did not sympathize with Chertkov's plan. His foreign publications would end up in Russia, resulting in the followers' arrest. Tolstoy felt he had no moral right to expose others to danger, while he lived in safety, "eating meals prepared with almond milk." His works were not worth dying for and he did not want his writings "to inflict suffering upon people who are dearest and closest to me." He asked Chertkov to at least postpone his plan: "Wait until I die . . ."[9] Chertkov dismissed these objections: "I absolutely and definitely refuse to fulfill your request to wait for your death . . ."[10] He asked Tolstoy to stop worrying about people who were making their own decisions; he also disagreed that Tolstoy's works were not worth dying for. Tolstoy replied that Chertkov's arguments were "very persuasive," but they did not change the way he felt: "I fear for the possible sufferings of close people."[11]

Tolstoy would continue to witness the arrest of his followers and petition for their release. In 1907, his secretary and follower, Nikolai Gusev, was detained for circulating his works; the writer was in torment. Chertkov wrote him that "imprisonment of one of us, your friends, is such a trifle, it results inevitably from our attitude to those in power . . ."[12] By then, Chertkov had switched sides, becoming an open critic of the regime and befriending revolutionary socialists.

In 1908, when a follower Vladimir Molochnikov was arrested, Tolstoy, aged eighty, wanted to travel to Petersburg to personally defend him in court. Chertkov wrote to dissuade Tolstoy and argued that taking part in government institutions was against his own teaching. (This was hypocritical: Chertkov continually made use of government institutions. In 1910, he would prevail on Tolstoy to sign a legal will, himself drafting it with his attorney.) Incapable of empathy, Chertkov wrote Tolstoy, "Actually, I always find it touching that you take the persecution of people who promote your writings so close to heart; but I cannot forgo my impression that you consider this to be too much of your *personal* issue."[13]

In October 1909, Chertkov informed Tolstoy that he wanted to reproduce his articles on a rotogravure, a printing machine with a huge capacity. The writer was horrified: "I don't like this at all: 1st, the need to conceal, and this alone is bad and unpleasant; 2nd, many such editions will be distributed, and people can be detained and will suffer."[14] Chertkov responded, yet again, that it was up to individuals to determine "the level of risk."[15] Such callousness was typical of Chertkov. Indifferent to the fate of those he recruited into Tolstoy's following, he would say: "In our movement we consider principles, but not people."[16] It's not clear, however, what sort of principles Chertkov had: his loyalties kept changing.

In 1895, Tolstoy and Chertkov became united in a major cause, aiding persecuted religious sectarians, the Doukhobors. In December 1894, Tolstoy first met with several members of this peasant sect, discovering that their pacifist beliefs were remarkably similar to his own. This sect also believed in non-resistance to violence, rejected war, and secular authority. In addition, they did not accept organized religion, ritual, and sacraments, and abstained from alcohol, tobacco, and meat. Living without government, army, police, and clergy they appeared to prove the validity of Tolstoy's theories, with which they were then unacquainted. For several centuries, the government had harassed and exiled these sectarians for refusing military draft. Beginning in 1841, the Doukhobors were relocated to the Caucasus, a violent region where the authorities expected Muslim tribes to exterminate them or force them to abandon their non-resistance principles.[17] But this did not happen. The Muslims discovered that their neighbors did not retaliate and that it was possible to coexist peacefully. In 1887, when conscription was extended to the Caucasus, the Doukhobors complied with the law, letting their young men join the army, although advising them not to engage in combat. This compromise was abandoned on instructions from their leader, Peter Verigin, who believed they must refuse army service altogether.

On June 29, 1895, several thousand Doukhobors in three separate regions of the Caucasus publicly burned their firearms. The government retaliated by sending in Cossack troops who conducted beatings and interrogations, resulting in the arrest of 200 sectarian leaders. Hundreds of others (according to Maude—an entire settlement of 4,000 people) were driven from their homes and dispersed. Forced to live in malarial valleys, prohibited from owning land or even looking for work, the "dispersed" Doukhobors were dying of starvation and epidemics. In addition, the authorities attempted to ban communication with these people, thus cutting them off from the outside world.

Meanwhile the Doukhobors, who had been conscripted, but refused military training, were either banished to the Far East or sent to penal battalions where some died after brutal floggings. The Russian press was forbidden from covering these events, but in August 1895 Tolstoy read a brief report about twelve Doukhobors sent to a penal battalion for refusing military service. It was published in *Birzhevye Vedomosti*, or Stock-Exchange News. Tolstoy needed more information about the Doukhobors and arranged with Chertkov's help for Biryukov to travel to the Caucasus and investigate the matter. Biryukov chose not to travel far, interviewing only people close to the Doukhobor leader, which is why he brought back only flattering information about the sect and their way of life. In October, Biryukov's account about the Doukhobors appeared in *The Times* in London, preceded by Tolstoy's letter, which stated that "450 Doukhobor families have been completely ruined and driven out of their homes only because they were not willing to act contrary to their religious beliefs."[18] Thus, information about the desperate situation of the sectarians was communicated to the outside world. Tolstoy also wrote a letter to a commander of a penal battalion asking to treat conscientious objectors with compassion; he called their refusal of military training "a great deed, most useful to mankind."[19] In addition, he began to raise funds for the dispersed Doukhobor families: 1,000 rubles, which Sophia set aside for charitable donations, was sent in the care of a Georgian acquaintance. Around this time, Demetrio Zanini from Barcelona wrote Tolstoy that his readers wanted to buy him an expensive inkwell. Instead, Tolstoy asked them to invest in a good cause. A significant sum was collected in Barcelona, but the money never reached the Doukhobors. The police knew about Tolstoy's efforts to provide material help for the sectarians, reporting in early 1897 that 32,000 francs had been collected in France, Sweden, and Spain.

Although the authorities prohibited contact with the Doukhobors and with other sectarians, Chertkov was able to collect ample information through his channels. Over the years, he assembled a valuable archive of sectarian manuscripts and other materials: by 1902, it contained 4,000 documents.[20]

❖

In 1895, Chertkov had two alternative plans. He considered buying land to settle permanently next to Yasnaya. He also considered relocating to England to publish Tolstoy's works, which were banned in Russia. Once he became involved in the Doukhobor affair, this second plan seemed more practical. In his letters to Tolstoy, Chertkov once again hinted at his possible persecution and exile. Tolstoy believed Chertkov exaggerated the danger, replying he had nothing to fear from the government: if he were to go abroad, Russian authorities would always let him back.[21] Nonetheless, Chertkov was already contemplating his separation from Tolstoy. That fall, he wrote Tolstoy that he would unlikely leave Russia willingly: "But *you*, going away from you, is such a hurdle . . . that only *the necessity* would make me overcome it. I wanted to tell you this, so you would know *what* you mean to me."[22]

Actually, Tolstoy did not need Chertkov's help to have his prohibited works disseminated abroad. By then, there were two publishers doing just that. In Geneva, a Russian émigré publisher, Mikhail Elpidin, had been producing Tolstoy's religious works in Russian for a decade. Elpidin, who published for the émigré audience, produced *A Confession*, Tolstoy's translation of the four Gospels, and *What I Believe*. There was also Tolstoy's English follower and publisher John Kenworthy. A former businessman, Kenworthy became influenced by Tolstoy's teaching, abandoned his career, and settled in London's East End to study the economic and social conditions of the poor. Tolstoy was impressed with Kenworthy's book *Anatomy of Misery: Plain Lectures on Economics* and arranged to have it translated into Russian. Kenworthy became an honorary pastor at the Brotherhood Church at Croydon. In March 1895, he launched the Brotherhood Publishing Company to produce inexpensive editions of Tolstoy's works and other literature of similar tendency in English. Upon receiving some of his translations, Tolstoy informed Kenworthy that "my friend Chertkov" also had this project in mind and that it would be good for them to get in touch.[23]

Chertkov at once invited Kenworthy to Moscow to meet with Tolstoy and even promised to pay half his travel expenses. Curiously, Tolstoy was unaware of this and upon learning, was upset with Chertkov's haste.[24] Chertkov was bringing Kenworthy through the back door with an apparent intention of helping his publishing company. Arriving with Kenworthy on Christmas Eve, Chertkov helped navigate the publisher's conversation with Tolstoy. It was a highly successful trip for Kenworthy, who unexpectedly obtained Tolstoy's exclusive support. After his departure, Chertkov composed a statement in Tolstoy's name, which read:

> My dear Friend,
>   Sympathizing with all my heart with the aims of your Brotherhood Publishing Co., I intend to put at your disposition the first translation of all my writings as yet unpublished, as well as forthcoming. Should you find it in any way expedient, as for instance in order to secure for them a wider circulation, to offer the first publication of any of my works to one of the English periodical papers or magazines, and should any pecuniary profit therefrom ensue, I would desire it to be devoted to the work of your Brotherhood Publishing Company.[25]

In February 1896, sending this statement to Tolstoy, Chertkov instructed: "You should copy and sign this little declaration, which I prepared and which expresses nothing more but the actual truth . . ."[26] Tolstoy apparently signed the paper without reading it. According to Maude, he "had no recollection of writing this letter."[27]

Theoretically, the document gave Kenworthy unprecedented publishing privileges. He could produce the first and most profitable editions of Tolstoy's works in English and sell the rights to English periodicals. In addition, he did not have to account for the proceeds. (But Kenworthy would never be able to profit from these privileges: his claim that Tolstoy had given him first translation rights to all his writings was understandably mistrusted in the publishing world.) It was precisely the arrangement Chertkov later secured for himself. Upon relocating to England, he launched the Free Age Press, an offshoot of Kenworthy's publishing company, and squeezed him out.

In fall and winter 1895, Tolstoy frequently complained of general fatigue and weakening intellectual energy. It was the year his beloved youngest son, Vanechka, died and Sophia suffered a major breakdown. That year, Tolstoy began his last major novel, *Resurrection*, but had no strength to continue it. He was still working on his catechism, which Chertkov wanted him to produce, and also needed his flagging energy to revise Chertkov's articles and write letters at his request.

In 1896, Chertkov sent Tolstoy his piece "Needless Cruelty," in which he advocated exemption from the military draft for religious minorities. Tolstoy revised all versions of the poorly written article in which Chertkov argued that it was not in the interests of the government to punish conscientious objectors and turn them into martyrs. That year, the article was published in London and copies were smuggled back into Russia. In addition, Chertkov compiled a brochure about persecution of sectarians, called "Christian Martyrdom in Russia." Tolstoy contributed an article to this brochure, which appeared in London in 1897.

By actively advocating the cause of religious minorities, Chertkov engaged in anti-government activity and thus was burning his bridges. In November 1896, he wrote an appeal on behalf of the Doukhobors jointly with Biryukov and Tregubov. The goal was to solicit donations and inform society and the government about the sect's desperate situation. The appeal would circulate illegally, in typewritten copies. Chertkov sent it first to Tolstoy, asking him to revise it and to contribute a conclusion, but the writer replied that the appeal was "not good." It was aloof and unconvincing and had to be rewritten.[28] Chertkov did not reply to this, so Tolstoy reminded him the following month: "We need to talk about the appeal and the Doukhobors, that's the main thing."[29] Chertkov ignored this letter as well.

Maude, then living in Moscow, remembers that Chertkov brought him the appeal and asked him to urgently produce copies on his hectograph: "He told me Tolstoy wanted to have [it] done quickly . . ." Maude and his wife spent the night printing copies of the illicit appeal behind drawn blinds. In the morning, Maude delivered them to Tolstoy, only to learn that "it was a document Chertkov had drawn up but Tolstoy did not approve of. It had to be rewritten before he could associate himself with it . . . I then got my first glimpse of the fact that Chertkov felt quite competent to try to make up Tolstoy's mind for him, and had no hesitation about using Tolstoy's name for his own purposes."[30] (Chertkov's appeal pictured the Doukhobors as saints and martyrs, an exceptional people who had achieved a Christian ideal. In the new year, Tolstoy revised the appeal and Chertkov published this new version in England.[31])

In early December, Tolstoy received Chertkov's letter urging him to travel to his Rossosh estate where he anticipated the arrival of two Doukhobors from Tiflis (Tbilisi). The sectarians were traveling without papers and risked arrest, so he advised Tolstoy to set out at once. Tolstoy replied in a telegram that he could not come.[32] It was wise of Tolstoy to refuse, since his visit would only alert the police.

In fact, Chertkov's estate was now also under surveillance. The police report stated that Biryukov and Tregubov had already arrived at his estate to confer with the Doukhobors who were traveling secretly and without passports. It also established that Chertkov was collecting information to produce an account about Doukhobor harassment. "Lev Tolstoy himself was expected to travel from Moscow, but declined."

After the meeting, Chertkov left for Petersburg with his family and Biryukov. Tregubov remained at the estate to guard the archive of sectarian materials. Chertkov was planning to present a full report on the Doukhobor situation to the Tsar and, supposedly, only then realized that he needed the sectarian archive he had left at his estate. Instead of returning, he urgently requested that Tregubov deliver the papers to Petersburg. The police intercepted Chertkov's message and followed Tregubov from the moment he set out to the station. On January 7, he was detained in Voronezh and the archive was seized. Tregubov explained to the police that Chertkov needed the papers to write a memo to the Tsar.

After the seizure of this illicit archive the authorities acted quickly. On January 31, the interior ministry issued a resolution about administrative exile for Chertkov, Biryukov, and Tregubov. On February 1, the Interior Minister Ivan Goremykin (later Russia's prime minister) invited Chertkov for a private meeting for the following afternoon. But early on February 2, the police searched the house of Chertkov's mother where he was staying (Simanskaya Street, No. 3). Additional papers were confiscated. After this search, Chertkov refused to meet the interior minister and sent him a mocking letter, writing that he must refuse himself the pleasure of meeting the minister. He had first considered keeping the appointment, believing that it could benefit his cause. But the search and confiscation of his papers demonstrated that finding understanding between them in matters of "goodness and truth" was impossible. The developments ruled out any opportunity of "communication, which you have desired to establish with me."[33] Later, when it would benefit Chertkov, he would himself establish communication with the interior ministry.

Chertkov's exile and the seizure of his archive would establish his reputation as Tolstoy's disciple and someone who suffered for the cause. Curiously, Chertkov did not lose any of his essential materials, which he had already shipped to England. The police may have simply seized duplicates. But during the search at his mother's house some of Chertkov's notebooks and personal papers were confiscated. Regarding this as a violation, Chertkov appealed to the interior minister from his English exile, even after his refusal to meet with him. His letter to Minister Goremykin of July 25, 1897, reveals that the police were instructed to only seize materials concerning the Doukhobors and Tolstoy's teaching. Chertkov was asking them to return his personal papers, which he said contained nothing forbidden, e.g., his research notes for a book about Dmitry Khilkov.[34]

Chertkov's detailed letter to General Otto Richter, head of the imperial chancellery and his mother's friend, reveals that the police also seized the copied extracts from Tolstoy's diaries. Chertkov, however, was more concerned about his own research notes for the book about Prince Khilkov. But as he wrote General Richter, the seizure of his personal papers would not prevent him from writing the book: "I have long sent all the *necessary* materials for this book abroad . . . I simply ask to return to me what is my own."[35] Thus, with his materials already in England Chertkov was fighting for the return of his papers only out of principle. He also tried to blackmail General Richter, informing him that failure to return his papers would inspire him to write negatively about the government.

Appallingly, Chertkov's handwriting can be found today on the secret police reports about the very meeting with the Doukhobor delegates, which he had wanted Tolstoy to attend, and about the seizure of his own archive from his friend, Tregubov. The reports with Chertkov's revisions were signed by the director of the police department, Sergei Zvolyansky. An anonymous official has identified the writing as Chertkov's. These documents are kept at the Manuscript Department of the Russian State Library in the file of Bonch-Bruevich, Lenin's secretary, who was also Chertkov's friend. Ever meticulous, Chertkov made several minor changes on the police documents to clarify, for example, that his archive was confiscated from Tregubov by the head of the *provincial* Voronezh Gendarmes.[36] Chertkov's revisions were made between January 10 and 20, 1897, around the time Tolstoy, unaware of what kept Chertkov in Petersburg, was asking:

> Why don't you write to me, dear friend? Are you all right? All right in your soul? I don't like what you are doing there. I'm afraid you are doing damage to your soul. I don't believe that a good, genuine job should be done with such preparations and preliminaries . . . Write to me, particularly about yourself and your soul . . .[37]

More than a decade later, on August 26, 1909, the German Socialist magazine *Vorwärts*[38], published an article by Vladimir Burtsev, "The Tsar and His Police." A Russian émigré journalist and editor, Burtsev became famous for his sensational exposés of the tsarist political police and its secret agents. In this article, he revealed the existence of the *Tsar's Leaflet*. A secret periodical, it was produced especially for Nicholas II to inform him about dissent in the empire and beyond. It was compiled by the members of the Petersburg Police Department and overseen by Interior Minister Goremykin, who personally endorsed every issue.

That same year, Burtsev published a volume of the *Tsar's Leaflet* for the year 1897 in the Paris historical review, the *Past*, which he edited. Without revealing his source, Burtsev mentioned obtaining the periodical from an "untrustworthy" Russian official. The police reports concerning the Doukhobors and the seizure of Chertkov's archive appeared in the January issue of the Tsar's periodical. (Chertkov's revisions on the original reports were incorporated into the text.)

In 1910, during his visit to the United States, Burtsev gave a copy of his publication to George Kennan. On February 20, 1910, *The New York Times* published Kennan's sensational article about the Tsar's own police gazette. Kennan wrote: "Through this periodical . . . we are able to see one side of Russian life exactly as the Tsar himself sees it; and to know, with absolute certainty, what things have been brought to his attention and what things have interested him in the wide field covered by the operations of the

Russian secret police."[39] Among items, which caught Kennan's attention, was the exile of Tolstoy's disciples for their support of religious minorities. From this publication, however, Chertkov emerged as someone who suffered for Tolstoy's cause, not someone who collaborated on the Tsar's police gazette.

Recently, it has been established that "the untrustworthy official" who delivered the issues of the Tsar's secret periodical to Burtsev was Vladimir Krivosh. (A friend of Chertkov, Krivosh was the expert cryptologist employed by the special section of the Petersburg Police Department to perlustrate foreign correspondence. It was sampled for the interior minister, who compiled his report for the Tsar.) In 1897, Krivosh and Burtsev first met at Chertkov's residence near London. This is when Krivosh, who introduced himself as a Russian censor, told Burtsev about the existence of the *Tsar's Leaflet*. In 1909, Krivosh, who had connections at court, later even working in the private library of Nicholas II, smuggled a few issues of the Tsar's periodical for Burtsev.[40] Krivosh was notorious for his love of money and Burtsev undoubtedly paid him well for the service. (It would be logical to suppose that Krivosh could also smuggle the pages of the original police reports with Chertkov's revisions. It is unknown though how these papers made their way into the private archive of Lenin's secretary Bonch-Bruevich. However, Bonch-Bruevich had collected dossiers on many people, knew Krivosh, and had worked for Chertkov in England.)

In early February 1897, Tolstoy and Sophia traveled to Petersburg to bid farewell to Chertkov and other disciples who were being exiled. The Tolstoys stayed in the vacant apartment of Count Adam Olsufiev on Fontanka 14. Incidentally, this house was near the headquarters of the police department, a long elegant building on Fontanka 16, which faced the river.

Unlike Biryukov and Tregubov, who were banished to remote towns in the Baltics, Chertkov would serve his term in England, a privilege granted by the Tsar himself. The news that the disciples were exiled for Tolstoy's just cause inspired an outpouring of public sympathy. Sophia describes the mood of the day in a letter to her sister Tanya:

> To my surprise and joy, the entire Petersburg society . . .
> reacted to the news of exile with indignation . . . The farewell

to Chertkov and Biryukov with friends was very moving and
solemn. Each day, up to 40 people, of all different ranks and
walks of life, came to see them: high aristocracy, muzhiks,
writers, wardens, scientists, musicians, kursistki [student girls],
the military, the dark ones [Tolstoyans], ladies . . . Some sewed
clothes for the road, others ran errands; some, perched on the
floor, made orations . . .[41]

(Sophia interceded on the exiles' behalf with Minister Goremykin; he
received her with due respect, but gave no promises.)

On a snowy morning of February 8, 1897, the Petersburg secret police
were following Tolstoy's every move. Three police agents had been watching
the house on Fontanka Street 14, and when he left trailed him throughout
the day. They collected data about his encounters and routine calls to a
drugstore, tobacco shop, curiosity shop, barber, the public library, book-
stores, and bakery. Tolstoy met acquaintances everywhere he went, keeping
the police busy.

Although Tolstoy was wearing his peasant garb, people on the streets
had no trouble recognizing him from his portraits. That morning, when
he took the horse-drawn tram from Fontanka to Nevsky Prospect (the
police traveling along), several students immediately approached him.
Tolstoy was their idol; they invited him to their gathering (he promised
to come) and, filled with awe, one student kissed the writer's hand. The
police reported the incident, supplying a visual account of Russia's most
famous man: "Count Tolstoy was in a patched sheepskin tied with an old
sash; in dark trousers, a knitted dark woolen toque, and a walking stick.
Surveillance continues."[42]

In the farewell group photos Chertkov is sitting or standing next to
Tolstoy. A separate picture shows the two together in Chertkov's yard.
Towering over Tolstoy, Chertkov is a handsome man in his forties, with a
cold impenetrable look. The photographer was Krivosh, Chertkov's friend.
(As Krivosh reported to the police department, Chertkov was among his
close Petersburg friends in 1896.[43])

The Chertkovs were allowed ten days for packing; they were leaving to
England with friends and family. Two peasant women, Annushka, a cook

and housekeeper, and Katya, a maid, were also going. Once in England, they stayed in Duppas Hill, a recreation area near Croydon. Tolstoy wanted to visit Chertkov in England, but feared that the Russian authorities would not let him back. The exile enhanced their relationship: Tolstoy now felt guilty that Chertkov had suffered on his behalf. Sophia, no doubt was relieved that Chertkov would be living at a distance, and now spoke lovingly about him and Galya. As Tolstoy wrote Chertkov, her change of heart "makes me very happy because to love you (and to forgive)—means to love goodness. This is why I was so unhappy when she expressed unkind feelings towards you."[44] (But Chertkov's exile does not establish his loyalty to Tolstoy. Secret police agents, who infiltrated the revolutionary movement, were also arrested, exiled, and would serve their terms. Such a ruse allowed the police to deflect suspicion from their undercover agents.[45])

In June 1897, Galya Chertkova wrote a letter to Krivosh to invite him to Croydon. Her letter does not survive, but judging from Krivosh's response she discussed their photographs with Tolstoy. Krivosh replied to her on June 16 in a chatty letter. He boasted of his success as a photographer and expressed hope that "Lev Nikolaevich and Vladimir Grigorievich [Chertkov] and other members of the group" will not mind that he gave their photographs to friends, all of whom "are wonderful people" and sympathize with the Tolstoyans. Along with the chatter, there were cryptic messages, e.g., ". . . I sent groups of 2, 4, and 150 people in every corner of the great Rus . . . [Russia] By group No. 1 I mean the group with a Cossack officer . . . Group 'A.K. and O.K. [Galya and her sister] is very unfortunate, but the group 'Shk. [Albert Shkvaran, a Tolstoyan] and the unknown in plain clothes,' improved after strengthening . . ." After discussing in this way all members of the group photograph, Krivosh wrote that his photo was in demand and many copies of it were made and passed around: "Such a 'success' I never expected from my *atelier photographique* . . ."[46] (The secret police used photographs of Tolstoy's followers for identification and surveillance. Otherwise, they relied on word descriptions.)

Krivosh visited the Chertkovs in Croydon in July. On September 13, he submitted a report about his trip to the director of the police department, Sergei Zvolyansky. In it he told that the political émigrés who visited the

Chertkovs gave him valuable information about smuggling illicit materials through the Russian border.[47]

Bonch-Bruevich tells in his memoir how he met Krivosh at Chertkov's house in Croydon. The house was visited by scores of political exiles and was under the surveillance of Okhranka agents. A Slovak, Krivosh was an intelligent and stocky man, with an impressive ability to speak in scores of foreign languages; he "took on responsibility as a translator. He spoke Hungarian, all of Slavic languages, German, French, English, Italian . . . He also spoke very good Russian."[48] Bonch-Bruevich, then active in Marxist circles, was in hiding, pursued by the Russian authorities. He came to Croydon to work for Chertkov, who was about to establish his own press, and to help him sort his valuable archive of sectarian manuscripts. (After the 1917 Revolution, the Soviet government recognized Bonch-Bruevich as an expert on religious sectarians.)

In 1906, Krivosh published a satirical play about his stay with Chertkov in Croydon, called *A Tolstoyan*. The play was successful in the interior ministry and praised as "the best work illuminating on Tolstoyism as a religious sect."[49] Versatile and corrupt, Krivosh was also an inventor, who had perfected the manufacturing technology for fake seals on diplomatic correspondence and created an electrical apparatus to produce steam for opening letters. He invented many more devices that could have been useful to the secret police, but which were not introduced because of bureaucratic obstacles. For his long service and technical inventions he received the order of St. Vladimir, 4th class, given to Russian nobility. Krivosh would maintain his employment as an expert cryptographer after the 1917 Bolshevik Revolution, working for Felix Dzerzhinsky, the founder of the Bolshevik secret police.

In August 1898, in a casual letter to Tolstoy, Chertkov complained of his boredom living abroad. "Indifferent to everything in the world . . . I like to stretch myself in bed with a newspaper and read the police news and a program of festivities . . . in Petersburg."[50] As usual, he was asking Tolstoy not to let anyone see his letters.

CHAPTER SEVEN

THE TSAR OF THE TOLSTOYANS

"'It is one big gap in my education,' the Tsar said to me, smiling; 'I don't know the price of things; I have never had occasion to pay for anything myself.'"
   —Alexander Mossolov, *At the Court of the Last Tsar*

"Chertkov, in the exercise of his power and influence as Tolstoy's representative, was not subject to any . . . healthy restraint. He acted in Tolstoy's name, and Tolstoy's reputation shielded him from criticism."
   —Aylmer Maude, *The Life of Tolstoy*

Upon Chertkov's departure to England, Tolstoy wrote him several sentimental letters. When Chertkov complained that he did not write frequently enough, Tolstoy replied with emotion: "In Yasnaya I constantly think about you. As I enter my study in the mornings, I remember the feeling I experienced when seeing you on the divan: a small annoyance that I'm not alone, and a great joy that you are with me. I don't know how I've helped you, but you've helped me to live better many times and in various ways. We all help each other when we love."[1]

In 1897, Tolstoy was completing his treatise *What Is Art?* Frail after a series of illnesses, he used his energy to write in the mornings. Afraid that Tolstoy could die in his absence, Chertkov arranged that daughter Tanya send regular updates about his health. Should there be further deterioration Chertkov would request a short visit to Russia: he felt that the authorities would allow him. "Of course, in the event of your sudden death," he wrote Tolstoy, "I would be unable to arrive promptly." Chertkov, however, wanted to make sure he had the latest information, so he asked Tolstoy that he himself write about his condition.[2] Chertkov's matter-of-fact style annoyed Tolstoy: "It's always unpleasant for me to think of illnesses and approaching death. All this—how, where, when we should die—belongs to the sphere beyond your reach, godly, and one shouldn't meddle in it. But since you so insist, I will try to satisfy your wish."[3] Chertkov, not easily satisfied, would still interrogate Tolstoy about his health.

Although Chertkov was in England, Tolstoy continued to receive his requests. During the four months following his departure the disciple sent fifteen letters, some running to twenty pages. His envelopes were stuffed, since he was also sending newspaper cuttings and updates about meetings at Kenworthy's commune. With his energy flagging, Tolstoy put aside some of these dispatches, and soon they were buried under other papers. In mid-June, Chertkov demanded answers to his letters Nos. 11–15. Tolstoy, feeling guilty that he had misplaced his friend's letters, was able to unearth them and read them dutifully. Chertkov's questions mostly concerned publishing permissions. He wanted to know whether he could publish Tolstoy's nonfiction drafts at his own discretion. Did Tolstoy allow him to publish extracts from his letters and diaries? (He reminded about his important task of compiling the compendium of Tolstoy's thoughts.) Would Tolstoy send everything he writes to Chertkov first thing? (Here Chertkov recalled his long and dedicated service to Tolstoy.) The writer responded to all this in two sentences: "Of course, yes, yes, yes . . . Everything I will write, I will certainly send first thing to you."[4] Tolstoy was making a promise he would come to regret, but he wanted to be completely selfless. Chertkov was running his causes and promoting his faith, and Tolstoy did not allow himself to hold doubts. So, when Chertkov asked whether Tolstoy *trusted* him to publish a draft of his unfinished article "Christian Teaching," the writer replied, with typical spontaneity, that "there can't be even a question of trust."[5]

Chertkov's other desire was to continue reading Tolstoy's diaries. Tolstoy should send his notebooks with travelers to England, Chertkov said. "You'd give me a great joy if you send your diaries. I'd make extractions and return them at a first opportunity . . . If possible, also send me your youthful diaries in which you asked me to delete the unwanted parts."[6] In late summer, Chertkov's friend, heading for England, stopped in Yasnaya to collect Tolstoy's diaries. Tolstoy patiently explained that he could not yet send the notebooks. (Chertkov had read Tolstoy's latest entries shortly before his deportation. In February, when Tolstoy arrived to see him off, Chertkov managed to read the diaries and even to seize a few original pages. Soon after, recalling that these entries were critical of daughter Tanya, Tolstoy asked him to destroy the pages.[7]) Disarmed by his philosophy, Tolstoy was unable to protect his own peace and privacy.

Chertkov's letters were filled with requests for favors and petty complaints about other followers. He would begin by describing his spiritual affinity with Tolstoy and their unbreakable bond. Then he proceeded with his requests. In 1897, Chertkov was already establishing his own enterprise, the Free Word Press, while still associated with Kenworthy's Brotherhood Publishing Company. At this stage, Chertkov wanted to secure the right to the first appearance of Tolstoy's treatise *What Is Art?* in English. In Russia, the work would be serialized in the journal *Questions of Philosophy and Psychology*.

Because Tolstoy enabled all publishers to produce his works for free, there was a fierce competition over his first and most profitable editions. Chertkov argued that Tolstoy should lend his exclusive support to the like-minded Brotherhood Publishing Company, which ran on his moral principles. The profit from publishing *What Is Art?* would merely cover their business expenses.

Because Chertkov wanted to publish his English version simultaneously with the Russian journal, he argued that Tolstoy should send all translators his way. If any foreign edition of *What Is Art?* appeared ahead of his publication, "it would ruin our entire undertaking."[8] Tolstoy soon found himself in the awkward position of helping Chertkov secure a publishing profit. As well, Tolstoy was not free to choose a translator. Before asking Maude to translate *What Is Art?*, he obtained Chertkov's consent. An excellent translator, keenly interested in Tolstoy's philosophy, Maude decided to translate for free.

Tolstoy's collaboration with Maude was fruitful and inspired, but in the middle of their exchange, Chertkov suddenly gave the project to another translator. Appalled by this, Maude wrote Tolstoy that Chertkov decided to give *What Is Art?* to a hack translator who would turn out the work sooner. Tolstoy, who had sent new chapters to Maude only recently, implored Chertkov to let him finish the project: he would make an excellent translation.[9] As with other endeavors before this, the quality did not concern Chertkov as much as speed: he was worried that someone would get hold of the serialized Russian original and issue an English version first.

Having launched a simultaneous publication schedule in English, Chertkov could not keep up with the Russian journal. When *Questions of Philosophy* published an installment ahead of him, Tolstoy received Chertkov's letter demanding he suspend publication in Russia.

> I just received your angry letter, my dear friend Vladimir Grigorievich. I understand you entirely, but I regret that you have no trust that I will do everything for the benefit of your—our cause . . . You are angry with me that I'm publishing it here, which you think is hurtful to your publication . . . As long as I published for money, printing each work was a joy; ever since I stopped taking money, printing each work has become a source of suffering.[10]

Tolstoy asked the editor of the Russian journal, Nikolai Grot, to delay printing the next installment to allow his English translator to catch up. The editor replied he did not care about Tolstoy's translator, "Why, do you have a contract with him?"[11] Hurt by this, Tolstoy complained to Maude: ". . . I am so tired of the disagreements and unsatisfied demands that have occurred with regard to the publication of my works ever since I placed them at everyone's disposal!"[12] Meanwhile, an offended Chertkov was punishing Tolstoy with silence.

Despite pressure, Tolstoy was writing this work with great enthusiasm and continued to perfect it in proofs. Sophia was copying his revisions to help meet deadlines, and Maude patiently revised his translation. In addition to *Questions of Philosophy*, the treatise was later produced by Intermediary and in Sophia's collected works; however, Russian publications were censored. As a result, Maude's translation of *What Is Art?* became the most accurate contemporary version. Brotherhood Publishing issued three editions of his translation to excellent reviews. A prominent theater critic, Arthur Walkley, who had worked with George Bernard Shaw, found Maude's translation to be "an admirable piece of work . . . scholarly, solid, conscientious." But Walkley was surprised that Tolstoy's fascinating book in superb translation was produced by an unknown publisher "in so unobtrusive—I had almost written surreptitious—a fashion . . . Evidently Mr. Aylmer Maude is too modest, too anxious to keep himself unspotted from the (commercial) world . . ."[13] Little did the reviewer know that neither Maude nor Tolstoy had a say in this. Maude would in future issue translations only through well-known firms, which also secured larger circulation for Tolstoy's works.

According to his initial agreement with Tolstoy, Chertkov was expected to publish only his banned non-fiction. But in October 1897, he was already asking to be allowed to issue Tolstoy's unfinished novellas *Hadji Murat* and "The Devil." Horrified by the prospect of publishing these raw drafts, Tolstoy replied it would be "unthinkable."[14] Had Chertkov prevailed, he would have nipped Tolstoy's ideas in the bud and the masterpiece, *Hadji Murat*, would have never been completed. Chertkov reckoned that the first editions of Tolstoy's fiction, even of his drafts, would secure a steady flow of cash for his emerging publishing enterprise. Upset with Chertkov's request for funding, Tolstoy was also afraid to annoy him, so he tried to reduce the impact of his refusal: "Please don't be upset with me. I'll try to please you with the novella [*Hadji Murat*] by sending it to you first."[15] But two years later, after witnessing his publishers' rivalry over profit, Tolstoy decided not to publish *Hadji Murat* and other new writings during his life.

In early February 1898, Chertkov drafted a plan to secure important publishing privileges for his press. The strategy required Tolstoy to release his foreign editions through Chertkov, who would orchestrate publications in other languages. Although the document stated that Tolstoy "desired" to make this arrangement, he was merely yielding to Chertkov's request.

> Now that my friend Vladimir Chertkov is living in England, it is into his hands that I desire to transmit all arrangements in connection with the first publication of my writings in foreign countries and therefore to him that I would refer all translators and publishers interested in the matter.[16]

In January 1898, when the Doukhobors obtained permission to resettle abroad, Tolstoy began to receive their requests for help. It was essential to learn which country would accept seven to ten thousand farmers, who wanted to settle as a community, and it was necessary to collect funds for the migration. Tolstoy wrote an open letter "Aid to the Doukhobors," hoping to solicit donations and advice on where to emigrate. But Russian publications were prohibited from discussing the matter and Tolstoy's letter was suppressed. Turning to the West to publicize the sectarian cause, Tolstoy wrote a plea to English and American newspapers. It was published on April 29 by London's *Daily Chronicle*: "I am now addressing myself to all good people in England and America, to ask their help, firstly with money, for which a great deal is needed for the transport alone of 10,000 people over a great distance, and secondly, with simple and direct guidance in the difficulties presented by the forthcoming resettlement of people who know no foreign languages and who never have been outside Russia."[17] In a postscript to Tolstoy's letter Chertkov asked that responses be sent to his address in England. He was planning to oversee the resettlement.

"The Doukhobor affair consumes me entirely," wrote Tolstoy to Chertkov in March.[18] With an ability to react quickly and organize people, Tolstoy wrote dozens of letters to Russian industrialists, the Quakers, and other Christian communities in America and England. The Doukhobor cause was quickly becoming an international affair. But in Russia, donations had to be collected clandestinely. When *The Russian Gazette* published an announcement that it was receiving donations in Tolstoy's name, the collection was stopped on orders from the Moscow chief of police, Trepov, and the paper was shut down for two months. Trepov demanded that the money and lists of donors' names be handed over to the authorities. ("Alas—Trepov!" Tolstoy wrote to Cherkov who maintained that his friend Trepov was a decent man.) The journal replied to the police that the funds had already been sent to Tolstoy.[19] Maude was among the donors, while Chertkov did not contribute.

When Sophia telephoned Esper Ukhtomsky, the editor of the influential *St. Petersburg's Gazette*, to whom Tolstoy initially turned for advice, he suggested emigrating to Manchuria (now Northeast China). Tolstoy seized on the idea. But once he told Chertkov about it, revealing with his usual frankness that it was Sophia who had received this advice, the idea was dead. Chertkov argued that the Quakers in London had established a committee to help the resettlement and that no one should interfere with their work.

Acting as an intermediary between the Quaker committee and Tolstoy, Chertkov gained considerable influence. "Send everyone to me," he instructed Tolstoy, "and I will pass them on to the committee." All letters concerning the migration had to be forwarded to Chertkov.[20] Beginning to dominate the cause, he amassed information as well as funding, and now wanted to make all decisions unilaterally. As he wrote Tolstoy, "I worry . . . that you'll be now receiving suggestions for the resettlement from all sides, one more thoughtless and impractical than the other . . ."[21] Maude, who was then living at Purleigh, Essex, and actively assisting the migration, tells that even though the Quakers established a special fund, Chertkov as Tolstoy's representative "controlled most of the money" for the resettlement.[22]

When the Quakers proposed Cyprus as a temporary destination, Chertkov weighed in. "I cannot imagine anything better than Cyprus,"[23] he assured. The main advantage was inexpensive transportation: the migrants would have to sail only a short distance from the port of Batum on the Black Sea to the Mediterranean island. But Tolstoy had doubts because it was only temporary and because of a deadly epidemic of yellow fever on Cyprus.[24] Chertkov, without ever having set foot on the island, dismissed his concerns.

Soon the expedition to Cyprus was underway: in May, the Doukhobor scouts, accompanied by Prince Khilkov, arrived in England. A former army officer who had lived among the Doukhobors in the Caucasus, knew their customs and farming methods, Khilkov was highly competent to choose a location. But instead of accepting his expertise, Chertkov quarreled with him and forbade him from approaching the Quaker committee; he also refused funding for the reconnoiter trip to Cyprus.

A follower of Tolstoy, Khilkov had transferred all his estates to the peasants and was now without means. He had suffered for his Tolstoyan beliefs when the authorities exiled him to the Caucasus and took away custody of his children because he refused to baptize them as Christian Orthodox. Tolstoy had intervened in his case and Chertkov had even wanted to write a book about his persecution. But because Khilkov was more popular among the followers, Chertkov was jealous and tried to discredit him. All this was happening during the resettlement, when the fate of thousands was at stake.

Tolstoy was receiving Galya's and Chertkov's letters reporting this and other quarrels and asking that he take their side. Realizing that his followers were fighting amongst themselves, instead of doing God's work, Tolstoy was grieved: "We are obviously deceiving ourselves! Our foes accusing us of hypocrisy are perfectly right."[25] Although the letter was addressed to Galya, Chertkov demanded Tolstoy's apology for speaking critically of him, which he received.[26]

The trip to Cyprus was managed without money from Chertkov. Returning from the island in July, Khilkov and the Doukhobor scouts said it was unsuitable for the migration. But in early August, when Khilkov's letter reached Tolstoy, the first ship with 1,139 migrants was already sailing to Cyprus. Over a hundred people would die there of yellow fever and typhus and the rest would be desperate to get out. At the height of the epidemic, Chertkov and Galya bombarded Tolstoy with letters insisting that relocating to Cyprus was "a necessary measure and not a mistake."[27] There was also financial waste: because Cyprus was a British colony, the government requested a 165,000 ruble (£16,500) surety for the immigrants, which the Quakers had to provide.

In mid-summer, James Mavor, professor of political economy at the University of Toronto, proposed resettlement to Canada. Mavor, who lobbied his government on behalf of the pacifist Russian farmers, generated interest and sympathy. When the government guaranteed religious freedom

Tolstoy and Chertkov in the writer's study, Yasnaya Polyana, 1909. Tolstoy is wearing a camel wool sweater Chertkov sent from England. *Photo by Thomas Tapsell. Courtesy the Tolstoy State Museum.*

ABOVE: Chertkov as Tolstoy's mighty follower, towering over the teacher in an ironic illustration by M. Nesterov, 1924. *Illustration courtesy the Tolstoy State Museum.* BELOW: Chertkov at 81, depicted as a tyrant by M. Nesterov. The painter refused Chertkov's plea to alter his features and draw a tear on his cheek, 1935. *Illustration courtesy the Tretyakov Gallery.*

and exemption from military draft, Canada emerged as the best choice. In October, two Doukhobor families sailed for Canada with Maude and Khilkov as interpreters and guides. Preposterously, Chertkov again refused funding to all involved in this major stage of the campaign. The Doukhobors were sponsored by a member of Kenworthy's commune in Purleigh.

The trip was a success: Maude secured an allocation of land from the Canadian government and arranged for cheaper fares with the Canadian Pacific Railway. Khilkov and the scouts chose places for future communal settlements. Meanwhile, Chertkov spitefully wrote Tolstoy that Khilkov was having an extra-marital affair and only went to Canada to stay away from his family.[28]

Because Chertkov was heavily in debt, trusting him with funds was unwise. In spring 1898, he borrowed 10,000 rubles from Tolstoy's son, Lev.[29] (In comparison, Tolstoy's advance for *Resurrection* from Russia's wealthiest publisher was 12,000 rubles.) But this did not solve Chertkov's financial troubles: he was establishing a press and his business expenses were growing. There was also his extravagant lifestyle, a habit of accommodating guests and enormous staff—secretaries, assistants, and acolytes. During this time, his mother cut his allowance to only 3,000 rubles.

Chertkov's impatience to receive funds is revealed in a letter he sent Tolstoy early in the campaign, urging him to "solicit donations, since we'll need lots of money . . ."[30] Having conducted a major international operation for famine relief, Tolstoy, of course, did not need Chertkov's advice. What he needed was information. Once Canada emerged as the only option for the migration of the pacifist sect (America and Argentina were briefly considered), Tolstoy needed an accurate estimate. On June 24, he asked Chertkov to find out the number of emigrants, how much money was collected, and what remained to be raised. Instead of replying, Chertkov sent a dreamy letter discussing theoretical questions of Tolstoyism. Tolstoy repeated his request, but to no avail. Meanwhile, the sectarians, impatient to relocate, were selling their property and livestock.

One of the major difficulties of organizing the resettlement was establishing reliable communication between two continents and different countries. Tolstoy was in Tula, Maude was about to leave for Canada, and Chertkov and the Quaker committee were in England. Timely exchange of information between these stations was essential. Tolstoy's young follower, Leopold Sulerzhitsky, was handling the difficult and dangerous task of connecting with the sectarians in three different regions of the Caucasus. (Russian authorities had prohibited all contact with these people.) But Tolstoy's exchange with Sulerzhitsky, who wrote from the Caucasus, was more fruitful than with Chertkov, in England.

In mid-July, with no news from Chertkov, Tolstoy decided to raise money by selling *Resurrection, Father Sergius,* and "The Devil" in Russia and abroad. But since *Resurrection* was merely drafted and would consume all his energy, he would publish the novel alone. As he wrote Chertkov, he wanted to sell his fiction "on the most profitable terms" to English and American periodicals. Tolstoy believed in Maude's practicality and wanted him to approach foreign publishers on his behalf. But afraid to provoke Chertkov's jealousy, he was asking to handle the matter in consultation with Maude and then report the publishers' terms back to him.[31] Again, there was no response, as if Tolstoy's letters simply vanished; Chertkov, however, was getting them all.

"It's been almost a month since I haven't received a single letter from you," wrote a bewildered Tolstoy, in mid-August. ". . . 4 weeks ago I wrote to you about my plan to sell my novellas for the benefit of the settlers and asked about a translator, of how and where it would be best to sell them, and I expected some kind of reply. Meantime, every day I receive [your] telegrams, from which I understand nothing." By then, Tolstoy had received information about the total number of migrants, allowing him to approximate the cost of transporting them over the Atlantic. The funding would come from several major sources: the sectarians themselves, who sold their property; the Quakers; Kenworthy's commune in Purleigh, who gave all the money it had for the resettlement; and Tolstoy. At this time, he pledged to raise 30,000 rubles, but would exceed this target.[32] Tolstoy waited to hear about offers from foreign publishers, but another week passed without Chertkov's reply "to the questions that are of great importance to me . . ."[33] On August 27, on the eve of his seventieth birthday, Tolstoy received Chertkov's telegram inquiring how many words there were in *Resurrection.* But Chertkov still failed to write him about the definite cost of the resettlement—"surprisingly, we still can't find out this most important point . . ."[34]

Around this time, Tolstoy asked an émigré journalist Ivan Pavlovsky to approach foreign publishers on his behalf. Pavlovsky was eager to help, but Chertkov, upon learning, warned Tolstoy not to trust this man, claiming that "everyone abroad considers him to be financially unreliable" and demanding he not make any arrangements "without my knowledge and consent."[35] As much as Tolstoy was moved with the selflessness of Kenworthy's commune and others helping the cause, he was distressed that the man closest to him—Chertkov—continued to send irrelevant letters and bizarre telegrams. By mid-October, Tolstoy had collected half of the sum he pledged and dispatched it to England. Chertkov sent telegrams insisting that Tolstoy urgently transfer the remaining half by telegraph. With that, he instructed Tolstoy to send *all* funds in your disposal and as soon as you collect them, to any bank in London, but *definitely* to my name . . . Transfer all the money at once . . . You can be sure I'll not use it thoughtlessly and carelessly . . ."[36] Because Tolstoy had no more funds at hand, Chertkov instructed him to borrow the remaining sum. To make things worse, Chertkov's incompetent and unnerving letters were arriving at the height of Tolstoy's work on *Resurrection*.

In September, Tolstoy's eldest son, Sergei, arrived in England to establish proper communication with Chertkov and the Quaker committee. From Sergei, Tolstoy soon learned that there was no urgency to send the money. The first steamship, *Lake Huron*, was expected to sail out of Batum either in late November or early December, so there was still time to make the payment. But these facts did not matter to Chertkov, who continued to insist, with the intensity and callousness of a psychopath, on urgently receiving a cash transfer. Tolstoy was astounded:

> I've just received your letter . . . and I won't conceal from you the fact, dear friend, that it made a painful impression on me which I'm trying to rid myself of, but can't at all. Firstly, your request to send you at once all the money there is. I already told you that in order to collect it (which is terribly difficult for me, morally) I need to have freedom of movement and a clear idea of what it's needed for, how much and when . . . Apart from that I'm closer to the scene of action here in Russia, and

I can know better than you what is needed and where . . . This was one unpleasant impression—unpleasant because I have to disagree with you, and that hurts me.[37]

Five days later, another telegram from Chertkov arrived. Tolstoy was surprised that it was "demanding money, with an inexplicable urgency." He curtly replied, "I am not sending and will not send [you] the money." But as Tolstoy was finishing this note, a desperate letter came from his friend Alexander Dunaev, the director of the Moscow Commercial Bank. Chertkov had sent him the same urgent telegram—requesting "money, and again immédiatement."[38] Dunaev, who at one time kept a small sum for the resettlement, had long sent it to Tolstoy.

It was time to face the truth: Chertkov was hindering rather than helping him. Tolstoy approached the subject with much diplomacy:

You are very proud of your efficiency, but I frankly don't trust it. I don't say that I'm right, but am only expressing my opinion. It seems to me that you always take on too much work, more than you are capable of, and the work doesn't make progress for that reason . . . .You are slow and dilatory, and then you take a lofty, grand seigneur view of everything and fail to see a lot for that reason, and besides . . . your mood is changeable—sometimes you are feverishly active, other times apathetic. Because of all this I think . . . you are a very valuable collaborator, but on your own—an inefficient worker.[39]

Having criticized his friend, Tolstoy dreaded his reaction. Chertkov's angry letter would unnerve him, as he knew from experience. Working with great intensity on *Resurrection*, he could not afford interruptions: "Dear friend Vladimir Grigorievich. I am writing to you with fear that my latest letters were unpleasant to you and that I'll receive from you an expression of these same unpleasant feelings, and this would paralyze me."[40] Determined to get what he wanted, Chertkov launched his offensive precisely at the moment when Tolstoy was most vulnerable. Herbert Archer, his competent manager, was urgently dispatched from England to Yasnaya with a cache of papers.[41]

It was an empty gesture: Tolstoy, who trusted people, would unlikely look at the documents for the resettlement. And because Archer was almost deaf, Tolstoy could not really interview him. Archer was expected to deal with financial details, while Chertkov explained nothing: instead, he sent Tolstoy a love letter. Written in ink, Chertkov's sentimental letter was stained with tears:

> Firstly and most importantly, don't you dare, dear friend, to ever write to me, as you have . . . 'don't stop loving me' or 'love me too' . . . etc. Such requests indirectly 'imply' that I can stop loving you and that I need to make some effort to 'love you too.' You, obviously, don't know that there's no one in the world who loves you more than I do . . . [six lines crossed out] . . . and my love for you cannot decrease, but it can only grow. P.S. If . . . you want to give me a little retribution, send me a few notebooks of your diaries (for the last three years) with Archer . . ."[42]

Chertkov's cold and confident post script suggests that his tears of emotion were false.

Apparently to end the ordeal, Tolstoy sent several letters, asking Chertkov to forget his criticism. This is when Galya intervened to reprimand Tolstoy, telling him about the difficulties her husband had encountered having to pay for the ship without the needed cash. "Yesterday, I received Galya's strict letter, which I humbly accept as deserved," Tolstoy wrote. To appease Chertkov, he sent his diaries with Archer. Nonetheless, Chertkov was silent. At the end of November, Tolstoy wrote to Galya, soliciting his friend's response: "It's a pity that Vladimir Grigorievich does not write; I want to hear and feel him."[43]

Because of his incompetence and inability to work with others Chertkov was only hurting the cause: much energy and funding was wasted through his involvement. When he failed to order the first vessel, the task was delegated to Sulerzhitsky in Batum. The first ship was booked for £5,500, but as Sergei Tolstoy points out in his memoir, ordering the ships from England would have been less expensive. The extra money went for a ten percent commission to Messagerie Maritime Agency, while a competent person in England could have handled it without an intermediary.[44] Although others did the work, Chertkov collected the money: the sectarians, who had sold their property, had to transfer the funds to him directly. However, he offered no accounting and was later publicly accused by Kenworthy of profiting from the cause.

At the end of November, thousands of migrants streamed to the port of Batum where Sulerzhitsky and Sergei Tolstoy were overseeing their departure. Both would also accompany the ships. Sulerzhitsky would sail with the first vessel, *Lake Huron*, which belonged to the Canadian company Beaver Line. Built in 1883, the steamer originally delivered mail between the continents. Later, it was relegated to transport "troops, cattle, emigrants, and various goods" over the Atlantic. *Lake Huron*, which would carry 2,100 emigrants, arrived in Batum on December 6. The multipurpose vessel had no bunks. The passengers were expected to build them and pay for the lumber. There were only three days for building and loading the luggage and provisions for the month-long voyage. All went off without a hitch. A former seaman as well as an artist, Sulerzhitsky designed the bunks that were constructed on all decks. The lower deck was damp, cold, and almost completely dark, and the decision as to who would sleep there and who would go to the middle deck was made by drawing lots. First and second class cabins on the upper deck were reserved for the sick and elderly. Several people were expected to die during the arduous voyage; ten people in fact died before reaching the New World. Sergei Tolstoy accompanied the second ship, *Lake Superior*. In 1898–1899, these two Canadian vessels would each make two trips transporting the 7,500 emigrants from Batum to Halifax, Canada.

In late December 1898, Chertkov resigned his task of overseeing the migration. He asked Tolstoy "to relieve me of this burden, which has become unnecessary to me." Maude would manage it better, he admitted, while "I just want to be free from all obligations . . . and from the Doukhobor affair."[45] Tolstoy had to ask Maude, still in Canada, to replace Chertkov, who "writes that he doesn't want to, and is unable to deal any longer with the Doukhobor business . . ."[46] Chertkov's intimacy with Tolstoy gave him the freedom to pick up causes and drop them at a whim.

Deciding to dedicate himself to publishing, Chertkov, however, had another surprise. The Free Word Press "has no money at all," he abruptly informed Tolstoy, and unless a sponsor was quickly found, the enterprise would be shut down. Tolstoy could also rescue them by granting the first right to publish "a little fictional work of yours, such as 'Irteniev' ["The Devil"] or some other . . ." Aside from the first release, Chertkov wanted to sell translation rights to the novella.[47] Tolstoy no longer wanted to publish this draft and, besides, there was a difference between raising funds for a cause and helping his friend's business operation. Chertkov's letter made "a sad impression" on Tolstoy, who did not realize that the Free Word Press was in such a precarious state.[48]

Initially it was agreed that Chertkov would publish his banned non-fiction, but, of course, publishing Tolstoy's fiction was more profitable.[49] So, Chertkov urged Tolstoy to put his shoulder to the wheel and help the Free Word Press, which needed his "impetus."[50] It was becoming a familiar motif: "Could you put at our disposal . . . one of your fictional drafts, so I could begin to negotiate publication around the world? A short novella of a few printer's pages . . . could yield *proportionally* more than . . . a large work. Your Caucasian novella [*Hadji Murat*] would be especially valuable in this regard." He even instructed Tolstoy to "complete as many novellas as possible" and submit "each manuscript to me, then begin working on the next novella in line."[51] (Tolstoy chose the lesser of the two evils, finding a sponsor for Chertkov's press. Upon receiving a loan, Chertkov happily reported that his printing shop was now well equipped.[52])

Chertkov's involvement in publishing *Resurrection* in Europe and in America had disastrous consequences for Tolstoy. Acting in his usual irresponsible and secretive way, Chertkov signed contracts without informing Tolstoy about the publishers' terms. Consequently, during his work on *Resurrection*, Tolstoy faced needless pressure, embarrassment, and public relations scandals.

Tolstoy, of course, knew that Chertkov's handling the matter would cost him dearly. However, it seemed easier to agree rather than disagree with him, for Chertkov would not let up: he would send a stream of strong, argumentative letters and demand response. For an aging writer, who was perennially ill, too much was happening at once—the resettlement and his work on the novel. He did not want to quarrel with Chertkov and had neither energy nor time to contradict him. Back in October 1898, Chertkov suddenly requested that Tolstoy send first chapters and a synopsis of *Resurrection*. Tolstoy was insulted: under Chertkov's agency, foreign publishers were treating him like a beginning writer.

> I found your request to give the first chapters to the publishers to read unpleasant and, I must confess, offensive. I would never agree to it, and I'm surprised that you agreed . . . I remember American publishers writing several letters with offers of a very big fee, and I assumed that the matter would be handled the same way by you . . . I can't agree to it, because it's unpractical, and, apart from the needless humiliation, it is moreover a way of cheapening the wares. And so I would ask you . . . to give up this business and leave it to me. I think I shall do it better; at least, I shan't be annoyed with anyone.[53]

But shortly after, Tolstoy received that tear-stained letter from Chertkov. He took his words back and, to make up with Chertkov, dictated the synopsis of *Resurrection* to his messenger, Archer. As a result, Chertkov would orchestrate publication of the novel abroad, aiding neither the cause nor Tolstoy.

In Russia, Tolstoy sold the first appearance of *Resurrection* to Adolf Marx, a wealthy Petersburg publisher and the proprietor of a popular weekly magazine *Niva* (The Cornfield), which had 200,000 subscribers. In October, when the contract with Marx was signed, Tolstoy received an advance of 12,000 rubles (£1,200) and on top of it was paid 1,000 rubles (£100) per printer's page. (It was double the amount Tolstoy had negotiated for *Anna Karenina*.) But while Marx paid the author an exorbitant amount for the serialized first appearance, Chertkov's press would publish a simultaneous edition for free.

As it later transpired, Chertkov was placing Tolstoy's novel in Europe and in America through his own literary agents. (His agent in London was Dillon Woony and in America—Reynolds.[54]) They sold the first publication of the novel to German, French, and American periodicals.

As contracts stipulated, translations had to appear simultaneously with the Russian weekly, which put an insurmountable pressure on Tolstoy and on *Niva*'s publisher. This crisis could have been avoided if the practical Maude had been involved in negotiations, as Tolstoy had asked from the start, or if Chertkov had openly discussed the contracts with the writer himself.

Resurrection was the only work Tolstoy wrote under pressure from many publishers simultaneously. In summer and fall 1898, Tolstoy felt a surge of creative energy: "I am working with an excitement I have not experienced for a long time," he wrote Chertkov.[55] After *Anna Karenina*, it was his first major novel in two decades. Tolstoy told Sophia that "he hasn't been in such a creative mood since writing *War and Peace* . . ."[56] But unlike with his first masterpiece, written at the height of his creative powers, Tolstoy was now under stress and continually ill.

Tolstoy had been writing *Resurrection* sporadically for over a decade. In the novel, an aristocrat Dmitry Nekhlyudov seeks redemption for the sin he committed as a young man. Tolstoy was drawing from a story told by a lawyer friend, Anatoly Koni, as well as an event that took place in his own youth. As a young nobleman, Tolstoy had seduced his sister's chambermaid, and she was dismissed for their liaison; unable to find employment, the girl ended up on the streets. Tolstoy's central character, Nekhlyudov, who has ruined a maid, Katyusha Maslova, later becomes transformed by his guilt. As a juror, he recognizes her in a prostitute being tried for theft and murder. Because of a legal mistake, Katyusha is convicted for crimes she has not committed and sentenced to four years hard labor. Nekhlyudov files an appeal on her behalf with a Petersburg lawyer. But before her case is reviewed, she is deported to Siberia and, determined to save her, Nekhlyudov follows. This plot allowed Tolstoy to show corruption in all levels of Russia's society, and mainly, in the government, judiciary, and privileged classes.

In 1895, Tolstoy read chapters of *Resurrection* to a gathering at home. His perspicacious editor and friend, Strakhov, recognized Chertkov in the main character. "It would be the story of Chertkov," he wrote Tolstoy.[57] Indeed, Tolstoy employed Chertkov's physical portrait and background: his hero was also an elite officer in the Guards, close to the Tsar, and was paid an annual allowance of 20,000 rubles. Like Chertkov, Nekhlyudov is pedantic and humorless, but other features, such as readiness to sacrifice and capacity for remorse are clearly Tolstoy's. The writer mixed his own features with Chertkov's to create the hero. "In Nekhludov, as in every man, there were two beings; one of the spiritual, seeking only that kind of happiness for himself which tends towards the happiness of all; the other, the animal man, seeking only his own happiness, and ready to sacrifice to it the happiness of the rest of the world."[58] Curiously, Tolstoy perceived a major similarity between his own traits and Chertkov's, having written him that their two characters were different from the rest. Unlike in other people, good and evil did not mix in Chertkov. And so it was with Tolstoy.[59] (This was also an allusion to Robert Louis Stevenson's novel *The Strange Case of Dr. Jekyll and Mr. Hyde*, which had impressed Chertkov and which Tolstoy had also liked.[60])

In January 1899, Tolstoy's energy and enthusiasm for the novel were waning; he wrote listlessly to Chertkov: "I received your letter, dear friend and Galya's letters. Forgive me if I won't reply to everything now. All through this rotten winter I had a great deal of work, and my health has worsened—my back hurts constantly and I have general fatigue."[61] Unwell and depressed, Tolstoy explained to the publisher of the *Niva* magazine, that in this state of mind and soul he could not send the awaited installments.[62]

Chertkov did not spare Tolstoy: that same month, he abruptly informed him about the migrants' desperate situation on Cyprus. They had to be urgently evacuated, and he expected Tolstoy to raise an additional sum of 40,000 rubles (£4,000). "You've puzzled and confused me very much," Tolstoy responded, "having written that 40,000 rubles is needed for their [the Doukhobors'] departure and that I should get the money . . . If possible, write what you are going to do about this. How much money is there? Are the Quakers giving a loan? . . ."[63] Tolstoy was still kept in the dark about his advances from foreign publishers, "how much will translations give, what's collected in America, I don't know."[64]

Even after he gave up the Doukhobor affair, Chertkov maintained his role as intermediary between the Quaker committee and Tolstoy, who continued to receive his confusing telegrams, along the lines: "Further postponement Cyprus very dangerous Thirty thousand rubles necessary immediately Can you borrow? If not how much?"[65] In the end, two women in Essex, both of them Tolstoyans, paid for the vessel that brought the Cyprus Doukhobors to Canada.

Meanwhile, Chertkov coordinated simultaneous publication in different languages, and directed that printing had to await his signal. At his request, Tolstoy was to postpone publication in *Niva* magazine until March.[66] For *Niva* there would be "no significant losses at all"[67] from this postponement, Chertkov claimed. He was misleading Tolstoy: *Niva* would be losing over 100 rubles for each day's delay.

Niva's publisher was trying to prevent the manuscript of *Resurrection* from being copied or stolen. The manuscript was sent to the printers under a different name and a fictitious title: "*Expectation*. Novella by V.G. Korolenko."[68] But even such precautions proved futile. When *Niva* published the first chapters, scores of newspapers and magazines reprinted them without respecting the magazine's exclusive rights. Tolstoy issued a statement asking to postpone reprinting until the whole novel appeared. In Russia, the novel was truncated by censors, but Tolstoy was prepared to publish a compromised version, since the full text would appear abroad.

During a productive period in February Tolstoy was trying to accomplish as much as possible. As his enthusiasm returned, Sophia told the art critic Vladimir Stasov: "Lev Nikolaevich is completely immersed in *Resurrection*, and the novel is moving towards the end. He is working with such surprising thoroughness, studying the smallest details in all spheres where he places his characters."[69] Tolstoy visited prisons, attended court proceedings, and interviewed a superintendent of the Moscow Butyrskaya prison, Vinogradov, asking about the inmates' routine and how the guards treated female convicts during the long journey to Siberian exile. He was writing the chapter of Katyusha Maslova's deportation from prison to a penal colony in Siberia: a crowd of over a thousand convicts, in chains, marches for miles in scorching heat to the station. Weakened by months in confinement, five convicts die of heat stroke on the way. Tolstoy was describing the actual occurrence and had a prison superintendent read his proofs and correct inaccuracies. This interesting period of Tolstoy's work was interrupted with an ugly quarrel between his publishers.

On February 27, two weeks before *Niva* published its first installment, Chertkov announced in the German newspaper, *Berliner Literärischer Echo*, that he alone had an accurate text, having received it directly from the author. This was meant to squeeze out other foreign publishers, who launched their versions, and to undermine *Niva*'s publication in Germany. Chertkov warned that *Niva*'s version was "abridged" and could not be trusted. The German publisher of Deutsche Verlags-Anstalt, F. Fontans, with whom Chertkov signed a contract, alleged that *Niva* would only publish one quarter of the novel.[70] These announcements produced an uproar in the publishing world.

On March 2, *Niva*'s publisher informed Tolstoy about the conflict and asked that Chertkov retract his statement, which he believed untrue and financially damaging to his magazine. Tolstoy asked that Chertkov satisfy the demand of *Niva*'s publisher. Chertkov did not reply and, after four anxious days, Tolstoy wrote again, explaining his position. He was pressed on all sides and afraid of disagreements. Yet, everyone was complaining and quarreling. Disheartened, Tolstoy was prepared to think that fundraising for the Doukhobor migration was a mistake: "It's all [because of] money. And the Doukhobors did not need money. It would be better if they lived as before and suffered for us and for the world."[71]

In response, Tolstoy only received an admonishing letter from Galya. He at once sent Chertkov an apology: "So, forgive me, dear Vladimir Grigorievich. How many times do I say this, more than 7, but 7 × 70. I kiss you."[72] Tolstoy referred to the epigraph in the novel: "Then came Peter to him, and said, Lord, how oft shall my brother sin against me, and I forgive him? Till seven times? Jesus saith unto him, I say not unto thee, Until seven times: but, Until seventy times seven."[73] But this did not soften Chertkov, who had previously explained that in order to forgive, one needs to love. "And there's so little love in me . . . I love people little . . ."[74]

Chertkov did not retract his statement in the German newspaper. Instead, he sent Tolstoy a full account of his quarrel with *Niva*'s publisher, Marx. He also claimed that the resulting polemic undermined his own reputation in the publishing world. Tolstoy was expected to support Chertkov by signing "a little power of attorney document." Drafted in Tolstoy's name, it stated that Chertkov was the writer's sole representative abroad and was producing his most faithful versions.

I believe it is necessary to add that my friend V. Chertkov disinterestedly and motivated only with his desire to help promote
the most accurate versions of my writings, has kindly agreed
to act as intermediary between myself and those foreign publishers who want to produce accurate versions of the first editions of my works. Therefore I ask to consider V. Chertkov my
immediate representative in the matter, who has my complete
trust, and to regard all his statements related to the matter as
completely truthful and accurate.[75]

Tolstoy signed the document on April 3 and it was published by scores
of Western newspapers. Publishers would think it came from the author
himself. What Tolstoy may not have realized was that none of the contemporary publishers, even his friend Chertkov, produced accurate versions
of *Resurrection*. Decades later, when a team of Russian scholars worked to
restore Tolstoy's genuine text, it was discovered that Chertkov's version
published by the Free Word Press was also inaccurate. He occasionally
employed proofs received not from Tolstoy, but from *Niva* magazine, and
was reproducing their censored version. Because Tolstoy kept revising the
novel, some changes arrived too late to be introduced. In addition, Chertkov
made his own stylistic changes without consulting the author: he believed
Tolstoy had given him carte blanche.[76]

Foreign editions Chertkov had contracted were also incomplete. In
America, he sold the first serial publication to the *Cosmopolitan Magazine*
for 10,000 rubles (£1,000). Because of moral censorship in America, sexual
content was cut and the scene of Nekhlyudov seducing Katyusha Maslova
was heavily edited. Upon discovering this, Chertkov broke the contract,
informing the author after the fact. Chertkov insisted that Tolstoy sign a
statement, saying that he disowns authorship of the piece. After signing
it, which was easier than arguing, Tolstoy asked that Chertkov refrain
from publishing it. He did not want to offend people and, besides, it was
impossible to intervene in every case where publishers altered his text.[77]
"Personally, I would not forbid publication," Tolstoy repeated in another
letter.[78] (In France, Chertkov sold the first appearance of the novel to
L'Écho de Paris, a conservative daily newspaper, for 12,000 francs. In

French translation a satirical scene depicting the Orthodox service in a prison church was entirely missing.) Chertkov did not heed Tolstoy's request, so there was soon conflict with *Cosmopolitan*'s publisher, John Brisben Walker. The publisher threatened to sue Chertkov, who broke the contract without consulting Tolstoy. In addition, he demanded that Chertkov return his portion of the advance.

Chertkov would not return the money, so the publisher complained to Tolstoy, to the latter's dismay. Tolstoy replied to Walker, in English, expressing confidence that the money would be returned. He also defended "my respected friend Mr. Chertkov, who . . . disinterestedly and with self-denial undertook the difficult task of procuring the money necessary to help the Russian exiles . . ."[79] Simultaneously, Tolstoy asked Chertkov to make sure the money was returned to the publisher. But Chertkov claimed he had returned the check to his American agent, Reynolds. The agent denied receiving it. Tolstoy was distressed by the new argument, again over money. In October 1899, Walker wrote that Chertkov still refused to return his advance. Chertkov shifted the blame to the American agent and severed his contract with him. Then he cheerfully wrote Tolstoy, "Now the matter lies entirely between Walker [publisher] and Reynolds [agent] and no longer concerns you and me."[80]

The first American publication was later expertly handled by Ernest Crosby, Tolstoy's friend and follower. An American lawyer and social reformer, Crosby became influenced by Tolstoy's ethical writings, resigning his position as judge in the International Court in Egypt. Crosby had visited Tolstoy in Yasnaya in 1894, corresponded with him, and promoted his works in America. In 1900, *Resurrection* in the authorized translation by Louise Maude was published by the reputable Dodd, Mead & Co. The publisher offered a generous advance (between $4,000 and $6,000), of which Crosby immediately informed Tolstoy. Before the arrangement could be made, Tolstoy formally asked for Chertkov's permission. This edition was also censored and when the publisher asked to alter sexually suggestive scenes, Tolstoy agreed.

During *Resurrection*, Tolstoy felt he was no longer the master of his life, but only a laborer.[81] As he wrote a friend, he felt besieged by translators and publishers, who were "hastening me and tearing me to pieces."[82] But even as he had "no energy, no desire to work," he was striving for quality. In May, sending revisions to Chertkov, Tolstoy apologetically explained why these were necessary. A clever portraitist or sculptor works to convey an expression of one's eyes and face. "For me, the most important is spiritual life expressed in scenes."[83]

Chertkov was relentlessly enforcing a simultaneous publication schedule. In July, when *Niva* printed several chapters ahead of foreign publishers, Chertkov demanded suspension of Russian publication. He had recently made several such requests and Tolstoy felt he could no longer bother *Niva's* publisher. Marx suffered losses for printing delays, so Tolstoy attempted to cut the Gordian Knot. He suggested breaking contracts and returning advances to foreign publishers, to which Chertkov calmly replied that such action would only result in publishers' lawsuits.[84]

That summer, Chertkov suddenly announced that he decided to live without money. Tolstoy replied that although he approved of the idea, he did not think such a life feasible for Chertkov, whose wife and son depended on his support.[85] Maude describes the Essex colony's reaction to Chertkov's decision:

> I remember how much amusement was caused by the conduct of . . . V.G. Chertkov, who was reported to have ceased to use money but allowed his wife to sign his checks, and his secretary to accompany him to the station to buy his railway tickets . . . I heard him deliver an impassioned oration on the wickedness of using money . . . I do not see that the evil is lessened by insisting that others should have the trouble, and bear the guilt, of owning the land, and the food-stuffs . . .[86]

Having witnessed Chertkov's practices during the publishing of *Resurrection*, Maude was doubtful of his moralizing: "If anyone was authorized to say what our 'principles' were, it was Chertkov, but within a course of a few months we found him ardently collecting money, refusing to handle money, desiring to obtain money from *Resurrection* and . . . neglecting to account for sums that passed through his hands."[87] In the end, Chertkov undermined the followers' faith in Tolstoyan ideals, having proved, although unintentionally, the unworkability of non-resistance principles by reverting "to autocracy undiluted and unashamed." Tolstoy inspired enthusiasm, and people were willing to assist him, but "our devotion was not transferable, and when Tolstoy passed it on to such a lieutenant, it dwindled away."[88]

Far from giving up money, Chertkov was expanding his publishing operations. In August 1899, he sent his housekeeper, Annushka, to Yasnaya. She carried Chertkov's publishing plan, along with an estimate, which "horrified" Tolstoy. Chertkov requested an annual subsidy of 15,000 rubles (£1,500), apparently expecting the writer's help. Tolstoy reacted by saying that Chertkov's plan was "unthinkable and ruinous." His press should be able to earn enough to cover expenditures. Even if the requested sum was "miraculously found" this time, next year the enterprise would only slide deeper into debt. The publisher of *Northern Herald*, Lyubov Gurevich, who recently went bankrupt, has accumulated an inconceivable debt of 200,000 rubles (£20,000). (Gurevich had also approached Tolstoy asking to bail out her magazine by letting it publish first editions of his various works.) Chertkov was now planning to produce a periodical, *Leaflets of the Free Word Press*, but Tolstoy felt he lacked the necessary journalistic ability. Chertkov was usually late with his coverage and discussed the news "as one should ponder eternal questions."[89]

Chertkov did not forgive this sarcasm, so Tolstoy apologized "that I wrote to criticize your activity."[90] (Ever after, he would only praise Chertkov's publishing efforts.) As well, Tolstoy was vaguely promising to help Chertkov's press, while saying that "the financial side of every enterprise horrifies, repulses, frightens me; it causes a physical sensation of fear, heartache, and shame."[91] Chertkov reassured that Tolstoy needn't be afraid for the Free Word Press. Publishing requires large investment, he emphasized. If Tolstoy finds a rich sponsor, he should ask him to send "the entire sum at once."[92] But even such selfish letters did not change their relationship. As Tolstoy earlier wrote Chertkov, nothing could "affect my love for you. The feeling is not in danger."[93] The relationship established through faith was unbreakable, although "since recently, all of these trifling affairs have overshadowed, obscured our bond."[94]

In summer 1899, the last and most crowded ship brought the migrants to Canada. The first year was particularly hard: the settlers had no money to buy horses and inventory. Tolstoy received reports that the Doukhobor women plowed the land by harnessing themselves twelve pairs to a plough. The women were also building villages, while men earned cash as laborers on outside farms. In November 1899, Tolstoy raised an additional sum and himself sent it to Canada. The Quakers in Philadelphia donated $30,000 to the Doukhobors.

In December, having completed the novel, Tolstoy was beginning to think, "with joy and hope," of what his next project would be.[95] Unsatisfied with *Resurrection*, especially with the final part, which he was composing in haste, he wanted to return to the novel, write a sequel, but this intention never materialized. Publishing *Resurrection* was an ordeal, from which Tolstoy would never recover.

CHAPTER EIGHT

"A GRAVEN IMAGE"

"I met Chertkov, 'his very self.' He was a tall, large-built, noble-looking individual with a small, very proud head; a cold, arrogant face; a tiny, hawk-like, well-shaped nose; and similarly predatory-looking eyes . . . Tolstoy's wife, Sofia Andreevna . . . used to refer to Chertkov as a 'graven image.' I saw him only once or twice, but I could never figure out precisely what kind of man he was. But the impression he made was indeed that of a 'graven image.'"
—Ivan Bunin, *The Liberation of Tolstoy*

"He's his universe, his hero;
He's lost in constant admiration, quotes him
On all occasions . . .
The fellow knows his dupe, and makes the most on't,
He fools him with a hundred masks of virtue,
Gets money from him all the time by canting,
And takes upon himself to carp at us.
. . . And how about Tartuffe?"

—Molière, *Tartuffe*

C hertkov's political loyalties were changing: in January 1899, Tolstoy read his article criticizing the upcoming First Hague Conference, proposed by Nicholas II. Tolstoy had openly disapproved of the Tsar's initiative because his call for an international peace conference was accompanied by an expansion of the Russian army.[1] But Chertkov's disapproval of the Tsar was news. Tolstoy found it regrettable that Chertkov had "so mercilessly depicted the role of Nicholas II; you're burning your bridges."[2] In England, Chertkov was befriending democratic socialists, many of whom were lodged in his houses in Croydon and Christchurch.

Among them was Lenin's future associate, Bonch-Bruevich. Chertkov had invited him to Croydon to look after his book warehouse and help establish his press. At twenty-four, Bonch-Bruevich had publishing experience and had studied natural sciences at the University of Zurich. He also had coordinated shipments of illegal revolutionary literature to Russia. Before emigrating from Russia, Bonch-Bruevich had met Chertkov and Tolstoy through his involvement with Intermediary.

Vera Velichkina, who had assisted Tolstoy during the famine relief, was also invited to stay with the Chertkovs in England. Like Bonch-Bruevich, whom she later married, Velichkina organized the transport of revolutionary literature to Russia. She translated works by Marx and Engels and contributed to Lenin's *Iskra*, launched in 1900. A medical student, who was qualified at the University of Bern, Velichkina was among physicians attending to Lenin after the Bolshevik Revolution.

In his memoir, Bonch-Bruevich tells that the Russian political colony in London regarded Chertkov as a curiosity. The close friend and associate of Tolstoy was believed to be something of an enigma. But his publishing activity and the fact that he disseminated Tolstoy's prohibited works inspired their respect. Although democratic socialists disagreed with Tolstoy's doctrine of non-violence, they circulated his works critical of the government and the Church.

Political émigrés were also drawn to Chertkov because he provided badly needed employment, housing, and food. In Chertkov's house one could meet people of diverse backgrounds: political émigrés, like Bonch-Bruevich and Velichkina, and a member of the secret police, Vladimir Krivosh, who introduced himself as a Russian censor. There were also aristocrats, Latvian democratic socialists (with whom Galya corresponded), and Tolstoyans. Albert Shkvaran, a physician and a Tolstoyan from Slovakia, whom Chertkov sheltered in England, had fled his home country where he had been jailed for refusing military service. He was a friend of Krivosh, also a Slovak. (Interestingly, Krivosh was a second cousin of Dushan Makovitsky, who would become Tolstoy's personal doctor.)

Bonch-Bruevich describes meeting Chertkov at the station in Croydon in 1897. Tall, big, in a brimmed hat and plain shirt without the starched collar commonly worn at the time, Chertkov attracted attention. His aristocratic charm and roman profile inspired his guest's curiosity. Chertkov himself drove the coach and they soon arrived to his three-story house, crammed with family and guests. At 8 o'clock, at the sound of the bell, everyone assembled for dinner in the enormous kitchen on the ground floor. Twenty-five were seated while Annushka, Chertkov's housekeeper and cook, served the food. Other domestics included Galya Chertkova's maid, Katya, and Mokei, a deserter from the Russian army. Miss Picard, a governess, also living with the family, instructed son Dima in English. In the mornings, Galya would appear in a soft robe of camel wool. In contrast to his thin, pale, and sickly wife, Chertkov was a picture of health. Bonch-Bruevich thought that "one needs a fortune to feed this multitude. And they had to be fed well, since everyone had healthy appetites and were on vegetarian diets, which required skillful preparation and considerable expense."

Galya was musical and had a magnificent voice, but Bonch-Bruevich felt her artistic nature was buried under the weight of Tolstoyism. "It seemed to me that she suppressed many of her own strivings by reading the works, which were supposed to reveal the meaning of life to her, but . . . which did not allow her . . . to be herself." Galya was helping Chertkov compile the "Compendium of Tolstoy's Thoughts," this "utterly boring, tedious, and useless tract . . ." Assisting Chertkov with his publishing enterprise, she read proofs and helped handle correspondence. Shkvaran, who had "a privileged position in the house," would sit beside Galya, looking bored, while pretending to write a memoir.

During his productive periods Chertkov, suffering from insomnia, worked feverishly day and night; then he plunged into apathy, both spiritual and physical sleep. When cheerful he amused guests with stories, which he told "masterfully," and performed tricks. He would heat up a needle over a candle and drive it into his hand or would pretend to bump his forehead with all his might against a doorframe.

Chertkov liked to condemn the government and upper classes, saying that "he was one of the . . . leeches sitting on the neck of the working people and sucking their blood..." He would talk about the need "to build a good life," but after preaching for a while, would become bored, get up, and walk away.

Bonch-Bruevich sarcastically describes a Tolstoyan colony, which Chertkov presided over, as "a Garden of Eden." As he wrote a friend in Moscow (the letter was intercepted by the secret police), the near-perfect Tolstoyans did not inspire him to join their paradise. Interested only in their cause, they were unlike Tolstoy himself, who, despite his age, remained open-minded and alert. "I had a chance to read his diary for the past three years, and found a response virtually to everything that's happening in the world."[3] Bonch-Bruevich relished his opportunity to sort through Chertkov's "colossal" archive, comprised of a collection of Tolstoy's manuscripts and diaries, sectarian papers, and correspondence with writers and artists. He knew that earlier in 1897, these papers had been seized by the police. "However, the archive survived. Chertkov preserved it intact." Explaining the mystery, Bonch-Bruevich tells that Chertkov had anticipated the search and deposited his original papers in the apartments that were "inaccessible to the gendarmes." The seizure of his archive in his mother's Petersburg apartment was initiated by Pobe-donostsev. (The Procurator of the Holy Synod believed Tolstoy's teaching was damaging to the authority of the Church. He was also behind the writer's excommunication in 1901.) Later, Chertkov's friends and family delivered his papers to England.[4]

Sophia Motovilova, a young philosophy student who visited the Chert-kovs in Essex, Purleigh, also left a memoir about her stay. Born in Simbirsk, like Vladimir Ulyanov (Lenin), Motovilova came from a middle-class family. In fact, the two families were close. At nineteen, she studied at universities in Weimar and Leipzig. Like many liberals of her day, she read Marxist literature, utopian socialists, and Tolstoy's non-fiction, of which *The Kingdom of God* impressed her most.

In Switzerland, she met Georgy Plekhanov, a leading Marxist thinker and publicist, and Mikhail Bakunin, a prominent revolutionary anarchist. Switzerland was a center of Russian political emigration and there she also met Biryukov, a prominent Tolstoyan. (In 1899, Biryukov was released from his exile in Bausk, a town on the Baltic, and allowed to emigrate.) Because Motovilova wanted to see "a real Tolstoyan colony," Biryukov suggested visiting Chertkov and his colonists near Purleigh. In May 1900, she wrote Chertkov from London; he replied coldly. A month later, she suddenly received Chertkov's telegram urgently inviting her to come. Arriving on the appointed day, Motovilova did not find Chertkov at home. His two-story house in Maldon (near Purleigh) looked ordinary. Inside, it resembled a peasant hut: the ground floor was occupied by a large kitchen, with a long table in the middle. As at the previous house everyone ate in the kitchen, peasant fashion. Most of Chertkov's guests were democratic socialists, rather than Tolstoyans.

Galya received Motovilova in her low-ceiling bedroom upstairs, which looked ascetic without carpets, paintings, and furniture. Pale, "her gaze dull and unfriendly," she was lying in bed. "I sit down beside the bed on a wooden chair and she starts examining me from head to toe. Then she begins to interrogate me, in the style of Soviet questionnaires: 'Who am I? What do I do? What am I doing in England? How much do I pay for staying in a boarding school? Why so little?' I explain. 'Who are my parents? What do they do? Who was my father? A landlord? How much land did he have?' I cannot reply to this last question—I don't know. During the interrogation my revulsion grows." (Galya was trying to establish Motovilova's status: the Chertkovs graded their guests according to social background. Publisher Sytin, a former peasant, was refused sheets when he stayed for the night, unlike the Chertkovs' aristocratic relatives, who were treated as equals.) "Then she [Galya] asks me whether I am interested in Tolstoyism. 'Why? . . .' She asks whether I read *Anna Karenina*. I reply coldly—yes. Later she told others that I was a superficial person and had nothing to say about my impression from *Anna Karenina*."

The following day, Chertkov returned from London; the domestics announced his arrival with servility: "Chertkov himself arrived!" Chertkov, who never traveled alone for fear of railroads, returned with his large retinue. Motovilova thought that something in his appearance resembled Ivan the Terrible from Repin's paintings: the same cold look in his bulging eyes and aquiline nose. "He was dressed strangely, in a jacket of camel wool, and wore a bag over his shoulder. He spoke briskly and did not even apologize for going away on the appointed day." Chertkov had traveled to see Prince Peter Kropotkin, a scientist and theoretician of anarchism, and at his house met a group of Spanish anarchists, recently released from jail.

After supper, Chertkov lay down on a couch and a student guest started playing the piano to amuse him; Mokei brought him a glass of tea on a tray. "I thought: 'If they are Tolstoyans, and they are equal, why is Chertkov resting on a couch and a muzhik is bringing him tea, not the other way?'"

Chertkov was not in a mood to discuss Tolstoyism, until one evening, when he plunged into an argument. "Chertkov was not so much explaining his Tolstoyan ideas to me; he was mostly attacking, censuring, and mocking me. His domestics, sitting around him, laughed approvingly at all his jokes, which were often rude . . . He ridiculed me for having studied philosophy in Leipzig. 'Who needs this philosophy? Physical work is all that matters, this soup, which a village woman can make, matters, and peasant labor matters more than any of the philosophical systems.' Books and science are unimportant, only physical work is important. 'But you have a publishing house,' I countered. 'You publish Tolstoy. If books are unimportant, why are you doing this?' 'So what, I am inconsistent,' Chertkov replied . . . Dinner was long over, but everyone stayed at the table listening to our debate and having a good time. Although I was alone, I boldly defended myself, but after Chertkov's particularly rude outburst I was reduced to tears. Everyone became frightened. They offered me a glass of water. I drank it; then someone gave me a glass of milk. I got up and, nervously clutching my fists, approached Chertkov, enraged: 'I came here hoping to find an exemplary Tolstoyan in you, a Christian who treats others lovingly; instead I found an arrogant nobleman, who allows himself to humiliate another human being.'"

That evening, Chertkov delivered a large envelope to the cottage where Motovilova was staying. Inside was a verbose letter. Chertkov was asking to forgive him. In the morning, there was a knock on the door. When Motovilova opened, "Chertkov just stood there, tall and aloof. He came to ask whether I had forgiven him. I am annoyed with this comedy. He asks to forgive him. He realizes he was at fault . . . He speaks dryly, without feeling: cold virtue." Chertkov returned on the following morning and again stood in the doorway, with a linen bag hanging over his shoulder. Like Tolstoy, Chertkov took a notebook and a pencil when heading for a stroll.

Chertkov returned daily, demanding to know whether he was forgiven. "He relishes his virtue . . . He, Chertkov himself, asks me, a virtual nobody, for forgiveness. Isn't it an act of heroic Christian submission? I feel uncomfortable. 'I've told you that I'm thinking about you.' But he just stands there, like a post. He will not leave until I tell him that I've forgiven him. I say something noncommittal. He leaves. Thank God, I think, I got rid of this comedian. But no! Two days later, he comes back and again asks for forgiveness."

Chertkov's attitude to property also struck her as hypocritical. When Chertkov needed a couch, he ordered it from his Voronezh estate, rather than buying it in England. This allowed him to claim that he did not use money, even though shipping a couch from Russia was more expensive than buying new. When someone pointed this out to him, Chertkov replied, "So what? I'm weak."[5] (Tolstoy would say of himself that he was weak and inconsistent; Chertkov parroted his words.)

Chertkov exploited his servants, employees, and guests alike. Annushka and Mokei never received a salary. When Tolstoy gave Annushka a tip for delivering Chertkov's letters from England, Chertkov was displeased. His servants and employees were taught that money was sinful. A Latvian democratic socialist, German Punga, who handled anything from accounting to washing dishes and tutoring Dima in arithmetic, worked unpaid. And so did a Latvian student, named Albin. He helped with editing and correspondence, tutored Chertkov's son, played chess with Chertkov, played the piano to amuse him, scripted scores for Galya's songs, and took his turn washing dishes. (His real name was Andropov; he later became a Bolshevik.) Like other émigrés staying at Chertkov's house, Albin was later arrested on the Russian border for smuggling illicit literature and imprisoned in the Peter and Paul Fortress in Petersburg. After Motovilova informed Chertkov about his detainment, he wrote to the fortress commandant, a good acquaintance of his father, but it is unknown whether this helped Albin.

Dmitry Abrikosov, a future diplomat, met Chertkov while visiting his brother, Hrisanf, in the Tolstoyan colony near Purleigh. The Abrikosov brothers, who knew Tolstoy, came from a famous family of factory owners, Abrikosov and Sons. This was one of the oldest and most reputable confection factories, which delivered sweets to the Imperial Court. Abrikosov Jr. reminisces about his stay with the Tolstoyans, who engaged in growing vegetables and proselytizing. "After three weeks of such life, I had enough. It all seemed senseless play; I could not understand how such a forcible character as Chertkov could be satisfied with it. In fact he probably was not, for he was always in bad temper and one could see what effort it cost him to control his passionate nature."[6]

At Chertkov's house Abrikosov met "the widow of a famous terrorist who had been executed for his part in the assassination of Emperor Alexander II."[7] (In 1881, five members of the terrorist revolutionary organization the People's Will were publicly hanged.) Abrikosov does not provide the name of the terrorist or his widow. But the fact that Chertkov accommodated someone so close to this notorious terrorist organization, despite his proximity to the Tsar, is astonishing. This was happening at the time when the foreign section of the Russian secret police was hunting down members of the People's Will in Europe and tracing their contacts with Russia. But whether Chertkov's house served as a setup for political émigrés is unknown.

Chertkov's association with revolutionaries troubled Tolstoy, who reminded him that "there are no people further apart from us." Although revolutionaries also stood for equality and rejected private ownership, they wanted to achieve their goals by violent means. Tolstoyans did not recognize the state, while revolutionaries wanted to destroy the state; Tolstoyans did not recognize property, while revolutionaries destroyed property.[8] On another occasion Tolstoy explained that a social order, established through violence, cannot become fair and just. Attained through a violent revolution, the new order "would have to be constantly supported by that same violence, i.e. by illegality and, consequently, it would inevitably and very quickly be corrupted just like the order it replaced."[9]

There was no consistency in Chertkov's views on the issue. To Tolstoy, he would say that his publishing provided an alternative to revolutionary propaganda. However, he also defended revolutionary socialists, which became particularly apparent in 1902, when he was publishing Tolstoy's article "To the Working People." Both Chertkov and Galya then attacked Tolstoy for his critique of revolutionaries in this article. Chertkov defended the need for the workers to strike and even wrote that he could see nothing wrong if factories became the property of the workers.[10] At the same time, Chertkov was not planning to allow the workers to expropriate his family's oil plant and land; on the contrary, he would be making every effort to sell them profitably in 1915, before the Revolution occurred.

In 1900, the Chertkovs bought Tacton House, an estate in Christchurch where they would live until the end of their exile. Next to the main mansion, Chertkov erected a brick building for his printing shop and editorial office. Later, he added a modern storage facility, equipped with a steel vault and an alarm for keeping his collection of Tolstoy's manuscripts. The expensive construction was completed in 1906. Describing the storage, Chertkov's employee recalled that it was equipped with several alarms, which were turned on at night. If someone accidentally touched the thick steel doors of the vault, deafening alarms would sound in the main house. The walls were built to withstand an earthquake.[11] Guarding his archive as a treasure, Chertkov hired a loyal man, Leonid Perno, to watch over the main house and storage in his absence.

In January, Tolstoy wrote Chertkov he was glad to have finished *Resurrection*. This "ended our business relationship . . . which has been always poisoning for me, your, our friendship."[12] Around this time Tolstoy confided with Maude that publishing *Resurrection* "and all that money business which I undertook and which I now repent, has been so tormentingly painful, that now that it is over I have decided to have nothing more to do with the matter, but to return completely to my former attitude towards the publication of my writings: that is, while letting others do what they please with them, stand quite aside from the business myself."[13] While Tolstoy, near the end of his life, became indifferent to practical affairs, Chertkov was establishing himself as his major publisher, agent, and collector of his manuscripts.

In February, Chertkov wrote to remind Tolstoy that more funds were needed for his periodical. Tolstoy's sympathy for their editions gave him and Galya "the reason to hope that we'll no longer be deprived of material support essential to our undertaking . . . especially if you, Lev Nikolaevich, will remember about it and on occasion direct this support to us."[14] Because Chertkov's periodical published extracts from Tolstoy's letters and diaries, it would be deeply embarrassing for him to approach donors. Chertkov claimed that he was no longer "seeking large royalties for the first appearance of your writings." Yet, he wanted to maintain his role as Tolstoy's sole publishing representative abroad. Chertkov reminded about the fifteen years of his disinterested service, of working "devotedly and doggedly . . . (year after year, sometimes entire days and nights) copying, collecting, and systematizing all of your writings, so that eventually I alone on earth would preserve a complete collection . . . of everything you have written . . ." During *Resurrection* "foreign publishers were becoming used to the idea that I'm your representative . . . In a word, I'm asking, Lev Nikolaevich, to maintain the existing agreement between us, to send all of your writings and copies of your letters 'in the first instance' directly to me." It was a "small prerogative," which naturally arose from Chertkov's dedicated service.[15] Tolstoy took almost two months to reply. Meanwhile, he had visitors from England: Alexander Konshin (a son of a textile factory owner and one of Chertkov's sponsors) and the followers Sulerzhitsky and Paul Bulanzhe. They told him that Chertkov was making money from the first publication of his writings.

But far from ending his business relationship with Tolstoy, Chertkov was enlarging his operations and driving out competitors. When Biryukov published a selection of Tolstoy's letters ahead of him, Chertkov at once complained to the writer about a violation of his rights. Allowed to handle Tolstoy's first editions in the past, Chertkov wanted to retain this privilege. Biryukov's publication deprived him of the opportunity to offer this same selection of Tolstoy's letters to popular periodicals in England and America.

Chertkov was forcing Tolstoy to choose: either he or Biryukov. Tolstoy's follower, biographer, and friend, Biryukov produced a journal in Switzerland to which the writer occasionally contributed articles. Chertkov continually complained that this journal provided "a needless competition" to his own periodical. But Biryukov was almost family to Tolstoy, having been engaged to Masha (before her marriage to Nikolai Obolensky in 1897.) Masha attempted to defy Chertkov, writing to him that she would be sending her father's letters on equal terms to all publishers. Tolstoy, knowing what Chertkov's reaction to this would be, tried to make peace: "I very much regret that Masha's letter has upset you; please, don't be angry with her and don't disapprove of her. And let's stop talking about this." He reassured Chertkov that he would continue to send him everything worthy of publication first thing and that he had no desires in this regard different from Chertkov's. "My attitude to you is . . . deeper than words," Tolstoy assured. However, his sympathy for Chertkov's publishing activity was diminishing because of the need to finance it.[16]

Masha, who had to apologize to appease Chertkov, later told Maude: "It is my father's weakness that he relies so much on Chertkov." When Maude included her remark in his biography of Tolstoy, Chertkov found out and demanded he delete the passage.[17] (Maude received a typewritten letter signed by Tolstoy and written in his name, but betraying Chertkov's style. Actually Chertkov kept blank sheets with Tolstoy's signature, still found today among his papers, and could type up any letter.) Maude would include Masha's remark in his 1930 edition of *The Life of Tolstoy*, along with Chertkov's profile.

Forced to compromise his loyalty to Biryukov, who had been involved in all his causes, including famine relief, Tolstoy stopped contributing to his journal in Switzerland. When Biryukov asked why, the writer replied that if he went on, it would be unpleasant to Chertkov. Tolstoy continued, "But you could say, why am I choosing Chertkov and not you—that's because you'd do more for Pasha Nikolaevna [Biryukov's wife] than for another, you'd be reluctant to deceive her expectations remembering all of those things she had done for you. That's how it is with me and Chertkov."[18] Biryukov's journal, *Free Thought*, ceased to exist in the fall of 1901. In spring, Tolstoy helped secure a loan for Chertkov's press: the money was donated by Kuzma Soldatenkov, a Moscow merchant and publisher.[19]

On March 10, in a letter to Chertkov, Tolstoy described his recent erotic dream. Chertkov's mother is reading aloud a sentimental German story. A priest and a deacon come in and put on their vestments, ready to begin a service. Chertkov is lying on a divan next to Tolstoy, and they all wait for his mother to finish her reading. But she goes on, and everyone feels awkward. Chertkov begins to say something to the priest, and Tolstoy is afraid that what he is about to say "might ruin you, deprive you of opportunity to return to Russia. And I'm . . . terribly sorry that I won't see you." At this moment Tolstoy woke up "with such pity and love for you."[20] Chertkov replied, "What you have written about me, touched me very much. I often see you in my dreams."[21] Earlier that year, in a rare display of genuine feeling, Chertkov wrote Tolstoy that, upon receiving his letter and a parcel, he shut himself in his room "to cry of my joy and love for you."[22] (Chertkov, who liked to express himself more ostentatiously, once wrote Tolstoy: "In the garden of my soul, waterfall fountains are beginning to run after a long drought."[23])

Tolstoy's dream, illuminating his intimacy with Chertkov, can be interpreted as a veiled reference to *War and Peace*. After joining the Masonic Temple, Pierre Bezukhov attempts to restrain his passions: he reads the Scriptures, shuns society, but is still sinning in his dreams. In one of them, he is lying in bed next to another Mason, his Benefactor: ". . . We were suddenly in my bedroom, where there was a double bed. He lay on the edge of it and I, as if burning with the desire to caress him, lay beside him. And he asked me: 'Tell me truly, what is your main predilection? Do you know it?"[24] In the same way, the exclusiveness of Tolstoy and Chertkov's faith inspired their physical attraction.

In *Resurrection* Tolstoy makes reference to homosexual love. The novel tells about a highly placed official, the head of a government department, who is deported to Siberia after his homosexuality is exposed. The case is said to have preoccupied all of Petersburg and was even discussed by senators. Opinions are divided as one senator says that homosexuality is a crime and another objects, "Why, where is the harm of it? I can show you a Russian book containing the project of a German writer, who openly proposes that it should not be considered a crime, and that men should be allowed to marry men . . ."[25] (Tolstoy was likely referring to the German writer Karl Heinrich Ulrichs, a pioneer of gay rights, who campaigned for sexual reform beginning in the 1860s.) In Siberia, the ex-government official is promoted to a local governor. Nekhlyudov meets him there, at a dinner given by the Governor General:

> He was plump, with thin, curly hair, soft blue eyes, carefully tended white hands with rings on the fingers, and a pleasant smile; and he was very stout in the lower part of his body. The master of the house valued this governor, because, surrounded by bribe-takers, he alone took no bribes. The mistress of the house, who was very fond of music and a very good pianist herself, valued him because he was a good musician and played duets with her. Nekhlyudov was in such good humor that even this man was not unpleasant to him, in spite of what he knew of his vices.[26]

Tolstoy's attitude to homosexuality is not easy to determine from this passage, especially that he had stated elsewhere that the sexual act inspired his disgust. But in his youthful diaries he discusses his attraction to men. In 1851, at twenty-three, he wrote: "I have never been in love with women . . . But I've often fallen in love with men . . ." In his youth Tolstoy was attracted to several men, including Dmitry Dyakov and Konstantin Islavin, Sophia's uncle.

> Of all these people I continue to love only Dyakov. For me, the main symptom of love is fear to offend or disappoint my beloved, simply fear. I was in love with men before I knew anything about the possibility of sodomy; but even after I learned about it, the thought about the possibility of copulation never came into my head . . . My love for Islavin has spoilt the entire 8 months of my life in Petersburg. Although unconsciously, I only cared about winning his love . . . I've always loved people who were cold towards me and only valued me . . . Beauty always had great influence over my choice; actually, Dyakov is one example; but I will never forget the night when we drove together from Pirogovo and I wanted to crawl under the blanket cover and kiss him and cry. There was also

sensuality in this feeling . . . but my imagination never drew pictures of physical love to which I have a horrible disgust.[27]

Tolstoy cared about winning Chertkov's love, was afraid to disappoint him, and was simply afraid of him. But he furiously denied Sophia's allegation that he and Chertkov had a homosexual relationship. Yet, Chertkov was his idol, to whom Tolstoy would continually sacrifice his other friendships, family ties, work, and principles.

As Tolstoy's close disciple, Chertkov could do no wrong. In July 1900, Tolstoy received a letter from Eliza Pickard, a Quaker and Chertkov's former employee. She complained about Chertkov's lack of accountability during the Doukhobor migration.[28] Tolstoy replied to Miss Pickard that it was pointless for others to tell him what they thought about Chertkov. "My opinion of him is formed and cannot change. It is founded on something much more than friendship."[29] (Tolstoy did not send this letter to Miss Pickard, but instead sent it to Chertkov.) The following year, the Quakers published "Account of Receipts and Expenditure," their audited report for the migration and the publishing of *Resurrection*. It revealed real problems, so in December 1901, Maude wrote an article exposing Chertkov's improprieties and failure to account for the funds. In addition he told about Chertkov hindering the work of the novel's translators and publishers.[30] Chertkov complained to Tolstoy that Maude was "relentlessly persecuting" him. He severed relations with Maude as he previously had with Kenworthy for accusing him of profiting from the cause.[31] When Maude sent a copy of his published article to Tolstoy, the writer replied: "I am very sorry you wrote it. You have thereby grieved and in no way strengthened the feeling of love—and that is the chief business of life—in the soul of Chertkov, a man near to you, but have on the contrary evoked in him an angry feeling . . . All considerations as to accounts and donations weigh as nothing in comparison with the infringement of love."[32]

This attitude suited Chertkov, who remained unaccountable for the money he made from Tolstoy's works. He gave vague promises to Tolstoy to stop selling his first publication rights: "Forgive me, dear friend, for upsetting you repeatedly in this regard . . . You'll be pleased to know that from now on, I decided, as a matter of principle, never to transfer the right for a first publication of your writings to anyone . . . Since I changed my attitude to money, it wouldn't be possible for me to receive payment for your writings; indeed, I haven't received any . . ." He would act "in full accordance with your views and wishes on the subject" in the future.[33]

Meanwhile, Chertkov tightened control over people close to Tolstoy, who were copying for him in Yasnaya. He managed to replace Masha with Galya's sister, Olga Dietrichs, who was married to Tolstoy's son, Andrei. In September, Chertkov found an even more reliable helper in Masha's husband, Obolensky, who promised to punctually send him copies of Tolstoy's diaries and letters.[34]

According to Maude, Chertkov had a true talent for obtaining free help from Tolstoy's sympathizers.[35] When Chertkov launched the Free Age Press to produce Tolstoy's works in English, his manager A. C. Fitifield worked there almost unpaid. During its heyday the Free Age Press issued a series of Tolstoy's articles, such as "Patriotism and Government," "Letters on War," "Thoughts on God," "Religion and Morality," and "Slavery of Our Time." Before Chertkov broke up with him, Maude translated Tolstoy's articles and contributed them to the Free Age Press gratis. But to be able to publish these articles elsewhere, Maude copyrighted his translations. Chertkov objected to this, demanding that all translators surrender copyright to his press. By doing so, he used Tolstoy's principles to his own advantage, as Maude points out:

> Tolstoy had renounced his rights in his own works, but had no desire to interfere with his English or other translators. Yet in England Chertkov, by a dexterous application of Tolstoy's 'principles,' endeavored to take from those who translated Tolstoy's new works, the control of their productions, even when, as in my case at that time, they were willing to let him have free use of their versions.[36]

Chertkov complained to Tolstoy that Louise Maude has copyrighted her translation of *Resurrection*, which in his view was a "regretful" violation of principle.[37] (Actually, Mrs. Maude had donated the fee from her translation to the Doukhobor Fund, so there was no contradiction with Tolstoy's principles.) Tolstoy felt obligated to defend Chertkov and, as a result, his relations with the Maudes, his best English translators, became strained. This happened at the time when Tolstoy received Maude's translations of his early prose, which delighted him: he read the volume with his *Sevastopol Sketches* and *Two Hussars* "as if it were something new that had been written in English."[38]

Explaining the unexplainable, why he needed Chertkov as an intermediary between himself and the publishing world, Tolstoy wrote to Maude: "I can't disappoint his expectations and hinder his work instead of helping him. My help in his work is limited to the fact that all my new writings . . . I distribute first of all through him, letting everybody, if they need to, make use of them afterwards as they please."[39]

Chertkov despotically insisted that Tolstoy should not send any of his works to Maude or his best French translator, Ilya Galperin-Kaminsky. Tolstoy had praised Galperin-Kaminsky's translation of *Resurrection*, but it was not commissioned by Chertkov, who dealt with another French translator. Resorting to blackmail, Chertkov advised Tolstoy not to trust Galperin-Kaminsky, who might be a good translator, but as a person was "outright dishonest."[40] Tolstoy was safe only with Chertkov and Galya who guarded his works from becoming the property of large publishing firms and were zealously "protecting your interests, so that no one could exploit the copyright, which you've relinquished."[41]

Yet, Chertkov's publications were often unpleasant and embarrassing to Tolstoy. For example, he insisted on publishing the parable "Walk in the Light, While There Is Light," of which Tolstoy could not hear without feeling ashamed. It was the very story on which Chertkov had "collaborated" with Tolstoy, having inserted the dialogues between a good Christian and a bad heathen. Chertkov was determined to produce it, despite Tolstoy's reluctance to have it published, while aware that "you're unhappy with it and almost renounce it . . ."[42]

Chertkov's periodical published extracts from Tolstoy's diaries, letters, and drafts: his thoughts on God, views on women, sex, etc. Upon reading his "Thoughts on God," Tolstoy wrote Chertkov that this "publication was premature." These thoughts "should be published after my death (not long). It's frightening to continue living with such a program."[43] In another letter, he admitted that he felt awkward reading Chertkov's compilation: "As if I'm showing off with my thoughts. One can only respectably do this from the grave."[44] More important, Chertkov's brochures did not represent Tolstoy's views and misinformed journalists and the public. When *La Revue Blanche* in France reprinted some pronouncements attributed to Tolstoy from Chertkov's brochure on sex, the writer published a refutation: "The opinions there attributed to me are grotesquely absurd, and are a careless, second-hand, and incorrect summary of a collection of articles and undated extracts put together and published by my friend, Vladimir Chertkov."[45]

But regardless of what Tolstoy felt about his publishing practices, Chertkov solicited his praise. Upon launching the Free Age Press, he nagged Tolstoy to write "a few words of approval" of its activity.[46] Tolstoy kept postponing the obligation, eventually submitting a paragraph of thanks to the manager of the Free Age Press, Fitifield. He thanked the press for publishing his works cheaply and making them widely accessible to the working masses.[47] This letter dissatisfied Chertkov, who sent Tolstoy a different version he composed. It emphasized that the Free Age Press alone did not profit from publishing Tolstoy's works and reproduced the most accurate versions of his writings, receiving them from the author, with whom the press maintained close personal contact.[48] Tolstoy was expected to copy this out, but the text struck him "like an advertisement. And it's so terribly disgusting . . ."[49] But Chertkov would not approve of anything that fell short of his expectations. In the end, Tolstoy wrote to endorse publications of the Free Age Press as "extremely neat and attractive," as well as cheap and widely accessible. He expressed his "heartfelt gratitude" to all employees of the press, "who in generous compliance with my objection to copyright of any kind" were issuing the English versions "of my writings absolutely free to all who may wish to make use of it."[50] This would allow Chertkov to claim his press was morally superior to other firms. But in fact, respected publishers did not reprint his translations precisely because they were not copyrighted.

Such small matters took time from Tolstoy's work on his new play, *The Living Corpse*, which he began in 1900. In September, his writing was disrupted with an assignment from Chertkov. Needing material for his periodical, he unearthed several unfinished articles and Galya was asking

Tolstoy to urgently revise them for publication. Tolstoy put aside his play to revise one of the drafts, called "Proclamation," which dealt with a familiar matter, that land should belong to those who work it. He could not deal with other drafts: "All this is old and badly expressed," he concluded. He allowed Chertkov to do "whatever you want" with these sketches.[51] Two weeks later, Galya sent Tolstoy another assignment. Tolstoy responded diplomatically: "You are positively not letting me amuse myself. Just as I began a frivolous drama, Galya sent these two articles. I'm very grateful for this."[52] Since he had mentioned the play, Chertkov wanted to publish it. Tolstoy replied he was not planning to complete it any time soon, maybe, never.[53] Because other publishers also wanted the play, he indeed left it unfinished, so as to avoid arguments.

The Living Corpse was based on an actual court case of a fake suicide, which Tolstoy learned from his friend Davydov, a local judge. Chekhov's play *Uncle Vanya* provided the inspiration. Tolstoy wanted to keep his work secret, but an alcoholic copyist he employed out of charity told the plot of *The Living Corpse* to a reporter he met in a pub.[54] Once the news appeared in the press, Tolstoy was besieged by editors, journalists, and theater directors asking to produce the play. He told everyone he was not planning to complete it. Meanwhile, Chertkov was reminding Tolstoy of his promise to send him all his new works "in the first instance." Chertkov heard a rumor that Tolstoy has completed his novellas *Hadji Murat* and *Father Sergius* and worried that the writer would send them to someone else. Tolstoy was struck with Chertkov's suspicion: ". . . Please have faith in me, for I not only trust you—no such word is possible between us . . . I'm simply glad that I have you and that you're doing the work, which we think is not ours, but *his* [God's]."[55]

In January 1901, Chertkov sent an exceptionally rude letter to Tolstoy. It arrived at the time when Tolstoy, in addition to being unwell, was grieving deaths in his family. (Three of the Tolstoys' grandchildren had died within one month, beginning in December 1900. Son Lev and his Swedish wife, Dora, née Westerlund, lost their son, Lyovushka. Tanya, who had married a family friend, Mikhail Sukhotin in 1899, gave a still birth. Coincidentally, Masha also delivered a stillborn baby in January.) Chertkov was attacking Tolstoy for his decision to support a literary journal, which his followers were about to launch in Russia. Since all Russia's publications were censored, dealing with them would involve an inadmissible compromise with the government. People who possess "some moral principles," Chertkov lectured, could not participate in a publication that is "subordinate to government demands." Chertkov called it "spiritual prostitution," an activity worse than running a brothel, since "spiritual prostitution is worse, more disgusting and harmful than physical."[56] Chertkov's letter was hypocritical, since he had willingly dealt with government censors in the past, considering himself to be an expert on the subject ("leave censorship to me," he wrote Tolstoy a decade earlier). However, this letter influenced Tolstoy to change his mind about participating in the journal. Chertkov never apologized for his rudeness even upon learning about the tragedies in Tolstoy's family. He maintained that he sent a "strict, but loving letter"; perhaps it was not at the right time, but he was right in essence.[57]

Chertkov had a poor reputation in the publishing world beyond Russia. His conflict over *Resurrection* with publisher Marx was not forgotten in Germany. In 1899, Marx had accused him of being "an impostor" who exploited Tolstoy's authority for personal gain. Reporting this to Tolstoy, Chertkov wrote that ever since Marx's allegation appeared in a respected Leipzig newspaper, which belonged to the union of publishers and booksellers, even "a mention of my name inspires not trust, but doubt . . ."[58] This is why Chertkov asked that Tolstoy send his own statement to the same German newspaper. As usual, Chertkov attached the text, which Tolstoy was to copy out by hand and dispatch to the newspaper. The text was familiar to Tolstoy: it was the statement Chertkov had him sign during the publishing of *Resurrection*. It authorized "my friend V. Chertkov" to be his representative with foreign publishers and translators. And it emphasized Chertkov's disinterested involvement and Tolstoy's "complete trust" in him. During the migration such a statement seemed to have been justified, but now Tolstoy had to use his authority simply to salvage his friend's reputation. As Tolstoy wrote Chertkov, signing this statement would be "horribly difficult and unpleasant." The text seemed to contradict his renunciation of copyright, especially the sentence, which Tolstoy deleted: *"I would not deal with anyone directly, but only through Chertkov."*[59] After a few revisions, Tolstoy still signed the statement and it was published on February 2, 1901.

The publishing world became convinced that Tolstoy had turned over his affairs to Chertkov.

At the end of January, an English newspaper reported that Tolstoy was seriously ill. Chertkov, with typical bluntness, asked Tolstoy to let him know whether "you feel the nearness of death." If Tolstoy was dying, Chertkov had to make urgent arrangements to visit Russia.[60] Tolstoy wrote he was feeling better: "I understand you want to come. Wait a while . . . I'm saying this despite the joy of seeing you."[61] Nonetheless, Chertkov applied for permission to make a short visit, but was refused.

On February 25, the front pages of newspapers across Russia printed the edict of Tolstoy's excommunication. Issued by the Holy Synod and signed by three metropolitans, it proclaimed that Tolstoy "has devoted his literary activity and the talent given him by God, to disseminating among the people teachings repugnant to Christ and the Church . . ."[62] Services to anathemize Tolstoy were held in churches across the country and newspapers were banned from publishing discussions. These measures further undermined the authority of the government institutions, of which the Synod was one, and of the official Church. The excommunication actually boosted Tolstoy's popularity: in fact, it was never so high. A contemporary wrote in his diary that there were two tsars in Russia, Nicholas II and Leo Tolstoy.[63]

Immediately upon Tolstoy's excommunication Sophia sent a letter of protest to the Holy Synod and the Metropolitans. Published by the *Church Gazette* and later widely reprinted, it was the first challenge by a woman to the heads of the Orthodox Church. Her letter received public acclaim, but Tolstoy reacted with indifference.

The government chose an unsuitable moment to attack him: there were widespread student disturbances in Petersburg, Kiev, and Moscow. Tolstoy received ovations when he went for walks. In Lubyanka Square, he met a large student march. They were protesting the government's draconian measure of sending student demonstrators to the army. Tolstoy was their champion: he was instantly recognized, and the crowd cheered: "Hail to the great man! Hurrah!" At the Wanderers' Exhibition, his portrait by Repin showing him at prayer in the forest was garlanded with flowers and applauded; four hundred people sent him a telegram from the exhibition.

There was a spirit of jubilation in the Tolstoys' Moscow house: when friends visited, the writer told them, "I positively decline to accept congratulations."[64] Tolstoy received baskets of flowers, telegrams, and letters from home and abroad. When deputations of women, students, and workers filled the yard around his house, Tolstoy advised against any violent action. He told all his visitors that people should unite together in love, not in enmity.

There were a few letters with death threats from extreme nationalists, but on the whole, public support was overwhelming. Tolstoy received a letter from employees of the Maltsev Glass Factory outside Moscow, who wrote: "You have shared the fate of many great people ahead of their time ... Let the hypocrite priests excommunicate you however they want. Russian people will always be proud, seeing you as their own . . ."[65] Tolstoy's "Reply to the Holy Synod's Edict" circulated in underground copies and was published by Chertkov in England. In it Tolstoy wrote: "I do not believe my faith to be the one indubitable truth for all time, but I see no other that is plainer, clearer, or answers better to all the demands of my reason and my heart. Should I find such a faith, I shall at once accept it; for God requires nothing but the truth."[66]

In early March, during protests in Petersburg, the governor ordered Cossacks to beat the crowd in Kazanskaya Square. After the clampdown Tolstoy wrote an "Appeal to the Tsar and His Chief Ministers." In it he argued that by suppressing demonstrations the government would not extinguish flames of unrest. The Tsar's position would be safe only if the government adopted measures to meet popular demands: equal rights for the peasants, liberty of education, freedom of conscience, and relaxation of administrative control. Earlier, he sent a letter to Nicholas II criticizing autocracy as a form of government that has long outlived itself.

In June 1901, Tolstoy became gravely ill with malaria and was not expected to live. The Russian interior minister instructed the police and administration across the country not to allow demonstrations and speeches in the event of Tolstoy's death. The Tolstoys received telegrams and letters from home and abroad inquiring about the writer's health. The French writer, Romain Rolland wrote that he read reports about Tolstoy's illness with despair, that Europe needed his intellect and sense of justice.[67] (The reports about the course of Tolstoy's illness were regularly published by

Chertkov, who received daily bulletins from Yasnaya.) There were also ongoing requests from Chertkov—to send him copies of all responses to the excommunication (this was unthinkable), to help secure an annual subsidy for his press (8,000 rubles), to let him publish *Hadji Murat* or "at least a small literary work of yours," to allow him to produce Tolstoy's complete collected works, etc.[68]

In late July, Countess Panina offered her estate in Gaspra, the Crimea, to help Tolstoy recuperate. Arriving in September, Tolstoy was amazed with the opulence of the palace, with its marble staircases, fountains, and parks. He wrote to everyone and to Chertkov that the place had every conceivable comfort of life and that he had never lived in such luxury. This mansion had previously belonged to Prince Golitsyn, minister of education for Alexander I.

In Gaspra, Tolstoy recuperated for a year, surrounded by doctors, his family, and friends. Here Sophia nursed him through pneumonia, which he developed in early 1902. Tolstoy had a stream of visitors and enjoyed stimulating discussions with writers Chekhov and Gorky, who came to see him from Yalta; he wrote articles on religion, the subject that concerned him most. In his essay "What Is Religion?" he defines faith as "a special state of the soul." Religion "is a relation, accordant with reason and knowledge, which man establishes with the infinite life surrounding him, and is such as binds his life to that infinity and guides his conduct."[69]

Tolstoy told his family that he should be asked, when he was dying, whether his faith remained unchanged. Perhaps, he began to doubt the validity of his ideals and principles. In any case, he thought that in his dying hour the truth would be revealed. He wrote Chertkov that if he still believed what he had, he would nod; if not, he would move his head from side to side; if he was hesitant, he would raise his eyes and head.[70] Ever pedantic, Chertkov inquired, what if Tolstoy could not move his eyes?[71]

Chertkov sent his recent photographic portrait, expecting that it would remind Tolstoy to write more often. Tolstoy thanked him for the picture, but replied that at his age, the German philosopher Kant took a year to write letters.[72] During his final decade, Tolstoy still wanted to accomplish many things, but knew there was little time. The great questions of life and his religious quest consumed him as before, and he recorded new fictional plots, which he knew he would never realize.

CHAPTER NINE

BEYOND THE GRAVE

"Our bond cannot be broken . . . by death."
—Tolstoy, in a letter to Chertkov[1]

"People will say: there's a man whom many people rate highly, and look what a scoundrel he was! So we ordinary people cannot be blamed for doing what he does. Seriously, when I began to recall all my life carefully and saw all its stupidity (actually stupidity) and vileness, I thought: what must other people be like, if I who am praised by many am such a stupid beast?"
—Tolstoy, in a letter to his biographer Biryukov[2]

In summer 1902, the Tolstoys returned to Yasnaya, where the writer would remain indefinitely. After a series of illnesses (malaria, followed by pneumonia in both lungs and typhus) he was too frail to be moved even to Moscow. Sophia attended to him with the help of doctors, and herself administered baths, medications, massages, and a special diet. A doctor was now constantly present in the house, which Tolstoy accepted on condition that he also provide medical help to local peasants.

Maude, who was working on the biography *The Life of Tolstoy*, visited in August. By then, Tolstoy was able to take two-hour walks, but returned exhausted. Maude would recall this visit to Yasnaya as one of the most enjoyable and stimulating events of his life:

> I cannot adequately describe the peaceful yet animated atmo-
> sphere of that home, crowded with vital interests, throbbing
> with life, overrun with visitors, but so influenced by the high
> and earnest tone of the great man whom they all looked up to,
> that I felt it more bracing and more peaceful than any circle
> I was ever in, and I see that, on leaving, I jotted down in my
> notebook: 'A remarkable and kindly family apart from Tol-
> stoy's genius . . . '[3]

While in Yasnaya, Maude met other visitors, such as Vladimir Stasov, head of the Petersburg's Imperial Public Library and art critic, who had supplied Tolstoy with historical materials for *Hadji Murat*; musician Sergei Taneev, who performed his new compositions; sculptor Ilya Ginzburg, who was modeling Tolstoy's bust, and Mikhail Stakhovich, a statesman and family friend, who was seeking Tolstoy's advice on a letter to the Tsar about religious tolerance. A Jewish clerk came to discuss some passages in the Talmud, which Tolstoy had read in Hebrew.

With Maude, Tolstoy could not avoid a conversation about Chertkov. Tolstoy said that Chertkov was hard to get along with, but that he "had done so much for the common cause and for him personally, that he could not but support him." By then, Chertkov had such influence with Tolstoy that it would not be possible for a biographer not to write about the relationship. Moreover, he would get hold of the manuscript "and if I did not confine myself to what Chertkov approved of, severe conflict would be inevitable." Maude postponed completing the biography until after Tolstoy's death, when he would be free to say what he wanted about Chertkov's character and methods. As a result, Biryukov was the one to produce an authorized biography, which presents an "official" view of Tolstoy's doctrine and his following; it had Chertkov's approval.

Tolstoy felt that while his body was wasting away, his spiritual life was growing. He no longer believed that life ended with death, imagining a transition: his expanding spirit would destroy the physical shell and be liberated from the body.[4] Chertkov discussed Tolstoy's illnesses and imminent death in a typically pragmatic way: the writer's experiences would yield new material and "you will share your spiritual acquisition with us."[5] Tolstoy was "an old man standing with one foot in the grave"[6] (here he repeated the writer's words about himself). He continued, cheerfully, that "physical death" would bring Tolstoy "respite and a welcome change" and would "vastly strengthen our spiritual union."[7]

Chertkov was beginning to enjoy some recognition and fame of his own. He was invited to give talks about Tolstoy. In Bournemouth, where he spoke to a large audience, people would begin to applaud at the mere mention of Tolstoy's name. An enthusiastic ovation broke out when Tolstoy's portrait was placed on stage.[8] Chertkov also received telegrams from newspapers requesting that he write Tolstoy's obituary or an article.

While still in the Crimea, Tolstoy wrote a few articles for Chertkov's periodical. Among them were two pieces on Christians and military service, with such unimaginative titles as "A Soldier's Leaflet" and "An Officer's Leaflet." After reading them, Chertkov reported his and Galya's reaction: they were "excited, moved, delighted."[9] (Chertkov had used these exact words when describing his and Galya's impression of *Resurrection*.)

As Tolstoy's editor, Chertkov continued to enjoy carte blanche. He usually advised the writer about changes, believing that "it would be inadmissible on my part to become some kind of an obstacle to free expression of your thoughts."[10] Chertkov's stylistic changes, even minor, would obfuscate the meaning of Tolstoy's sentences. (Tolstoy typically rejected such revisions.) When publishing the article "What Is Religion?" Chertkov asked to exclude an entire chapter, which discussed religion and science. Tolstoy did not agree, and the chapter remained. As for minor revisions, Chertkov had greater freedom.

His publishing affairs did not go well: he periodically informed Tolstoy that his press was on the brink of financial ruin. Shortly after excommunication, Tolstoy received a desperate letter from Chertkov, who wrote that unless money was found within two weeks, his press would have to be liquidated.[11] This time, by exaggerating his circumstances Chertkov managed to get Tolstoy's permission to produce his collected works. He expected that the profitable project would finally make his press self-sustainable.

However, the following year, he informed Tolstoy that publishing his collected works was moving along slowly for lack of donations.[12] Despite Tolstoy's exclusive permissions and the support of the wealthy Konshin family, Chertkov was perennially short of funds. He now wanted a special subsidy to publish Tolstoy's translation of the four Gospels. It was unclear where all the money was going. Around this time, Galya described their near destitution (no money for the dentist) to the manager of the Chert-kovs' estates, Alexander Ertel. (A gifted writer, Ertel had also followed in his father's footsteps as manager of the Chertkovs' estates. Ertel Sr. had supervised the vast estates of their uncle Pashkov.) Now that income from the family estates was diminishing, Ertel advised selling the land, which was worth one million rubles.[13]

Around this time, Chertkov quarreled with the efficient manager of the Free Age Press, Fitifield, and his resignation led to a gradual decline of the production of English editions. Later, Mrs. Fitifield published a sketch, depicting Chertkov during a temper tantrum when his speech resembled "a mountain torrent" and he "allowed himself to say whatever anger and contempt suggested to him."[14] Tolstoyans, who also witnessed his mood swings and rages, believed he suffered from mental illness. Chertkov's employees would not stay long. His inability to maintain relationships and his persecution complex can be gauged from a typical letter to Tolstoy, in which Chertkov writes that his soul is full of "anger for all the unfairness, insults and lies, which I have to bear."[15] After reading Chertkov's report about the conflict with Fitifield, Tolstoy reminded him that relationships are more important than practical affairs.[16]

Chertkov was asking for yet another favor. He wanted Tolstoy's official permission to publish his private correspondence of many years.[17] As usual, Chertkov included the text for the permission, which Tolstoy had to copy with his own hand. Because Tolstoy addressed these letters to other people, Chertkov wanted a document to protect him from litigation.[18]

The request was unpleasant to Tolstoy, who did not want his private letters published during his life, so he tried to decline. He felt these letters were personal, not to be read by the public. If Chertkov insisted on publishing them, he would have to request consent from the people with whom Tolstoy corresponded. About a year later, when Tolstoy forgot all about it, he received a twenty-page letter from Chertkov arguing the significance of publishing his private correspondence. Frightened with Chertkov's contentious tone and wishing to put the matter behind him, Tolstoy signed the needed permission.

But this did not save him from the endless flow of Chertkov's letters, in which he reiterated his exclusive privilege of publishing Tolstoy's first editions. His persistent rhetoric projected the same message that Tolstoy was safe only with Chertkov, who protected the integrity of his no-copyright principle. Chertkov exaggerated the dangers of having Tolstoy's writings produced by "various commercial hawks," who only cared about squeezing more profit.[19] In fall 1902, interrupting Tolstoy's work on *Hadji Murat*, Chertkov drew him into another conflict with the Maudes. Because Louise Maude's translation of *Resurrection* was copyrighted, Chertkov refused to include it in the collected works and instead decided to procure a new one. Maude informed Tolstoy that Chertkov had negotiated the new translation with an amateur interpreter just because she would not copyright her work.[20] Nonetheless, Tolstoy backed Chertkov. Actually, none of these arguments about the copyright interested him: he simply wanted an end to the conflict.

"So little time is left, and so much it seems to me that I need and want to say, but I waste it [the time] so idly," Tolstoy wrote at seventy-six.[21] Escaping into the world of ideas, Tolstoy contemplated the importance of increasing love among people. In the Gospel from Matthew, Jesus speaks to his disciples on the Mount of Olives about the signs of the end of the world: "For nation shall rise against nation, and kingdom against kingdom: and there shall be famines, and pestilences, and earthquakes . . ."[22] And "lastly, as of the greatest calamity, that love in people will grow cold."[23]

Hadji Murat was Tolstoy's last fictional masterpiece and the novella he cared about most. Beginning in 1896, he worked on it for over a decade and was protective of the manuscript, always keeping it in his desk. He still occasionally revised it in 1910, during his final year, but even then maintained it was uncompleted. Over the years, Chertkov had nagged him to publish the novella but as long as he continued to polish it, Tolstoy could refuse publication. In 1902, when he finished the draft, Chertkov immediately requested a copy. Tolstoy reluctantly allowed him to have it, but insisted that publishing it was unthinkable. That same year, in summer, Tolstoy put *Hadji Murat* aside to write a proclamation, "To the Working People," for Chertkov's periodical.

Trying to explain why it took so long for Tolstoy to write "his beloved *Hadji Murat*" Sophia commented: "In my view, artistic works always demanded his full tranquility, both physical and spiritual. Without it his work would not flow." Over the years, there were fewer and fewer opportunities for peaceful work, she remarked.[24]

The novella drew from Tolstoy's experiences of the war in the Northern Caucasus, in which he participated as a young man. Russia's attempt to subjugate the Muslim tribes met with fierce resistance in Chechnya and Dagestan, which resulted in a protracted war of four decades. Shamil, the imam who united the Muslim tribes, led the anti-Russian resistance in the name of "hazavat," or jihad.

When in 1851, at twenty-three, Tolstoy arrived in Chechnya, the war entered its fourth decade.[25] In December, Tolstoy witnessed a major event when Shamil's bravest and most popular commander, Hadji Murat, fell out with his leader and switched to the Russian side. Tolstoy was in Tiflis (Tbilisi) precisely at the time when Hadji Murat arrived to meet with the Russian authorities. Tolstoy, however, did not see him. Describing the event, which occupied everyone in the Northern Caucasus, Tolstoy wrote his brother, Sergei Nikolaevich, that Hadji Murat, the second man after Shamil and the most skillful and fearless warrior in all of Chechnya, "behaved basely" by switching sides.[26] For the Russians Hadji Murat's participation was important, but they also mistrusted him.

Decades later, Tolstoy saw the complexity and tragedy of Hadji Murat's situation. He was caught between the two autocratic leaders, the imam, and the Russian emperor. While researching the novella, Tolstoy interviewed people who had met this legendary commander and realized that he was not free to choose sides. After Shamil had killed his brothers, it fell upon Hadji Murat to avenge their blood. In the novella, Hadji Murat promises the Russians to defeat Shamil, but asks that they first help him rescue his family, which the imam held hostage. But the Russians procrastinate, suspecting that Hadji Murat might switch sides again. After failing to secure support for his family, Hadji Murat escapes to the mountains; he is pursued by the Russian units and killed in a battle. His head is severed from the body by his tribal enemy who had also switched to the Russian side.

Aside from Hadji Murat's character and fate, Tolstoy wanted to depict "the psychology of despotism."[27] His idea was to show two poles of absolute power, the Asian and the European models, the imam versus the Russian emperor. Tolstoy collected information about the two protagonists, Imam Shamil and Nicholas I, and read numerous published and unpublished sources. With the help of librarians, who delivered archival materials to Yasnaya, Tolstoy was able to access documents that acquainted him with the Tsar's routine, love life, character, and intrigues. Tolstoy also examined hundreds of sources to understand Nicholas I's domestic and foreign policy. He even considered writing a separate novel about Nicholas I, whose policies illustrated "what I write about state power."[28] The strategy in the Caucasus was establishing domination through oppression and forceful conversion of ethnic minorities.

Tolstoy read archival documents illuminating the decisions the Tsar would make on a single day. The chapter about Nicholas I lists several of his verdicts. The Tsar orders a student to run a caning gauntlet of one thousand men, twelve times. This was death by torture, skinning this man alive. Nicholas I also decides on a similar punishment for mutinous peasants who refuse to convert to Orthodoxy. Parallelism between the two tyrants is achieved when Imam Shamil determines the fate of Hadji Murat's wives, mother, and son. The imam orders the boy be blinded and the women sent to the villages to be raped.

Tolstoy invested years researching the politics and culture of the Caucasus, revealing in the novella that Russia's official policy involved deliberate and systematic destruction of the minorities. Aside from regular raids on the Chechen villages, soldiers were ordered to fell forests and destroy food supplies to deprive the locals of their means of survival. Tolstoy describes a raid, which he had witnessed as a young man: Russian soldiers burn wheat fields, houses, beehives, fruit orchards, and poison a well. They kill a boy with a bayonet and desecrate a mosque—acts that inspire in the locals a feeling "stronger than hatred. It was not hatred, but a refusal to recognize these Russian dogs as human beings, and such loathing, disgust, and bewilderment before the absurd cruelty of these beings, that the wish to exterminate them, like the wish to exterminate rats, venomous spiders, and wolves, was as natural as the sense of self-preservation."[29]

Tolstoy found the key to the character of Hadji Murat through a metaphor. In 1896, on a walk in Yasnaya, he spotted a cotton thistle with a striking maroon flower. He wanted to pluck the flower for his bouquet, but the hard stem refused to yield. This brought back the memory of the war in the Caucasus. "'What energy!' I thought. 'Man has conquered everything, destroyed millions of plants, but this one still does not surrender.' And I remembered an old story from the Caucasus, part of which I saw, part of which I heard from witnesses, and part of which I imagined to myself.'"[30]

Hadji Murat fascinated Tolstoy with his religious fanaticism: he intended to show the "deception by faith."[31] As well, Tolstoy was interested in the changeability of human nature: ". . . The same man is now a villain, now an angel, now a wise man, now an idiot, now a strong man, now the most impotent of creatures . . . That's the way to show Hadji Murat: as a husband, a fanatic, etc."[32]

Tolstoy had volunteers helping him collect information in Russia and in the Caucasus. But while many felt privileged "to find materials for our dear writer," Tolstoy doubted his project's importance and even called the novella "silly *Hadji Murat.*" As a man of religion, he was "ashamed" to write fiction for his own "amusement." The struggle in his heart is apparent from his words to daughter Tanya: "The entire time, while I was writing *Hadji Murat,* I felt ashamed of it, but now, as I finished [drafting] it, I want to go on doing artistic work." He also told daughter Masha that it was shameful to revise the novella: he was standing "at the edge of the grave" and should have more appropriate thoughts. But the novella drew him irresistibly. "I will be doing it on the sly from myself," he concluded.[33] When it was read to a gathering of family and friends, Tolstoy was split between his desire to know their impression and his need to moralize. He emerged at the end of the reading, to say that the novella was "a piece of trash." To Sukhotin's question, "So, why have you written it?" Tolstoy replied, "But it's not ready yet. You came to my kitchen and naturally, there are cooking fumes and it stinks."[34] When during his last years, Biryukov asked what he was writing, Tolstoy whispered, as if admitting to a sin, that he was revising *Hadji Murat*.[35]

In Russia, the novella appeared in 1912, after the writer's death, in Chertkov's three-volume edition of Tolstoy's previously unpublished works. Chertkov himself dealt with censors at the very top, sending it to the Department of Press Affairs as well as the Ministry of the Imperial Court and the Tsar. Naturally, the parts critical of Nicholas I, the great-grandfather of the Tsar, were eliminated. Nicholas II communicated to Chertkov his wish to personally censor Tolstoy's works. (This was an obsession with the Russian tsars, ever since Nicholas I himself censored the work of Alexander Pushkin. Alexander III, Nicholas II's father, had also aspired to become Tolstoy's censor.)

Chertkov published the uncensored version of *Hadji Murat* in the West. As the executor of Tolstoy's will, he presided over publications in other languages. Maude received a contract from Chertkov's agency, Curtis Brown, Ltd., to make an English translation. Maude later discovered that the contract took away his copyright. The American publisher, L. C. Page & Co., informed him that they had purchased the copyright of his version from the executor of Tolstoy's will, Chertkov.[36]

❖

In spring 1903, during a Jewish pogrom in Kishinev (Chişinău, now the capital of Moldova), then a part of the Russian Empire, fifty people were killed, many more injured, and seven hundred houses looted and destroyed. The Jewish writer Sholem Aleichem (the pen name of Solomon Rabinovich) asked Tolstoy to contribute his prose to a Yiddish anthology they were producing for the benefit of the victims. On May 6, Tolstoy wrote Aleichem: "The terrible crime perpetrated in Kishinev made a painful impression on me . . . We recently sent a collective letter from Moscow to the mayor of Kishinev expressing our feelings about this terrible affair." This letter, from Russia's intellectuals, for which Tolstoy suggested the text, expressed condolences to the victims of violence, horror for the brutal actions of the Russian people, and disgust towards those who incited the mob. Having first learned about the tragic events from a brief newspaper report, Tolstoy correctly assumed that the true culprit of the terrible crime was the Russian government along with fanatical clergy and a gang of corrupt officials. He was bewildered by the actions of the beastly mob of so-called Christians and felt disgust towards the educated people who had incited the violence.[37]

The pogroms were not only tolerated by the government, but in fact organized by the Petersburg Police Department and the interior ministry, in conjunction with the local authorities. They began on a mass scale in the early 1880s, under the nationalist Tsar Alexander III. The goal was to keep minorities in submission. During several days of rioting in Kishinev the police did not interfere, allowing the mobs to kill and rape, and burn Jewish property.

The riots began on April 19, Easter Sunday, when mobs stormed Jewish businesses and homes. At the Easter service a priest spoke about blood libel, claiming that the Jews use the blood of Christian babies for preparing matzo during Passover. Prior to the pogrom the secret police distributed anti-Semitic proclamations. The police department had a secret printing shop where such literature was mass produced. Captain M. Komissarov, who was in charge of printing services, said they could organize a pogrom on any scale—for ten or ten thousand people.

General Dmitry Trepov, then the head of the Moscow police, was actively involved in organizing the pogroms in Kishinev and elsewhere: local authorities consulted him directly. In 1905, Trepov's role was exposed by a representative of the Russian Duma, Prince Sergei Urusov, who publicly called Trepov "*a pogromshchik* by conviction."[38] Chertkov maintained his relationship with Trepov until his friend's death in 1906.

In 1903, Tolstoy contributed three stories for the Yiddish collection edited by Aleichem: "Esarhaddon," "Three Questions," and "Work, Death, and Illness." In September, he informed Chertkov that the stories would be published for the benefit of the victims in Russian and Yiddish. He was hoping that Chertkov would not interfere with the success of the edition.[39] When Aleichem asked Maude to translate these stories into English, Tolstoy again asked Chertkov to avoid conflict: "I'm confident that you would not object to his [Maude's] translation . . . and this matter would not trigger the worsening of your relations with him."[40]

Tolstoy's request fell on deaf ears. Chertkov effectively impeded Maude's version by informing Aleichem that he himself would translate the stories, for which, he claimed, he had Tolstoy's permission. To Tolstoy, Chertkov sent a forceful letter, again using the principle of no-copyright to defeat Maude. He argued that Tolstoy's principle of no-copyright was established once and for all:

> Dear LN, there's a sad truth in your words that since you renounced your copyright you always anticipate trouble when publishing your new work. But what can be done: apparently, this is one of the trials you're destined to suffer . . . I have to suffer even more, having to implement your decision that concerns renouncing your literary property. . .[41]

Chertkov insisted that Tolstoy himself inform Maude that the project was taken away from him. The disciple did not relent until Tolstoy sent a telegram to Maude asking him to stop translating the stories.[42] "Your loyalty . . . is one of the greatest joys of my life," mused Chertkov in a letter to Tolstoy earlier that year. "Without boasting and false modesty, I feel that I deserve your trust . . . And if one day someone, somewhere, would express dissatisfaction with my handling of your writings, this may happen only because of personal jealousy . . ."[43]

Chertkov was now establishing unilateral control over publishing Tolstoy's new works in Russia. Earlier that year, Tolstoy gave his story "Three Deaths" for inclusion in the *Cycles of Reading*, his inspirational calendars with tales and wise sayings for every day, produced by Intermediary. However, Chertkov would not allow Intermediary to publish the story. In a letter to Tolstoy, he argued that it had been earlier placed "at my full disposal." Chertkov also informed him that his English agent was already negotiating the first publication of "Three Deaths" with periodicals abroad and that he had his plans for publishing the story in Russia.[44] Publication of even a minor story was now out of Tolstoy's hands.

Around this time, Chertkov advised Tolstoy on what to write next. To persuade him to go back to parables and moralistic stories, he used the same argument, which never failed to impress Tolstoy, that it was what people "need most." Chertkov explained that in Tolstoy's decline, it was a manageable project. To illustrate how little effort it required, he resorted to a metaphor: producing parables was like picking ripe fruit. Tolstoy would merely touch it with his fingertips, the fruit would fall "and would be ready for our consumption."[45] Tolstoy replied he had no energy to write fiction.

Around this time, Tolstoy jotted in his diary that he wanted to write a novel about Nicholas I, "about his ignorance and self-assurance, and about what a terrible thing it is that people of inferior spiritual strength can influence and even control people of superior strength."[46] He still dreamt of writing a sequel to *Resurrection*, in which his hero, Nekhlyudov, joins an agricultural commune: "His work, exhaustion, reawakening aristocratic habits, temptation by a woman, fall, mistakes, and all this against a backdrop of a Robinson commune."[47] And he was planning to resume his memoir, the project he believed important. Time was running out, and Tolstoy sensed the pressure to accomplish more, and his inability to realize the many projects and plots. In January 1904, he remarked: "Health is good, but death is near."[48]

Early in 1904, Japan launched a sudden attack on the Russian Far Eastern fleet. For the next eighteen months Tolstoy closely watched the events of the war, which would have disastrous consequences for Russia and bring heavy casualties to both sides. On January 27, he observed in his diary:

> The war, and hundreds of arguments about why it has come about, what it means, what will result from it, etc. Everyone is arguing about it, from the Tsar to the lowest trooper. And apart from arguments about what results the war will have for the whole world, they will all have to face the argument about what must *my, my, my* attitude be to the war? But nobody is arguing in this way.[49]

Tolstoy made a powerful indictment of war in the article "Bethink Yourselves!" It was published by newspapers across Europe: "Again there is war!.. Men who are separated from each other by thousands of miles—Buddhists whose law forbids the killing not only of men but even of animals, and Christians professing a law of brotherhood and love . . . seek one another out on land and sea like wild beasts, to kill, torture, and mutilate one another in the cruelest possible way."[50]

The siege of the main Russian naval base, Port Arthur, its defense and surrender brought back Tolstoy's experiences of the Crimean War and the siege of Sevastopol. The Russian commander surrendered the port to the Japanese without consulting his officers and despite having three months' provisions and adequate supplies of ammunition. Tolstoy spoke about this incident and the destruction of the Russian Baltic Fleet as some of the most painful events in his life.

Russia's defeat in the war intensified popular discontent and produced a surge in revolutionary activity. Tolstoy was convinced that a revolution could not bring liberation to the masses. Once in power, revolutionaries would establish just another corrupt and violent government. As he would write in "A Letter to a Revolutionary," throughout history revolutions helped replace one despotic government with another, while the situation of the working people remained the same.[51] In another piece, Tolstoy compared Russia's revolutionary activity with the sport of hunting dangerous animals. Revolutionaries were drawn to their sport with a sense of danger, much like hunters of lions.[52] Chertkov argued that Tolstoy's analogy between revolutionary activity and hunting could offend a revolutionary worker: "This little article produced more doubt and unease in me than any other piece."[53] Tolstoy agreed not to publish it, since "it would be too painful to provoke people's hatred before dying."[54]

As if to prepare Tolstoy for what would come next, Chertkov philosophized: ". . . Life is not about freedom, but about submission—submission to one's own will or to god's will or to what we recognize as the highest human law. And for the most part we are guided not by our own free choice, but by pressure from one of these sources."[55] In May 1904, Charles Briggs, a Unitarian priest and Chertkov's part-time secretary, arrived in Yasnaya. Briggs delivered Chertkov's questionnaire, which Tolstoy was expected to read secretly from his family. The matter was of great importance to Chertkov: he needed to know whom Tolstoy would appoint as his literary heir. His questions suggested that he should choose none other than Chertkov. The paper could well have been composed by a notary: it referred to Tolstoy's death in every clause:

1. Do you wish your statement in *The Russian Gazette* of September 16, 1891 [of renouncing copyright] to remain in force both now and *after your death*?
2. Who do you wish should have the final decision about problems connected with the editing and publishing of your writings *posthumously* . . . ?
3. Do you wish that the written authority given to me by you as your only foreign representative should remain in force after *your death* . . . ?
4. Do you put *at my complete disposal* even *after your death* all your manuscripts and papers which I have received and shall receive from you before *your death* . . . ?
5. Do you wish that I should be given the opportunity of looking through in the original all your manuscripts . . . which may be in the hands of Sofya Andreevna or members of your family *after your death*?[56]

Tolstoy did not care what would happen to his papers after he died. He replied in two letters. In the first, he gave the answers Chertkov had wanted him to provide. He entrusted sorting his papers to Chertkov because of "your great love for me and your moral sensibility" and because of "our complete agreement over a religious understanding of life."[57] Tolstoy slightly deviated from Chertkov's script by mentioning that he wanted him to consult Sophia about publishing his works. This "official" letter was meant to posterity and did not express what Tolstoy felt upon receiving Chertkov's brutal questionnaire.

This is why Tolstoy also wrote a genuine reply, in which he did express his feelings and thoughts. Addressing Chertkov alone, it was meant to remain confidential:

I won't hide from you, my dear friend Vladimir Grigorievich, that the letter you sent with Briggs was unpleasant to me. Oh, those practical affairs. It was not unpleasant that my death or my overrated and worthless papers were discussed. It was unpleasant because there's in it a kind of entrapment, coercion, distrust, and meanness toward people. And I feel . . . I'm being drawn into doing something unpleasant, which may generate evil. I've written answers to your questions and I'm sending them. But if you'll write that you've torn them up, burnt them, I'll be very pleased."[58]

Tolstoy apparently expected that Chertkov might be influenced by his message of goodness and give up his ambition to possess his manuscripts. It was a moment when Tolstoy could prevent an ugly struggle over his legacy, which Chertkov generated during his final years. He could reply decisively and deter Chertkov's advance. But as usual, he gave Chertkov freedom of choice. The disciple did not burn Tolstoy's forced answers. Instead, he suppressed Tolstoy's genuine reply, hiding it in a folder with "secret" inscribed on the cover. This letter was only discovered among Chertkov's papers in 1961.[59]

Back in 1903, something of an inventory was conducted in Yasnaya at Chertkov's insistence. The writer's archive at his house was checked against the list of manuscripts Chertkov kept in England, so that not a single paper would get past him.[60] Chertkov was establishing total control over the writer's legacy—beyond the grave.

Chertkov was one of those people whom Tolstoy aptly describes in his memoir as a "wild" type, the ones who are never satisfied with what they've got. Interestingly, Tolstoy's father, Nikolai Ilyich, was also attracted to such characters, becoming attached to the brothers Petrusha and Matyusha, his former serfs, whom he had freed. The brothers accompanied Nikolai Tolstoy on hunting expeditions and he showered them with favors and money. Later, the shady circumstances around the sudden death of Tolstoy's father generated gossip that these same brothers had poisoned and robbed him. Tolstoy thought this was not impossible. There were cases when former serfs, whom their masters had freed and who suddenly rose to positions of power, would later kill their benefactors.[61]

❖

The year 1905 began with Bloody Sunday. On January 9, a peaceful demonstration of Petersburg workers with their families marched to the Winter Palace carrying church banners, icons, and the Tsar's portraits. They were petitioning the Tsar to end the war and grant an eight-hour working day. The marchers were led by Father George Gapon, a priest, who was also a secret police collaborator.

The police department, warned of the march, had alerted Nicholas II and his family to leave the capital. The workers expected to meet the Tsar, but he, in fact, was outside Petersburg in Tsarskoe Selo. Although the Tsar was safe and the march was peaceful, troops were called in to defend the Winter Palace. When the demonstrators disregarded orders to stop, the Tsar's uncle, Grand Duke Vladimir Alexandrovich, who commanded the Petersburg garrison, ordered the troops to fire at the crowd. Over a hundred people were slaughtered, among them women and children.[62] The massacre dealt a fatal blow to the regime. In response, half a million workers went on strike. From 1905 to 1907, a wave of political terrorism, peasant unrest, and mutinies swept the empire.

A strong man was needed to restore order, and General Trepov, who was such a man, was appointed as governor general of Petersburg and assistant minister of the interior. As a favorite of Nicholas II, Trepov became a virtual dictator. His power extended far beyond the capital, recounts Witte: "It was Trepov who in fact controlled the Ministry of the Interior." Also appointed a commandant of the Imperial Court, Trepov moved to the Winter Palace. "It was not long before Trepov had the Emperor under his thumb . . ."[63] According to Witte, who became Russia's first prime minister in 1905, Trepov Jr. advised Nicholas II on both domestic and foreign affairs. At the height of his career, Trepov Jr. controlled the army and political police; he was relentless in crushing opposition and persecuting minorities. Today, he is best remembered for his infamous instruction to the police forces during the social unrest of 1905, "Do not spare the bullets."

With Trepov's rise to the top, Chertkov was allowed to visit Russia. On May 9, 1905, he crossed the Russian border. At the station of Verzhbolovo[64], passengers had to disembark to face Russian customs and have their baggage searched. In 1871, when Dostoevsky returned to Russia from Dresden, his baggage was subjected to a meticulous search by officials because he was a former political convict. An exile, Chertkov was entering Russia during revolutionary unrest. A senior gendarme officer, a "phenomenally stupid man," told Chertkov that he had instructions from Petersburg to search him. What happened next, Chertkov describes in a humorous letter to Galya, beginning it with the words: "I will now tell you about my triumphant arrival in Russia, of which you may have already learned from the Russian newspapers..." Chertkov followed the gendarme officer to a spacious room, which looked like an entrance to the Tsar's waiting rooms. He was asked whether he carried any papers. Sitting on a chair, with two gendarme officers standing before him, Chertkov replied that he refused to participate in the activity, which he regarded as an evil act of coercion, and refused to answer the questions of the gendarmes. The officers proceeded to unpack his trunks and to search Chertkov. "They found nothing, except a few letters from Trepov concerning my arrival, which I deliberately kept in my pocket." Realizing their mistake, the gendarme officers returned Chertkov's papers, along with a socialist proclamation, which he also kept in his pocket. But Chertkov's article about Tolstoy's anarchism, he was told, had to be first sent to the Petersburg Police Department. After shaking hands with the senior gendarme, Chertkov told him that he had nothing against him personally, "but your activity makes me feel deeply ashamed." In Petersburg, Chertkov met with Trepov, who "was outraged that I was subjected to a search after he said he took personal responsibility for me." Concluding his letter to Galya, Chertkov wrote that Trepov "was very willing to take any requests from me on behalf of others, so if any of our friends need something, *now is the moment* . . ." Trepov offered to extend the duration of Chertkov's visit, but "I refused. I don't want . . . to stay away from home longer than the agreed month."[65]

On May 24, Chertkov was arriving in Yasnaya by an evening train. Everyone went outside to meet him. Tolstoy walked away from the rest further into an alley, to greet Chertkov separately. Doctor Makovistky, now staying permanently with the family, knew that Tolstoy was excited: he hasn't seen Chertkov for eight years. "L.N. was moved, perhaps, he cried," remarks Makovitsky, who was keeping detailed notes of all events and conversations in Yasnaya. His perennial scribbling annoyed Tolstoy, so Makovitsky, trying to be unobtrusive, learned to write with his hand in his pocket where he kept small pencils and paper. His *Yasnaya Polyana Notes* would yield four sizable volumes.

Makovitsky documented Chertkov's arrival and his conversations with Tolstoy and others. Chertkov said that his mother had attained permission for him to visit Russia. He mentioned the search on the border (but not the instance when Trepov's letters and provocative article on socialism were found in his pocket). He told about meeting Trepov in Petersburg: he came to inquire whether he could return to Russia for good. Trepov suggested that Chertkov should file an official application. Chertkov replied that since he did not recognize government authority he would not be applying. Tolstoy asked Chertkov about his relationship with Trepov. Chertkov described Trepov as a "truthful man," who at one time sympathized with Tolstoy's views. Now, Trepov believed that his violent measures against revolutionaries were justified.[66]

Tolstoy told Makovitsky that he was happy to see Chertkov, who "changed little," except that he has grown heavier. During the ten days of his stay, Chertkov played chess with Tolstoy and joined him for swims. He complimented Tolstoy, saying that he played chess like a true Christian by trying to accommodate his partner: "You reveal your plans and give advice."[67] On June 4, when Chertkov was leaving, there was an emotional farewell and Tolstoy wept. A few days later, Tolstoy wrote in his diary that he had felt very good with Chertkov, beyond expectations.[68]

Chertkov's visit brought back Tolstoy's memories of "the first period of our closeness."[69] Recently, they also became related. Tolstoy's son, Andrei, and Galya's sister, Olga Dieterichs, had two children, Sonya and Ilyushok. Tolstoy's grandchildren were Chertkov's nephew and niece. The writer kept Chertkov's portrait with Ilyushok by the armchair in his study.[70] Earlier, in a letter to Chertkov, Tolstoy intimated: ". . . I looked at your portrait with Ilyushok, and remembered you so vividly and with love, that I wanted to write to you: simply to tell you that I value our friendship and spiritual closeness."[71] Tolstoy never forgot the impression of his first meeting with Chertkov, two decades earlier, when his life was illuminated with newly found faith. In June, remembering Chertkov's recent visit, Tolstoy wrote him: "Our meeting was very good. It [the bond] exists and will exist forever."[72]

"I'm standing up to my waist in the grave, and there's no need for me to pretend and also no need to care what people say about me," Tolstoy wrote.[73] But his relationship with Chertkov was entangled and he often had to pretend. In September 1905, trying to flatter him, Tolstoy expressed his happiness at the good fortune to have found such a friend and companion in Chertkov.[74] And there was no sincerity on Chertkov's part: he collected every piece of evidence to prove that Tolstoy regarded him as his close friend. He even had Tolstoy sign a statement: "Anna Konstantinovna [Galya] and Vladimir Grigorievich [Chertkov] are my closest friends and not only do I always approve of their entire activity on my behalf and their publishing of my writings, but [this activity] also inspires my most sincere and deepest gratitude towards them."[75] Chertkov knew that his friendship with Tolstoy would be questioned, which is why he needed written proof. It is surprising that Tolstoy, so sensitive to falsehood, failed to detect it in the person closest to him. Alexandrine tells in her reminiscences that she had read Chertkov's letters to Tolstoy early on and found them so insincere that she was sickened by her reading.[76]

In October 1905, Chertkov sold the rights to the first publication of Tolstoy's collected works to William Heinemann.[77] This was a clear violation of the writer's beliefs. A decade earlier, replying to Heinemann's inquiry, Tolstoy stated, in English: "I never sell the right of translation of my books and everybody is welcome to translate and to publish them."[78] Now Chertkov unilaterally decided to sell the first appearance of Tolstoy's works to the publisher who, in turn, sold foreign rights.

What is more, Chertkov concealed these arrangements from Tolstoy and the translators, who would learn about it the hard way. In 1905, Tolstoy sent some stories from *The Cycle of Reading* to his Slovak follower and translator, Shkvaran. The latter translated Tolstoy's stories into German, only to learn that Heinemann objected to their publication. In January 1906, Tolstoy received a desperate letter from Shkvaran who asked to give him written permission to publish his translation. Tolstoy could only explain that he had turned his publishing affairs over to Chertkov. Simultaneously, Tolstoy begged Chertkov not to deprive Shkvaran of his only way of making a living:

It's sad that such worthless things as publishing [editions] can disunite such people . . . as you and Shkvaran. I know you well and I believe there's some misunderstanding here. He [Shkvaran] is poor and feeds himself with such projects, and, of course, you would not want to deprive him of this income. But please forgive me if there's something I've misunderstood or did not put right.[79]

Later, Shkvaran also translated Tolstoy's article "Bethink Yourselves!" into German. Chertkov, who knew about this, secretly commissioned another translator to do the work. Shkvaran was stunned when, days before the publication of his version, he received Chertkov's dispatch with another German translation of "Bethink Yourselves!" The rival version deprived Shkvaran of the opportunity to publish his. Chertkov was punishing a Tolstoyan, who was also his friend. Refusing to believe that Tolstoy had no influence in his publishing affairs, Shkvaran decided to try yet again. This time, he also obtained Chertkov's permission to translate some of Tolstoy's minor fiction, which the writer had sent to him. But again, Chertkov informed him, after he completed the work, that the German rights to these same stories had been sold. Heavily in debt, Shkvaran, in addition, had now damaged his reputation with publishers.[80] By then, Chertkov alone decided who should publish and translate Tolstoy's works, and was merciless with competitors.

Chertkov was also settling old scores with the Slovak translator, who had uttered unorthodox thoughts about their movement. Back in the days when they were close, Shkvaran wrote sarcastically about Tolstoy's dogmatic followers, who loved God more than they loved people. He ridiculed the precise following of the commandments, which in his words was the road "to the Devil, rather than to God." And he was open about sexual misconduct among the Tolstoyans: despite their vows of chastity, there was more sinning among the "brothers" of the movement than "in brothels and in pubs." Shkvaran ridiculed this hypocrisy, "lying before God." Chertkov never forgave such revelations and punished this heretic at an opportune moment.

In October 1905, faced with revolutionary unrest, Nicholas II agreed to restrict his authority. His October 17 manifesto guaranteed basic political and civil liberties and established the first Russian parliament, the Duma. But since the Tsar retained his power to declare war and appoint ministers, the Duma had no real independence from the monarchy. Nicholas II's powers were restricted only symbolically: instead of "unlimited autocrat," he was now called "an autocrat."

Censorship was abolished (although temporarily) and political exiles were allowed to return. There was no longer any need for Chertkov to remain in England and no justification for his publishing activity abroad, since most works could now appear in Russia. In March 1906, Chertkov was informed that he was free to repatriate, but it would take him another two years to wrap up his affairs. In summer, he again traveled to see Tolstoy. Sophia allowed him to stay in a separate wing of the house, reserved for the family in the past. She photographed Tolstoy with Chertkov on a bench. Tolstoy, in his white flannel shirt, looks ahead morosely; a beefy Chertkov, towering over him, his head turned, gazes formidably. In this photograph they resemble two conspirators rather than friends. Chertkov was also photographing Tolstoy—alone in the park and with some family (but not with Sophia). He was planning to buy property near Yasnaya and Tolstoy, as always, offered to help with practical arrangements.[81]

In November 1906, learning that Chertkov had pneumonia, Tolstoy was "frightened and pained" that his friend could die before he did, which proved "how strongly I'm bound to you, just how much I love you."[82] Chertkov recovered, but only ten days later, Tolstoy's beloved daughter, Masha, developed lobar pneumonia, a particularly vicious kind. Tolstoy was at her bedside when Masha died on November 27, at thirty-five. Grief-stricken, he wrote Chertkov that he lost his best friend in Masha and that his only solace was thinking that "I won't have to live long without her."[83] Tolstoy spent much of December in bed with bronchitis.

During the writer's illness Chertkov sent anxious telegrams, which arrived even at night, disturbing everyone in the house, including Tolstoy. Asking Chertkov to stop sending telegrams, Tolstoy promised: "I'll write to you myself when things will begin to look like I'm dying . . ."[84] Early in the New Year, Tolstoy sent him a telegram to reassure about his health:

"*Convalescent mais faible.*"[85] In February 1907, Tolstoy was still weak, easily tired, and had no energy for intellectual work. Around this time, he had fainting spells "with a complete loss of memory,"[86] as daughter Tanya informed Maude. The so-called fainting spells left Tolstoy emotionally vulnerable: he would cry when reading a book.

On March 14, Galya's brother, Iosif Dieterichs visited Yasnaya. He had been in Canada where he met with the Doukhobor leader, Peter Verigin. Dieterichs described him as a duplicitous, despotic man, who had no religion at all. Tolstoy replied to this, calmly: "What business is it of ours? We are all human."[87] The Doukhobors were in trouble with the Canadian government for refusing to swear allegiance to King Edward VII. (Chertkov, secretly from Tolstoy, had sent them a handbook instructing them to disobey the government and advising against swearing the oath.[88])

Dieterichs had also been in England visiting his sister and Chertkov. He said the Chertkovs were building houses and buying land at £300 an acre. Chertkov was giving talks and spent much time playing soccer. He hosted regular soccer practices, playing with teenaged son Dima and his friends; they played even at dusk, under the lanterns. Galya was managing practical affairs and the press.[89]

But the main news was that Chertkov had negotiated publication of Tolstoy's collected works in Russia with publisher Sytin, who was also his friend. Tolstoy was unaware of this; upon learning, he was unpleasantly struck. Sytin was now among the wealthiest publishers in Russia, one of those to whom Chertkov referred as "commercial hawks." Tolstoy did not want to be associated with Sytin and was disappointed that he was not consulted; he said impulsively: "That's the first time I hear about this. It's always unpleasant to me when the Chertkovs launch into business . . . The result is deeply regretful and disgusting. And why, what for? I can't understand this."[90] Soon after, Tolstoy received a letter from Chertkov, who quoted these same words back to him and complained about his criticism. Tolstoy told doctor Makovitsky that he received "an extremely long letter from Chertkov who meticulously explains why he is dealing with Sytin, a reliable bookseller," and why he doesn't want to do business with Intermediary, which is perishing.[91] Tolstoy allowed Intermediary to produce his calendars, *The Cycles of Reading,* to support it financially.

When Chertkov turned this project over to Sytin, he dealt a serious blow to Intermediary, the non-profit publishing venture he had founded with Tolstoy two decades earlier.

In April 1907, in a letter to Chertkov, Tolstoy explained that he did not want to be associated with "such wheeler-dealers as Sytin . . ."[92] Chertkov ignored this wish and on his next visit to Russia arrived in Yasnaya with the publisher in tow. By then, Chertkov had already prevailed on Tolstoy to give written approval for the exclusive permission to Sytin to produce his complete works. Sytin promised to take care of all expenses and to pay the editorial team "a certain (small) percentage from the sale of your books."[93] Chertkov claimed that he had invested his own money producing Tolstoy's works and now his budget was stretched thin. (As it later emerged, Sytin paid Chertkov 10 percent from the sale of Tolstoy's works.) It was with disarming frankness that Chertkov intimated to Tolstoy that with people like his late friend Trepov, Ertel (his estate manager), and Sytin he had more in common than with his fellow Tolstoyans.[94]

That year, Makovitsky and daughter Sasha were regularly copying Tolstoy's diary for Chertkov. Before sending him copies, they would read the entries aloud to check against the original. Tolstoy lost privacy even at home. What is more, he no longer could write in his diary what he felt. Upon finding some disapproval of his own or Galya's activity, Chertkov would insist on destroying the entry. (In 1905, Chertkov demanded that Tolstoy rub out a comment in his diary where he complained that Galya was pestering him over an interview he had given to a newspaper in Philadelphia. Tolstoy agreed to delete the "nasty" passage.[95]) This was mind control, to which Tolstoy consented for the sake of his so-called spiritual unity with Chertkov.

At seventy-nine, Tolstoy rarely had an uninterrupted day of work. There were scores of visitors asking for material help or advice and a flow of correspondence. He still read many of the letters himself, afraid to miss something of interest. Daily, he would write six to fifteen letters, leaving the rest to daughter Sasha and other helpers. When people asked for his autograph, Tolstoy willingly inscribed their postcards, while saying, "I'm beginning to believe in my fame." But most of his correspondents asked for money. He received requests to help pay for education and even to help buy some property. Someone even asked Tolstoy to send 25 rubles for fencing lessons.[96] In September 1907, Tolstoy published an open letter explaining that he had renounced his property and money and asked the public not to approach him with material requests. This made no difference: requests kept pouring in, only that now some correspondents also complained about Tolstoy's open letter.

In summer 1907, Chertkov sent two telegrams to Yasnaya advising he was arriving with his family. One telegram was delivered at night. Chertkov requested certain carriages to be sent to the station. At dinner, Tolstoy was agitated and kept talking about Chertkov's arrival. When someone asked why he was so excited, Tolstoy replied that he hadn't seen Galya for a long time.[97] He recently sent a telegram to Chertkov: "Inexpressively happy. Give assignments. We're at your disposal."[98] He rode to the station to meet Chertkov, his wife, and son.

That summer, Chertkov bought 62 acres from daughter Sasha, in Telyatinki, which was only three miles from Yasnaya. Upon learning that Chertkov wanted to build so close to their estate, Tolstoy disclosed "a secret": Sophia did not welcome the idea. Chertkov replied that "we want to build near Yasnaya" because it's the main place of Lev Nikolaevich's activity and "we like people there."[99] Tolstoy's objection, that there was no need to move into the neighborhood because he would soon die, was also dismissed.

In 1908, on the eve of Tolstoy's eightieth birthday, Chertkov moved into his newly built two-story mansion, which would accommodate his family and a throng of secretaries and acolytes. Chertkov's arrival spelled the end of peaceful life in Yasnaya. The writer and his family were facing the greatest trial of their lives.

CHAPTER TEN

THE GREATEST LITERARY SCANDAL

"I despised all secret activity, plots, flights."
—Tolstoy, in a letter to Alexandrine, 1862

"Around your writings, preaching love and harmony, a scandal unparalleled in literary history would flare up."
—Chertkov, in a letter to Tolstoy, 1910[1]

"He is motivated primarily by the need to dominate and humiliate."
—Ethel Spector Person, "Manipulativeness in Entrepreneurs and Psychopaths"[2]

I n September 1907, during Chertkov's stay in Yasnaya, the *Russian Word* published an article by Vasily Rozanov, a prominent writer and religious philosopher. Without mentioning Chertkov's name, but simply identifying him as Tolstoy's "narrow-minded, dogmatic friend from London," Rozanov spoke of his "Mephistophelian" influence. In this article he describes the mysterious unions of writers with religious zealots, something of a phenomenon in Russian literary history. Tolstoy's predecessor, Nikolai Gogol, subordinated himself to his confessor, Father Matvei. A religious fanatic and, some say, a masochist, Father Matvei compelled Gogol to believe his literature was sinful. Gogol burned the unpublished sequel of his last novel and died soon after. Rozanov argued that the relationship with Chertkov had a similar detrimental effect on Tolstoy's art. (Chertkov called himself "Tolstoy's confessor," making the parallel with Gogol more striking.) When pianist Alexander Goldenweiser, a frequent guest at Yasnaya, asked Chertkov what he thought about this article, the latter replied, "How disrespectful of Lev Nikolaevich!"[3]

Rozanov's article produced a strong impression on Tolstoy's close circle and was discussed by Yasnaya inhabitants in Chertkov's and the writer's absence. Chertkov's domineering influence was impossible to deny, and those gathered agreed that each would provide an example of it. Tolstoy's new secretary, Nikolai Gusev, said that the writer did not publish anything without Chertkov's consent. Sukhotin remarked that Chertkov did not allow Tolstoy to criticize revolutionaries. Daughter Sasha, now closest to Tolstoy after Masha's death, had more to say. She observed that Chertkov behaved despotically towards her father, disturbed his peace, took away his manuscripts and diaries, and did not leave him alone on his walks, following him around with a camera. Makovitsky summarized the discussion: Chertkov's influence on Tolstoy was "tremendous" and "despotic."[4] Sukhotin later wrote in his diary:

> If I would begin to recount those actions of L.N., which people found most irritating, it would appear they were made under pressure from Chertkov . . . That statement, which L.N. made long ago [in 1891] about placing his works into the public domain, has long lost all its meaning. In reality, L.N.'s works belong to Chertkov. He takes them away, sells them abroad, gives them to translators he himself finds suitable; insists that L.N. revise what he, Chertkov, does not like. He publishes them [the works] in Russia with whomever he likes, and only after Chertkov releases them, do they become public property.[5]

In the fall, when Chertkov had returned to England, Tolstoy spoke about their relationship in his close circle, with Makovitsky and Sophia present: "There is a weak man in me who sympathizes with Chertkov, his activity, and another one who does not sympathize with him and with his desire to put himself forward. I'm strict in this regard . . . But the weak Lev Nikolaevich in me is happy with Chertkov's activity."[6] That weak man in Tolstoy now had the upper hand: he continually praised Chertkov, even saying he was "not worthy of such a man . . . who employs all his energy and resources to help me."[7] The Yasnaya inhabitants realized it was the other way round: Tolstoy was investing his remaining time and dwindling energy to help Chertkov.

While in Yasnaya, Chertkov presented Tolstoy with the entire compendium of his thoughts comprising thirty-six volumes. Tolstoy was childishly impressed, sharing his delight with his secretary Gusev: "Here's what Chertkov is doing for me! Thirty-six huge volumes of the 'Compendium' . . . If only I was worthy of this!"[8] Tolstoy was moved by the amount of labor that went into producing the volumes, which seemed to illustrate Chertkov's personal dedication to him. "This is a history of my thoughts," he said. However, when skimming through the volumes, he found that his ideas had changed significantly: "When I wrote *Translation and Unification of the Four Gospels*, I was a Christian, but now I am more broad-minded."[9] Chertkov, in producing the compendium, was attempting to prevent Tolstoy's ideas from developing. His main concern was consistency, and he continually warned Tolstoy against deviations from his own doctrine, as formulated back in 1884. Now that Tolstoy had the compendium in his study, Chertkov instructed him to check the volumes when producing his inspirational calendars, the *Cycles of Reading*, to avoid contradicting his views: "You should consult the table of contents in the Compendium of your thoughts, which I compiled..." In addition, Chertkov assigned Tolstoy to reread "Christian Teaching" and the *Gospel in Brief,*[10] force-feeding the writer with his own thoughts.

Like Pygmalion, who fell in love with the statue he carved, Tolstoy loved Chertkov for echoing his views. Chertkov was really Tolstoy's brainchild, his creation: responsible for his rise and outlook, he was inclined to see only goodness in his disciple. Tolstoy sent him a sentimental letter after his brief visit in winter 1908: "It feels strange and sad without you. . . . These dots mean all [those things] that I think and feel about you, but don't want to spoil with words."[11] Tolstoy also dictated a letter to Chertkov into the phonograph in Yasnaya: "I love you—that's all I wanted to say to you."[12] He then listened to his recording, and the player shouted the words back. Tolstoy's affection for Chertkov went beyond Christian love, which the writer well realized: "You also love me unlawfully, more than brotherly, like I love you."[13] During that same visit, Makovitsky observed Tolstoy as he went to Chertkov's bedroom to say good-night. When Tolstoy emerged, the doctor offered to take his pulse, as usual. Tolstoy declined and changed the topic.[14] Tolstoy was fond of Chertkov and was letting him know how much he enjoyed his company: "S'il n'y avait pas Tchertkoff, Il faudrait l'inventer. Pour moi du moins, pour mon bonheur—lots—pour mon plaisir . . ." ("If Chertkov did not exist, one would have to invent him. At least for me, for my happiness—lots—for my pleasure . . .")[15]

Tolstoy liked to display technical inventions, which visitors brought to Yasnaya. Chertkov recently gave him an American clock: inside the glass display were small digital cards with numbers printed on them, which flipped every minute.[16] When showing off the clock with its flipping cards, Tolstoy would say, "They terribly remind one of how time slips by."[17]

In March 1908, Tolstoy fainted in his study. He remained unconscious for a minute or two, but his memory loss was more frightening: he could not remember any events that day. In April, he fainted again and his amnesia and confusion lasted longer. He failed to recognize family and friends, and talked about his dead brother, Dmitry, thinking he was in Yasnaya with them. But in a while, Tolstoy regained his memory, reading his correspondence in all European languages. In addition, he soon acquired new ones—reading in Polish, Czech, and Bulgarian. As Tolstoy told Makovitsky, he was often thinking in French, which he learned in childhood.

Already becoming used to the idea that Chertkov would settle close by, Tolstoy gave advice about building a house in Telyatinki. However, Chertkov hired an architect, who surprised the Yasnaya inhabitants by showing his sketch for the two-story house with thirty-two bedrooms. A sitting room in Chertkov's house was three times the size of the family room in Yasnaya. Upon hearing the estimate, 35,000 rubles, Tolstoy sighed.[18]

Sasha, twenty-three, said she regretted selling her land to Chertkov, who would build a huge and expensive house on it. Sasha and her friend, Varvara Feokritova, who was a typist in Yasnaya, were Chertkov's harshest critics. But Chertkov would soon turn them into his staunch supporters, enlisting them in his coalition against Sophia. When Chertkov's construction was discussed in Sophia's presence, she asked, "But why are they building? They have houses in Rzhevsk, Lizinovka, and in England."[19] (Actually, Chertkov's mother owned a palace at Southbourne, Hants, a resort town by the sea where Chertkov would take his family for a vacation. In the 1920s, Chertkova's residence, called "Slavyanka," became one of the buildings of the Southbourne Missionary and Conference Centre for evangelical Christians.[20]) Tolstoy tried to justify his friend's ambitious construction in Telyatinki: the new house was meant for Chertkov's son, Dima. This did not convince Sukhotin, who quipped that it was an example of how Tolstoyans should not build. All materials were top quality, with no attempt to save. Later that year, when Chertkov moved into his new house, his stables, a bathhouse, and shops were set afire. According to rumors, which Chertkov denied, the fire was set by a contractor, whom he threatened to fine for delays. It could also have been set by local peasants, out of spite: it was a time when landowners' estates were burning across Russia.

During a wave of violence in 1905–07, hundreds of government officials were killed and estates robbed and burned. The government responded with mass executions. On May 9, 1908, Tolstoy read a brief report in *The Russian Gazette* that twenty peasants were hanged for allegedly plundering an estate. Tolstoy was struck by the triviality of the report, suggesting that death sentences had become a regular occurrence. His powerful short article, "I Cannot Be Silent," made Russians feel the horror of mass executions. The recently granted freedom of the press was short-lived and several newspapers were fined for printing this article without a censor's approval. It circulated in underground copies.

On the eve of Tolstoy's eightieth birthday Yasnaya resembled a sanatorium: local doctors and professors from Moscow were attending to the writer, who was suffering from bronchitis, phlebitis, and intestinal problems. The doctors refused to accept payment from the great man, believing it an honor to treat him. Tolstoy was no longer afraid to die, claiming he had reached his nirvana: "What happiness it would be to die now!"[21] Almost never alone, he treasured a few solitary evenings and the occasions when he could simply enjoy music. When Goldenweiser played his beloved Chopin, Tolstoy told him that he felt as merged with the melody as if he had composed it.

On August 28, Tolstoy received hundreds of telegrams and letters from Russia and around the world. Charles Theodore Wright, the secretary and librarian of the London Library and Tolstoy's translator, arrived from England to deliver a letter signed by over 700 English admirers. Wright was present at the family dinner, served at a long table outside. Tolstoy was sitting separately from the rest, in his wheelchair, and scribbling in his notebook.

In the fall, Tolstoy's condition improved and he resumed his walks and rides, now in Chertkov's company. Sukhotin observed in his diary, "Chertkov not only adores Lev Nikolaevich, but also orders him around; Lev Nikolaevich admires Chertkov and obeys him in everything." He was alone privileged to enter the writer's study even during his working hours. Despite his healthy physique, Chertkov walked around with an expression of "world sadness" on his face: he had made Tolstoy's perennial dissatisfaction with himself into a principle. Tolstoyans were not supposed to enjoy life. In his diary Sukhotin referred to Chertkov as "son of Zebedee," an ironic parallel between Apostle John, the closest disciple to Jesus, and Tolstoy's chosen disciple.

> . . . [Tolstoy's] favorite pupil brings with him a spirit of misery. I always feel oppressed in his presence, which comes from real-izing an exaggerated role of this strong, but extremely narrow-minded man . . . In his absence, everyone criticizes him, tells various anecdotes about his insincerity, an incongruity between his Tolstoyan views and a lifestyle as a rich daydreamer . . . L.N. alone adores him and in his presence no one can criticize Chertkov . . .[22]

That fall, Sukhotin wrote an article about Tolstoy for an almanac, quoting Tolstoy's criticism of revolutionaries. Chertkov demanded the removal of these remarks, as a censor would. In protest, Sukhotin withdrew his article, remarking that Chertkov was Tolstoy's "chief censor." Tolstoy defended Chertkov's position by saying his criticism of revolutionaries was careless. (In fact, Tolstoy had once sympathized with revolutionary ideals. But over the years, his attitude changed and he described their activity as futile: "The whole first half of the nineteenth century is full of attempts to destroy despotic state regimes by revolutionary violence. All attempts ended in reaction, and the power of the ruling classes only increased."[23])

Although Chertkov came daily to Yasnaya, staying for dinner, he treated Sophia with contempt. "She had never said and never will say a word of truth," he told Makovitsky with typical intolerance. "She has no religion."[24] This was a reference to Sophia's different faith: she remained Christian Orthodox, which made her morally inferior in the eyes of Tolstoyans. In December 1908, Chertkov confronted Sophia at an opportune moment. She unwisely began to speak with Tolstoy about his posthumous copyright in Chertkov's presence. According to Makovitsky, Sophia said that the family should have exclusive right to produce his unpublished works, of which Chertkov had made a copy. Chertkov immediately took out his notebook and began scribbling. He produced a transcript of their conversation, which reads, like a play. Chertkov later sent these notes to Tolstoy to persuade him to write a secret will.

. . . Sophia Andreevna addressing Leo Nikolaevich, irritably asserted that the copyright of all his unpublished writings, whenever written, belongs to the family. Leo Nikolaevich objected . . .

Leo Nikolaevich. 'You imagine that our children are some sort of scoundrels, who will wish to counter my wishes about what is most precious to me.'

Sophia Andreevna. 'Well, I don't know about the scoundrels, but . . .

Leo Nikolaevich—firmly. No, let me finish . . . You know that I had grounds which caused me to renounce these rights—the bases of my faith—and what now? Do you wish these grounds to appear like a hypocrisy?[25]

Chertkov jumped into this conversation to condemn Sophia, which Tolstoy heard with indifference. Later, Chertkov admitted to Makovitsky that he was surprised that Tolstoy did not try to defend his wife. Actually, he never defended her even in the past, when they were close, and now would do almost anything to oppose her. Tolstoy told Chertkov that he felt nothing but pity towards Sophia.

Around this time, taking advantage of Sophia's weakness, Chertkov began to build a coalition against her. He argued that Tolstoy's family could not be trusted to carry out his posthumous wishes, which is why a proper will must be drafted. According to Maude, "no one could put his case more persuasively or ingeniously" than Chertkov.[26] His ability to antagonize people was also unmatched: with Chertkov around, Tolstoy's family split into feuding camps.

When in 1909, Maude visited Yasnaya, it was a different place. All conversations were centered on the conflict over Tolstoy's posthumous legacy. Maude felt that Tolstoy and his wife would have resolved the matter peacefully, if not "for the interference of that remarkable man, V. G. Chertkov. I never knew anyone with such a capacity for enforcing his will on others. Everybody connected with him became his instrument, quarreled with him, or had to escape."[27] Daughter Sasha, by then completely in Chertkov's power, zealously protected his interests. She was antagonistic towards her mother and treated Maude "as belonging to the enemy's camp." Chertkov "had a talent for making people believe that by obeying him they performed a high moral duty. When he spoke, the will of God, the law of non-resistance, the teachings of Tolstoy, and service rendered to Chertkov, merged into each other and became one."[28]

Chertkov was a busy man: aside from fueling the conflict in Tolstoy's family, he also proselytized. His new mansion accommodated his secretaries, Tolstoyans, and village lads, who received a salary for listening to him preach. Chertkov also distributed prohibited literature, which got the authorities' attention. In March, the police entered Chertkov's house and read an order for his expulsion from Tula province. Chertkov received unlikely support from Sophia, who made a gesture of good will to restore peace. In a letter to *The Russian Gazette* of March 11, 1909, she described Chertkov's banishment as an unlawful act, since it was made "without establishing his guilt and taking the matter to court." Sophia believed that Chertkov had suffered for his proximity to Tolstoy and spreading his ideas, but she was unaware that he also engaged in anti-government propaganda. Sukhotin was annoyed with her letter, commenting in his diary that Chertkov "preached many of those things that could not be tolerated by any government."

Sophia's letter was reprinted by scores of newspapers, creating publicity for Chertkov. Liberal papers rushed to interview him. Chertkov told reporters that he was destroying "revolutionary nests" around his estate and that the government should thank him, instead of deporting him. To another reporter he said that he had invested all his funds into building his Telyatinki house and could not afford to settle elsewhere with his family. Tolstoy, who read these reports, was upset with the lack of truth.[29]

In April, Chertkov joined his mother in Petersburg, staying at her apartment on Millionnaya 16 (the Millionaires' Street). He attended Verdi's *La Traviata*, his favorite opera. While in Petersburg he appealed to the prime minister, Pyotr Stolypin, to review his case. At Tolstoy's request, daughter Tanya also traveled to meet Stolypin, who promised to investigate. When Tanya left for Petersburg, Tolstoy wrote Chertkov, "How happy I am, my dear, dear friend, that Tanya is going. I'm not saying that I expect something [will come out of it], but I'm happy for her, for you, for myself, for the love that unites us . . . Please don't show my letter to anyone. Only to you, knowing how partial you are to me, I allow myself to write whatever comes to mind."[30]

After Chertkov's expulsion Tolstoy had sent him a series of nostalgic letters: "I'm writing a few words just to tell you how close and dear you are to me . . ."[31] ". . . I think of you incessantly, and of your return."[32] Unable to respond emotionally, Chertkov stated that Tolstoy's love moved him "to the bottom of my heart."[33] Tolstoy no longer restrained his feelings: "Our bond cannot be broken not merely by Stolypins, but also by death."[34]

"Last night, I dreamt of you, that you returned . . . I'm writing this on my walk, with your pen and in your little notebook."[35]

"The longer I'm separated from you, the more and more I miss you. I don't think it's because you love me, more so because I love you."[36]

The relationship now entered a new stage: Tolstoy and Chertkov would begin seeing each other secretly. In June, Tolstoy traveled to Tanya's and Sukhotin's estate in Kochety, accompanied with his secretary Gusev, doctor Makovitsky, and a servant, Ilya Sidorkov. Tolstoy spent three weeks in Kochety, playing chess with Sukhotin and resting from visitors in Yasnaya. He asked Sukhotin to critique his new article, "The Inevitable Overturn." In it he argued that "the law of violence" would become inevitably replaced with "the law of love." The idea struck Sukhotin as completely unrealistic. Tolstoy's expectation that people would suddenly become united in love, at a time of unprecedented violence, was unfounded. When Sukhotin expressed these objections, Tolstoy agreed, also saying that the article was weak and repetitive.

Tolstoy expected Chertkov to write whether he was allowed to return to Tula province.[37] Instead, Chertkov sent a business letter, asking for permission to publish Tolstoy's unfinished story, "The Devil," in an almanac produced by the Literary Fund. Chertkov had been frequently asking to publish this particular work, which describes Tolstoy's affair with a peasant woman, Aksinya, by whom he had a son before marriage. Tolstoy had been hiding this erotic piece from Sophia, which is why Chertkov insisted on publishing it. Now, Chertkov alleged that Sophia was "burning with a desire" to make money from this story and wanted to include it in her collected works. He reminded that the story was written after 1881, when Tolstoy had renounced his copyright, which is why Sophia must not be allowed to have it.[38]

Tolstoy was upset with Chertkov's tedious arguments: "It's disappointing that you're not writing anything definite about yourself, while I'm waiting. It's also disappointing, even unpleasant, what it says there about my writings from such and such year. The 'devil' take all these writings, so that they'd not cause unkind feelings!"[39] Shortly after, Chertkov informed that his appeal to return to Tula province was rebuffed. Tolstoy at once wrote to express sympathy and assuage his criticism: "I feel sad for you, Galya, Dima, the friends in Telyatinki, and for myself."[40]

It was agreed to meet in neighboring Oryol province. Tanya rented a peasant hut within two miles from Kochety, where Tolstoy was staying. Chertkov kept changing his mind about the date and was sending frequent telegrams. This was unnerving and expensive, since Tolstoy's family had to pay for their delivery. On July 1, the much anticipated "joyful meeting" took place in Suvorovo village. Chertkov arrived with his English photographer, Thomas Tapsell. At Chertkov's insistence, Tolstoy brought his latest diary to be copied.[41] (Tolstoy had recently repeated his wish to keep the diary for himself, but yielded to Chertkov.[42])

"Chertkov is my alter-ego,"[43] observed Tolstoy in his diary, in October 1909. Around this time, he told his family that Lev Tolstoy (the artist, driven by ambition) was "the man most alien to me."[44] Chertkov represented another part of his personality (the man of religion, driven by altruism), and which Tolstoy thought was his better self. He admitted his sense of duality to Chertkov:

> I'll write to you, dear friend, about what has happened very recently to L.N. Tolstoy. What has happened is that as well as Tolstoy, somebody else has appeared who has completely taken possession of Tolstoy and allows him no freedom of movement. As soon as Tolstoy states a willingness or, on the contrary, an unwillingness to do something, this somebody, whom I call 'I', decides the matter for himself and sometimes agrees, but usually, on the contrary, refuses permission to do what Tolstoy wants or tells him to do what Tolstoy doesn't want . . . And the surprising thing is that ever since I've clearly understood that this *I* is far more important than Tolstoy and that it's necessary to listen to him and that good will come out of it, I immediately listen to him as soon as I hear his voice.[45]

Chertkov had appeared to penetrate his unconscious mind and take the upper hand.

In late July, Chertkov and his family moved to his uncle Pashkov's luxurious estate near Moscow, Krekshino. Tolstoy felt meeting him there would be "a joyous dream . . . .You're close, close to me, and it's joyous not only to be with you, but even to think of you."[46] He mentioned that Sophia was nervously ill and daughter Tanya was looking after her.

On September 3, Tolstoy and his retinue (his servant, daughter Sasha, Goldenweiser, Makovitsky, and Chertkov's son Dima) set out for Krekshino. His departure was filmed by the French cinematographic firm Pathé. Arriving in Moscow, where he has not been in a decade, Tolstoy was overwhelmed with traffic, the noise from cars and trams. Taking a walk downtown, he spoke of how the city had grown, telling Goldenweiser that he yearned to express his new feelings in an artistic work. (It was not to be.) Tolstoy and his companions visited Yuly Zimmerman's music shop. A reputable supplier of music instruments, Zimmerman owned factories and stores across Europe and in Russia. Recently, he started manufacturing mechanical music instruments and self-playing pianos. Tolstoy was curious about his popular mechanical piano "Mignon," which used music rolls. The store owner readily showed it to his eminent guest and took photographs. One picture shows Tolstoy listening to Chopin's Polonaise "Heroique" and Straus Waltzes. He shrieked with delight while hearing performances by the best pianists.[47] A practical Chertkov arranged to deliver the instrument to Krekshino for the duration of Tolstoy's stay.

Krekshino was one of Russia's most prosperous estates. Unlike Yasnaya, the spacious mansion had running water and bathrooms, and was surrounded by an English-style park. Greenhouses, fruit orchards, an apiary, and numerous outbuildings were well maintained by numerous staff. Far from criticizing Chertkov for such luxury, Tolstoy found something to praise. He was impressed that Chertkov and his family were eating at the same table with servants. (However, there were different menus, reflecting one's status. While Chertkov and his family feasted on asparagus and Swiss cheese, the servants, at the other end of the table, received only porridge.) Tolstoy believed the Chertkovs were more democratic than his family. In Yasnaya, meals were served by a lackey in white gloves, whereas in Krekshino, Annushka cooked and served meals.

During the two weeks of Tolstoy's stay, Krekshino was besieged by photographers, a cinematographer, and visitors. Chertkov hosted a feast for 200 peasants and had Tapsell photograph this occasion. In the evenings, in addition to the mechanical piano, Goldenweiser played live music. Almost never left alone, Tolstoy was happy to take a solitary walk.

Sophia, who arrived in Krekshino for a short visit, was surprised with a warm welcome: "It was all very friendly, gracious and comfortable."[48] During her stay Tolstoy signed the first redaction of his secret will, which Chertkov had been pressing him to make and which concerned renouncing his posthumous copyright. On September 17, on a walk with Tolstoy, Chertkov spoke at length about his children's supposed intentions to profit from the works, which he had put in the public domain. Tolstoy responded in his diary: "I don't want to believe it."[49] Nonetheless, the testament was drafted the following day, on September 18. Tolstoy proclaimed all his works public property and gave editorial executorship to Chertkov, who in addition would take possession of the writer's papers. Sasha copied the document and it was signed by Tolstoy, Goldenweiser, Alexei Sergeenko (Chertkov's closest assistant), and Alexander Kalachev, a vagabond. The conspirators managed to conceal the business from Sophia, although she was in the same house. But the ordeal was not over: to satisfy Chertkov, Tolstoy would have to sign several more redactions of this will. It would deprive Sophia of the posthumous copyright even to *War and Peace* and *Anna Karenina*, which she had helped Tolstoy produce.

Having acted behind his wife's back, Tolstoy felt bad and decided to return to Moscow separately. But when he told Sophia that she should travel alone, she became miserable and he changed his mind: "She's very pitiful, ill, and weak."[50] Chertkov had announced the date of Tolstoy's return in a newspaper, which drew a rapturous crowd of five thousand to the Moscow station. They crammed the square, hung from posts, and stood on railcars. Chertkov was clearing the way for Tolstoy, Sophia, and Sasha. "A huge crowd, we were nearly crushed," Tolstoy later remembered. "Chertkov was saving the situation; I feared for Sonya and Sasha."[51] Overwhelmed, Tolstoy fainted on the train. Back in Yasnaya, he fainted again and was attended by one of his expert doctors, Grigory Berkenheim. Tolstoy's speech was slurred, and there was another frightening and lasting loss of memory. But a few days later, he resumed his walks and read letters, although he remained weak and complained of "lack of mental activity."[52]

In October, he told Makovitsky and others that he felt his teachings were having no effect and that he wanted to die.[53] Tolstoy conveyed this wish to Chertkov as well: "I don't know whether it's good or bad, but since recently I desperately want to die, mainly because of the terrible disagreement between my view of the world and the actual world of living people, hopelessly uncooperative and contradictory."[54] Indeed, he had dreamt that his teachings would enable people to live in peace; instead, he was witnessing malice, intrigue, and strife.

Chertkov responded in a series of banal questions. Was Tolstoy's wish to die inspired by his family's conditions of luxury? Why did Tolstoy yearn to depart society at age 81? What ideas and plots remained unrealized and which ones passed vividly before his mind's eye?[55] Chertkov would not relent until Tolstoy provided answers, which took almost a year.

When in a brighter mood, Tolstoy liked to talk about his dreams. During his last year, he dreamt of dancing at a ball. He told Sukhotin how much he enjoyed dancing mazurkas and waltzes in his dreams, although sensing that his style had become outdated. "Life is a dream," Tolstoy would say. Truly spiritual life lies beyond death, and "the closer I approach death, the more and more I wake up, and when I'll begin to die, I'll become fully awake."[56] Chertkov now insisted that Tolstoy should record his dreams. Overhearing one of Chertkov's conversations with Tolstoy (about prayer), Sophia remarked in her diary: "What a narrow-minded individual this Chertkov is, what an unimaginative view he takes of everything! He is not even interested in the psychology of Lev Nikolaevich's soul . . . All Chertkov ever does is to *collect information, make notes*, and *take photographs*."[57] Nonetheless, Chertkov had utmost power over Tolstoy and kept him under his thumb.

In November, he sent an envoy to explain that another redaction of the secret would have to be made. Chertkov's Moscow attorney found the will invalid: Tolstoy did not designate an heir. Upon learning that Chertkov wanted the attorney to redraft the will, Tolstoy complained in his diary: "The conversation . . . was painful on account of Chertkov's demands, because it's necessary to have dealings with the government."[58] As usual, Tolstoy agreed to do what was asked of him, "but I regret that I haven't said that it was very hard for me, that not doing it was best."[59] Days after, on November 1, he signed the second draft, in which Sasha was formally chosen as heiress.

Although Chertkov had consulted one of Moscow's most brilliant and experienced lawyers, Nikolai Muravyov, this new redaction of Tolstoy's will was also flawed. Provisions in the event of Sasha's death were not made. The little glitch allowed Chertkov to draft another version in summer 1910. But Chertkov would claim that it was also incomplete, supplying a codicil, in which he was named sole executor of Tolstoy's literary estate. This was his goal from the start.

Muravyov, who handled major literary and publishing lawsuits, was among the six best Moscow attorneys. Tolstoy knew him personally because Muravyov also defended peasants and religious minorities. It would be impossible for the highly qualified lawyer to make basic mistakes in Tolstoy's testament. Chertkov, however, was interested in continually redrafting the document. As he later explained to Tolstoy, the different redactions would later "serve as confirmation of the fact that your will was not written under any momentary impulse or temporary impression, but on the contrary quite deliberately and persistently, since you gave yourself the trouble on different days, over a prolonged interval of time, to set out in your own handwriting one and the same deposition three times over."[60] This strategy would help Chertkov to persuade the public that the secret testament was Tolstoy's idea. To strengthen his case, he put the ailing writer through the painful trial of signing different redactions. Devised in his psychopathic mind, the intricate scheme would mislead Tolstoy's biographers and the public for over a century.

In January 1910, Sukhotin wrote in his diary that Tolstoy looked more withdrawn and spiritually alone. He had another memory lapse, now failing to recognize his grandchildren, who were staying in his house, and his daughter-in-law. When Tolstoy's memory returned, he looked embarrassed and depressed, muttering it was the beginning of the end, "C'est le commencement de la fin."[61]

During his last year, Tolstoy's relations with Sophia had become cold and distant. Sukhotin felt that he was completely indifferent to her. In fact, the secret will deepened the gap between them. Tolstoy now felt uncomfortable in her presence, and she suffered from the awareness that she was no longer loved. Nearing sixty-six, Sophia was nervously ill. She had lived through numerous crises: her continual pregnancies, thirteen births, the deaths of six children, and Tolstoy's difficult moods. Chertkov had many advantages over her, the main one being that he had Tolstoy's undivided attention. She was jealous of Chertkov and spoke mockingly about him, and this further damaged her relations with Tolstoy.

In March 1910, the Yasnaya inhabitants were reading Alexandrine's correspondence with Tolstoy. Alexandrine had recently died and a volume of these letters, which she prepared for publication, was carried to Yasnaya. Her introduction to the volume had insights into Tolstoy's character. Thus, she observed that Tolstoy often prized opinions of people who were inferior to him morally, if they shared some of his beloved ideas. Upon reading this, Sukhotin remarked in his diary that Tolstoy loved it when people repeated his ideas and words to him; such repetition made the matter of sincerity superfluous.[62] Chertkov, who had spent decades collecting and copying Tolstoy's pronouncements, thus catered to the writer's narcissism. (Before meeting Chertkov, Tolstoy had been deeply influenced by his sons' tutor, Vasily Alexeev, a man twenty years his junior, with whom he discussed his religious and social views. In 1875, Alexeev emigrated to America with a group of young intellectuals, whose beliefs combined socialist theory with Christian ethics. They set up an agricultural commune in Kansas to promote their view of a morally good life. When the utopian experiment failed, Alexeev returned to Russia. In 1877, Tolstoy, upon discovering that Alexeev's ideals corresponded to his own, hired him. Tolstoy also became infatuated with the young man and later wrote him repeatedly about his love. Sophia expelled the tutor in 1881, after he persuaded Tolstoy to send an appeal to Alexander III, interceding on behalf of the revolutionary terrorists who had assassinated the Tsar's father, Alexander II.)

Tolstoy's attraction to his young admiring followers is apparent from Gorky's essay, which describes him during his convalescence in the Crimea. The sight of Tolstoy standing in their midst, was etched in Gorky's memory:

> It was strange to see L.N. amongst the 'Tolstoyans'; he stands in their midst like some majestic belfry, and his bell tolls out ceaselessly to the whole world, while all around him scamper small, stealthy curs, yelping to the tones of the bell, and eyeing one another mistrustfully, as if to see which of them was yapping best. I always felt that these people filled both the house

at Yasnaya Polyana and the mansion of Countess Panina with the spirit of hypocrisy, cowardice, bargaining, and the expectation of legacies . . . One day a certain individual related eloquently at Yasnaya how easy his life had become, and how pure his soul, since adopting the doctrines of Tolstoy. L.N. bent towards me and said softly, 'He's lying, the rascal, but he's doing it to give me pleasure.'[63]

"I want to see you very much," Tolstoy wrote Chertkov in winter. "It's strange, but you are so close to me that it even feels awkward [for me] to write to you. I need to tell you so many things."[64] Writing letters to his alter-ego must have felt like writing to himself. Praising Chertkov, who repeated his thoughts, may have felt awkward as well. In January 1910, Tolstoy cried over Chertkov's letter: "Perhaps, it's because you praise me so much, but I hope it's because I love you so much."[65]

In early summer, Tolstoy visited Chertkov at his luxurious rented dacha near the village of Meshcherskoe, on the road to Moscow. This time, Sophia was not invited. Tolstoy set out with his usual retinue and his new secretary, Valentin Bulgakov. During the two weeks at Meshcherskoe, Tolstoy visited a local psychiatric clinic to research his article, "On Insanity." He spent days interviewing patients and doctors. Mental illness had long interested him: he had described his own struggle with depression and suicidal thoughts in "Notes of a Madman" and in *A Confession*. Now, he jotted in his notebook that the mentally ill always achieved their goals better than healthy people because they have "no moral barriers: no shame, no conscience, no truth, or even fear."[66] Tolstoy summarized his impressions from visiting the hospitals by focusing on one characteristic that the mentally ill shared: "This feature is a blind, crude egotism," which enables them to see nothing but themselves.[67] The profile would also fit Chertkov, but Tolstoy may have been too partial to see this.

On June 23, Tolstoy was summoned to Yasnaya with Sophia's anxious telegrams: she was desperately lonesome and implored him to return immediately. He replied to her first telegram: "More convenient return morning 24th. If necessary, will take night train." Sophia at once detected "the cold style of the hard-hearted despot Chertkov in that 'more convenient.'" It was indeed the phrase Chertkov commonly employed. The idea that Tolstoy was using Chertkov's style drove her to the "limits of endurance." She fired off another telegram: it was necessary for Tolstoy to return by the night train.

When Tolstoy came back, "in a disgruntled and unfriendly mood," the two had "a painful" conversation. She was jealous of Chertkov, who had taken her place beside Tolstoy. But "while I regard Chertkov as having come between *us*," she observed in her diary, "both Lev Nik. and Chertkov regard me as having come between *them*." Sophia "said everything that was on my mind"; Tolstoy, hunching on a chair, listened in silence. "What could he have said? There were moments when I felt dreadfully sorry for him," she admitted. She talked, of course, about Chertkov, and that Tolstoy was entirely in his power. Once she brought this up, "a wild beast suddenly leapt out of Lev Nik., his eyes blazed with rage and he said something so cutting that at that moment I hated him and said: 'Ah, so that is what you are really like!' And he grew quiet immediately." Next morning, the two made peace, embraced, and wept, and Tolstoy, although reluctantly, agreed to take a short trip with Sophia. She cheered up: "There was some small ray of happiness in just being *together*."[68]

But days later, Chertkov received permission to return to his Telyatinki estate, neighboring Yasnaya. (He had appealed directly to Nicholas II and his mother also used her connections.) Upon returning, Chertkov sent a message to Tolstoy requesting to see him. Tolstoy asked to postpone the meeting: in the morning he had to accompany Sophia to son Sergei's estate. Chertkov disobeyed, arriving before 8 A.M. to meet Tolstoy privately during his walk in the park.

Around this time, Sophia discovered the disappearance of Tolstoy's diaries for the past decade. Tolstoy claimed he did not know where the notebooks were, but it transpired that Chertkov had them. Yet, Tolstoy had promised that Chertkov would not be allowed to keep these diaries, containing spiteful comments about her and the children. When Sophia demanded to have the notebooks returned, Tolstoy inquired why she needed them. "Because I am your wife, the person closest to you." Tolstoy countered: "Chertkov is the person who is closest to me . . ."[69] These words confirmed Sophia's suspicion that Tolstoy and Chertkov had been having a love affair all along. On June 22, she poured her despair into her diary:

". . . I am disgusted by his senile affection toward Chertkov . . . I want to die and I am afraid of suicide . . . My heart, head, soul—everything hurts . . . Love is lost, ruined."[70] (This entry and others like it have been long suppressed for fear of compromising Tolstoy.) That same summer, she shared her inkling about Tolstoy's homosexuality with Makovitsky, Biryukov, and Bulgakov. They refused to believe her allegation because of the esteem they held for Tolstoy as a man and writer. When she brought up the subject with Tolstoy himself, he turned white and "flew into a terrible rage such as I have not seen for a long, long time."[71]

Yet, the bizarre events in the Tolstoys' household that summer suggest that Sophia's suspicion was not unfounded. It was a rivalrous triangle: Chertkov was determined to humiliate and squeeze her out. He spurned Tolstoy's request to return the diaries and formulated his objections in a dry and ambiguous response: "Considering your desire to get back your diaries, which you had given me so that I could destroy information you've specified, I will hasten to complete this work and will return the notebooks as soon as I complete it."[72] Chertkov was revising Tolstoy's diaries to destroy information he did not want included; he also photographed passages critical of Sophia. In July, Chertkov vaguely explained to Tolstoy how he edited his diaries: "I destroyed . . . some parts, which could cause distress to those whom they concern [likely, the remarks critical of Chertkov and Galya]. As for Sophia Andreevna, I did not have to strike anything out, since . . . in these diaries you have not written anything essentially *unkind* about her."[73] In fact, Chertkov would be the first to publish these same disparaging entries about Sophia in his book *The Last Days of Tolstoy*.

Chertkov created an unbearable situation in Tolstoy's family by holding on to the diaries for two weeks. He further escalated tensions by arriving in Yasnaya to confer with Tolstoy and Sasha behind closed doors: they were deciding "what we should do about the diaries."[74] Some entries contained vague references to the secret will and Chertkov did not want this information to fall "into the enemy hands." Sasha, now completely under Chertkov's spell, repeated after him that the secret will was "the matter of tremendous importance . . . for the entire Russia."[75] Tolstoy's opinion on what to do with the diaries was not even sought.

On July 1, Chertkov attacked Sophia in Yasnaya, shouting that he would use Tolstoy's diaries "to unmask" her and the children: "If I really wanted to I could really *drag you and your family through the mud!*"[76] Sophia reflected in her diary: "How insulting that my husband did not even stand up for me when Chertkov was so rude to me. How he fears him! How he has subjugated himself to him! The shame and the pity of it!"[77] Weeping and trembling, she implored Bulgakov to meet Chertkov and ask him to return the diaries.

Bulgakov arrived at Chertkov's "palazzo" in Telyatinki as Sophia's messenger. Fixing his large restless eyes on Bulgakov, Chertkov asked whether he or Sophia knew where the diaries were kept. "And with these words, to my utter amazement, Vladimir Grigorievich [Chertkov] made a hideous grimace and stuck out his tongue at me." Learning that Bulgakov did not know his hiding place, Chertkov was relieved: "Oh, now that is wonderful!"[78] Bulgakov was shown the door.

When Sophia threatened to commit suicide, Tolstoy commissioned Sasha to retrieve the notebooks. Tanya had deposited the diaries in the State Bank in Tula and Sukhotin kept the key for the deposit box. Sophia now could not hear Chertkov's name without convulsions, referring to him only as "the devil Chertkov." She wrote Tanya, "This despot has spiritually enslaved the old man, who cannot undertake anything without his permission . . ."[79]

After less than a year in Yasnaya, Bulgakov had a good grasp of the conflict: Chertkov aimed "at the moral destruction of Tolstoy's wife in order to get control of his manuscripts."[80] Sophia also realized this, having written to Chertkov himself: "You've *published* Lev Nikolaevich's writings, for which you deserve praise. But why are you constantly taking away his *manuscripts?*"[81]

Sophia was a serious rival, and Chertkov did not spare effort to compromise her. In July, he conspired with Sasha to have a psychiatrist examine her mother in Yasnaya. A professor of the Moscow University, neurologist Grigory Rossolimo, was invited against Sophia's wishes: she felt he would come only to certify her insane. Before Rossolimo's arrival, Chertkov attempted to influence the Tolstoys' family doctor, Dmitry Nikitin, who would be present during the assessment. Chertkov asked Tanya to arrange the clandestine meeting for him: "I'd be ready to come instantly to Yasnaya and see him at least . . . in the stable . . ."[82] Tanya replied that her mother did not want to be examined. This is when Sasha, secretly from Sophia, summoned Rossolimo.

Arriving at the height of dramatic events in Yasnaya, when Sophia kept talking about the conspiracy against her, intrigues by "the devil Chertkov," and Tolstoy's homoerotic relationship with his disciple, Rossilimo diagnosed her with hysteria, paranoia, and dementia. Immediately after, Chertkov and Sasha began to publicize her diagnosis. Sasha wrote to Maude that her mother's hateful remarks about Chertkov must be interpreted in the light of her paranoia.[83] When the writer Vladimir Korolenko visited Yasnaya, Sasha spoke with him at length about her mother's alleged mental illness. She felt it was her duty to "defend Chertkov and father" and expose her mother's "unfounded hatred towards Chertkov."[84] Galya was actively involved, persuading Tolstoy to discuss his family situation with Korolenko. After Tolstoy's death, when Chertkov launched a legal battle for possession of his manuscripts, Sophia's diagnosis became expedient. Chertkov, with Sasha in tow, approached Rossolimo, asking for a certificate about Sophia's "irresponsible state."[85] Realizing that the document could be used for defamation, the doctor refused to provide it.

In 1910, Chertkov was screening visitors to Tolstoy, isolating him from all other influences. That summer, a group of evangelical Christians arrived from England, headed by Pastor William Fetler. Deciding to spend a day in Tolstoy's neighborhood, they first visited Chertkov's "small colony." Chertkov discouraged them from visiting Tolstoy, who was in a "weak state of health." Soon after, Sophia arrived, saying that Tolstoy had invited the group to Yasnaya. Chertkov "vetoed the proposal," declaring that Tolstoy could not have sent such a message in his state of health and that "the excitement would . . . be too much for the old man." Before the missionaries' departure, Chertkov produced some photographs he had taken of Tolstoy and offered them to the group as consolation.[86]

Chertkov also established close surveillance over Yasnaya, receiving daily bulletins from Sasha, her friend Feokritova, and others, instructing them to "incessantly record *as a digest*, everything that's happening . . ."[87] They informed Chertkov about Sophia's alleged wrongdoings and everything spoken in the house. This intelligence, along with Chertkov's comments, was then presented to Tolstoy. As well, Chertkov continued to read Tolstoy's entries, which Sasha copied, and used them to monitor his mood.

On July 21, in the forest near the village of Grumont, Tolstoy, sitting on a stump, signed the third redaction of his secret testament. Because of Chertkov's paranoiac fear that Sophia would uncover the plot, the matter was handled in "absolute secrecy." A few days later, Tolstoy wrote in his "Diary for Myself Alone": "Chertkov has involved me in a struggle, and this struggle is both very depressing and very repugnant to me."[88] But he still signed Chertkov's codicil to his testament, underneath the words: "I completely agree with the content of this declaration, which was drafted at my request and which completely expresses my wishes."

During that summer and fall, Chertkov controlled Tolstoy's every move to prevent him from changing his mind about the will. Tolstoy was trying to do just that. In early August, Biryukov was in Yasnaya. Upon learning about the secret testament, he told Tolstoy it would have been better to gather his family and announce his wishes openly. This would correspond more with the spirit of Tolstoy's teaching. Immediately after, Tolstoy wrote Chertkov: "It was bad that I acted secretly, assuming bad things about my heirs and, most important, I undoubtedly acted badly in making use of the institutions of the government I renounce in drawing up the will properly."[89] Chertkov responded in a long letter of August 11, 1910, reminding Tolstoy of all the circumstances necessitating the will. Running twenty-five pages, Chertkov's letter was designed to intimidate an ailing Tolstoy. Chertkov claimed that without a formal will Tolstoy's family would launch a lawsuit against his "devoted friends," who would be trying to implement his posthumous wishes.

And not only would your nearest and most devoted friends suffer, but around your writings, preaching love and harmony, a scandal unparalleled in literary history would flare up and, above all, enmity and strife between those who are in one or other way most closely connected with you. And the only cause of all this would be that during your lifetime you had not drawn up a will so definite and irrefutable, even on its formal side, as not to admit of the least doubt. If, on the contrary, you drew up such a will, you would thereby forestall all these evils and sufferings. On the legal side it would be impossible to deprive it of validity, and you would therefore have done all in your power to prevent any litigation or prosecution in connection with your writings.[90]

In other words, Chertkov guaranteed a scandal if Tolstoy attempted to renounce the secret will. Tolstoy knew it was not an idle threat. He sent a repentant letter to Chertkov, took his words back, and apologized "for having caused you pain . . ."[91]

That summer, Sophia was ready to surrender her right to Tolstoy's posthumous legacy, having told Tanya that she made a note about this in her diary.[92] But nobody was listening: Chertkov had undermined trust within Tolstoy's family. At the end of August, Sophia briefly visited Tolstoy in Kochety, Tanya's and Sukhotin's estate. As she was leaving, she managed to get through to him. Tolstoy then wrote her from the heart: "You have moved me deeply, dear Sonya, with your good and genuine words as we parted . . . I felt sad and dejected all evening. I think of you incessantly."[93]

Tolstoy immediately wrote Chertkov that he felt "terribly sorry" for Sophia. "When you think what it's like for her alone at nights, more than half of which she spends awake with the . . . painful awareness that she isn't loved and is a burden to everyone except the children, you can't help being sorry for her."[94] Chertkov was unmoved by this: having skimmed Tolstoy's letter for information, he underlined passages with a blue pencil, as he would do when some matter required urgent attention. Soon after, he organized a stream of denunciation from members of the Yasnaya household. Sukhotin read one of the reports, penned by Feokritova and forwarded to Tolstoy by Goldenweiser, for credibility. Feokritova alleged that Sophia had spoken of her plan to violate her husband's posthumous wishes regarding the copyright, vowed to take revenge on Chertkov, and spoke of her revulsion towards Tolstoy. Sukhotin thought the report was concocted collectively in Chertkov's house. "Having read this disgusting, fake, and boorish denunciation written with an apparent goal to intimidate L.N . . . I felt nauseous and was unable to sleep for a long time. But L.N. surprised me by showing great interest in this filth. Next day, when he asked my opinion, I told him what I thought in this regard, explaining it was a pure provocation . . ." Sukhotin realized that Tolstoy would do nothing about it: he was old, ill, and no longer loved Sophia, although he was still bound to her by "the strength of habit."[95] However, Tolstoy wrote to Goldenweiser that it was unpleasant to him when strangers gave him advice on what he should do.[96]

Around this time, Sophia prevailed on Tolstoy to end his meetings with Chertkov. But once he gave her this promise, he received a flood of reproaches from Chertkov, who called their separation "ugly and unnatural" and urged Tolstoy to be firm with Sophia. In turn, Galya expressed her outrage with Sophia's "monstrous" request, which was crueler than the exile imposed on their family by the Russian government.[97]

Chertkov also flattered Tolstoy, describing his marriage as a trial sent to him by God and comparing his sufferings to those of Christ: "Crosses, bonfires, executions, all kinds of torture—we know it all and nothing new is possible in this regard . . . But your situation is particularly trying . . ."[98] Tolstoy responded that Chertkov's effort to understand him showed "that you love me genuinely."[99]

On September 22, the couple's 48th wedding anniversary, Tolstoy reluctantly agreed to pose for a picture with Sophia. Sasha criticized him for agreeing to take this photo. Chertkov expressed his disappointment in a long letter. In his "Diary for Myself Alone," which he now kept secretly, Tolstoy wrote: "A letter from Chertkov with accusations. They are tearing me to pieces. I sometimes think that I should go away from them all."[100]

The denouement was approaching: Chertkov was making Tolstoy's stay at home unbearable. On September 24, the disciple insisted that they should resume their meetings, "otherwise I'd be *ashamed* for both of us."[101] Chertkov mocked Tolstoy for needing his wife's permission to see such a close friend. "Your letter, my dear friend Vladimir Grigorievich, made a painful impression on me," Tolstoy replied. "I fully agree . . . that I've made a mistake and ought to correct it, but . . . I must decide the question alone, in my own heart, before God . . . I was hurt by your letter; I felt I was being torn in two directions . . ."[102] Tolstoy's request to stop discussing how he should behave at home was dismissed. Chertkov cheerfully returned to the subject: "No, dear Lev Nikolaevich, I cannot stop discussing my letter, which has painfully affected you . . . After sending this letter, I kept worrying, would it give you pain?"[103]

Tolstoy's fainting spells (or transient ischemic attacks), now occurred approximately every six weeks. On October 3, his loss of consciousness was accompanied by powerful seizures. Sophia, who found him sitting in bed and staring vacantly, warned Makovitsky that he was about to have an attack.[104] When Tolstoy fainted, his body twitched and quivered. During one powerful seizure he was thrown across the bed and three men could hardly hold his legs down. Makovitsky and Sophia used their arsenal of home remedies, applying icy compresses to his forehead, and hot water bottles and mustard plasters around his feet and legs. The day after, when Tolstoy was recuperating, Sophia invited Chertkov to visit, but he declined. On October 5, Galya wrote Tolstoy: "We are happy and rejoice [to learn of] your physical resurrection . . ." Chertkov added a few words to establish conditions for their rendezvous, advising Tolstoy that "my *first* meeting with you must be tête-à-tête . . . And if I come, you should agree in advance with S.A. that we'd be given an opportunity to speak in private for as long as it's necessary for you and me."[105] In the weeks and days that remained Tolstoy was powerless to influence events. On October 12, Sophia found his "Diary for Myself Alone" and learned about his secret will. "I am hurt by Chertkov's evil *influence*, hurt by all their endless secrets, hurt that Lev N.'s 'will' is going to give rise to a lot of anger, arguments, judgments and newspaper gossip over the grave of an old man who enjoyed life to the full while he was alive but deprived his numerous direct descendants of everything after his death."[106] A week later, Tanya attempted to bring the family together and discuss Tolstoy's posthumous wishes openly. In a letter to Sasha, which she also intended for Tolstoy to read, Tanya expressed her belief that her mother and brothers should freely release the works to the public domain, without being forced.[107] But instead of sharing her sister's letter with Tolstoy, Sasha gave it to Chertkov, who forbade Tanya, if she cared about her father's peace, to have any discussions of the will.[108]

According to Mikhail Stakhovich, an old family friend and Duma deputy, Tolstoy felt bad about his secret testament. Stakhovich visited Yasnaya on October 15, two weeks before Tolstoy's departure. Like daughter Tanya and Biryukov, Stakhovich considered the will to be "undoubtedly a violation" of Tolstoy's basic beliefs. What is more, Tolstoy knew his opinion and cared about it. As Stakhovich was leaving, Tolstoy took him aside and asked to promise that he would visit again in November, when Tanya would also be in Yasnaya. "We will talk it over with her. This is of great importance to me," Tolstoy said. Pondering Tolstoy's words later on, Stakhovich observed: "This last conversation indicates to me beyond doubt that he had yielded to outside pressure in the question of a will, and that this was worrying him."[109]

On October 19, Chertkov circulated an open letter, entitled "Why L.N. Tolstoy Hasn't Departed From His Wife." It was written in response to Christo Dosev, Tolstoy's dogmatic follower in Bulgaria, who wondered why Tolstoy remained at his estate for so many years. All disciples agreed in their interpretation of Tolstoy's marriage: they blamed it for his failure to implement his doctrine. Dosev, who had never met Sophia, referred to her as "a stupid and vulgar woman," who had enslaved Tolstoy by forcing him to live in luxury, and who had separated him from his friends and humanity. Chertkov had promoted these ideas for many years: having a common enemy helped unite the followers. In his reply to Dosev, he describes Sophia as Tolstoy's "pitiless tormentor," the woman "crazed with egotism, greed, and wrath." In addition, Chertkov compiled some entries in Tolstoy's diaries where he had spoken of his wish to flee from his estate. He argued it was Tolstoy's long-standing dream to live out his final days in "a humble dwelling," in peace and solitude. At his age and with his illnesses Tolstoy could die after leaving home, something Chertkov viewed as both a sacrifice and "an attractive" way to end his life.[110]

Over the years, Tolstoy received letters from his fanatical followers who criticized him for what they saw as a major contradiction of his life: while he renounced property and money, he remained at his estate. Although Tolstoy was now eighty-two, they still expected him to provide an example of complete material renunciation by escaping what was described as "conditions of luxury" and going into the world to preach, in a manner of Christ or Buddha.

Tolstoy's followers needed a lasting legend of their own, and Chertkov urged him to provide it. Tolstoy read his letter to Dosev on October 22, six days before his escape. He replied that although reading it was unpleasant, the letter has "clarified the past and the future."[111] Around this time, Tolstoy began to plan his departure, and Sophia, suspecting a new conspiracy, initiated surveillance of his comings and goings. On October 25, Tolstoy wrote in his "Diary for Myself Alone": "Suspicions, spying, and the sinful desire on my part that she should give me an excuse to go away. That's how bad I am. I think of going away, and then I think of her situation, and I feel sorry and I can't do it."[112] Next day, in a letter to Chertkov, Tolstoy described his dream, in which he was pre-experiencing his flight and imminent death:

> Today, for the first time I felt with a special clarity—and sadness—how much I miss you . . . There is a whole sphere of thoughts, feelings, which I cannot share with anyone as naturally as with you, knowing that I'm completely understood. Today, I had several such thoughts-feelings. One of them I experienced in my sleep: last night, I felt a thrust in my heart, which awoke me and, upon becoming awake, I remembered a long dream, how I was going down the hill, holding onto the branches, but still slipped and fell, i.e., woke up. This entire dream, like the past, appeared for a moment, and the thought that in my dying moment there will be such a thrust of heart in a somnolent state, the moment outside of time, when the entire life will become this retrospective dream.

In this same letter, Tolstoy mentioned his plan of escape, which was already familiar to Chertkov: "Sasha has told you about my plan, which I consider sometimes at moments of weakness . . . If I will embark on something, I will, of course, let you know. Perhaps, I will even need your help."[113]

On October 27, Tolstoy rode with Makovitsky, taking a new route—along the railway and through the forest to the edge of a ravine. Makovitsky noticed that Tolstoy was silent and looked troubled. It was decided to cross the ravine. Tolstoy dismounted, gave his horse to Makovitsky, and began to descend on foot. Perhaps he was remembering his dream and experiencing déjà vu. Makovitsky made it over with both horses. Tolstoy moved slowly and with great difficulty. When he climbed onto the road, he was suffocating. That evening, Tolstoy asked Makovitsky whether he knew when the first morning train was leaving south. Makovitsky at once realized Tolstoy had made up his mind to escape.[114] Tolstoy had talked to him about his possible departure and even asked if Makovitsky would accompany him. The date of his flight, October 28, was also decided: Tolstoy superstitiously believed these two numbers were providential for him. But in his diary, he blamed his departure on Sophia. He describes that at night, upon hearing her footsteps and rustling noises in his study, he concluded that she was rummaging through his papers. In this famous entry he told nothing about his plan of escape, which he had discussed with Chertkov and Sasha.

On October 28, at 3 A.M., Tolstoy woke Makovitsky, told him of his decision, and directed the doctor to accompany him. Their train ride to Kozelsk, in Kaluga province, was excruciatingly slow: it took six and a half hours to cover seventy miles. Tolstoy insisted on traveling third class, but the coach was packed and more than half the passengers were smoking. Tolstoy sought fresh air on the cold and drafty platform between coaches. From Kozelsk, he sent a telegram to Chertkov, informing him of his flight and location, signing it "Nikolaev," as was agreed with Sasha.

Tolstoy chose to stay at the Optina Monastery, a place where he could live and write in peace. From Optina, he wrote a long letter to Sasha. He asked to send him some books—Montaigne's *Essays*, the second volume of Dostoevsky's *The Brothers Karamazov*, and Maupassant's *Une Vie*. "Tell Vladimir Grigorievich that I'm very happy and very afraid for what I've done. I'll try to record my dreams and ideas for future artistic works."[115] Tolstoy jotted down ideas for several plots, of which two were love stories.[116]

On October 29th, Tolstoy visited his sister Maria Nikolaevna, a nun, in the neighboring Shamardino convent. They hadn't seen each over for a year and had a happy reunion. Tolstoy wanted to remain in Shamardino, staying in a nearby village, but this was not to be.

That day, Sergeenko delivered a letter from Chertkov, who congratulated Tolstoy on his flight: "I cannot express in words the joy I feel in hearing that you have gone away." The Chertkovs had been long anticipating it: Galya even dreamt of Tolstoy's home leaving the night before.[117] (Chertkov also wrote Sasha that Tolstoy's departure "was the only *rightful* way out" and that any outcomes of this step, "even the most undesirable—all will be for the best."[118])

Sergeenko told Tolstoy about Sophia's attempted suicide, news that struck him painfully. But on October 30, Sasha and Feokritova arrived to persuade Tolstoy that Sophia was faking her condition and in reality was organizing her pursuit with son Andrei.

Tolstoy was already unwell and wanted to stay in the monastery, but when told that he was being followed, he decided to travel further. (The idea of pursuit was a pure invention: after attempting to drown herself, Sophia was in bed, closely watched by two nurses.) In the morning of October 31, Tolstoy, accompanied by Makovitsky, Sasha, and Feokritova, boarded a train heading to the Caucasus. By mid-afternoon, Tolstoy developed high fever and Makovitsky, suspecting pneumonia, insisted on leaving the train at the next station, Astapovo.

Tolstoy spent the last week of his life in a small, overcrowded station-master's house, which allowed for neither solitude nor peace. On the first night, before the owner and his family moved out, fourteen people slept in the poorly ventilated hut, heated by a single smoking stove and infested by mice. It was noisy, filthy, and suffocating. In the daytime, he was disturbed by creaking and slamming doors and conversations.

On November 1, Tolstoy dictated a telegram to Chertkov and a letter to his eldest children, Sergei and Tanya. He did not disclose his location to the children and asked to forgive him for not inviting them to come. "You will both understand that Chertkov, whom I did ask to come, occupies a special position in relation to me. He has devoted his whole life to the service of the cause which I have also served for the last 40 years of my life." His final words were about Sophia: "Try to calm your mother, for whom I have the most genuine feeling of compassion and love."[119]

Tolstoy's family did not know where he was. The first to learn, Chertkov secretly left for Astapovo with his secretary Sergeenko. He arrived in the morning of November 2, when Tolstoy was diagnosed with pneumonia. Before leaving, Chertkov forbade Bulgakov, who remained in Yasnaya, to reveal Tolstoy's state of health and location. Bulgakov, however, told Tanya that Tolstoy was dangerously ill.

Also on November 2, Sasha sent a telegram to her brother Sergei, in Moscow, asking to urgently bring doctor Nikitin to Astapovo. Tolstoy was glad to see Sergei, surprised that he found him, and deeply moved when Sergei kissed his hand. That same day, a reporter for the *Russian Word* informed the family that Tolstoy was critically ill in Astapovo. When Sophia and the children arrived, the place was already besieged by correspondents and police. Tolstoy was not told that Sophia was there; his opinion on whether he wanted to see her was not sought. Sophia was photographed by the stationmaster's house peeking at her husband through the shuttered window. A reporter wrote: "It was the wife of the great Lev Tolstoy, Countess Sophia Andreevna. They did not let her in to see the sick man."[120]

Makovitsky registered Chertkov's arrival to the stationmaster's house. "L.N. needs rest, but Chertkov and Sergeenko arrived . . . Vladimir Grigorievich tired L.N. with conversations and by reading letters, to which L.N. dictated a reply."[121] Chertkov, who remained near Tolstoy the entire time, decided who should see the sick man.

Tolstoy was happy to see Tanya: "When I came in, he was fully conscious. He told me some tender words, and then asked: 'And who stayed with mama?' The question was posed in a way that I did not have to compromise the truth when replying. I said that mama is now with the sons, and that a doctor and a nurse are also with her. But then I said, 'Perhaps, this conversation is disturbing you?' He interrupted: "Speak, speak, what can be more important for me?" And he continued to ask questions about her." Tanya, like the rest, was afraid that meeting Sophia would distress Tolstoy. One day before he died, he told Tanya: "Many things are falling on Sonya. We managed things badly." Tanya asked whether he wanted to see Sophia, but Tolstoy had already slipped into unconsciousness.[122] Tolstoy's younger sons, Ilya, Andrei, and Mikhail looked at him through the open door while he slept, so as not to disturb him. On November 7, shortly before Tolstoy died, Doctor Berkenheim proposed to call in Sophia. She was only admitted when Tolstoy drew his last breath.

Chertkov remained dispassionately calm even during the most difficult moments of Tolstoy's suffering. He did not ask Tolstoy, as he was dying, the vital question about his faith—whether he still believed as he had. Makovitsky was finishing his chronicle. He registered the precise moment when Tolstoy died. Chertkov and his retinue were hurriedly packing to catch the train. The doctor and Nikitin washed and dressed the body: "We donned a linen undershirt, underpants (Chertkov's), knitted stockings, wide linen trousers, and a dark blouse . . ."[123]

Chertkov reached Yasnaya before the family returned for the funeral. On November 8, Bulgakov witnessed an appalling incident. Chertkov, in his long overcoat, mounted chairs in Tolstoy's study and searched the bookshelves, looking behind the books and even the family portraits. Bulgakov left the room, so disgusted with the spectacle that he failed to ask what Chertkov was looking for.[124]

Bulgakov would spend decades trying to fathom, "How *such a man* as Tolstoy could love *such a man* as Chertkov?"[125] In 1912, Sukhotin shared his understanding with Bulgakov: "L.N. loved V.G. [Chertkov] with exceptional tenderness, partially and blindly; this love drove L.N. to become completely subordinated to Chertkov's will. Chertkov also loved L.N. very much, not only strongly but also *tyrannically*; his despotism drove L.N. to make an act, which completely disagreed with his beliefs (e.g., the secret will)." Sukhotin did not blame Chertkov for his "pernicious influence" over his teacher, "just as I cannot blame a cuckoo bird for failing to sing like a nightingale. I'm far more surprised and saddened by the nightingale, who forgot his gorgeous singing out of love for a cuckoo bird and was trying not to sing . . ."[126] In his reminiscences about Tolstoy, Bulgakov quotes a remark of the statesman Alexander Kuzminsky, who was Sophia's brother-in-law. In 1914, in a conversation about Chertkov, Kuzminsky said: "He was a despot, a true despot! If he were on the throne, it would be disastrous for the people!"[127] This was, of course, a reference to Chertkov's closeness to the tsars.

As Gorky would remark, Chertkov was one of those people who profited from scandal. After Tolstoy's death, he launched a smear campaign against Sophia. Claiming she violated conditions of the will, he battled for the custody of Tolstoy's original manuscripts. To strengthen his position, Chertkov drew Sasha into what her sister Tanya called "a shameful and unworthy struggle with her own mother."

In 1911, Tanya decided to reveal some facts about Chertkov and explain that her mother had deposited Tolstoy's manuscripts in a museum for public use. "All that my mother wished was that the manuscripts given to her by my father and collected by her should be under the protection of some public institution, and should not fall into the uncontrolled hands of Chertkov whom she did not trust, as she feared that they would be altered." Tanya gave examples of Chertkov's "unceremonious treatment" of Tolstoy's text. When preparing Tolstoy's letters for publication, Chertkov purged from them positive remarks about Sophia and suppressed the writer's negative comments about himself. When Tanya noticed the missing information and asked Chertkov about it, he replied: "Chertkov does not remember what he struck out . . ." More important, Tanya admitted that her father had suffered from Chertkov's intrusion into his life and work. She and her sisters often talked about his despotic influence, but "we did not interfere into their relations." Chertkov brought "much that was difficult and inexplicable into our family." She, however, was not at liberty to disclose all she knew: she was bound by her "promise of silence."[128] Then, just before publication, Tanya withdrew her letter from the *Russian Word*, saying that she wanted to keep her hands "clean of all newspaper polemics." Perhaps, she realized that Chertkov would not leave her letter unanswered and his response would generate more controversy. As a result, Chertkov's version of events prevailed and the public at large never learned the truth about Tolstoy's secret will and his flight; as they never learned what motivated Sophia in the infamous struggle for Tolstoy's manuscripts, which she had deposited in the museum to protect them from falling into the hands of a maniac.

CHAPTER ELEVEN

CHERTKOV VS. TOLSTOY'S YOUNGEST DAUGHTER

"I agree that I am a monster and a disgusting one."
—Chertkov, in a letter to Sasha, 1920s

T he news of Tolstoy's death had made headlines around the world
and reverberated in many hearts. "Lev Tolstoy is dead," wrote Gorky
in November 1910. ". . . I wept from pain and grief . . ."[1] But in
Chertkov's family the events in Astapovo were discussed in terms of how
they affected his reputation. On November 11, his mother wrote Chertkov
from Cannes that the newspapers were portraying him negatively. She had
collected a pile of clippings and complained that the newspapers published
"many lies." Having read the reports that Sophia was not admitted to her
dying husband, she asked Chertkov whether he had anything to do with
this. Did Tolstoy ask him to come to Astapovo? Did he quarrel with Tolstoy's sons? Chertkova was sending a hug to Sasha and was also gossiping:
"I was so struck with fate's retribution: she [Sophia] had driven you out of

Yasnaya . . . and declared that you'd never see him [Tolstoy] again, and it turned out that when he was dying, you were by his bedside and she [Sophia] was not admitted. Clearly, these ignoble characters [reporters] imagine that you've revenged on her."[2] Chertkova decided to give up her trip to Italy and return to Petersburg to be closer to her son and help influence public opinion. That was all the mother and son had to say about Tolstoy's death. On December 1, Chertkov sent her a newspaper cutting in which he thanked people who expressed condolences to him personally "in connection with the death of Lev Nikolaevich Tolstoy."[3] He also discussed mundane matters, thanking his mother for the ointment to treat his eczema. Apparently, the events in Astapovo exacerbated his chronic condition.

Chertkova had never forgiven Tolstoy for taking away her son. Having perceived irreconcilable differences between Tolstoy's and Lord Radstock's interpretations of the Gospels, she had relegated the writer "to the camp adversarial of Christ."[4] Although she had learned to tolerate her son's close relationship with the writer, she was apparently relieved it was over.

Chertkova's only disagreement with her son was over money. She had often begged him to reduce his expenses. Chertkov maintained three estates—Lizinovka, Tuckton House, and the Telyatinki mansion. (On top of this, Chertkov was holding on to the Free Word Press, which he funded until 1913.) Lizinovka produced little income in 1910. Chertkova had heard that local villages were stricken with epidemics and mortality was high, especially among children. "Could you make inquiries whether this is true?" she asked Chertkov. There was still an ambulatory and a small clinic in Lizinovka, established decades ago. The doctor had written for permission to hire a female medical attendant, who was Jewish; Chertkova's opinion was that "one needs to stay away from Jewesses."[5]

Chertkov's inability to manage money had always been a problem. His mother contended that he needed to sell or rent Tuckton House. Because he continually complained about his debts, Chertkova wondered: "Have you estimated the cost of running your enormous house in Telyatinki, with all the upgrades and renovations, and how much is spent on poor Galya and her staff?"[6] (According to Bulgakov, Chertkov's "palazzo," after the upgrades, cost him 60,000 rubles. This was twice the value of the Tolstoys' house in Moscow.) In the fall of 1910, Chertkov was trying to persuade his mother to pay him an annual allowance of 12,000–15,000 rubles. He argued that he was entitled to the interest from their ancestral capital. Although his father had disinherited him, this happened decades earlier, when he was still a young man, "whereas now I'm approaching old age."[7] As for selling Tuckton House, Chertkov was in no hurry, since it was an investment. This estate and their other property in England could be profitably sold in the future.[8]

Chertkov kept borrowing money, but it all slipped through his fingers. In August 1910, he had asked Sasha to lend him 5,000 rubles. Meanwhile, his mother paid 3,000 rubles for the wedding of Chertkov's son Dima, who, much to the family's frustration, married a peasant girl. In addition, Chertkova paid for a greenhouse for Dima, costing 300 rubles (as much as a purebred English stallion).

"The Chertkovs' Telyatinki house was, of course, one of the most unusual houses ever," remembers Bulgakov. Aside from his small family it accommodated Chertkov's young male assistants, secretaries, and Tolstoyans, all of whom he fed and clothed. Three peasant lads stayed permanently to amuse son Dima with folk dances and singing. Life in the "palazzo" was disorderly, especially at night, when the bohemian members of Chertkov's "commune" invited visitors. In addition to the "palazzo" Chertkov built two cottages in the woods, reserving one for his assignations. Despite his own extravagance, Chertkov imposed austere measures on others, persuading his English photographer, Tapsell, to give up his copyright on Tolstoy's photographs.[9]

Chertkov's Tolstoyism was a façade. He traveled first class and bought expensive leather suitcases, but once a year, would pick up a scythe and mow. He never gave up his expensive tastes or his love of Swiss cheese, cocoa, chocolate, walnuts, and asparagus. According to Bulgakov, in his house one could find a crude, unpainted wooden stool, peasant style, and an expensive American bureau, which would look more appropriate in a bank, but which Chertkov used as a writing desk. The bureau was a present from his mother, whom Chertkov wrote to thank in February 1910: "I'm sitting at the beautiful desk you've given me . . . It's very comfortable and considerably eases my occupations."[10]

During Tolstoy's life, Chertkov hired his secretaries and paid their salaries; although they helped the writer, they also served as Chertkov's eyes and ears. In addition, Chertkov paid employees of the Free Word Press, run by Alexander Sirnis, a Latvian democratic socialist. (Sirnis's daughter, Melita Norwood, later became an important intelligence source, spying for the Soviets in Britain. A secretary for the British Non-Ferrous Metals Research Association engaged in nuclear weapons development, she photographed documents for Stalin. Working for the Soviets from 1937 and remaining undiscovered for decades, Melita was described as "the most important female agent ever recruited by the USSR."[11])

⁘

After Tolstoy's death, Sasha had the difficult task of working with Chertkov to execute her father's will. The two interpreted Tolstoy's wishes differently. Chertkov understood the will in a way that suited him best, so this created problems at every step of the process. Tolstoy had long wanted to transfer the land around Yasnaya to the local peasants. This became possible in 1912, after publisher Sytin paid Sasha 300,000 rubles for the exclusive right to produce Tolstoy's works for three years. She used the money to purchase two-thirds of the Yasnaya land from her brothers Ilya, Andrei, and Misha. (Sophia bought the remaining land from her sons to preserve Yasnaya as a museum.)

Chertkov argued against buying Yasnaya land from Sasha's brothers. He did not want Tolstoy's children to profit and either out of principle or out of spite insisted that land for distribution should be bought elsewhere. However, this would disregard Tolstoy's wish to dispense the land that had belonged to his serf-owning ancestors. Sasha defended her father's request, explaining that Tolstoy wanted to "expiate the sin he could not remedy during his life."[12] After the land was given to the Yasnaya peasants, Chertkov created new difficulties.

In December 1913, Sasha received Chertkov's bizarre proposal. He suggested selling Tolstoy's works and diaries to the highest bidder and using the profit to buy more land, which could be distributed among a larger number of peasants. (Perhaps, Chertkov dreamt of generating enough money from

Tolstoy's works to redistribute land across Russia, while remaining unaccountable in the process.) It took Sasha a month to reply. Her task, as she saw it, was implementing her father's wishes. Tolstoy's attitude to money was known: he considered it an evil in itself. Distributing land was a matter of great complexity. In Yasnaya, she had her father's instructions about allocating their family's land. Buying and handing it over on a broader scale was an unfeasible task and it was not clear where to put limits. She refused to support Chertkov's fantastic project.

Faced with this rebuff, Chertkov toughened his rhetoric: he argued that as executor of Tolstoy's will, he was entitled to make financial decisions alone. He reminded Sasha that she was only a formal heiress, a nominal figurehead. But dealing with Sasha proved more difficult than with Tolstoy. She focused on fulfilling her father's wishes and ignored Chertkov's grumbling. And since she was the heiress, Chertkov needed her signature with all his appeals.

That year, Chertkov requested a subsidy for the Free Word Press from the newly formed Tolstoy's Fund, which had branches in Russia and in England. Sasha had a decisive voice and could support or refuse funding. In England, the fund was managed by Sir Charles Wright, the secretary and librarian of the London Library, who had visited Tolstoy during his 80th anniversary. Sasha helped compile financial reports of the fund. In 1913, she supported Chertkov's request to fund publications of the Free Word Press, allocating 18,000 rubles.

Chertkov, however, didn't want to be accountable for the money, which was deposited to Galya's private account in England. He tried persuading Sasha to make no mention of the loan in the financial report. It was essential, he argued, that his and Galya's names were omitted because "some people might imagine" they used the money for their personal benefit.[13] By then, Sasha had a better grasp of Chertkov's character and refused to withhold information in the report.

She rejected yet another request, which concerned Tolstoy's manuscripts. In 1913, Chertkov had transported a part of Tolstoy's archive from Tuckton House, depositing it, with much fanfare, in the Academy of Sciences in Petersburg. But in summer 1914, at the start of the war, he asked Sasha to support his appeal to the Academy about relocating the papers (in a view of "possible bombardment") to safer storage. Chertkov's new scheme involved moving the papers into a rented basement of a bank, for which Tolstoy's Fund would provide a loan. But it was "essential to arrange it in a way that the manuscripts would remain registered as remaining at the Academy."[14] If Chertkov succeeded in this deception, the manuscripts would fall into his hands. Sasha did not give him carte blanche as he had asked.

At the start of the Great War, Sasha enlisted as a nurse with the Red Cross. She wrote a will appointing her sister, Tanya, as her heiress. Chertkov promptly declared Sasha's instructions to be "a direct violation of Tolstoy's wishes" and demanded the will be destroyed. Chertkov argued that the true meaning of the secret testament was known only to Tolstoy, Sasha, and Chertkov himself. "After LN's death it's known only to the two of us."[15] Chertkov made it clear that he wanted to appoint his own successor.

He never expressed personal concern for Sasha who could be killed at the front. "War" was a dirty word and he avoided it altogether. What concerned Chertkov was how to get hold of the key to the deposit box where Tolstoy's original diaries were kept. He wrote Sasha in October: "Considering that you, as I heard, are soon planning to leave to such places where written communication with you might be difficult, I endeavor to ask to provide me the key from the metal deposit box in the bank where the originals of Lev Nikolaevich's diaries are kept, so I could photograph them and make necessary inquiries for my edition."[16] Despite Sophia's request to wait for twenty-five years, Chertkov began publishing Tolstoy's diaries in 1913, when he sold an installment to the newspaper the *Russian Word*. At the start, he consulted Sasha and her brother Sergei about sensitive family material, but soon after, declared that Tolstoy had entrusted editing the diaries to him alone. Chertkov claimed that Tolstoy had "appointed" him as his editor and trusted him to know what to strike out from the diaries, "in the interests of his soul, the readers, i.e., the entire thinking humanity."[17]

By now Chertkov no longer concealed that he wanted to control the proceeds from publishing Tolstoy's works. Beginning in 1913, he complained that Tolstoy had trusted him to manage the profit and that by changing the arrangement Sasha had violated his wishes. Sasha received letters in which he complained about his material difficulties and demanded the restoration of his right "given to me by L.N. to manage the publishing profit." He alleged that Sasha took away this privilege because of "worsening relations" between them.[18] In a draft to this letter, Chertkov wrote: "By taking away my right, given to me by LN, to dispose of the profit, you are destroying the entire meaning of my publishing activity."[19] Reminiscing about her collaboration with Chertkov, Sasha describes his famously difficult character, "senseless stubbornness and stupid dictatorial ways . . . There was no flexibility in Chertkov . . . He was heavy-handed in his singleness of purpose... His conduct, his actions, his mind, all were focused in one direction and permitted no compromise. Chertkov had no sensitivity, there was no warmth in him . . ."[20]

In the fall of 1914, Tolstoyans campaigning against the war were arrested and jailed. Bulgakov, who was staying in Yasnaya, wrote and circulated an anti-war petition *Come to Your Senses, Brothers!* It was signed by twenty Tolstoyans, including doctor Makovitsky. On the night of October 28, the anniversary of Tolstoy's flight, the police searched the house and arrested Bulgakov. Sophia sent her protest to the deputy interior minister and the chief of the Okhranka, General Vladimir Dzhunkovsky, who replied that Bulgakov "was properly arrested" for circulating "criminal appeals," but, of course, arrest and search could have been conducted in daytime.[21] Makovitsky was detained in December. Chertkov surprised the Tolstoyans by supporting the war, despite his much publicized pacifism. However, he continued to believe that Tolstoyans should be exempt from military draft. (There was no contradiction here: Chertkov apparently thought that Tolstoyans possessed higher moral qualities than the rest, which is why they should not become cannon fodder.) Chertkov obtained an exemption for his son Dima. According to Bulgakov, the provision was made by Nicholas II himself.[22] (Chertkov had maintained his ties to the interior ministry: when in 1913, local authorities in Tula discovered where he stored prohibited literature, he went to Petersburg and settled the matter with the chief of gendarmes, Dzhunkovsky.)

In 1915, with war refugees streaming to Russia's midlands and Voronezh province, Chertkov was trying to protect his Lizinovka estate, the garden, and the forest from pillaging. Because some refugees were felling trees, he instructed his manager, Pyotr Apurin, to evict them from his land. This had to be handled humanely, Chertkov instructed: he was even prepared to cover some transportation costs, if a subsidy could not be obtained from the local government. In another letter, Chertkov gave instructions to save on medications and reduce the number of patients at the estate's clinic. If refugees were using "our medications," Apurin had to see that the *zemstvo* officials covered the cost.[23] Apurin was Chertkov's former pupil, the very peasant lad whom he had instructed in the Gospels in 1883. Back then, the two were intimate: Apurin slept in Chertkov's bedroom and traveled with him everywhere. Later, Apurin became Chertkov's secretary, treasurer, estate manager, servant, agent, and more. Irreplaceable because of his honesty, intelligence, and versatility, he served Chertkov for the privilege of maintaining a grocery shop on his land. A loner and alcoholic, a sin Chertkov would never fail to point out, Apurin had endured much abuse. In 1918, explaining to Chertkov why he never left him, he remembered their days together, when "I became so strongly attached to you that over thirty-seven years nothing could force me to separate, i.e., to sever relations with you, despite the unfairness I had to suffer."[24] Apurin managed the Chertkovs' practical affairs, bought and sold property. In 1912, Chertkov sent a telegram requesting him to immediately finalize "a profitable purchase of land."[25] Three years later, Apurin oversaw renovations of the Telyatinki "palazzo," which he had to prepare for sale. In February 1915, Chertkov also instructed him to find a buyer for the family's profitable oil plant in Vladimirovka estate, which "we firmly decided to sell (minimum 100,000 rubles)."[26] Because Chertkov held firmly to the price, during the economic chaos produced by war, the sale fell through.

In March 1917, after the abdication of Nicholas II, the provisional government came to power. During this time of economic and political uncertainty, Chertkov was desperate to liquidate his and his mother's Russian assets. He was persuading Apurin that during inflation people will hasten to invest in real estate and that the time was ripe to sell Vladimirovka with its oil plant. There were rumors of land reform, that land would be confiscated from major owners. But Chertkov believed this would not concern factories and plants. Therefore, the value of his family's oil plant could double: Chertkov was now asking 200,000 rubles.[27] (By then, Chertkov and his family lived in Moscow where in 1914 he bought a two-story house at Lefortovsky Lane, 7.) Apurin was able to sell the

Telyatinki "palazzo" and found a buyer for the oil plant, but much of the family's property was lost. Rzhevsk estate was set afire, and there were no buyers for Lizinovka, which Chertkov had been trying to sell since 1915. (On the eve of the 1917 Bolshevik Revolution, Lizinovka peasants were asking Chertkov to sell them parcels of land. Later, in his letters to the Soviet government Chertkov would claim that he transferred his land to the peasants, although this was not the case. Even Apurin was not rewarded for his dedicated service: Chertkov had neither given nor sold him the lot on which his grocery shop was built.)

❖

In May 1915, Chertkov spent an evening with a famous literary couple, Zinaida Gippius and Dmitry Merezhkovsky, the co-founders of a new literary movement, Symbolism. Their Petersburg salon in the early twentieth century was at the center of Russia's spiritual life, the place where culture was collectively created. Chertkov sought their opinion on his manuscript, *The Last Days of Tolstoy*, his account of the writer's secret will and the flight. In it, Chertkov assembled all the negative comments Tolstoy ever made about Sophia and added his own interpretation. The theme is familiar: Tolstoy's martyrdom was suffered at home. The sufferings were inflicted by Sophia's opposing her husband and surrounding him with luxury at their estate. All her activities were "purposely calculated to wound, insult and revolt him [Tolstoy] more and more in his most sacred feelings." Her treatment of Tolstoy was comparable to "the tortures of the Inquisition, and exceeding them in their uninterrupted persistence and prolongation." By bearing his sufferings meekly, Tolstoy gave examples of "great heroism" in his family life. He remained "a voluntary prisoner in his wife's house for . . . many years," thus proving the validity of his non-resistance principles. His eventual decision to flee "all the injustice, all the sinfulness of the surroundings of his home life" was commendable. Chertkov now held Sophia responsible for Tolstoy's home leaving, claiming it was impossible not to run away from such a wife.[28] The book was cleverly compiled: all of Chertkov's assertions were supported with quotations from Tolstoy's diaries.

Gippius describes the manuscript as "astounding . . . and *beyond belief.*" The book breathed hatred towards Tolstoy's wife, showing her spying, searching for the secret will, and making hysterical scenes. Gippius felt there was something insulting in Chertkov's impatience to publish his concoction while Sophia was still alive. "Insulting for Tolstoy? I don't know. But certainly for Tolstoy's love towards this woman." Chertkov's request "not to copy any part of this text" was absurd: copying it would not occur to Gippius or Merezhkovsky. Having met Sophia in Yasnaya, Gippius felt that she was a strong woman, a good wife and mother, and that Chertkov's opus had little to do with the truth. It was really an example of "what Chertkov does with truth."

Chertkov had circulated his manuscript in the literary community and among Tolstoy's children, all of whom, including Sasha, were offended. Tolstoy's letter to Sasha of October 29, 1910, was at the center of the book. It was written in response to Sasha's question whether Tolstoy regretted his flight after Sophia's attempted suicide. He replied that remaining at home "was not simply disagreeable to me but utterly impossible, and that if somebody has to drown himself, it is I, not she, and I only want one thing—to be free of her, and of the falsehood, pretense and malice which permeated her whole being." In this same letter, Tolstoy accused Sophia of her "simulated hatred of the man who is closest and most necessary to me . . ."[29]

In the writers' community Chertkov's manuscript (and Tolstoy's letter and diary entries) were producing shock. Mark Aldanov wondered whether Tolstoy wrote that letter on the spur of a moment, with "a demon driving his hand." Gippius responded in her diary: "It could be a demon. We don't know *who* Chertkov is." Chertkov was not the "closest and most necessary man" to Tolstoy. At least not to a genuine Tolstoy, who believed in love and truth, not in hatred and revenge.[30]

Sophia died in 1919, and three years later, Chertkov was able to publish his magnum opus. He wrote in the book's opening: "Now that Tolstoy's wife is dead, the chief obstacle to revealing the true causes of his [Tolstoy's] going away from Yasnaya Polyana is removed."[31] In Soviet times, Chertkov's myth of Tolstoy's marriage became influential. His presentation of the family conflict in black and white—Tolstoy rejecting his property and Sophia holding onto it—was perfectly relevant in the new Soviet era.

Because the Bolsheviks presented the propertied class as evil, portraying Sophia negatively became expedient. With the help of Chertkov's myth-making Tolstoy was included in a gallery of the new Soviet saints. Chertkov had no problem adjusting to Soviet ideology. In 1922, in the spirit of the day, he wrote that Tolstoy gave "his whole working time to intense spiritual labor in the interests of the working masses."[32] As Tolstoy's disciple, Chertkov found himself on the right side of history.

Shortly after the Bolshevik Revolution, Sasha returned from the front, decorated with two St. George medals for bravery. (She had managed a field hospital.) Banks were nationalized, and nearly all her money was lost. She experienced "neither terror nor disappointment," losing property meant little, but it was unclear how to live: "Food was my greatest need." The Revolution swept away the old life, and the new had to be built. "What was to become of the old world in the process?"[33] Chertkov never pondered such philosophical questions: he was well received at the court of the Red Tsar.

CHAPTER TWELVE

WORKING FOR THE SOVIETS

"From the age of uniformity, from the age of solitude, from the age of Big Brother, from the age of double-think—greetings!"

—George Orwell, *1984*

"The celebration of the Day of Unanimity, long awaited by all, took place yesterday. The same Well-Doer who so often has proved his unshakable wisdom was unanimously re-elected for the forty-eighth time. The celebration was clouded by a little confusion, created by the enemies of happiness."

—Evgeny Zamyatin, *We*[1]

"The greatest empire of all: over the human mind."

—Judith Shklar, *Ordinary Vices*

I'd like to know how Chertkov lived after the Revolution, what became of him, of his wife and son," mused Sophia Motovilova, who had visited Chertkov's Tolstoyan colony in Purleigh in 1900. After the

Revolution Motovilova worked under Lenin's wife, Nadezhda Krupskaya, who was deputy to the People's Commissar of Education. In 1918, in Krupskaya's reception room, Motovilova met Chertkov. He was there with publisher Sytin to discuss producing a comprehensive collection of Tolstoy's works. "I approached Chertkov, but he, of course, did not recognize me at first—18 years have passed since we've met—but then he remembered."[2] They only had time to exchange a few words: Chertkov was called in for his appointment. (Krupskaya was against publishing Tolstoy's religious writings, which she considered harmful: she even demanded they be removed from shelves.[3] Chertkov, however, soon befriended Krupskaya's boss, the Commissar of Education, Anatoly Lunacharsky.)

In 1918, Chertkov was sixty-four. That summer, Nicholas II and his family were executed by the Bolsheviks in Ekaterinburg. Chertkov's mother, a close friend of the dowager Empress, had left Bolshevik Russia forever. From Petersburg, where her apartment was expropriated, she escaped to Finland. Communication between Bolshevik Russia and the West was severed; however, Chertkov was able to correspond with his mother until her death in 1922. In January 1919, he instructed her to write him through the Russian envoy in Sweden and address her letters to Bonch-Bruevich, who was now Lenin's secretary. The Bolsheviks had reintroduced the system of perlustrating letters and would detect aristocratic handwriting; knowing this, Chertkov advised his mother to let someone else address the envelope.[4]

Curiously, Chertkov and Lenin had some family connections. Chertkov's grandfather, Ivan Dmitrievich, had christened Lenin's mother, Maria Blank. Maria came from the family of a Russian-Jewish physician, Alexander Blank, who was a good acquaintance of Chertkov's grandfather. Ivan Chertkov was a *stallmeister* in the court of Nicholas I and an adjutant to the Tsar's brother, the Grand Duke Mikhail Pavlovich. In February 1835, he attended the christening of Blank's daughter, Maria, becoming her godfather. In childhood Maria played with the Chertkov children in their Petersburg mansion on Millionnaya, 32. In 1900, Lenin visited this same house, which by then accommodated the German Consulate: he needed a German visa to emigrate.[5] But in 1918, Chertkov had not yet met the Red Tsar.

That year, Chertkov attained Lunacharsky's support to produce Tolstoy's most complete edition, to incorporate everything he had written, including drafts. In December, despite the civil war, the government decided to provide 10 million (inflated) rubles for the project, which was endorsed by Lenin. Chertkov instantly composed a memo, outlining his conditions, e.g., full editorial and financial autonomy. Although the subsidy would come from the state, Chertkov wanted to manage the funding, arguing that Tolstoy had allowed him to produce his works on such conditions. Chertkov proposed creating a special fund, named "Tolstoy's People's Publishing Fund," and depositing the entire sum "for my disposal." An advance of 400,000 rubles was to be paid immediately.[6]

But during the civil war, which followed, and with the economy in shambles, cultural projects were superfluous. The promised sum was never paid: the Bolsheviks, who had no money, would be soon seizing and selling the property of the Orthodox Church. Nonetheless, Chertkov assembled his own editorial team, comprising 30 scholars as well as secretaries and typists. In 1918, he secured, with Bonch-Bruevich's help, 30,000 rubles to pay salaries.[7]

For a while there were two independent teams preparing Tolstoy's comprehensive edition. Even before Chertkov began to lobby the government, work was already underway. Sasha, her eldest brother Sergei, and Tolstoy's former secretaries Bulgakov and Gusev had been elected to the editorial board of the edition, which they expected to fund through subscription. Their team sorted Tolstoy's manuscripts in unheated rooms of the Rumyantsev Museum. There was no fuel to heat the buildings and no food for the museum staff and board members.

Chertkov, however, was far better equipped to carry out the project. He found a patron in Lunacharsky, who sympathized with evangelical Christians and even considered integrating the evangelical wing of the Church into Soviet ideology.[8] Lunacharsky's support was essential to secure editorial office space for Chertkov's team. Despite severe housing shortages in Moscow, the city government provided a wing adjacent to Chertkov's roomy house at Lefortovsky Lane, 7. The former residents of this wing were ordered to leave and were later resettled. The editorial office was even renovated at city expense.[9] Having secured government support Chertkov was able to take the leading role in the project.

In July 1919, the Bolsheviks issued a decree that nationalized the manuscripts of Russian writers deposited in libraries and museums. This included Tolstoy's papers Sophia had deposited in the Rumyantsev Museum as well as Chertkov's collection in the Petersburg Academy of Sciences. The government was also preparing a decree that would give the state a monopoly over publishing Russian classics. Chertkov protested the measures in a letter to the government, arguing that an exception should be made in Tolstoy's case and explaining that such a monopoly on publishing his works contradicted the writer's renunciation of copyright. The Council of the People's Commissars (Sovnarkom) did not reply. Chertkov turned to Bonch-Bruevich, who held a high-level position at Sovnarkom. For years to come, Bonch-Bruevich would remain an important contact, navigating Chertkov through the corridors of Soviet power.

On September 8, 1920, Bonch-Bruevich arranged for Chertkov to meet Lenin. When discussing Chertkov's publishing project, Lenin agreed that Tolstoy's no-copyright principle should be formally recognized. Chertkov received permission to publish an inscription on the volumes that any part of the text could be freely reprinted.[10] But with tightening ideological control all publishing soon became state business.

During their meeting Chertkov and Lenin also discussed an exemption from military draft for Tolstoyans and other religious pacifist groups. In January 1919, the government issued a decree permitting conscientious objectors to work in medical units, primarily in hospitals for contagious diseases.[11] (In his official letters Chertkov would mention that he had helped prepare this decree.) The previous year Chertkov became the head of the newly formed United Council of Religious Communities and Groups. The Council was entrusted to oversee implementation of the government decree concerning religious objectors. Lenin's hostility was directed against the official Church, not the Tolstoyans or evangelical Christians. For a while, the Bolsheviks guaranteed freedom of religious conscience: even the Salvation Army was permitted in Moscow until 1920.[12]

But by 1922, the situation changed for the worse: the rights of religious objectors were no longer recognized. Even earlier, the Council proved ineffectual: in 1919 it failed to save one hundred Tolstoyan objectors from execution by firing squad.[13] Although the Council ceased to exist in 1923,

Chertkov continued to collect information on violations of the government decree.

In 1920, Chertkov also met Felix Dzerzhinsky, the Commissar of Internal Affairs and chairman of the Cheka, the Bolshevik secret police. The Cheka had a formal right to conduct executions without sanction and due process. Answerable to nobody, except Lenin, the repressive organization was headed by this fanatic, whom decades later the Soviet secret police would consider their role model.

Chertkov came to Lubyanka to persuade Dzerzhinsky that Tolstoyans and other evangelical Christians, such as the Shtundists, were harmless to the state. Later, he penciled a brief reverential memoir about this meeting: Dzerzhinsky heard him "with remarkable attention, sensitivity, and exceptional interest." When Chertkov mentioned Bolshevik sympathizers (those who were neither friends nor foes), Dzerzhinsky interrupted with the remark: "'Do you think there're no sympathizers down there?!' Having said this, he energetically threw his left hand, pointing his thumb down. This gesture implied the Cheka basements, in which the arrested were kept."[14] Chertkov was apparently awed with Dzerzhinsky's power over life and death, which was no different than in the Roman Empire, where that same gesture determined a defeated gladiator's fate.

Dzerzhinsky himself drove out to make arrests and interrogate prisoners. The British agent Robert Bruce-Lockhart portrays him as a ruthless and cold-blooded psychopath: "His eyes deeply sunk, they blazed with a steady fire of fanaticism. They never twitched. His eyelids seemed to be paralyzed."[15] Chertkov was drawn to a strong dictatorial type, like Dzerzhinsky, whom he attempted to depict as a sensitive man. (In 1921, Chertkov requested another meeting with Dzerzhinsky, to inform him about persecution of Tolstoyans and other religious sectarians, but the appointment was not granted.[16])

Having met the heads of the secret police under the tsars and under the Soviets, Chertkov could draw parallels. Actually, the Okhranka and the Cheka had much in common. The former head of the tsarist secret police, General Dzhunkovsky, had by then volunteered his services to the Cheka, teaching them about counter-subversion. It was a technique that worked well under Sergei Zubatov (and Trepov) in the Tsar's Ministry of the

Interior. It involved drawing factions into illegal opposition and manipulating subversives to work for the state.[17] Chertkov had met General Dzhunkovsky in 1913; he would also meet and correspond with the chairman of the OGPU[18], which replaced the Cheka, the nobleman Vyacheslav Menzhinsky.

Chertkov's old friend, Vladimir Krivosh, the very expert cryptographer employed by the Okhranka, was now working in the Special Department of the Cheka under Dzerzhinsky as a translator-decoder. Although Dzerzhinsky mistrusted those who had served in the tsarist secret police, he did recruit a few. Krivosh, who joined the Cheka in 1919, was also valuable with his knowledge of languages. When the Cheka interrogated foreigners, he was asked to translate.[19]

Although perlustration was technically illegal under the tsars and under the Soviets, it was widely practiced. But in Soviet times, services of perlustrators were in greater demand. In 1882, perlustrators in Russia's "black offices" read 38,000 letters annually. In 1923, the OGPU opened and read 5 million letters and 8 million telegrams.[20]

In the fall of 1922, some of Russia's most prominent intellectuals—philosophers, historians, doctors, agronomists, economists, linguists, and editors of academic journals were deported to Stettin, Germany, on two ships. Lenin, who initiated the move, had compiled the lists of what he called "active anti-Soviet intellectuals" and sent these lists to the OGPU. In September, Dzerzhinsky wrote a memo arguing that in addition to deportation intellectuals must be divided into groups according to their expertise. This would make it easier to track them down: "Each intellectual must have a file." The deportations prompted a protest from the German chancellor that "Germany was not Siberia."[21]

Tolstoyans were also harassed: Sasha was arrested three times. In 1919, she was incarcerated in the Lubyanka prison on a mere suspicion of counter-revolutionary activity. Later, officially appointed by Lunacharsky as the Commissar of Yasnaya Polyana, she did not feel safe: "Today I am a commissar, tomorrow I may be in prison."[22] But it was different with Chertkov whom the authorities spared even despite his closeness to the royal family and his fervent anti-Bolshevik propaganda.

The Cheka kept surveillance over the two-story house in Gazetny Crescent, which accommodated the Moscow Vegetarian Society and the

Tolstoy Society, along with their library and club. As the head of these organizations, Chertkov gave talks, which were quoted in police reports. In August 1920, at a gathering of Tolstoyans, Chertkov called for disobeying the Bolsheviks, accusing them of "bloody repression." In 1921, he accused the Bolsheviks of seizing power and holding on to it with the help of the Cheka. On November 25, Chertkov compared the Bolsheviks to "assassins" and declared that people who collaborated with such a government were "assassins as well." In 1922, he went even further, saying that "nowadays communists" were "a gang, which seized power," whereas the Quakers were "true communists." On December 2, Chertkov was present at a gathering of Baptists along with Valentin Bulgakov, who delivered a report about society and the individual. Bulgakov argued that public debate was essential in a free society, and that communists, instead of forming party organizations, should participate in these discussions on equal terms with the rest.[23]

Six days later, the Cheka searched Bulgakov's and Chertkov's homes. Both were required to provide a written undertaking not to leave Moscow. Bulgakov signed such a document, but Chertkov refused. When summoned to Lubyanka for further questioning, Chertkov declared that he did not recognize "any violent state power." He also demanded the return of papers confiscated in the search.

Both Chertkov and Bulgakov were sentenced to three years of administrative exile. Bulgakov, who was by then a director of the Tolstoy Museum, was deported with his family to Czechoslovakia in 1923 and allowed to return only in 1949. Chertkov refused to appear in Lubyanka. Upon receiving a summons, he replied that his religious beliefs did not allow him to deal with government institutions and that by coming to Lubyanka he would place himself "in a false and difficult position." Instead, he invited the prosecutor for "a private conversation in my house." Meanwhile, Chertkov appealed to his diplomatic contacts in England and in a short while, the OGPU received a letter from Maxim Litvinov, Deputy Head Commissar for Foreign Affairs, who explained that Chertkov's arrest and deportation would only benefit the West in their propaganda against the Soviet Union. Chertkov's exile abroad was substituted with an administrative exile to the Crimea under police surveillance. (The Soviet government was practically sending him to a resort.) But Chertkov would have none of it. He appealed to Avel Enukidze, a member of the Central Committee and Stalin's friend, arguing that he was busy producing Tolstoy's comprehensive edition. An administrative exile would jeopardize this important cultural project, which had "universal significance."[24] (Chertkov had befriended Enukidze. In spring 1920, when son Dima traveled to England on the train of the British Red Cross, Chertkov wrote Dzerzhinsky that Enukidze knew his family well and could confirm "we are utterly apolitical."[25]) Following his appeal to Enukidze, Chertkov was allowed to remain in Moscow.

The story of son Dima and his trip to England deserves to be told because it shows Chertkov's ability to do well under any regime. In 1920, Chertkov Jr. was an employee of the Central Union of Consumer Cooperatives (Centrosoyuz). During his trip to England, he had to inspect his father's archive and the family's property. As Chertkov explained to Lunacharsky, the trip was closely related to Tolstoy's publishing project. Because the project was sanctioned by Lenin, Chertkov Jr. was traveling with a Soviet trade delegation and on a train provided by the English Red Cross (the civil war was still on). Although space on the train was limited, Chertkov appealed to Dzerzhinsky to allow his son's wife to travel along. In March, he wrote to the head of the Cheka: "As Comrade Menzhinsky told me yesterday, there will be no objections on the part of the Special Department to my son's trip, but that the question whether his wife can accompany him, depends on you alone." Chertkov claimed that his son's poor health did not permit him to travel by himself. (Being a vegetarian, Chertkov Jr. preferred to travel with his peasant wife who was his personal cook. Chertkov troubled the head of the Cheka, the People's Commissariat for Education, and the Commissariat for Foreign Affairs to make this arrangement.) Since he was asking for a favor, Chertkov proposed using "my connections in England" and his son's services as a translator for the Soviet trade delegation.[26] Chertkov's connections would interest the head of the Cheka and his deputy chairman, Menzhinsky. Under Menzhinsky, the Soviet secret police would spread its influence abroad to recruit Russian émigrés and Soviet sympathizers.

That same year, when after a three-month journey Chertkov Jr. and his wife Matryona (Motya) were returning home, the Soviet mission in Berlin refused to give them a visa because they traveled without passports. (Before leaving abroad, in compliance with a bureaucratic requirement of the day, they had to leave their passports with the Soviet authorities, traveling with only a visa.) Overcoming Soviet bureaucracy, Chertkov pressed the Commissariat for Foreign Affairs to telegraph permission to issue visas for his son and daughter-in-law; that both sides on the German and Soviet border be "immediately" informed; and that no problem arise with his son's luggage.[27] (Chertkov Jr. was likely transporting papers from England.)

❖

In the early 1920s, Chertkov wrote several letters to Lenin to remind him about his publishing project. On November 27, 1922, shortly before Lenin's second stroke, Chertkov sent a detailed memo asking to lift the state monopoly on publishing Tolstoy's works. (The letter was signed by Chertkov and Sasha.) There was no reply, so Chertkov wrote again, in January 1923. In this letter, running six typewritten pages, Chertkov told about the obstacles to producing Tolstoy's comprehensive edition and difficulties dealing with the state publishing house. At sixty-nine, Chertkov was impatient to see publication of at least Tolstoy's diaries and letters, which he prized. He spoke about the need to speed up this work, since Tolstoy had entrusted the "confidential work" of editing his diaries "to his close friend" alone. Chertkov claimed he had "no moral right" to relegate this task to someone else.[28] By then, Lenin was gravely ill and this letter also remained unanswered.

After Lenin's death in 1924, Chertkov attained an audience with Stalin. The centenary of Tolstoy's birth was approaching and Chertkov came to discuss publishing the Jubilee Edition. This edition would eventually comprise 90 volumes, to include everything Tolstoy had written, even his religious tracts. Producing these works in a limited circulation was important to the county's prestige in the world, Chertkov argued. (A marginal publication of Tolstoy's religious works could attest to freedom of conscience in the Soviet Union and could serve as a propaganda tool.) Apparently, Stalin was persuaded: in June 1925, the government passed a resolution allocating 1 million rubles (of after-inflation money) for the project.

However, Chertkov would receive only crumbs of the promised sum. This was in spite of his persistence: over the years, he kept reminding Stalin about his pledge. But Tolstoy's non-fiction, critical of the dictatorial state, could only frighten the state publisher: Gosizdat would neither sign the contract nor release the funding. Chertkov insisted on an urgent installment of 100,000 rubles: he needed to pay salaries to his scholarly team. Although Stalin did not reply, the State Bank released a fraction of the requested amount.

In March 1928, months before Tolstoy's centenary, Chertkov again appealed to Stalin. Sprinkling his letter with flattery, he expressed his "confidence that the Soviet authorities at the very top, who had decided to produce this edition," would consider the impact it would make "on public opinion around the world" and would want this project to succeed. Chertkov expressed his "highest gratitude" to Stalin for his personal involvement.[29] This time Chertkov prevailed: Stalin gave a signal to the state publisher, and the contract was signed. Chertkov appointed himself as the general editor. When an announcement about the Jubilee Edition appeared in foreign press, Maude read it in disbelief: "Should the Soviet Government really publish in full what Tolstoy wrote in condemnation of Governments that employ violence or interfere with religious liberty and the freedom of the Press, it will be one of the strangest occurrences in their strange career."[30]

The year of Tolstoy's jubilee also marked the beginning of Stalin's mass trials and the peasant genocide. Chertkov received peasant letters, which gave harrowing accounts of how the villagers were herded into kolkhozes, with authorities seizing their inventory and crops.[31] (They wrote to Chertkov because of his reputation as Tolstoy's friend.) With typical duplicity, Chertkov expected the tyrant to subsidize publication of Tolstoy's works, which denounced violence. By then, Sasha had distanced herself from Chertkov's undertaking, convinced that her father would not have wanted the state to publish his writings. She also felt that a limited subscription and unaffordable price of 300 rubles were against Tolstoy's beliefs. In 1929, when the first volume appeared, Sasha left for Japan, never to return to Russia. It would take thirty years and many editorial teams to produce all ninety volumes. Chertkov did not live to see the completion of this colossal project.

Galya died in June 1927 and the following year, Chertkov had his first stroke. In May, he summoned his attorney, Muravyov, the very one who had drafted Tolstoy's secret testament. Muravyov was now expected to make a power of attorney document for Chertkov's chosen successor, Nikolai Rodionov, who was entrusted "to watch over the implementation of Lev Nikolaevich's will." At thirty nine, Rodionov was an impoverished descendant of the aristocratic Shakhovskoy clan. A former bank inspector, he organized village cooperative banks in the 1920s. At one time, he also collaborated on the Tolstoy edition, although he had no literary expertise. Chertkov made Rodionov a member of the editorial board, which comprised prominent literary scholars. While these academics were barely paid, Chertkov guaranteed a salary of 200 rubles a month to his successor. (An average worker's salary was then around 55 rubles.[32]) To his credit, Rodionov found this offer embarrassing and declined it, but Chertkov insisted, saying he would pay out of his own pocket.

Rodionov was entrusted an important task of editing Tolstoy's letters for 1910, the year Chertkov believed vital. As he told Rodionov, "I reserved this year for myself, since I don't want to admit strangers to this important period in L.N.'s life, and I'm passing it on to you."[33] Clearly, Chertkov wanted his account of the secret will and the flight to be consistent with Tolstoy's diaries and letters. To achieve this, certain things had to be edited out. When Rodionov accepted the job, Chertkov hugged him and cried: "Thank you! Don't leave me . . . I'm alone. I always believed that you're the most trustworthy, I will never forget that you . . . supported me at a critical moment. Even my son has betrayed me."[34] After the stroke, Chertkov suffered from insomnia, his speech was erratic, and tears stood in his red swollen eyes.

Tolstoy's former secretary, Gusev, who also helped prepare the writer's diaries for publication and would later become a major authority on Tolstoy, received the same instruction. In 1932, Chertkov wrote him: "After my death you will remain the only person on our editorial committee who personally knew him [Tolstoy] and worked with him . . ."[35] Gusev was then the head of the L.N. Tolstoy State Museum, which became the main depository of the writer's papers and those of his family. In this capacity, Gusev suppressed positive information about Tolstoy's wife. As a result, Sophia's memoir, her other prose, and much of her correspondence remained unpublished for a century.

Chertkov was still residing at Lefortovsky Lane, 7, in the house adjacent to his editorial office. He shared his living quarters with his son, who did not get along with him, his daughter-in-law, and several secretaries and assistants. Chertkov Jr., wanting to reduce the number of tenants and guests who dined in their house, requested that they pay 40 kopecks for each meal. Galya's sister, Olga, and Rodionov had to pay as well. "That's very strange," remarked Rodionov in his diary, "why, with all this education and heredity!"

In July 1928, one month before Tolstoy's centenary, Chertkov suffered a second stroke. When Rodionov came, Chertkov asked him, "Have you heard of my little stroke? But that's only a fainting spell, not a stroke, right?" Chertkov likely remembered Tolstoy's final years and his "fainting spells." Unlike with Tolstoy, Chertkov's stroke left him partly paralyzed: he lost control of his right arm and could barely walk. At the end of the month, he was learning to write in a lined student notebook. Chertkov could no longer handle mental tasks and in October, entrusted Rodionov with editing Tolstoy's youthful diaries as well.

In November, Rodionov arrived daily to work "on the intimate sections" of Tolstoy's youthful diaries under Chertkov's supervision. Tolstoy's eldest son, Sergei, then a professor at the Moscow Conservatory, was pleasantly surprised when he was allowed to see the changes. (Detail about Tolstoy's sex life and the course of his venereal disease had to be taken out: Chertkov believed this would make a poor impression on the reader.)

Chertkov now worried that Tolstoy's children—Sergei and Sasha— would write unfavorably about him in their memoirs. He read Sasha's manuscript and kept it at home. Once, when he misplaced it, Chertkov complained that God was punishing him "for one bad deed." Rodionov watched him cry "inconsolably": Chertkov complained it was impossible to return to the past and "redo what was wrong."[36]

Concerned for his image posthumously, Chertkov was trying to influence his portrayals by artists. In 1926, the Tolstoy State Museum, which mostly employed the writer's followers, assigned a talented sculptor, Anna Golubkina, to make Chertkov's bust. After meeting Chertkov, Golubkina told the portraitist Mikhail Nesterov: "How can I sculpt him? He is as hard as stone." Nesterov, who had known Chertkov for many years, quipped: "A stone guest! Just try and sculpt the face of a stone guest."[37] (He was referring to Pushkin's poetic drama, of the same title.) Around this time, Nesterov described Chertkov in a letter to a friend: "This formerly handsome officer of the Guards has become a complete wreck, but his main features—stubbornness, impenetrable dull-wittedness, narrow-mindedness—remain. And this makes him strikingly different from Tolstoy, who was always young, renewing himself spiritually . . ." (Nesterov had painted Tolstoy in 1907.)

During his last years Chertkov told people close to him that he had realized his mistakes, had restrained his character and love of power, and had become meek. Golubkina saw him cry at a meeting of Tolstoyans when Chertkov spoke about a follower who had committed suicide. This emotion, a manifestation of humanity, suggested the key to the portrait: Golubkina agreed to sculpt Chertkov. Arriving at her studio, Chertkov would sit on a chair in the middle of an elevated wooden circle. While he was napping, the sculptor carved his bust from a birch stump. Golubkina rendered Chertkov's complexity, secrecy, solitude, and a shadow of repentance through the gaze of his downcast swollen eyes.

Nesterov admired Golubkina's artistry, but remained unconvinced that Chertkov was capable of a genuine sentiment. "Chertkov is all about pretense, but she [Golubkina] saw a different Chertkov . . ." Having met Chertkov in 1890, Nesterov had made several sketches depicting him as Tolstoy's dogmatic disciple, with a single strong wrinkle between his brows. In 1924, the Tolstoy Museum asked the portraitist to design a card for Chertkov's seventieth birthday. Nesterov painted Chertkov with Tolstoy on a walk in an idyllic countryside. Towering over the writer, Chertkov's domineering and sinister figure makes him look more like a guard. Nesterov could not forgive Chertkov for "seducing Tolstoy" with Tolstoyism and for taking him away from his art.

Nonetheless, in 1934, Chertkov wanted none other but Nesterov to paint his new portrait. Nesterov had painted Russian saints and philosophers, and Chertkov needed a spot in this gallery. Before Chertkov's eightieth birthday, his secretary Sergeenko visited Nesterov. He brought Chertkov's photograph. Sporting a white beard, a righteous Chertkov is reading a book.

Nesterov did not like the photo, which, in fact, imitated Repin's portrait of Tolstoy with a book. But he agreed to paint Chertkov.

In January 1935, when Nesterov arrived for a first session, Chertkov was recuperating after yet another stroke, which now impaired his speech. Having seated Chertkov in an armchair with green and gray stripes, the portraitist had him don a brown velvet jacket. For Nesterov, who had painted frescos in the Orthodox cathedrals, brown symbolized carnal passions, while the blend of green and gray represented emotional sensitivity and spiritual emptiness respectively. Nesterov painted Chertkov as a tyrant, whose character remained unchanged despite old age. During the last session he lengthened Chertkov's fingers to show his grip on power.

When someone told the painter that his Chertkov resembled Ivan the Terrible, Nesterov replied, "But that's what he is like. What power . . ." Chertkov was upset with the lack of softness in his features and offered to bring his recent photographs to prove the portrait inaccurate. The artist was adamant: "And that's how *I* see Chertkov." When Chertkov asked to draw a tear on his cheek, Nesterov refused: "I did not see any tear . . . If I haven't seen it, I can't paint it." Sergeenko tried, but failed to convince the artist to paint a copy of the same portrait, with a tear.

Despite his antipathy to Chertkov, Nesterov admired him as an interesting model: working with zeal, he completed the portrait in just three sessions. Wondering at the source of his inspiration and the magnetism Chertkov held for Tolstoy, he muttered, "What mystery... Why is it? What mystery..." When later comparing Nesterov's portrait to the one made by Repin in 1885, Chertkov Jr. wondered which artist was a better judge of his father's character. Repin's painting shows Chertkov as an idealistic young man, "with Christ-like face," shortly after he met Tolstoy. Surprised with the vast difference between the two portrayals, Chertkov Jr. wondered whether Nesterov, who showed his father as Ivan the Terrible, was more perceptive.

❖

In 1930, Chertkov participated in resettling one thousand farmers, members of Tolstoyan agricultural communes reluctant to join state collective farms. For the second time since the Doukhobor migration to Canada he became an intermediary between the government and religious sectarians. But the resettlement under Stalin had tragic consequences.

Tolstoyan communes had sprung up across the country beginning in 1921, developing into successful farms. During the famine, which followed the civil war, the People's Commissariat for Agriculture had officially encouraged religious sectarians to launch their farming communes on unsettled lands. A geologist and gulag survivor, Boris Mazurin, later told about the destruction of his commune "Life and Labor." Launched by several families near Moscow, it quickly became successful and expanded. By the mid-twenties, "Life and Labor" was the main supplier of vegetables and milk to Moscow's hospitals. Not all commune members were Tolstoyans: some were Communists and anarchists. They were united in their pacifist beliefs and rejection of state interference in their affairs. For example, they refused to pay taxes and register their residency, which became mandatory under Stalin. In 1928, with the beginning of Stalin's collectivization, most Tolstoyan communes were dismantled. Ironically, during the writer's centenary, Tolstoyans were officially pronounced "the most harmful sect." But a few communes, including "Life and Labor," lasted longer than the rest.

The government used various, often contradictory regulations, as pretexts to liquidate Tolstoyan farms. In 1929, the Tolstoyan commune "New Jerusalem" was accused of being financially self-sufficient and failing to take government loans. Soon after, "Life and Labor" was accused of the opposite, of taking a government loan to buy cattle. The true reason was that both communes refused to enter kolkhozes. From this moment on, authorities relentlessly persecuted them. The Tolstoyan communes were similar to collective farms with no private ownership of inventory and livestock. But none of this mattered to the state, which needed to establish its ideological control over every aspect of life. When the authorities shut down "Life and Labor," its inventory was taken away and given to a neighboring collective farm. The commune leaders appealed for justice to the Central Committee, since they launched their farms at government initiative. But they found no justice: instead, criminal charges were brought against them.[38]

Around this time, Chertkov engineered his plan to resettle Tolstoyan communes on the edge of the country and sent a proposal to the Central Committee. In February 1930, the government passed a resolution concerning relocation of Tolstoyan communes. But it immediately became apparent that Tolstoyans would not be allowed to maintain pacifist beliefs anywhere in the Soviet Union. When Mazurin's group met with Chertkov's main contact in the Central Committee, Pyotr Smidovich, the Party boss read the commune's constitution, e.g., refusal of military draft and a pacifist curriculum in schools, with sinister comments: "We will arrest you for this . . . We will fine the parents." Upon finishing his reading, Smidovich asked, "So, do you want to live without Soviet power?"[39]

Despite such reception at the top, Chertkov continued to persuade Tolstoyans to relocate. In 1930, he began producing a monthly newsletter, "Letters to Friends," typed on onion skin and sent by registered mail to Tolstoyans. The first February issue reported the Party resolution, which sanctioned the resettlement. Chertkov wrote: "Recently, I've sent my proposal to the Government asking to allow our friends to relocate to unsettled lands and organize their own collective farms on the principles that do not contradict their conscience."[40] In subsequent issues Chertkov published extracts from letters of peasant sectarians, or "friends." These told about abuses and arrests among religious sectarians, who had resisted collectivization; about deportation of "our friends" (Tolstoyans and evangelical Christians) to far north labor camps. Chertkov quoted some letters, in which addressees complained that "the life of a Soviet citizen is not free, since he is a slave to the state," and published accounts of forced collectivization. Emigration was no longer an option, Chertkov explained; this made resettlement the only escape from persecution.

Chertkov was at once helping Tolstoyans and risking their safety. Under Stalin, his subversive newsletter, critical of collectivization, could land one in the gulag. Chertkov, who knew that correspondence with Tolstoyans, treated with suspicion by the authorities, could be opened and read, continued to endanger lives. When sending out his new issues, Chertkov asked whether his addressees wanted to keep receiving the newsletter and encouraged them to send money to cover his expenses. Chertkov was doing more harm than good with his activity, but whether he was simply reckless or treacherous is not known. He pursued his own agenda and acted out of opportunism.

Having announced the start of relocation in his newsletter, Chertkov reported that the government's deadline to complete it was January 1, 1932. In early 1931, groups of Tolstoyans journeyed from Moscow to Western Siberia, covering over 2,400 miles by train, horse, and on foot. Chertkov inspired them by quoting Tolstoy's letter to the Doukhobors of February 27, 1900, written upon their immigration to Canada: "You suffered and were exiled, and are still suffering want, because you wished, not in words but in deeds, to lead a Christian life. You refused to do any violence to your neighbors, to take oaths, to serve as police or soldiers . . . and in spite of all persecution you remained true to the Christian teaching."[41] The example of the Christian martyrs, persecuted for their pacifist beliefs under the tsars, was meant to inspire Tolstoyans under the Soviets. However, Chertkov's provocative newsletter may have contributed to the demise of the Tolstoyan communes after their relocation.

In spring and summer 1931, after traveling by dirt roads to their destination beyond Novokuznetsk (the city on the Tom River), the settlers began to arrive in Siberia. Many came with families and without means. They had to establish their farms without inventory and subsidies. According to government regulations, settlers were exempt from government procurement quotas for three years. But the authorities ignored this guideline. During the first year, Tolstoyans faced unrealistically high requisitions for timber and hay. When they failed to meet them, an investigation was launched and several members were arrested. In 1932, during the first full growing season, the procurement quota for grain exceeded what could realistically be produced on the designated land. But the commune's complaint to Moscow was met with new repressive measures.

A district inspector arrived, threatening to shut down the communal school, which did not follow the mandatory curriculum. But in 1935, despite having followed such a curriculum (minus military instruction) several teachers were arrested and accused of religious propaganda. A female teacher was charged with reading *The Kreutzer Sonata* to her students, said to be "a religious song," and sentenced to one year of imprisonment.[42] Mass arrests began in 1936, the year Chertkov turned eighty-two.

Earlier, Chertkov Jr. helped the commune representatives write a petition to Mikhail Kalinin, a member of the Politburo and one of few in the Stalin government with peasant origins. By then, the Tolstoyan commune in Siberia was fulfilling government targets, supplying vegetables to the city of Novokuznetsk (already renamed Stalinsk). Kalinin, who received pleas from across the country, could not help even if he wanted: at the height of purges, he kept a low profile. Chertkov, in his final letter to "Life and Labor," written in January 1935, advised commune members to show more tolerance as well as "submission and love."[43] In 1937, with all its useful members in the gulag, "Life and Labor" seized to exist.

Simultaneously, Chertkov acted as an angel for those sectarians who were sent to the gulag for refusing military draft. In 1929–1930, he compiled lists, each comprising some twenty names and itemizing religious sect, date and reason for arrest and charge, and location of concentration camp. Chertkov had his secretary deliver the lists along with his cover letter to Smidovich in the Central Committee, with a request to have the cases reviewed. (Smidovich, a nobleman, joined the Bolsheviks before the Revolution.) In June 1929, sending list No. 9 to Smidovich, Chertkov commented that most of the sectarians on it were sentenced to eight or nine years in the Solovki prison camp for refusing military draft and that some were serving second and third terms for the same offence. Chertkov wrote that recently, sentences for conscientious objectors had become unjustifiably harsh.[44] It is unknown whether Smidovich helped to alleviate the fate of some prisoners on Chertkov's lists.

In 1930, Chertkov also interceded on behalf of the peasant sectarians who were dispossessed and deported in the course of Stalin's collectivization. Those deported to Russia's far north near the Arctic Circle, pleaded to let them join Tolstoyan agricultural communes in Siberia. In September, Chertkov compiled three lists of these deported sectarians, and had his secretary deliver the petition to Smidovich. This time, Smidovich was so annoyed with Chertkov's petition that he shouted at the messenger. He returned the petition with the words that Chertkov was only "a private person" and it was high time for him to stop his activity.[45] It was a time when a million dispossessed well-off peasants, branded as *kulaks*, faced starvation in camps or special settlements in the far north. Tens of thousands of middle-income peasants, caught up in a wave of arrests and deportations, appealed to be freed from labor camps. Later, Stalin would mention to Churchill that collectivization cost ten million lives.[46]

In February 1930, Chertkov appealed to Stalin on behalf of five Tolstoyans who were serving long sentences in Solovki, the notorious prison camp on the Solovetsky Islands in the White Sea.[47] They had been arrested in Moscow on October 29, 1929. Among them was Chertkov's personal secretary, Ivan Bautin. The Tolstoyans were sentenced to five years in Solovki for objecting to military service. All five had already served sentences for the same offense. Chertkov wrote to Stalin that, according to his sources, the Tolstoyans were being treated with extreme cruelty and subjected to torture. He attached a memo with information about their treatment in the camp. Chertkov urged Stalin to send a telegram to Solovki that excessive punishment of Tolstoyans be stopped. He also asked to allow these sectarians to serve their sentences in a different camp, where they could feed themselves by doing agricultural work. Chertkov ended by expressing hope that his letter would not displease Stalin.[48]

Whether Chertkov's letter had any impact is unknown, but that same year, an OGPU delegation was sent to Solovki to investigate rumors about torture on the island. When these were confirmed, the commission executed nineteen perpetrators.[49] By then, official policy towards the gulag prisoners had changed: if in the early 1920s they were sent to the camps for "re-education," by now OGPU was concerned with prisoners' productivity. Regarded as slave labor, inmates were expected to build roads, make bricks, and fulfill production norms in timber. Under these new circumstances, extreme torture of prisoners would be viewed as sabotage.

Despite old age, Chertkov preserved his grip on events and a passion for collecting information. The rigid censorship in the gulag would not pass letters with complaints, but Chertkov found a way to circumvent it. His friend Krivosh could help establish contact with Solovki. Purged in 1924 and sentenced to eight years in Solovki prison camp, he was granted early release after serving half his sentence. The state needed his expertise: upon discharge, Krivosh was reinstated in his position as a cryptologist at the Special Department of OGPU-NKVD. In Solovki, Krivosh was for a while employed as a censor, perlustrating foreign correspondence.[50] Chertkov would be able to receive information about Tolstoyans in Solovki through some of Krivosh's contacts.

While helping arrested Tolstoyans, Chertkov also requested benefits from the regime. In October 1931, Chertkov wrote Bonch-Bruevich, asking to help him attain access to the restricted distribution system for Soviet and Party elite. Later, during the widespread famine, brought on by Stalin's collectivization, Chertkov petitioned to have his Kremlin vouchers renewed and was able to receive the best quality food at lower cost. In 1933, he applied for "a personal pension," then granted on an individual basis by the Central Committee. The beneficiaries were also Soviet and Party elite as well as prominent members of the intelligentsia whose services were considered valuable to the state. Chertkov emphasized his material need and the fact that he had been publishing Tolstoy for 50 years. His application was supported by the musician Goldenweiser, attorney Muravyov, and prominent scholars, who worked on the Jubilee Edition.[51] Taking no chances, Chertkov sent his application through Bonch-Bruevich, expecting him to forward it to his Party contact, Enukidze. Aside from money, recipients of "a personal pension" acquired higher status and a package of benefits, such as access to better hospitals and polyclinics. In 1934, Chertkov requested a government car with a driver, writing to a Party functionary: "In recent years I saw so much attention from the highest echelons of the Soviet Government in regards to the project I supervise [Tolstoy's edition], and attention to myself personally, that I feel I have the right to write directly to you and hope that my request will be satisfied as soon as possible."[52]

But Chertkov had additional, more important, privileges, which remained unmatched under Stalin. He was holding on to an enormous archive in a day when others were afraid to keep private diaries. Chertkov amassed information—hundreds of documents—concerning persecution of conscientious objectors under Lenin and Stalin. These were files with serial numbers that included detailed personal information; he also kept illicit documents concerning deportations of peasant sectarians. Chertkov, of course, presented himself to the authorities as an expert on the sectarian question and could say that he was working on government assignment. (This would not be farfetched: Chertkov participated in resettling religious sectarians, a government project.) However, there were no such private investigators under Stalin and no Soviet citizen could keep the documents, which are found today in Chertkov's archive. Only the secret police had the privilege to collect information about those arrested and deported. What's more, Soviet authorities knew about the existence of Chertkov's archive: he attached copies of some documents to his petitions. Chertkov's other exclusive privilege was also unrivaled: he was allowed to access the revenue from the sale of his property in England. In 1933, Chertkov wrote to Bonch-Bruevich that Tuckton House was sold.[53] The Tolstoy State Museum keeps Chertkov's letter to the editorial board of Tolstoy's Jubilee Edition, in which he promises to pay salaries from his proceeds in England.

In the late 1920s, when most Moscovites lived in cramped communal apartments, a cooperative settlement, "Sokol," was being built in the city's northern suburb.[54] Designed for only 140 cottages, it was the first Soviet cooperative for well-to-do artists as well as government officials, economists, and other professional elite. The down payment of 10 *chervontsy*, or gold rubles, was equivalent to 10,700 rubles, which only the very rich could afford. Payments were spread over the years; regardless of the cottage size, its total cost was 600 *chervontsy*. In 1932, Chertkov moved to "Sokol" with his son's family. The settlement combined advantages of rural and urban living. It was inspired by the book of the British urban planner, Sir Ebenezer Howard, *Garden Cities of To-morrow*, which describes such a utopian city. In the early 1930s, the community had two grocery stores, a library, several sports grounds, a dining hall, a kindergarten, and even its own cemetery with a chapel. Streets were named after Russia's famous painters and each house was individually designed. By the standards of the time, Chertkov's two-story cottage on Levitan Street was an unimaginable luxury. In the 1930s, several apartment houses were built here especially for secret police employees, many of whom were purged soon after.

As the general editor of the Jubilee Edition, the project sanctioned by Stalin, Chertkov attained the status of member of the Soviet elite. In August 1930, his library, paintings (of Chertkov), and personal archive were transported from Tuckton House to Moscow at government expense. Chertkov claimed that his archive was indispensable to publishing the Tolstoy edition and promised to donate it to the Tolstoy State Museum. Bonch-Bruevich secured the help of Grigory Sokolnikov, the Soviet ambassador to England. (During the Great Purge Sokolnikov was arrested and charged as a Trotskyist and died in prison.) The valuable cargo, comprising 21 boxes, was loaded on the steamer *Siberia* and transported under the captain's personal supervision. Sokolnikov, who arranged the shipment, assumed they were transporting Tolstoy's manuscripts. But the writer's papers had been moved to Russia in 1913. Once the archive arrived to Moscow, Chertkov arranged with Bonch-Bruevich to retrieve some materials of personal significance, which he could not donate.[55] In the event, even not all of the paintings would remain in the museum. In a note to Bonch-Bruevich, Chertkov explained that he would let the museum keep his own youthful portrait by Kramskoy, Nesterov's drawings, and Golubkina's bust. But Chertkov wanted his son to inherit Repin's portrait and another painting of himself, as a baby. Although museums did not return gifts, he insisted, in a letter to Andrei Bubnov, the new Commissar for Education, that "perhaps an exception can be made in this case."[56]

Chertkov never played by the rules: he created his own, persuading even the Soviet authorities of the importance of his undertakings. His publishing project was arguably the most controversial ever sanctioned by Stalin's government. Gosizdat, afraid to produce the Jubilee Edition, took three decades to complete the task. Every line in Tolstoy's non-fiction argued against violent dictatorship; his religious works were also unacceptable in the atheist state.

As with all publications in the Soviet Union, Tolstoy's edition had to be endorsed by censors. Bonch-Bruevich, then employed as the Commissariat for Education, had to watch that introductory articles and commentaries were ideologically sound. In 1935, he was troubled with the volume that included Tolstoy's articles on the famine, a sensitive subject under Stalin. Bonch-Bruevich requested that the commentary incorporate Lenin's "remarkable" pronouncements on the famine. The "issue of pacifism" also had to be explained from the new Soviet perspective.[57]

In 1933, Bonch-Bruevich objected to the phrase "political crime." He argued that this usage had become obsolete: political crimes existed only under the tsars. However, the terms "political inmate," "political prisoner," or "political" were still relevant. (This linguistic gymnastics reflected Soviet double-think.) The word "religious" had to be struck from scholarly articles: Tolstoy was not seeking "religious truths," since none existed.[58]

There was also something positive in Bonch-Bruevich's involvement: he knew that Chertkov took liberties with Tolstoy's text, becoming in effect his personal censor. In his turn, when Bonch-Bruevich became Chertkov's censor, he ensured that Tolstoy's original text was restored, especially in *Resurrection*.[59]

The issue with funding Tolstoy's edition was, perhaps, the most entangled of all. In 1930, Chertkov had Bonch-Bruevich provide a letter, which stated that his editorial office worked "entirely on government assignment" and therefore had to be viewed as a state-funded organization, financed by the Commissariat for Education. Over the years, Chertkov pressed the government for money. In February 1934, he reminded Vyacheslav Molotov about the government pledge of 100,000 rubles annually. Chertkov wrote that he was prepared to accept three quarters of the sum and expressed hope the Soviet government would help him "complete the task entrusted to me by my late friend Lev Nikolaevich Tolstoy, the task which at the same time became . . . a historical undertaking by the Soviet government."[60] With no response from Molotov, Chertkov appealed to Stalin. In a letter of May 27, he emphasized the importance of Tolstoy's edition, which was launched on Stalin's own initiative. Referring to the government subsidy, Chertkov wrote: "I believe one word from you would be enough to settle the formal side of my request." In July, with no reply from Stalin, Chertkov's son petitioned the dictator. Chertkov Jr. wrote that speedy permission to release the funding would bring his ailing father "tremendous joy and calm." This time, Chertkov did not even wait for a reply: days later, he sent a deranged letter to Stalin. Whether his mind was indeed failing as a result of strokes, or he pretended to be mad to further his cause, Chertkov informed Stalin about the course of his illness (sclerosis), mentioned that he recently revised Tolstoy's secret testament and sent this new redaction to comrade Enukidge. After such a preamble Chertkov articulated his request for the annual subsidy and expressed deep gratitude to Stalin for his attention in the past. The bizarre letter was effective: a fortnight later, the government transferred the requested sum, also promising to increase the circulation of Tolstoy's edition.[61] (Chertkov's questionable methods aside, he put together a team of experts who, decades later, produced the most important academic edition of Tolstoy's works, supplying it with priceless biographical information. Recently, this 90-volume edition became available on the internet.) Tolstoy, of course, would not have wanted a dictator to sanction publication of his works.

During his final years, a frail Chertkov was taken for walks in a wheelchair. He seems to have made a special arrangement even for his death. Chertkov died in 1936, at age eighty-two, like Tolstoy, and also in November. His obituary appeared in *Izvestia*, the second most prominent Party newspaper after *Pravda*. The article announced his passing in a style reserved only for important people: Chertkov's heart stopped beating on November 9, at 13:22. Chertkov was described as "the closest friend of the great writer Lev Nikolaevich Tolstoy" and the editor of the Jubilee Edition of his works.[62] The Council of the People's Commissars decided that Chertkov should receive a state funeral. A special government commission was appointed. On November 12, *Izvestia* reported that the funeral would be held at Vvedenskoe Cemetery in Lefortovo. (It was a main burial ground for Catholics and Protestants in the city.) "God is not in strength but in truth," reads the epitaph on Chertkov's tombstone, recounting the motto on the Intermediary editions.

Like his father, Chertkov Jr. enjoyed a special status. In 1937, less than one year after Chertkov's death, he ventured to Europe. At the height of the purges, travel abroad became unfeasible even to Sergei Prokofiev, among other celebrities. Chertkov Jr. was merely a senior researcher at the State Literary Museum (headed by Bonch-Bruevich). In April, he applied to the State Commissariat for Foreign Affairs for permission to take a four-month trip together with his wife. He intended to visit England, France, and Denmark. In England, he needed to sort his father's remaining archive and sell the rest of the family property. "In England my father has inherited a small piece of land (12 acres) and 2 cottages, receiving them from his mother, and which now should come into my possession. My father had asked me to use the money from the sale of this property in England for publishing L.N. Tolstoy's works."[63] In 1937, no one would dare tell the authorities about ties to the West. Thousands were purged and executed on mere accusation of being foreign spies. Chertkov Jr. was living in a bubble:

he was chatting with the State Commissariat for Foreign Affairs about his relatives abroad. In France, he wanted to visit his father's elderly cousins, the Pashkovs. (Chertkov had corresponded with the two aristocratic ladies until 1936.) In addition, he wanted to attend the World Exhibition in Paris and an international peace conference in Denmark. He intended to travel with his wife because she can "cook vegetarian meals for me."[64]

In the early 1950s, when Chertkov Jr. was selling his father's papers to several Moscow archives, Olga Golinenko, an employee of the Tolstoy State Museum, visited him in "Sokol." Chertkov Jr. rented the second floor of his family cottage to a hack artist who painted Stalin's portraits. Golinenko was awed by the sight of a headless dummy sitting on a chair in Stalin's military jacket.

⁂

Chertkov's survival and public career under Stalin, despite his closeness to the tsars, is puzzling and nothing short of miraculous. But his lasting intimacy with Tolstoy presents the biggest mystery of all. Maude, who had tried to unveil it, commented in his biography of the writer: "It would be outrageously unjust to compare Chertkov to Judas Iscariot, but the fact that one of Jesus's chosen disciples was a traitor, shows us that even the trusted friend of the greatest and the best man may have flaws in his character."[65]

ABBREVIATIONS

GMT, L.N. Tolstoy State Museum
RGALI, Russian State Archive of Literature and Art
RGB, Russian State Library
ALT, Alexandra L'vovna Tolstaya, Tolstoy's youngest daughter
(also referred to as Alexandra Tolstoy in notes)
LN, Tolstoy
SA, Sophia Tolstoy
TA, Tatyana Kuzminskaya (Sophia's sister)
VG, Vladimir Chertkov

A NOTE ABOUT MY SOURCES

All citations from the 90-volume edition of Tolstoy's works, or the Jubilee Edition, are translated by the author.

I also translated Tolstoy's letters and entries from the Jubilee Edition not included in the editions of his Letters and Diaries edited by R. F. Christian. Chertkov's letters to Tolstoy come from the Jubilee Edition and from the L.N. Tolstoy State Museum (GMT). Unless otherwise indicated, translations of various sources are my own.

ENDNOTES

Prologue

1. Aylmer Maude, *The Life of Tolstoy: Later Years* (London: Oxford UP, 1930), vol. 2, 146–47.
2. Tolstoy's (LN) letter to Chertkov (VG), December 12, 1900. In L.N. Tolstoy, *Polnoe sobranie sochinenij*, ed. V.G. Chertkov, 90 vols. (Moscow-Leningrad: Goslitizdat, 1928–58), vol. 88, 126. In future, *Jubilee Edition*.
3. Mikhail Sukhotin's letter to Bulgakov, June 5, 1912. *Yasnopolyanskij sbornik* (Tula: Yasnaya Polyana, 2006), 280–81.
4. *Jubilee Edition*, vol. 89, 231.
5. Tatyana Sukhotina's letter of 1911. *Yasnopolyanskij sbornik* (Tula: Yasnaya Polyana, 2006), 268.
6. *Tolstoy's Letters*, ed. and trans. R. F. Christian (London: The Anthlone Press, 1978), vol. 2, 716.

Chapter I

1. *Tolstoy's Letters*, vol. 2, 454.
2. Valentin Bulgakov, *O Tolstom: Vospominaniya i rasskazy* (Tula, 1964), 193–94.
3. *The Memoirs of Count Witte*, trans. Sidney Harcave (New York: M.E. Sharpe, 1990), 462.
4. Dominic Lieven, *The Aristocracy in Europe, 1815–1914* (New York: Columbia University Press, 1997), 44–45.
5. Ronald Rayfield, *Anton Chekhov: A Life* (London: HarperCollins Publishers, 1997), 3.
6. Approximately £208,000.
7. Lieven, *The Aristocracy in Europe*, 36.
8. Information about Prince Alexander Chernyshev comes from Dominic Lieven's *Russia Against Napoleon: The True Story of the Campaigns of War and Peace* (New York: Viking, 2009).
9. Alexander Mossolov, *At the Court of the Last Tsar*, trans. E. W. Dickes (London: Methuen, 1935), 116.

10. *Tolstoy's Letters*, ed. and trans. R. F. Christian (New York: Charles Scribner's Sons, 1978), vol. 1, 141.

11. *Jubilee Edition*, vol. 48, 30.

12. Ibid., vol. 34, 351.

13. *Tolstoy's Letters*, vol. 2, 520.

14. Dominic Lieven, *Nicholas II: Emperor of All the Russias* (London: John Murray, 1993), 34.

15. Chertkov's (VG) letter to Tolstoy (LN), mid-April 1884. Unless otherwise specified, Tolstoy's and Chertkov's letters come from the *Jubilee Edition*.

16. M.V. Muratov, *L.N. Tolstoy and V.G. Chertkov*, trans. Scott D. Moss (Tenafly: Hermitage Publishers, 2002), 30.

17. Upon her marriage to Alexander II Princess Dolgorukaya's name was changed to Yurievskaya.

18. Muratov, *L.N. Tolstoy and V.G. Chertkov*, 40.

19. *Tolstoy's Letters*, vol. 2, 576.

20. Richard S. Wortman, *Scenarios of Power: Myth and Ceremony in Russian Monarchy* (Princeton: Princeton University Press, 2000), vol. 2, 118.

21. Chertkov, "Stranitsa iz vospominanij" in *Vestnik Evropy* (St. Petersburg, 1909), 141–45.

22. Mossolov, *At the Court of the Last Tsar*, 197.

23. A.A. Polovtsev, *Diary of a State Secretary* (Moscow: Nauka, 1966), vol. 1, 168.

24. Ibid., 208.

25. Wortman, *Scenarios of Power*, vol. 2, 132.

26. Ibid., 156.

27. Chertkov, "Avtobiografiya." Quoted in Georgy Orekhanov, *V.G. Chertkov v zhizni L.N. Tolstogo* (Moscow: PSTGU, 2009), 17–18.

28. Wortman, *Scenarios of Power*, vol. 2, 132.

29. Chertkov, "Stranitsa iz vospominanij," 140–61.

30. Orekhanov, *V.G. Chertkov v zhizni L.N. Tolstogo*, 17.

31. *The Memoirs of Count Witte*, 44.

32. LN letter to VG, August 10, 1909.

33. Granville Waldegrave, 3rd Baron Radstock.

34. Edmund Heier, *Religious Schism in the Russian Aristocracy 1860-1900. Radstockism and Pashkovism* (The Hague: Nijhoff, 1970), 52.

35. Ivan Turgenev, *Polnoe sobranie sochinenij i pisem*, 28 vols. (Moscow –Leningrad: Nauka, 1964–68), vol. 12, 555.

36. Heier, *Religious Schism in the Russian Aristocracy*, 46.

37. *Tolstoy's Letters*, vol. 1, 294.

38. Heier, *Religious Schism in the Russian Aristocracy*, 84–85.

39. *Tolstoy's Letters*, vol. 1, 295.

40. Tolstoy, *Anna Karenina*, trans. Richard Pevear and Larissa Volokhonsky (New York: Penguin Books, 2002), 127.

41. Rosamund Bartlett, *Tolstoy: A Russian Life* (Boston: Houghton Mifflin Harcourt, 2011), 270.

42. *Tolstoy's Letters*, vol. 1, 124.

43. Bartlett, *Tolstoy: A Russian Life*, 271–72.

44. Heier, *Religious Schism in the Russian Aristocracy*, 110.

45. Bulgakov, *O Tolstom: Vospominaniya i rasskazy*, 117.

46. Leo Tolstoy, *Resurrection*, trans. Louise Maude (Oxford: Oxford University Press, 1994), 19.

47. *Tolstoy's Letters*, vol. 2, 340.
48. Ibid., 363.
49. *Jubilee Edition*, vol. 85, 25.
50. Ibid., 7.
51. *Tolstoy's Letters*, vol. 2, 347.
52. Chertkova's letter to VG, November 25, 1883. RGB, f. 435, 149, 4.
53. VG letter to Peter Shuvalov, July 7, 1881. RGB, f. 435, 142, 21.
54. *Memoirs of Count Witte*, 98.
55. VG letter to Chertkova, December 20, 1883. RGB, f. 435, 138, 6.
56. The Tsar's uncle and the youngest son of Nicholas I.
57. Born Cecilie Auguste, Princess and Margravine of Baden (1839–1891).
58. Chertkova's letter to VG, February 17, 1883. RGB, f. 435, 149, 4.

CHAPTER 2
1. *Tolstoy's Letters*, vol. 1, 295–96.
2. Quoted in Rosamund Bartlett, *Tolstoy: A Russian Life,* 113.
3. *The Diaries of Sophia Tolstoy*, trans. Cathy Porter (New York: Random House, 1985), 1000–1001.
4. *Jubilee Edition*, vol. 85, 68.
5. VG letter to Chertkova, October 31, 1883. RGB, f. 435, 138, 6.
6. *Tolstoy's Letters*, vol. 1, 294.
7. LN letter to VG, December 5, 1883.
8. VG letter to LN, December 7, 1883.
9. VG letter to Chertkova, November 24, 1883. RGB, f. 435, 138, 6.
10. Chertkova's letter to VG, November 11, 1883. RGB, F. 435, 149, 4.
11. VG letter to Chertkova, November 18, 1883. RGB, f. 435, 138, 6.
12. Sophia Tolstaya, *Moia Zhizn'* (Moscow: L.N. Tolstoy State Museum, 2011), vol. 1, 441.
13. VG letter to LN, January, 1884.
14. LN letter to VG, February 17, 1884.
15. VG letter to LN, February 18, 1884.
16. LN letter to VG, end of February, 1884.
17. *Jubilee Edition*, vol. 85, 29.
18. VG letter to LN, February 18, 1884.
19. *Jubilee Edition*, vol. 23, 551.
20. VG letter to LN, March 6, 1884.
21. *Tolstoy's Diaries*, ed. and trans. R. F. Christian (London: The Anthlone Press, 1985), vol. 1, 204.
22. *Jubilee Edition*, vol. 49, 70.
23. *Tolstoy's Diaries*, vol. 1, 209.
24. LN letter to VG, March 4–6, 1884.
25. Leo Tolstoy, *Childhood, Boyhood, and Youth*, trans. Aylmer Maude (London: Oxford University Press, 1928). In Tolstoy Centenary Edition, vol. 3, 218.
26. Tolstoy, *Childhood, Boyhood, and Youth*, 384, 381.
27. Valentin Bulgakov, "Zamolchannoe o Tolstom." In *O Tolstom: Vospominaniya i rasskazy* (Tula, 1964), 106.
28. *Jubilee Edition*, vol. 82, 87–88.
29. Tolstoy, *Childhood, Boyhood, and Youth*, 219.
30. Ibid., 266.

31. *Jubilee Edition*, vol. 2, 378.
32. Jean-Baptiste Alphonse Karr (1808 – 1890), a French novelist and journalist.
33. Tolstoy, *Childhood, Boyhood, and Youth*, 218.
34. VG letter to LN, April 9, 1884.
35. VG letter to LN, December 8, 1884.
36. *Tolstoy's Letters*, vol. 2, 521.
37. Ibid.
38. VG letter to LN, April 18, 1884.
39. LN letter to VG, April 18, 1884.
40. *Tolstoy's Letters*, vol. 2, 372–73.
41. VG letter to LN, March 13, 1884.
42. *Jubilee Edition*, vol. 49, 107.
43. Maude, *The Life of Tolstoy*, 146–47.
44. VG letter to LN, April 8, 1884.
45. *Tolstoy's Diaries*, vol. 1, 209.
46. *Jubilee Edition*, vol. 85, 53.
47. Polovtsev, *Diary of a State Secretary*, 209.
48. VG letter to LN, April 25, 1884.
49. LN letter to VG, May 19, 1884.
50. *Jubilee Edition*, vol. 85, 60.
51. LN letter to VG, March 4–6, 1884
52. VG letter to LN, April 18, 1884.
53. *Jubilee Edition*, vol. 63, 165.
54. Ibid., vol. 85, 55.
55. VG letter to LN, September 15, 1884.
56. LN letter to VG, May 7–8, 1884.
57. *Tolstoy's Letters*, vol. 2, 372–73.
58. Ibid., vol. 2, 562.
59. *Jubilee Edition*, vol. 85, 83.
60. *Tolstoy's Letters*, vol. 2, 370.
61. Luke, 3: 10–11. (All quotations from the Gospels are from the KJV.)
62. LN letter to VG, May 19, 1884.
63. LN letter to VG, June 6, 1884.
64. VG letter to LN, May 31, 1884.
65. LN letter to VG, September 22–23, 1884.
66. VG letter to LN, September 2, 1884.
67. LN letter to SA, October 23, 1884. Tolstoy's letters to his wife are quoted from the *Jubilee Edition*.
68. *Jubilee Edition*, vol. 85, 63–64.
69. LN letters to VG, June 6 and July 11, 1884.
70. VG letter to LN, June 18, 1884.
71. Ibid.
72. *Tolstoy's Diaries*, vol.1, 220.
73. VG letter to LN, August 18, 1884.
74. LN letter to VG, October 1, 1884.
75. *Tolstoy's Letters*, vol. 1, 323.
76. VG letter to LN, June 18, 1884.

77. VG letter to LN, September 21, 1884.
78. LN letter to VG, November 7, 1884.
79. LN letter to VG, May 7–8, 1884.
80. LN letter to VG, August 28–29, 1884.
81. LN letter to VG, September 5–7, 1884.
82. VG letter to LN, September 25, 1884.
83. Ibid.
84. VG letter to LN, July 4, 1884.
85. LN letter to VG, October 31, 1884.
86. LN telegram to VG, November 3, 1884.
87. LN letter to VG, November 7, 1884.
88. LN letter to VG, November 7–8, 1884.
89. LN letter to VG, December 2, 1884.
90. LN letter to VG, December 8, 1884.
91. LN letter to VG, December 17, 1884.
92. *Jubilee Edition*, vol. 85, 133.

CHAPTER 3

1. Leo Tolstoy, *Plays: Volume Three, 1894–1910*, trans. Marvin Kantor with Tanya Tulchinsky (Evanston: Northwestern University Press, 1998), 40.
2. Ivan Sytin, "Iz perezhitogo. Avtobiograficheskie nabroski" in *Polveka dlya knigi. Literaturno-hudozhestvennyi sbornik* (Moscow, 1916).
3. Paul Biryukov, "Avtobiografia," http://birlife.narod.ru/.
4. LN letter to VG, October 3, 1884.
5. *Tolstoy's Letters*, vol. 2, 404.
6. VG letter to LN, February 16–17, 1885.
7. Maude, *The Life of Tolstoy*, vol. 2, 267.
8. *Jubilee Edition*, vol. 85, 140.
9. Ibid., 142.
10. LN letter to VG, February 5–6, 1885.
11. *Jubilee Edition*, vol. 85, 276–78.
12. VG letter to LN, March 23, 1885.
13. Maude, *The Life of Tolstoy*, vol. 2, 162.
14. VG letter to LN, February 9–10, 1887.
15. VG letter to LN, April 16, 1885.
16. LN letter to VG, February 24, 1885.
17. *Tolstoy's Letters*, vol. 2, 400–01.
18. VG letter to LN, October 19, 1885.
19. VG letter to LN, April 4, 1886.
20. VG letter to LN, April 6, 1886.
21. VG letter to LN, May 22, 1885.
22. VG letter to LN, February 24, 1885.
23. VG letter to LN, August 8, 1886.
24. Maude, *The Life of Tolstoy*, vol. 2, 188.
25. VG letter to LN, July 7, 1885.
26. LN letter to VG, May 10–11, 1885.
27. *Tolstoy's Letters*, vol. 2, 391.

28. LN letter to VG, December 17, 1885.

29. *Tolstoy's Letters*, vol. 2, 393–99.

30. SA letter to Tatyana Kuzminskaya (TA), December 20, 1885. Sophia's letters to her sister come from GMT, f. 47, inv. 37872.

31. LN letter to VG, April 16, 1885.

32. *Jubilee Edition*, vol. 85, 169.

33. LN letter to VG, January 19–21, 1887.

34. VG letter to LN, January 24, 1887.

35. VG letter to LN, December 9, 1885.

36. LN letter to VG, January 23, 1887.

37. *Jubilee Edition*, vol. 86, 30.

38. Ibid., 146.

39. VG letter to LN, May 16, 1887.

40. LN letter to VG, July 21, 1887.

41. VG letter to LN, July 26, 1887.

42. VG letter to LN, May 2, 1887.

43. Maude, *The Life of Tolstoy*, vol 2, 239.

44. LN letter to VG, April 11, 1886.

45. *Jubilee Edition*, vol. 85, 341.

46. SA letter to VG, April 14, 1886.

47. *The Diaries of Sophia Tolstoy*, October 27, 1886.

48. *Jubilee Edition*, vol. 26, 721.

49. Ibid., vol. 26, 722–23.

50. VG letter to LN, February 13, 1887.

51. LN letter to VG, February 6–7, 1887.

52. VG letter to LN, February 4, 1887.

53. Matthew 5:28.

54. LN letter to VG, July 23–24, 1885.

55. LN letter to VG, September 5–7, 1884.

56. Matthew, 4:7.

57. VG letter to LN, September 9, 1884.

58. LN letter to VG, September 22–23, 1884.

59. VG letter to LN, July 25, 1886.

60. *Jubilee Edition*, vol. 63, 385.

61. Ibid., 399–400.

62. Tatiana Sukhotin–Tolstoy, *The Tolstoy Home,* trans. Alec Brown (London: Harvill Press, 1950), 90.

63. *Tolstoy's Letters*, vol. 2, 419–20.

64. LN letter to VG, November 6, 1886.

65. *Jubilee Edition*, vol. 85, 402.

66. Ibid., 401.

67. Maude, *The Life of Tolstoy*, 229.

68. VG letter to LN, January 26, 1887.

69. VG letter to LN, April 9, 1887.

70. *Tolstoy's Letters*, vol. 2, 475.

71. Ibid., 401.

72. Ibid., 420.

CHAPTER 4

1.   *Tolstoy's Letters*, vol. 2, 403.
2.   *The Diaries of Sophia Tolstoy*, 75.
3.   *Tolstoy's Letters*, vol. 2, 393.
4.   *The Diaries of Sophia Tolstoy*, 79.
5.   *Jubilee Edition*, vol. 26, 765–66.
6.   VG letter to LN, April 9, 1887. .
7.   VG letter to LN, July 26, 1887.
8.   LN letter to VG, January 4–8, 1890.
9.   Laughing gas, or nitrous oxide (N2O), began to be commonly used in dentistry and surgery in Europe in the 1860s. It was first used on laboring mothers in the 1880s. The gas became more widespread in the 1930s in Great Britain when it was possible for women to self-administer it through a mask. See more: http://www.slate.com/articles/double_x/doublex/2011/05/get_this_woman_some_laughing_gas.html
10. LN letter to VG, October 16, 1887.
11. Ibid.
12. LN letter to VG, November 13, 1887.
13. LN letter to VG, June 24, 1884.
14. VG letter to LN, December 21, 1887.
15. LN letter to VG, December 19, 1887.
16. LN letter to VG, March 4, 1888.
17. VG letter to LN, March 7, 1888.
18. LN letter to VG, March 11, 1888.
19. LN letter to VG, March 19, 1888.
20. SA letter to TA, April 11, 1888.
21. VG letter to LN, May 1, 1888.
22. LN letter to VG, June 10, 1888.
23. Maude, *The Life of Tolstoy*, vol. 2, 271.
24. Tolstoy, *The Kreutzer Sonata*, in *Tolstoy's Short Fiction*, ed. and trans. Michael R. Katz (New York: Norton, 1991), 191.
25. *Tolstoy's Diaries*, vol. 1, 231, 233, 235, 258.
26. *The Diaries of Sophia Tolstoy*, 123.
27. *Jubilee Edition*, vol. 27, 563.
28. Matthew, 19:12.
29. LN letter to VG, November 6, 1888.
30. *Tolstoy's Diaries*, vol. 1, 271.
31. Mikhail Sukhotin, *Diary* (Moscow: *Literaturnoe nasledstvo*, 1961), 206. In future, *Literaturnoe nasledstvo*.
32. Strakhov's letter to Tolstoy, April 24, 1890.
33. Quoted in Rosamund Bartlett, *Tolstoy: A Russian Life,* 329.
34. Ivan Bunin, *The Liberation of Tolstoy: A Tale of Two Writers*, trans. Thomas Marullo and Vladimir Khmelkov (Evanston: Northwestern UP, 2001), 55.
35. *Tolstoy's Diaries*, vol. 1, 275.
36. Maude, *The Life of Tolstoy*, vol. 2, 282.
37. Sukhotin-Tolstoy, *The Tolstoy Home*, 146.
38. *The Diaries of Sophia Tolstoy*, 144.
39. LN letter to VG, April 10, 1889.

40.   VG letter to LN, May 15, 1889.
41.   *Tolstoy's Diaries*, vol. 1, 272.
42.   *Jubilee Edition*, vol. 27, 593–94.
43.   *Tolstoy's Diaries*, vol.1, 304.
44.   *Tolstoy's Letters*, vol. 2, 476–77.
45.   VG letter to LN, January 7, 1890.
46.   *The Diaries of Sophia Tolstoy*, 141.
47.   Ibid., 133–34.
48.   Sophia Tolstoy, *Moia Zhizn'*, vol. 2, 134.
49.   VG letters to LN, October 27–28, 1889.
50.   *Tolstoy's Diaries*, vol. 1, 267.
51.   *Tolstoy's Letters*, vol. 2, 451.
52.   VG letter to LN, April 12, 1890.
53.   LN letter to VG, April 24, 1890.
54.   Quoted in Maude, *The Life of Tolstoy*, vol. 2, 271.
55.   *Jubilee Edition*, vol. 51, 85.
56.   VG letter to LN, October 3, 1887.
57.   LN letter to VG, October 10, 1887.
58.   LN letter to VG, February 1, 1890.
59.   VG letter to LN, May 1, 1888.
60.   *Jubilee Edition*, vol. 86, 250.
61.   LN letter to VG, April 24, 1890.
62.   *Tolstoy's Letters*, vol. 2, 458.
63.   *Jubilee Edition*, vol. 86, 39.
64.   LN letter to VG, July 28, 1890.
65.   *Jubilee Edition*, vol. 86, 39.
66.   VG letter to LN, August 5, 1890.
67.   Sukhotin-Tolstoy, *The Tolstoy Home*, 198.
68.   VG letter to LN, August 1, 1889.
69.   V.D. Bonch-Bruevich, "Iz Moskvy za granitsu," memoir, RGB, f. 369, 6, 1.
70.   Maude, *The Life of Tolstoy*, vol. 2, 283.
71.   *Tolstoy's Letters*, vol. 2, 386–87.
72.   SA letter to TA, fall 1885. F. 47, 37872.
73.   VG letter to LN, February 20, 1887.
74.   George Kennan, "A Visit to Count Tolstoy" in *Americans in Conversations with Tolstoy: Selected Accounts* (Jefferson, NC: McFarland, 2006), 13
75.   Maude, *The Life of Tolstoy*, vol.2, 427–28.
76.   Ibid., vol. 2, 437.
77.   *Tolstoy's Letters*, vol. 2, 489.
78.   SA letter to TA, January 8, 1892.

CHAPTER 5
1.   VG letter to LN, December 25, 1889.
2.   LN letter to VG, July 1896.
3.   VG letter to LN, January 26, 1887.
4.   *The Diaries of Sophia Tolstoy*, 890.
5.   *Tolstoy's Letters*, vol. 2, 451.

6. *Jubilee Edition*, vol. 87, 8.
7. Ibid.
8. *Jubilee Edition*, vol. 86, 382.
9. *Tolstoy's Diaries*, vol. 1, 315.
10. VG letter to LN, February 14, 1891.
11. LN letter to VG, February 16, 1891.
12. *Jubilee Edition*, vol. 31, 260.
13. LN letter to VG, August 31, 1902.
14. VG letter to LN, October 1890.
15. VG letter to LN, April 29, 1891.
16. LN letter to VG, May 8, 1891.
17. VG letter to LN, May 18, 1891.
18. *Tolstoy's Letters*, vol. 2, 488.
19. LN letter to VG, December 14, 1891.
20. *Jubilee Edition*, vol. 28, 356.
21. Ibid., 359.
22. LN letter to VG, February 3, 1893.
23. LN letter to VG, November 5, 1893.
24. LN letter to VG, December 17, 1893.
25. VG letter to LN, February 13, 1894.
26. LN letter to VG, March 5–7, 1892.
27. LN letter to VG, February 5, 1892.
28. *Jubilee Edition*, vol. 28, 363.
29. Ibid., 326.
30. VG letter to Bonch-Bruevich, June 26, 1901. RGB, f. 369, 363, 13.
31. LN letter to VG, October 24, 1893.
32. Maude, *The Life of Tolstoy*, vol. 2, 325.
33. *Jubilee Edition*, vol. 87, 138.
34. LN letter to SA, November 25, 1891.
35. *The Diaries of Sophia Tolstoy*, 895.
36. LN letter to SA, February 28, 1892.
37. VG letter to LN, March 8, 1892.
38. LN letter to VG, April 19, 1892.
39. Ibid.
40. VG letter to LN, February 20, 1892.
41. VG letter to LN, October 1, 1892.
42. VG letter to LN, December 20, 1892.
43. VG letter to LN, October 1, 1892.
44. S.A. Tolstaya, *Pis'ma k Tolstomu: 1862–1910* (Moscow–Leningrad: Academia, 1936), 525–26. Sophia's letters to Tolstoy come from this edition.
45. LN letter to VG, December 26, 1892.
46. *Jubilee Edition*, vol. 87, 203.
47. SA letter to LN, January 30, 1884.
48. LN letter to VG, April 1885.
49. Valentin Bulgakov, *O Tolstom: Vospominaniya i rasskazy*, 193–94.
50. *Jubilee Edition*, vol. 87, 235.
51. VG letter to LN, March 28–31, 1893.

52. VG letter to LN, April 8, 1893.
53. LN letter to VG, October 24, 1893.
54. LN letter to VG, June 22, 1893.
55. VG letter to LN, June 16, 1893.
56. *Jubilee Edition*, vol. 87, 242.
57. LN letter to VG, August 23, 1893.
58. LN letter to VG, June 4, 1893.
59. VG letter to LN, May 29, 1893.
60. LN letter to VG, June 4, 1893.
61. VG letter to LN, May 29, 1893.
62. V.G. Chertkov, *Tainyj porok. Trezvye mysli o polovyh otnosheniyah* (Moscow: 1908), 5–7.
63. *Jubilee Edition*, vol. 87, 185, 264.
64. LN letter to VG, March 18, 1894.
65. LN letter to SA, March 27, 1894.
66. LN letter to VG, April 7, 1894.
67. LN letter to VG, March 30, 1893.
68. VG letter to LN, December 25, 1888.
69. LN letter to VG, January 2, 1889.
70. LN letter to VG, April 28, 1894.
71. *Jubilee Edition*, vol. 87, 270–71.
72. LN letter to VG, April 30, 1894.
73. LN telegram to VG, May 5, 1894.
74. *Jubilee Edition*, vol. 87, 278.
75. LN letter to VG, May 12, 1894.
76. *Tolstoy's Diaries*, vol. 1, 332.
77. Sukhotin-Tolstoy, *The Tolstoy Home*, 248.
78. Ibid., 207–08.
79. Ibid., 256.
80. VG letter to LN, April 10, 1893.
81. *Tolstoy's Diaries*, vol. 1, 337.
82. LN letter to VG, August 9, 1894.
83. *Tolstoy's Diaries*, vol. 1, 205–12.
84. *Tolstoy's Letters*, vol. 2, 520–21.
85. VG letter to LN, October 24, 1894.
86. LN letter to VG, November 26, 1894.
87. VG letter to LN, October 24, 1894.
88. *The Diaries of Sophia Tolstoy*, 174.
89. Ibid.
90. VG letter to LN, October 20, 1895.
91. *Jubilee Edition*, vol. 53, 102.
92. SA letter to LN, September 11, 1894.
93. *Jubilee Edition*, vol. 68, 15.
94. *Tolstoy–Strakhov, Complete Correspondence* (Ottawa: Slavic Research Group at the University of Ottawa, 2003), vol. 2, 977.
95. VG letter to LN, January 25, 1895.
96. *The Diaries of Sophia Tolstoy*, 180.
97. VG letter to LN, January 25, 1895.

98.   LN letter to VG, February 2, 1892.
99.   VG letter to LN, February 14, 1895.
100. *Jubilee Edition*, vol. 87, 312.
101. *Tolstoy's Letters*, vol. 2, 517.
102. LN letter to VG, March 8, 1895.

CHAPTER 6

1.   *Tolstoy's Letters*, vol. 1, 163–64.
2.   V. Chisnikov, "Agenty Ohranki v Yasnoi Polyane," *Sotsialisticheskaya zakonnost'*, No. 11, 1988.
3.   "L.N. Tolstoy i department politsii" in *Byloe*, No. 9, 1918.
4.   Chisnikov, "Agenty Ohranki."
5.   V. Chisnikov, "L.N. Tolstoy and S.V. Zubatov" in *Russkaia klassika: problemy interpretatsii. Materialy nauchnoi konferentsii*, Lipetsk: 2002, 78–87.
6.   *Jubilee Edition*, vol. 69, 104–05.
7.   "Moskovskaia ohranka o Tolstom i tolstovtsah" in *Golos minuvshego* (Moscow, 1918), 284.
8.   A. Zdanovich, V. Izmozik, *Sorok let na sekretnoi sluzhbe: zhizn' i priklyucheniya Vladimira Krivosha* (Moscow: Iks-History Kuchkovo pole, 2007).
9.   LN letter to VG, October 7, 1895.
10.   VG letter to LN, October 13, 1895.
11.   LN letter to VG, October 25, 1895.
12.   VG letter to LN, December 27, 1907. GMT, f. 1. (At the time of my research, in 2010–12, Chertkov's letters were being catalogued at the Tolstoy State Museum and had not yet been assigned inventory numbers.) In future, GMT.
13.   VG letter to LN, May 8, 1908. GMT.
14.   LN letter to VG, October 24, 1909.
15.   VG letter to LN, October 29, 1909. GMT.
16.   Maude, *The Life of Tolstoy*, 267.
17.   Aylmer Maude, *A Peculiar People: The Doukhobors* (New York: Funk & Wagnalls Company, 1904), 23.
18.   *Tolstoy's Letters*, vol. 2, 522.
19.   *Jubilee Edition*, vol. 69, 190–92.
20.   Georgij Orekhanov, *Chertkov v zhizni Tolstogo* (Moscow: 2009), 43.
21.   LN letter to VG, October 7, 1895.
22.   VG letter to LN, October 23, 1895.
23.   *Jubilee Edition*, vol. 68, 116.
24.   LN letter to VG, December 1, 1895.
25.   *Tolstoy's Letters*, vol. 2, 534.
26.   VG letter to LN, February 1, 1896.
27.   Maude, *The Life of Tolstoy*, vol. 2, 360.
28.   LN letter to VG, November 25, 1896.
29.   LN letter to VG, December 2, 1896.
30.   Maude, *The Life of Tolstoy*, 356.
31.   Maude, *A Peculiar People: The Doukhobors*, 60–63.
32.   LN letter to VG, December 5, 1896.
33.   RGB, f. 435, 118, 39.

34. Prince Dmitry Khilkov was Tolstoy's follower, who resigned from the army, gave up his land to the peasants, and was banished to the Caucasus for his beliefs. In 1893, his mother, helped by the authorities, seized his children, whom he refused to baptize as Christian Orthodox. Tolstoy protested this violation and Chertkov promised to bring the case to the Tsar's attention.

35. RGB, f. 435, 118, 39.

36. RGB, f. 369, 411.

37. LN letter to VG, January 12, 1897.

38. Berlin's Social Democratic magazine founded by Wilhelm Liebknecht.

39. *The Tsar's Leaflet*: Paris, 1909, 39.

40. Zdanovich, Izmozik, *Sorok let na sekretnoi sluzbe*, 100.

41. SA letter to TA, February 19, 1897.

42. GMT, f. 302, 3, 9.

43. Zdanovich, Izmozik, *Sorok let na sekretnoi sluzbe*, 98.

44. LN letter to VG, February 15, 1897.

45. Frederic S. Zuckerman, *The Tsarist Secret Police in Russian Society, 1880–1917* (New York: New York University Press, 1996), 52.

46. RGB, f. 435, 189, 14.

47. Zdanovich, Izmozik, *Sorok let na sekretnoi sluzbe*, 98.

48. Ibid., 96.

49. Ibid., 103.

50. VG letter to LN, August 18, 1898. GMT.

CHAPTER 7

1. LN letter to VG, May 7, 1897.

2. VG letter to LN, July 20, 1898. GMT.

3. LN letter to VG, July 14, 1898.

4. LN letter to VG, June 19, 1897.

5. LN letter to VG, July 15, 1897.

6. VG letter to LN, August 19, 1897. GMT.

7. LN letter to VG, February 15, 1897.

8. VG letter to LN, July 28, 1897. GMT.

9. Maude's translation of *What Is Art?* was published as a separate book in 1898.

10. LN letter to VG, December 13, 1897.

11. *Jubilee Edition*, vol. 88, 68.

12. Maude, *The Life of Tolstoy*, vol. 2, 374.

13. Ibid., 378.

14. LN letter to VG, October 26, 1897.

15. LN letter to VG, February 25, 1898.

16. *Jubilee Edition*, vol. 71, 287.

17. *Tolstoy's Letters*, vol. 2, 567–70.

18. LN letter to VG, March 18, 1898.

19. LN letter to VG, April 6, 1898.

20. VG letter to LN, April 12, 1898. GMT.

21. VG letter to LN, April 12, 1898. GMT

22. Maude, *A Peculiar People: The Doukhobors*, 46.

23. VG letter to LN, April 17, 1898. GMT.

24. LN letter to VG, April 4, 1898.
25. LN letter to the Chertkovs, June 30, 1898.
26. LN letter to VG, July 6, 1898.
27. LN letter to the Chertkovs, September 11, 1898.
28. VG letter to LN, August 5–6, 1898. GMT
29. *Jubilee Edition*, vol. 88, 108–09.
30. VG letter to LN, April 3, 1898. GMT.
31. LN letter to VG, July 14, 1898.
32. LN letter to VG, August 12, 1898.
33. LN letter to VG, August 17, 1898.
34. LN letter to VG, August 27, 1898.
35. VG letter to LN, September 15, 1898. GMT
36. VG letter to LN, October 18–19, 1898. GMT
37. *Tolstoy's Letters*, vol. 2, 574.
38. LN letter to VG, October 20, 1898.
39. LN letter to VG, October 16, 1898.
40. LN letter to VG, October 20, 1898.
41. Archer was a good and unselfish worker, who would travel to Canada to assist the Doukhobors upon their arrival.
42. VG letter to LN, November 4, 1898. GMT.
43. LN letter to the Chertkovs, November 23, 1898.
44. *Sergei Tolstoy and the Doukhobors: A Journey to Canada* (Ottawa: University of Ottawa, 1998), 49.
45. VG letter to LN, December 21, 1898. GMT.
46. *Tolstoy's Letters*, vol. 2, 578–79.
47. VG letter to LN, December 21, 1898. GMT
48. LN letter to VG, December 31, 1898.
49. VG letter to LN, March 12, 1899. GMT.
50. VG letter to LN, May 8–9, 1899. GMT.
51. VG letter to LN, September 22, 1898. GMT.
52. VG letter to LN, February 24, 1899. GMT.
53. *Tolstoy's Letters*, vol. 2, 574–75.
54. Chertkov referred to his agent, Reynolds, only by his last name. The man was, apparently, obscure: his full name is unavailable from other sources.
55. LN letter to VG, August 31, 1898.
56. *The Diaries of Sophia Tolstoy*, 352.
57. *Jubilee Edition*, vol. 33, 347.
58. Tolstoy, *Resurrection*, 58.
59. LN letter to VG, May 28, 1899.
60. LN letter to VG, July 15–16, 1886.
61. LN letter to VG, January 12, 1899.
62. *Jubilee Edition*, vol. 33, 366.
63. LN letter to VG, February 5, 1899.
64. LN letter to VG, February 12–19, 1899.
65. VG letter to LN, March 12, 1899. GMT.
66. VG letter to LN, September 22, 1898. GMT.
67. VG letter to LN, November 21, 1898. GMT.

68.   *Jubilee Edition*, vol. 33, 365.
69.   Ibid., 378.
70.   *Jubilee Edition*, vol. 72, 87.
71.   LN letter to VG, March 9, 1899.
72.   LN letter to VG, March 15, 1899.
73.   Matthew, 18: 21–22.
74.   VG letter to LN, February 13, 1899. GMT.
75.   *Jubilee Edition*, vol. 33, 416.
76.   Ibid., vol. 32, 521–22.
77.   LN letter to VG, April 25, 1899.
78.   LN letter to VG, May 5, 1899.
79.   *Jubilee Edition*, vol. 72, 157.
80.   Ibid., 158–59.
81.   LN letter to VG, May 28, 1899.
82.   *Jubilee Edition*, vol. 33, 422.
83.   LN letter to VG, May 5, 1899.
84.   VG letter to LN, July 28, 1899. GMT.
85.   LN letter to VG, July 28, 1899.
86.   Maude, *The Life of Tolstoy*, vol. 2, 203–04.
87.   Ibid., 392.
88.   Maude, *The Life of Tolstoy*, vol. 2, 392.
89.   LN letter to VG, August 8, 1899.
90.   LN letter to VG, September 6, 1899.
91.   Ibid.
92.   VG letter to LN, November 15, 1899. GMT.
93.   LN letter to VG, September 12, 1898.
94.   LN letter to VG, May 28, 1899.
95.   LN letter to VG, December 15, 1899.

CHAPTER 8
1.   Maude, *The Life of Tolstoy*, vol. 2, 423.
2.   LN letter to VG, January 24, 1899.
3.   Bonch-Bruevich's letter to Lidiya Morozova, August 13, 1897. RGB, f. 369, 363, 16.
4.   Vladimir Bonch-Bruevich, *Iz Moskvy za granitsu: Moi Vospominaniya*. RGB, 369, f.1., 6, 1.
5.   Sophia Motovilova, "Reminiscences." RGB, f. 786, 1, 20.
6.   Dmitri Abrikosov, *Revelations of a Russian Diplomat* (Seattle: University of Washington Press, 1964), 63–64.
7.   Ibid., 63.
8.   *Tolstoy's Letters*, vol. 2, 405.
9.   Ibid., 540.
10.   *Jubilee Edition*, vol. 88, 272, 274.
11.   Orehanov, *Chertkov v zhizni Tolstogo*, 64.
12.   LN letter to VG, January 1, 1900.
13.   Maude, *The Life of Tolstoy*, vol. 2, 405.
14.   VG letters to LN, February 7, 10, 12, 1900. GMT
15.   VG letter to LN, February 10, 1900. GMT.
16.   LN letter to VG, February 28, 1900.

17. Maude, *The Life of Tolstoy*, vol. 2, 432–33.
18. *Jubilee Edition*, vol. 73, 36.
19. *Jubilee Edition*, vol. 88, 194.
20. LN letter to VG, March 10 (?), 1900.
21. VG letter to LN, March 9, 1900. GMT.
22. VG letter to LN, January 21, 1900. GMT
23. VG letter to LN, June 24, 1900. GMT.
24. Leo Tolstoy, *War and Peace*, trans. Richard Pevear and Larissa Volokhonsky (New York: Alfred A. Knopf, 2007), 444.
25. Tolstoy, *Resurrection*, 300.
26. Ibid., 466–67.
27. *Jubilee Edition*, vol. 46, 237–38.
28. *Jubilee Edition*, vol. 72, 413.
29. Ibid., 412.
30. *Jubilee Edition*, vol. 73, 173.
31. VG letter to LN, November 30 and December 26, 1901. GMT.
32. Maude, *The Life of Tolstoy*, vol. 2, 421–22.
33. VG letter to LN, March 26, 1900. GMT.
34. VG letter to LN, September 4, 1900. GMT.
35. Maude, *The Life of Tolstoy*, vol. 2, 395.
36. Ibid., 394.
37. VG letter to LN, October 26, 1899. GMT.
38. Maude, *The Life of Tolstoy*, vol. 2, 422.
39. *Tolstoy's Letters*, vol. 2, 590–91.
40. VG letter to LN, September 4, 1900. GMT.
41. VG letter to LN, December 19, 1900. GMT.
42. VG letter to LN, November 4, 1900. GMT.
43. LN letter to VG, September 6, 1900.
44. LN letter to VG, February 19, 1901.
45. Maude, *The Life of Tolstoy*, vol. 2, 431–32.
46. VG letter to LN, September 4, 1900. GMT.
47. LN letter to VG, October 2–3, 1900.
48. VG letter to LN, November 14, 1900. GMT.
49. LN letter to VG, November 5, 1900.
50. *Jubilee Edition*, vol. 72, 540.
51. LN letter to the Chertkovs, September 29–30, 1900.
52. LN letter to VG, October 13, 1900.
53. LN letter to VG, December 12, 1900.
54. *Jubilee Edition*, vol. 34, 540–42.
55. LN letter to VG, December 12, 1900.
56. VG letter to LN, January 15, 1901. GMT.
57. VG letter to LN, January 20, 1901. GMT.
58. VG letter to LN, January 26, 1901. GMT.
59. LN letter to VG, January 19, 1901.
60. VG letter to LN, February 5, 1901. GMT.
61. LN letter to VG, January 28, 1901.
62. Maude, *The Life of Tolstoy*, vol. 2, 410.

63. Nikolai Gusev, *Letopis' zhizni i tvorchestva L'va Nikolaevicha Tolstogo, 1891–1910* (Moscow: Gosizdat, 1960), vol. 2, 373.
64. Maude, *The Life of Tolstoy*, vol. 2, 412–13.
65. Bartlett, *Tolstoy: A Russian Life*, 390–91.
66. Maude, *The Life of Tolstoy*, vol. 2, 412–13.
67. Gusev, *Letopis'*, vol. 2, 384.
68. VG letters to LN, March–June 1901. GMT.
69. Maude, *The Life of Tolstoy*, vol. 2, 426.
70. LN letter to VG, November 6, 1901.
71. VG letter to LN, November 30, 1901. GMT.
72. LN letter to VG, November 6, 1901.

CHAPTER 9

1. LN letter to VG, May 12, 1909.
2. *Tolstoy's Letters*, vol. 2, 621.
3. Maude, *The Life of Tolstoy*, vol. 2, 435–37.
4. LN letter to VG, May 27, 1902.
5. VG letter to LN, March 20, 1902. GMT.
6. VG letter to LN, March 20, 1901. GMT.
7. VG letter to LN, February 26, 1902. GMT.
8. VG letters to LN, February 15 and 22, 1902. GMT.
9. VG letter to LN, January 8, 1902. GMT.
10. VG letters to LN, August 27, 29, 1902. GMT.
11. VG letter to LN, March 16, 1901. GMT.
12. VG letter to LN, April 26, 1902. GMT.
13. Ertel's letter to Anna (Galya) Chertkova, June 6 (19), 1901. RGB, f. 349, 6, 1.
14. Maude, *The Life of Tolstoy*, vol. 2, 395.
15. VG letter to LN, April 26, 1902. GMT.
16. LN letter to VG, March 26–28, 1902.
17. *Jubilee Edition*, vol. 88, 277.
18. VG letter to LN, August 12, 1902. GMT.
19. VG letters to LN, August 27 and 29, 1902. GMT.
20. LN letter to VG, June 30, 1903.
21. LN letter to VG, October 6, 1903.
22. Matthew, 24:7, 17.
23. LN letter to VG, March 23, 1902.
24. *Jubilee Edition*, vol. 35, 590.
25. The fighting lasted from the 1820s until 1864.
26. *Jubilee Edition*, vol. 35, 583.
27. Ibid., 628.
28. Ibid., 621.
29. Leo Tolstoy, *Hadji Murat* in *The Death of Ivan Ilyich and Other Stories* trans. Richard Pevear and Larissa Volokhonsky (New York: Alfred A. Knopf, 2009), 450.
30. Ibid, 375.
31. *Jubilee Edition*, vol. 35, 589.
32. *Tolstoy's Diaries*, vol. 2, 457.
33. *Jubilee Edition*, vol. 35, 620.

34. Ibid., 625.
35. Ibid., 628–29.
36. Maude, *The Life of Tolstoy*, vol. 2, 485–86.
37. Gusev, *Letopis'*, vol. 2, 450–51.
38. *The Memoirs of Count Witte*, 404.
39. LN letter to VG, September 6–7, 1903.
40. LN letter to VG, October 6, 1903.
41. VG letter to LN, October 12, 1903. GMT.
42. LN telegram to VG, October 10, 1903.
43. VG letter to LN, May 10–15, 1903. GMT.
44. VG letter to LN, March 9, 1903. GMT.
45. VG letter to LN, March 23, 1903. GMT.
46. *Jubilee Edition*, vol. 53, 65–66.
47. *Jubilee Edition*, vol. 55, 65–66. Tolstoy referred to *Robinson Crusoe*.
48. *Tolstoy's Diaries*, vol. 2, 516.
49. Ibid., 517.
50. *The Works of Leo Tolstoy*, trans. Aylmer Maude (London: Oxford University Press, 1937), vol. 21, 205.
51. Tolstoy, "A Letter to Revolutionary," *Jubilee Edition*, vol. 38, 264–65.
52. LN letter to VG, May 20, 1904.
53. VG letter to LN, July 6, 1904. GMT.
54. LN letters to VG, July 1 and July 3, 1904.
55. VG letter to LN, June 2, 1904. GMT.
56. *Tolstoy's Letters*, vol. 2, 643. Italics are added by the author.
57. *Tolstoy's Letters*, vol. 2, 1904.
58. *Literaturnoe nasledstvo* (Moskva: Izdatel'stvo Akademii Nauk, 1961), vol. 69/1, 554–55.
59. Alexander Fodor, *The Quest for a Non-Violent Russia: The Partnership of Leo Tolstoy and Vladimir Chertkov* (Lanham MD: University Press of America, 1989), 107.
60. Orehanov, *Chertkov in Tolstoy's Life*, 60.
61. *Jubilee Edition*, vol. 34, 374.
62. Lieven, *Nicholas II: Emperor of All the Russias*, 140.
63. *The Memoirs of Count Witte*, 406.
64. In German, Wirballen; in Polish, Wierzbołów.
65. VG letter to Anna (Galya) Chertkova, May 25, 1905. RGB, f. 435, 137, 27.
66. Dushan Makovitsky, *Yasnopolyanskie zapiski* (Moscow: Nauka, 1979), vol. 1, 293.
67. Ibid., vol. 2, 488.
68. *Jubilee Edition*, vol. 55, 144.
69. LN letter to VG, December 24, 1905.
70. *Jubilee Edition*, vol. 89, 16.
71. LN letter to VG, April 17, 1905.
72. LN letter to VG, June 16, 1905.
73. LN letter to VG, January 22, 1905.
74. LN letter to VG, September 4, 1905.
75. RGALI, f. 552, 1, 2863.
76. Orehanov, *Chertkov in Tolstoy's Life*, 68.
77. *Jubilee Edition*, vol. 76, 78.
78. *Jubilee Edition*, vol. 67, 14.

79.   LN letter to VG, January 1, 1906.
80.   RGALI, 552, 1, 2804. Shkvaran's letters to VG come from this fond in RGALI.
81.   LN letter to VG, October 3, 1906.
82.   LN letter to VG, November 13, 1906.
83.   LN letter to VG, November 26, 1906.
84.   LN letter to VG, January 4, 1907.
85.   LN letter to VG, January 10, 1907.
86.   Maude, *The Life of Tolstoy*, vol. 2, 449–50.
87.   Makovitsky, *Zapiski*, vol. 2, 395.
88.   Maude, *The Life of Tolstoy*, vol. 2, 386–87.
89.   Makovitsky, *Zapiski*, vol. 2, 395.
90.   VG letter to LN, April 12, 1907. GMT.
91.   Makovitsky, *Zapiski*, vol. 2, 408.
92.   LN letter to VG, April 6, 1907.
93.   VG letter to LN, April 12, 1907. GMT.
94.   VG letter to LN, April 26–30, 1907. GMT.
95.   *Jubilee Edition*, vol. 55, 489.
96.   Makovitsky, *Zapiski*, vol. 2, 572.
97.   Ibid., vol. 2, 456.
98.   LN telegram to VG, June 15, 1907.
99.   Makovitsky, *Zapiski*, vol. 2, 500.

CHAPTER 10
1.   Maude, *The Life of Tolstoy*, vol. 2, 494.
2.   *Unmasking the Psychopath: Antisocial Personality and Related Syndromes*, ed. William H. Reid, Darwin Dorr (New York and London: W.W. Norton & Company, 1986), 265–66.
3.   Makovitsky, *Zapiski*, vol. 2, 495.
4.   Ibid., vol. 3, 437.
5.   Quoted in Orehanov, *Chertkov v zhizni Tolstogo*, 150–51.
6.   Makovitsky, *Zapiski*, vol. 2, 537.
7.   Ibid., vol. 3, 10.
8.   Ibid., 233.
9.   Ibid., vol. 2, 580.
10.   VG letter to LN, December 20, 1907. GMT.
11.   LN letter to VG, September 16, 1907.
12.   LN letter to VG, March 25, 1908.
13.   LN letter to VG, June 2, 1908.
14.   Makovitsky, *Zapiski*, vol. 3, 20.
15.   LN letter to VG, June 9, 1908.
16.   Most likely, the Plato Clock, precursor of the first digital clock; it was patented by Eugene L. Fitch in New York City in 1903.
17.   Makovitsky, *Zapiski*, vol. 2, 582.
18.   Ibid., vol. 3, 21.
19.   Ibid., 74.
20.   A. McCaig, *Wonders of Grace in Russia* (Riga: The Revival Press, 1926), 65.
21.   Makovitsky, *Zapiski*, vol. 3, 94.
22.   Quoted in Orehanov, *Chertkov v zhizni Tolstogo*, 150–51.

23. *Tolstoy's Diaries*, vol. 2, 504.
24. Makovitsky, *Zapiski*, vol. 3, 174.
25. Quoted in Maude, *The Life of Tolstoy*, vol. 2, 492–93.
26. Ibid., 458.
27. Ibid., 455–56.
28. Ibid., 467.
29. *Literaturnoe nasledstvo*, 213.
30. LN letter to VG, April 30, 1909.
31. LN letter to VG, April 26, 1909.
32. LN letter to VG, April 27, 1909.
33. VG letter to LN, May 4, 1909. GMT.
34. LN letter to VG, May 12, 1909.
35. LN letter to VG, May 6, 1909.
36. LN letter to VG, May 25, 1909.
37. LN letter to VG, June 18, 1909.
38. VG letter to LN, June 19, 1909. GMT.
39. LN letter to VG, June 23, 1909.
40. LN letter to VG, June 24, 1909.
41. VG letter to LN, May 28, 1909. GMT.
42. LN letter to VG, May 25, 1909.
43. *Jubilee Edition*, vol. 57, 155.
44. *Literaturnoe nasledstvo*, 220.
45. *Tolstoy's Letters*, vol. 2, 686.
46. LN letter to VG, July 22, 1909.
47. Alexander Goldenweiser, *Lev Tolstoy: Vospominaniya* (Moscow: Zakharov, 2002), 274.
48. *The Diaries of Sophia Tolstoy*, 647.
49. *Jubilee Edition*, vol. 57, 141.
50. Ibid., 142.
51. Ibid., 143.
52. *Tolstoy's Diaries*, vol. 2, 664.
53. Makovitsky, *Zapiski*, vol. 4, 75.
54. LN letter to VG, October 12, 1909.
55. VG letter to LN, October 23, 1909. GMT.
56. *Literaturnoe nasledstvo*, 219.
57. *The Diaries of Sophia Tolstoy*, 493.
58. *Tolstoy's Diaries*, vol. 2, 638.
59. *Jubilee Edition*, vol. 58, 161.
60. Quoted in Aylmer Maude, *The Life of Tolstoy*, vol. 2, 495.
61. *Literaturnoe nasledstvo*, 217.
62. Ibid., 221.
63. Gorky, "Lev Tolstoi" in *Literary Portraits*, trans. Ivy Litvinov (Moscow: Foreign Languages Publishing House, 1982), 81.
64. LN letter to VG, January 14, 1910.
65. LN letters to VG, January 28 and February 6, 1910.
66. *Jubilee Edition*, vol. 58, 184.
67. *Jubilee Edition*, vol. 38, 395–411.
68. *The Diaries of Sophia Tolstoy*, 495–97.

69. Ibid., 498.
70. From unpublished portions of Sophia Tolstoy's *Diaries* kept at the Tolstoy State Museum, f. 47.
71. *The Diaries of Sophia Tolstoy*, 536.
72. VG letter to LN, July 1, 1910. GMT.
73. VG letter to LN, July 14, 1910. GMT.
74. Alexandra Tolstoy, *The Daughter* (Moscow: Vagrius, 2000), 158.
75. Quoted in *Ukhod L'va Tolstogo* (Moscow: Gosudarstvennyj myzei L.N. Tolstogo, 2011), 375. In future, *Ukhod*.
76. *The Diaries of Sophia Tolstoy*, 502.
77. Ibid., 537.
78. Valentin Bulgakov, *The Last Year of Leo Tolstoy* (New York: The Dial Press, 1971), 158.
79. *Ukhod*, 359.
80. Valentin Bulgakov, *The Last Year of Leo Tolstoy*, 179.
81. *Ukhod*, 490–91.
82. Ibid., 392.
83. Ibid., 316.
84. Ibid., 258.
85. Quoted in Maude, *The Life of Tolstoy*, vol. 2, 520.
86. McCaig, *Wonders of Grace in Russia*, 78–80.
87. *Ukhod*, 392.
88. *Tolstoy's Diaries*, vol. 2, 678.
89. *Tolstoy's Letters*, vol. 2, 703.
90. Quoted in Maude, *The Life of Tolstoy*, vol. 2, 393–94.
91. *Tolstoy's Letters*, vol. 2, 704.
92. *Ukhod*, 461–62. Sophia's statement does not appear in her published diaries. However, not all her entries are published to this day.
93. LN letter to SA, August 29, 1910.
94. *Tolstoy's Letters*, vol. 2, 705.
95. RGALI, f. 508, 4, 12.
96. Dushan Makovitsky, *Zapiski*, vol. 4, 355.
97. *Ukhod*, 391.
98. Ibid., 483–85.
99. Ibid., 486.
100. *Tolstoy's Diaries*, vol. 2, 683.
101. *Ukhod*, 495–96.
102. *Tolstoy's Letters*, vol. 2, 708.
103. *Ukhod*, 498.
104. An epileptic seizure may occur in the wake of a stroke.
105. *Ukhod*, 505–06.
106. Ibid., 577.
107. Ibid., 523–24.
108. Ibid., 536–37.
109. Quoted in Maude, *The Life of Tolstoy*, vol. 2, 521–22.
110. *Ukhod*, 525–31.
111. LN letter to VG, October 22, 1910.
112. *Tolstoy's Diaries*, vol. 2, 687.

113.   *Jubilee Edition*, vol. 89, 231.

114.   Makovitsky, *Zapiski*, vol. 4, 397.

115.   *Ukhod*, 551.

116.   *Jubilee Edition*, vol. 89, 231.

117.   *Jubilee Edition*, vol. 58, 573.

118.   RGB, f. 435, 133, 21.

119.   *Tolstoy's Letters*, vol. 2, 717.

120.   Quoted in the almanac *Dni Nashei skorbi* [*Days of Our Mourning*] (Moscow: 1911), 112–13.

121.   Makovitsky, *Zapiski*, vol. 4, 429, 430.

122.   *Ukhod*, 71–73.

123.   Makovitsky, *Zapiski*, vol. 4, 432.

124.   Valentin Bulgakov, "Zloi genij geniya" in *Slovo*, No. 9–12, 1993, 17.

125.   Ibid., 11.

126.   *Yasnopolyanskij sbornik* (Tula: Yasnaya Polyana, 2006), 280–81.

127.   Bulgakov, *O Tolstom: Vospominaniya i rasskazy*, 266.

128.   Tatyana Sukhotina's letter to SA of January 29, 1911 in Maude, *The Life of Tolstoy*, vol. 2, 519–23.

CHAPTER II

1.   Gorky, "Lev Tolstoi," 68–69.

2.   Chertkova's letter to VG, November 11, 1910. RGB, f. 435, 140, 4. Chertkova's correspondence with VG and his letters to her for 1910 come from this fond.

3.   VG letter to Chertkova, December 1, 1910.

4.   *Jubilee Edition*, vol. 85, 82.

5.   Chertkova's letter to VG, October 20, 1910.

6.   Chertkova's letter to VG, October 14, 1910.

7.   VG letter to Chertkova, October 1, 1910.

8.   VG letter to Chertkova, October 4, 1910.

9.   Bulgakov, "Zloi genij geniya," 10.

10. VG letter to Chertkova, February 15, 1910.

11. http://www.telegraph.co.uk/news/uknews/1492935/Unrepentant-Soviet-spy-Melita-Norwood-dies-at-93.html

12. A.Tolstaya's (ALT's) letter to VG, January 20, 1914 in *Tolstovskij ezhegodnik* (Moskva: GMT, 2001), 464–65.

13. VG letter to ALT, October 9, 1913. RGB, f. 435, 133, 21.

14. VG letter to ALT, July 20, 1914. RGB, f. 435, 133, 22. VG letters to Sasha for 1914 come from this fond.

15. VG letter to ALT, September 10, 1914.

16. VG letter to ALT, October 1, 1910.

17. VG letter to ALT, May 16, 1914.

18. VG letter to ALT, September 10, 1914.

19. RGB, 435, 133, 25.

20. Alexandra Tolstoy, *Out of the Past*, ed. Katharine Strelsky and Catherine Wolkonsky (New York: Columbia University Press, 1981), 13–14.

21. *The Diaries of Sophia Tolstoy*, 981.

22. Bulgakov, "Zloi genij geniya," 10.

23. VG letter to Apurin, May 8 and October 29, 1915. RGB, f. 435, 114, 52.
24. RGALI, f. 552, 1, 221.
25. VG telegram to Apurin, October 4, 1912. RGB, f. 435, 114, 52. VG letters to Apurin come from this fond.
26. VG letter to Apurin, February 21, 1915. RGB.
27. VG letter to Apurin, April 4, 1917. RGB.
28. Vladimir Chertkov, *The Last Days of Tolstoy* (London: William Hienemann, 1922).
29. *Tolstoy's Letters*, vol. 2, 712–13.
30. Zinaida Gippius, "Okolo Tolstogo," *Voskresenie*, No.3, 1998, 55–61.
31. Chertkov, *The Last Days of Tolstoy*, ix.
32. Ibid., 14, 21.
33. Alexandra Tolstoy, *Out of the Past*, 81.

CHAPTER 12

1. Evgeny Zamyatin, *We*, trans. Gregory Zilboorg (New York: Dotton & Co., Inc., 1952), 138.
2. Sophia Motovilova, *Vospominaniya*, RGB, f. 786, 1, 20.
3. Vitaly Shentalinsky, *Donos na Sokrata* (Moskva: Formika-C, 2001), 54.
4. VG letter to Chertkova, January 5, 1919. RGB, f. 369, 5.
5. Vladlen Izmozik, *Peshkom po Millionnoi* (St. Petersburg: Znanie, 2004), 165–66.
6. Chertkov's memo about publishing Tolstoy's works in Soviet Russia, 1918–19. RGB, 369, 411, 44.
7. Ibid.
8. Donald Rayfield, *Stalin and His Hangmen* (London: Viking, 2004), 119.
9. Lev Osterman, *Srazhenie za Tolstogo* (Moskva: Grant, 2002), 27–28.
10. Ibid., 10–11.
11. *Jubilee Edition*, vol. 85, 17.
12. Rayfield, *Stalin and His Hangmen*, 119.
13. Bartlett, *Tolstoy: A Russian Life*, 431.
14. RGB, f. 435, 8, 9.
15. Rayfield, *Stalin and His Hangmen*, 462.
16. VG letter to Dzerzhinsky, 1921. RGB, f. 435, 78, 24.
17. Rayfield, *Stalin and His Hangmen*, 136–37.
18. Unified State Political Administration.
19. Zdanovich, Izmozik, *Sorok let na sekretnoi sluzhbe*, 206.
20. Rayfield, *Stalin and His Hangmen*, 119.
21. Ibid., 115–17.
22. Alexandra Tolstoy, *Out of the Past*, 101.
23. Shentalinsky, *Donos na Sokrata*, 56–64.
24. Ibid.
25. VG letter to Dzerzhinsky, March 29, 1920. RGB, f. 435, 113, 2.
26. Ibid.
27. RGB, f. 435, 113, 2.
28. RGALI, f. 552, 4, 7.
29. VG letter to Stalin, March 13, 1928. RGALI, f. 552, 4, 336.
30. Maude, *The Life of Tolstoy*, vol. 2, 525.
31. Nikolai Rodionov's Diary, RGB, f. 691, 1, 8. June 6, 1928.

32. http://45f.ru/sse/zarabotnaya-plata/.
33. Rodionov's Diary, RGB.
34. Ibid.
35. VG letter to Gusev, August 8, 1932. RGB, 435, 119, 16.
36. Rodionov's Diary, November 27, 1928, RGB.
37. N. Zaitseva, "Obrazy Chertkovyh v tvorchestve Nesterova" in *Yasnopolyanskij sbornik* (Tula: Yasnaya Polyana, 2000), 359–70. The story of Nesterov's painting comes from this source.
38. Boris Mazurin, "Rasskaz i razdum´ia ob istorii odnoi tolstovskoi kommuny 'Zhizn´ i trud.'" *Novy mir*, No. 9, 1988, 180–226.
39. Mazurin, "'Zhizn´ i trud,'" 192.
40. RGB, f. 369, 363, 26.
41. "A Letter from Tolstoy to the Canadian Doukhobors" in Maude, *A Peculiar People: The Doukhobors*, 270.
42. Mazurin, "Zhizn´ i trud," 215.
43. Chertkov's letter to "Life and Labor" commune, January 29, 1935. RGB, f. 369, 363, 26.
44. RGB, f. 435, 81, 9.
45. RGB, f. 435, 94, 30.
46. Rayfield, *Stalin and His Hangmen*, 185.
47. http://www.solovki.ca/camp_20/tolstoy.php. Solovki was the first camp of the gulag, which functioned since 1923.
48. GARF, f. 8409, 1, 406, pp. 71–78. http://www.solovki.ca/documents/letters_004.php.
49. Anne Applebaum, *Gulag: A History* (New York: Doubleday, 2003), 37.
50. Zdanovich, Izmozik, *Sorok let na sekretnoi sluzhbe*, 240.
51. RGB, f.435, 2, 24.
52. RGB, f. 369, 364, 6.
53. VG letter to Bonch-Bruevich, April 28, 1933. RGB, f. 369. The letter is found in Bonch-Bruevich's fond.
54. The subway station, "Sokol," was later built in this district.
55. RGB, f. 369, 222, 9.
56. VG letter to Bubnov, March 23, 1932. RGB, f. 369.
57. RGB, f. 369, 222, 12.
58. Bonch-Bruevich's letters to Chertkov, 1930s. RGB, f. 369, 222, 14.
59. RGB, f. 369, 222, 9.
60. RGALI, f. 552, 4, 3.
61. Lev Osterman, *Srazhenie za Tolstogo*, 32–34.
62. *Izvestia*, November 10, 1936, No. 260.
63. V. Chertkov's letter to Commissariat for Foreign Affairs, April 20, 1937. RGB, f. 435, 113, 2.
64. Ibid.
65. Maude, *The Life of Tolstoy*, vol. 2, 456.

INDEX

299

ABOUT THE AUTHOR

Alexandra Popoff is the author of the award-winning *Sophia Tolstoy: A Biography*. Her biography *The Wives: The Women Behind Russia's Literary Giants* became a *Wall Street Journal* Best Book for 2012. She has written for Russian national newspapers and magazines in Moscow and, as an Alfred Friendly Press Fellow, published articles in the *Philadelphia Inquirer* and its Sunday magazine. She has also contributed to *Huffington Post*, the *Boston Globe*, *The Globe and Mail*, and *National Post*. Popoff lives in Canada.